Hospitals

What They Are and How They Work

Fourth Edition

Edited by

Donald J. Griffin, MBA, MS, MS, JD, FACHE
Assistant Professor
School of Health Administration
Texas State University
San Marcos, Texas

JONES & BARTLETT
LEARNING

World Headquarters
Jones & Bartlett Learning
40 Tall Pine Drive
Sudbury, MA 01776
978-443-5000
info@jblearning.com
www.jblearning.com

Jones & Bartlett Learning
Canada
6339 Ormindale Way
Mississauga, Ontario L5V 1J2
Canada

Jones & Bartlett Learning
International
Barb House, Barb Mews
London W6 7PA
United Kingdom

Jones & Bartlett Learning books and products are available through most bookstores and online booksellers. To contact Jones & Bartlett Learning directly, call 800-832-0034, fax 978-443-8000, or visit our website, www.jblearning.com.

Substantial discounts on bulk quantities of Jones & Bartlett Learning publications are available to corporations, professional associations, and other qualified organizations. For details and specific discount information, contact the special sales department at Jones & Bartlett Learning via the above contact information or send an email to specialsales@jblearning.com.

Production Credits
Publisher: Michael Brown
Associate Editor: Catie Heverling
Editorial Assistant: Teresa Reilly
Associate Production Editor: Lisa Lamenzo
Associate Production Editor: Laura Almozara
Senior Marketing Manager: Sophie Fleck
Manufacturing and Inventory Control Supervisor: Amy Bacus
Composition: Datastream Content Solutions, LLC
Cover Design: Kristin E. Parker
Cover Image: © ERproductions Ltd/age fotostock
Printing and Binding: Malloy, Inc.
Cover Printing: Malloy, Inc.

Library of Congress Cataloging-in-Publication Data
Griffin, Donald J., 1949-
   Hospitals : what they are and how they work / [edited by] Griffin, Donald.—4th ed.
      p. ; cm.
   Includes index.
   ISBN-13: 978-0-7637-9109-4 (pbk.)
   ISBN-10: 0-7637-9109-1 (ibid)
   1. Hospitals.   2. Hospitals—Administration.   3. Hospitals—United States.   I. Title.
   [DNLM: 1. Hospitals—United States.   2. Hospital Administration—United States.   WX 100]
   RA963.S57 2011
   362.11068—dc22
                                                              2010028461

6048

Printed in the United States of America
15 14 13 12 11   10 9 8 7 6 5 4 3 2

Table of Contents

Acknowledgments xiii
About the Editor xv
Contributors xvii
Background to the Fourth Edition
    of *Hospitals* xxi
Foreword xxiii
Introduction to the Fourth Edition xxv

Part I   **An Overview of Hospitals** **1**

Chapter 1   **History of Hospitals and Health Care** **3**
The Very Early Days 3
Early American Hospitals: From the Founding
    of the New World Through World War II
    (1500–1945) 6
The Modern Era: Post–World War II
    to the Present (1945–2010) 11
Summary 12
Chapter Review 12

Chapter 2   **Hospitals and Important Hospital Trends** **13**
Background 13
How We Classify Hospitals 13
Trends in General Acute-Care
    Community Hospitals 14
Summary 24
Chapter Review 24

Part II   Leadership **25**

**Chapter 3   Organizational Structure, the Governing
                  Body, and the CEO** **27**
                  Theories of Organization, Introduction
                      of Concepts 28
                  Organization Chart 30
                  Team of Three—A Very Important Concept 33
                  Corporate Restructuring of the Hospital 34
                  Multihospital Systems 34
                  Alliances 35
                  The Governing Body—A Deeper Discussion 35
                  Functions of the Board of Trustees 38
                  The Chief Executive Officer 42
                  The Future for CEOs 48
                  Chapter Review 48

Part III   Accessing the Hospital **51**

Chapter 4   Doorways into the Hospital **53**
                  Introduction 53
                  Objectives 54
                  Entering the Hospital—Planned
                      or Unplanned 54
                  The Emergency Department 57
                  The Trauma Department 59
                  The Golden Hour 61
                  Cost of Running Emergency Departments
                      and Trauma Centers 62
                  Summary 63
                  Chapter Review 63
                  References 64

Part IV   The Hospital Team **65**

Chapter 5   The Medical Staff **67**
                  Introduction 67
                  Becoming a Physician 68
                  Continuing Medical Education 70
                  Organized Medicine 70

Medical Staff Organization 70
Closed and Open Medical Staffs 73
Medical Staff Committees 73
The Medical Director 75
The Hospitalist 75
Allied Health Personnel 75
Legal Restrictions on Physicians 76
Chapter Review 76

Chapter 6   **Physician Extenders** **79**
Introduction 79
History of Physician Assistants 79
Specialties 80
What Is a Nurse Practitioner? 81
Responsibilities of the Nurse Practitioner 81
What Is a Midwife? 82
Chapter Review 83
References 83

Chapter 7   **Nursing Services** **85**
Introduction 85
Early Traditions 85
Nursing Education 86
Modes of Nursing Care Delivery 92
Terms and Standards 95
Staffing 96
Nurse Staffing Issues 97
Scheduling 98
Department Organization 101
The Patient-Care Unit 102
Special-Care Units 105
Telemonitoring and Bedside Terminals 109
Chapter Review 110
References 111

Chapter 8   **Older Patients in the Hospital—Geriatrics** **113**
The Field of Aging 113
Services to the Elderly 114
Understanding Aging 114
Role of the Hospital/Staff 114

Specialized Departments: A Multidisciplinary
  Approach 115
Chapter Review 116
References 116

Part V   Key Ancillary Services 117

Chapter 9   The Clinical Laboratory and the Pathologist 119
Introduction 119
Structure and Function of the Clinical Laboratory . . . 120
Clinical Laboratory Certification 120
Clinical Laboratory Accreditation 121
Proficiency Testing 122
Personnel 122
Quality Improvement 124
The Future of the Clinical Laboratory 125
The Professional Laboratorian 126
Chapter Review 126

**Chapter 10   Diagnostic Imaging and Therapeutic
                 Radiology Departments 127**
Introduction 127
Mission of the Department 128
Diagnostic Imaging Department 128
Specialties Within the Diagnostic
  Imaging Department 130
Other Specialties of Diagnostic Imaging 131
Summary 133
Chapter Review 134

Chapter 11   Physical Therapy 135
Introduction 135
Historical Perspective 137
Services Provided by the Physical
  Therapy Department 137
Personnel 138
How the Patient Is Affected 139
Special Considerations 141
Chapter Review 143
References 144

Chapter 12   **The Respiratory Therapy Department** **145**
Introduction 145
Chapter Review 157

Chapter 13   **Speech-Language Pathologists** **159**
Chapter Review 165
References 166

Chapter 14   **The Pharmacy** **167**
Introduction 167
Function of the Pharmacy 168
Telepharmacy 168
The Pharmacy Staff 168
Pharmacist Education 169
Pharmacy and Therapeutics Committee 170
Drug Distribution System 170
Medication Dispensing Errors 172
Control of Narcotics and Barbiturates 173
Generic Versus Brand-Name Drugs 173
Selling Drugs to Hospitals 174
Security of Drugs 174
Quality Improvement 175
Summary 175
Chapter Review 176
References 176

Part VI   **Patient Support Services** **177**

Chapter 15   **Hospital Essentials** **179**
Introduction 179
Reception. 179
Telecommunications 181
Dietary Services 182
Pastoral Services 183
Patient Transportation Services 185
Patient Representatives 186
Interpreters 186
Volunteer Services 187
Summary 188
Chapter Review 189

Chapter 16   **The Social Services Department** **191**
Introduction 191
The Social Services Department and
    Functions of Medical Social Workers 192
Compliance and Regulation Issues: Licensure,
    Education, and Training of Medical
    Social Workers 194
Social Services and Patient Care 196
Summary 197
Chapter Review 197
References 198
Suggested Readings 199

Chapter 17   **Health Information Management** **201**
Introduction 201
Purpose of the Patient Record 202
Privacy, Confidentiality, and Security 204
The HIM Department 206
Patient Record Storage and Archiving 210
Summary 211
Chapter Review 211
References 212

Part VII   **Facilities Support and Security** **213**

Chapter 18   **Supporting the Medical Center** **215**
Introduction 216
Materials Management Department 216
Environmental Services Department 219
Laundry Department 221
Maintenance Department 222
Plant Engineering 224
Parking Facilities 224
Biomedical Engineering Department 225
Contract Services 226
Chapter Review 226

Chapter 19   **Safeguarding the Hospital** **227**
Introduction 227
Security 228

General Safety 232
Fire Safety 233
Emergency Management 234
Summary 237
Chapter Review 238

Part VIII   **Administrative Services and Issues** **239**

Chapter 20   **Human Resources Department, Risk Management,**
Legal Services, and Corporate Compliance . . .**241**
Introduction 242
Functions of the Human Resources Department . . . 242
Salaries, Wages, and Benefits 244
Employee Performance Appraisal 245
Important Laws, Acts, and Issues 245
Hospitals and Unions 248
Occupational Licensure 248
Risk Management, Legal Services, and
Corporate Compliance Risk Management 249
Medical Malpractice 249
Defensive Medicine 250
Hospital Liability for Physicians' Acts 250
Ending Medical Errors 251
US Versus European Operating Rooms 253
Additional Legal Issues 253
Corporate Compliance 254
Chapter Review 254

Chapter 21   **The Importance of Diversity in a**
Healthcare Organization **255**
Introduction 255
The Role of Leadership 258
The Business Case for Diversity 259
The Organizational Approach to Diversity
and Inclusion 260
Chapter Review 262

Chapter 22   **Hospital Accreditation and Licensing** **263**
Introduction 263
The Joint Commission 264

Accreditation Overview 266
Accreditation in More Detail 267
What Does Accreditation Really Mean
    to a Hospital? 268
Sentinel Events 268
Joint Commission International 269
Licensure 269
Medicare Certification 270
Medicare Surveys 270
Registration 270
Chapter Review 271

Chapter 23   **Hospital Marketing** **273**
Introduction 273
What Is Marketing? 274
Sales 278
Branding 278
Market Research 278
Market Studies and Audits 279
Fundraising 281
Chapter Review 282

Chapter 24   **Strategic Planning** **283**
Introduction 283
The Evolution of Planning 284
The Hospital's Long-Range Plan 284
Who Should Do the Planning for the Hospital? . . . 285
Levels of Long-Range Planning 287
Benefits of Planning 287
Planning New Facilities 287
Chapter Review 288

Part IX   **Hospital Financial Issues** **289**

Chapter 25   **Finance** **291**
Introduction 292
Section A: Billing and Collection 292
Section B: Financial Management 298
Section C: Budgeting 307

Chapter Review 317
References 318

Chapter 26   **Generating Revenue—Third-Party Payers**
                   by Types and Percentages **319**
                   Introduction 319
                   History of Third-Party Payment 320
                   Managed Care Enters the Scene 321
                   Setting Charges 322
                   Methods of Payment 322
                   Chapter Review 324
                   References 324

Part X   **Evaluating and Ensuring the Quality**
                   of Care **325**

Chapter 27   **Compliance and Performance**
                   Improvement in Hospitals **327**
                   Introduction 327
                   Peer Review Organizations 328
                   System Failures 328
                   HIPAA and OIG 329
                   To Err Is Human 329
                   Accreditation 330
                   Quality Improvement Organizations 330
                   Keeping Patients Safe 331
                   PSOs 331
                   IHI and ISMP 331
                   Where Are We 10 Years After *To Err Is Human?* . . .331
                   Winkler County Nurses .332
                   Continuing Need to Promote Patient Safety 332
                   Summary 334
                   Chapter Review 334

Chapter 28   **The Importance of Bioethics** **335**
                   Introduction 335
                   Definition and Principles of Bioethics 336
                   Bioethics Issues for Hospitals 339
                   Hospital Ethics Committees and Bioethics 341

Hospitals, Patient-Centered Care, and Bioethics . . . 344
Summary 348
Chapter Review 348
References 348

Appendix A   **Case Studies** **351**
Appendix B   **Glossary** **383**
Appendix C   **Useful Websites** **421**

Index **423**

Acknowledgments

Any team is stronger than any individual. With that in mind, I wish to thank the following people:

- Dr. Ruth Welborn, dean of the Texas State University–San Marcos College of Health Professions; Dr. Michael Nowicki, director of the School of Health Administration; and the 24 faculty members of the College of Health Professions for coming together on this project. Without the help of these experts, the fourth edition of *Hospitals* would be much more limited in scope . . . thanks, everyone!
- My wife, Polly, for the many sacrifices she's made for this book, for keeping my nose to the grindstone, and for her contributions in editing this work.
- My father, Richard Griffin, the CEO of several hospitals and my role model.
- Jeff and Kevin with AeroAir who taught me several new things about managing.
- Mike Brown and the staff of Jones & Bartlett Learning for again having faith.
- And especially the members of healthcare faculties around the world, who guide and teach the next generation of healthcare leaders.

About the Editor

Donald J. Griffin, MBA, MS, MS, JD, FACHE

Don has spent more than 20 years managing hospitals in the United States, Saudi Arabia, the United Arab Emirates, and China. He has been on the faculty of 3 universities teaching healthcare administration courses, and has also practiced law in Texas and Oklahoma.

Don and his wife, Polly, have made their home in San Marcos, Texas, where he is on the faculty of Texas State University teaching courses in the School of Health Administration.

The author invites you to contact him at grif67@hotmail.com.

Contributors

Sue Biederman, MSHP, PhD,
    RHIA, FAHIMA
Associate Professor and Chair
Program of Health Information
    Management
College of Health Professions
Texas State University

Susan H. Fenton, MBA, PhD,
    RHIA
Assistant Professor and HIT
    Institute Director
Program of Health Information
    Management
College of Health Professions
Texas State University

Tina Fields, MPH, PhD
Assistant Professor
School of Health Administration
College of Health Professions
Texas State University

Valarie B. Fleming, PhD,
    CCC-SLP
Assistant Professor
Department of Communications
    Disorders
College of Health Professions
Texas State University

Melvin V. Greene, BS
Director of Diversity and Inclusion
Seton Family of Hospitals
Austin, Texas

Polly Griffin
Research Assistant
San Marcos, TX

Jason Hardage, PT, DScPT,
    GCS, NCS
Assistant Professor
Department of Physical Therapy
College of Health Professions
Texas State University

Attila J. Hertelendy, MS,
    MHSM, NREMT-P, PhD
Assistant Professor
School of Health Administration
College of Health Professions
Texas State University

Peggy Johnson, MPH
Assistant Professor
School of Health Administration
College of Health Professions
Texas State University

Lolly Lockhart, RN, PhD
Associate Professor
St. David's School of Nursing
Texas State University

Yvonne Lozano, MSG, LBSW,
    LMFT
Assistant Professor
School of Health Administration
College of Health Professions
Texas State University

Andrew T. Marks, LMSW
Senior Clinical Lecturer
School of Social Work
Texas State University

S. Gregory Marshall, PhD, RRT,
    RPSGT
Associate Professor and Chair
Department of Respiratory Care
College of Health Professions
Texas State University

Jacqueline Moczygemba, MBA,
    RHIA, CCS
Associate Professor
Program of Health Information
    Management
College of Health Professions
Texas State University

Tondra Moore, MPH, PhD, JD
Assistant Professor
School of Health Administration
College of Health Professions
Texas State University

Eileen E. Morrison, MPH, EdD,
    CHES
Professor and BHA Program
    Director
School of Health Administration
College of Health Professions
Texas State University

Rosamaria Murillo, PhD, LMSW
Graduate Adjunct Lecturer
School of Social Work
Texas State University

Danette Myers, MBA, RHIA
Clinical Assistant Professor
Program of Heath Information
    Management
College of Health Professions
Texas State University

Michael Nowicki, MHA, EdD,
  FACHE, FHFMA
Professor and Director
School of Health Administration
College of Health Professions
Texas State University

Divya Pandurangadu
Graduate Assistant
School of Health Administration
College of Health Professions
Texas State University

Thomas L. Patterson, MS, MT
  (ASCP)
Assistant Professor
Clinical Laboratory Science
  Program
College of Health Professions
Texas State University

Jana Proff, MS, CCC-SLP
Lecturer
Department of Communication
  Disorders
College of Health Professions
Texas State University

Geronimo Rodriguez, Jr. JD
Vice President
Diversity and Community
  Outreach
Seton Family of Hospitals
Austin, Texas

Cheryl Rowder, RN, PhD,
  CCRC
Assistant Professor
St. David's School of Nursing
Texas State University

Jim Summers, MA, PhD,
  LFACHE
Professor
School of Health Administration
College of Health Professions
Texas State University

Megan Trad, MSRS, RT(T)
Assistant Professor
Program of Radiation Therapy
College of Health Professions
Texas State University

Tiankai Wang, PhD
Assistant Professor
Program of Health Information
  Management
College of Health Professions
Texas State University

Betsy Wisner, PhD, LMSW
Assistant Professor
School of Social Work
Texas State University

Background to the Fourth Edition of *Hospitals*

When I was teaching healthcare administration courses in Houston around 2002, it occurred to me that although students can take courses in healthcare finance, law, economics, and other healthcare-related subjects, they do not learn about the daily operations of a hospital until they undertake their residency or internship. At that point, their education becomes remarkably like the fable of the six blind men and the elephant. Each blind man touches the elephant and describes what he touched as being the whole elephant—for the blind man who touched the elephant's knee, the elephant is like a tree; for the man who touched the tail, the elephant is like a snake, etc. Each was right, while all were wrong. During their internship or residency, students see the hospital only as the particular department to which they are exposed.

I believed that a formal course addressing all aspects of the hospital was sorely needed, and fortunately my dean agreed with me. After she approved a course in how the pieces of a hospital fit together and operate, I set out to find a suitable text. Coming across a description of Don Snook's book, *Hospitals: What They Are and How They Work, Second Edition,* I sadly noted that it was 14 years out of date. In seeking to understand why this was so, I learned from Mike Brown of Jones & Bartlett Learning that Mr. Snook was deceased. During our conversation, I mentioned to Mr. Brown that I had been the CEO of a hospital, and we struck a deal to update the text to a third edition.

As so often happens when we are planning for other things, however, life intervened: within a few months of that conversation I found myself in Saudi Arabia on a 3-year hospital consulting project. Lacking any references and working alone, I completed the third edition, but in a rather "thin" fashion. Often I would struggle to engage every hospital topic from memory.

Fast-forwarding a few years to 2010, I am again in academia, this time at Texas State University. I find myself embedded in the vibrant College of Health Professions, headed by a dean and director of the School of Health Administration who are both committed to encouraging the best efforts of every faculty member. With their help and the enthusiastic support of 24 other faculty members who are experts in their fields, we stand together to offer an updated fourth edition, illustrating what hospitals are and how they work.

Foreword

The quest to enhance the quality of patient care in our healthcare institutions has been the guiding principle for healthcare professionals since the early 18th century, when hospitals were being established in the United States. The participation and collaboration of all providers of patient services were essential at that time and remain today a salient factor in the delivery of those services. With the increased complexity of healthcare systems, taking into consideration economic and regulatory factors, healthcare professionals who are staffing various departments and units in hospitals are constantly asked to do more with less. We do more with less now because we care and are committed to excellence while recognizing that all entities involved in the delivery of patient services must work as a team to achieve the common goal of quality patient care.

As the dean of a college of health professions at a large public university with a history of preparing healthcare professionals, it gives me a great sense of pride to present this pertinent and relevant book. The chapters were written by faculty who recognize the importance of all healthcare professionals working together to maintain a relationship among quality, efficiency, and cost. As a reader of this 2010 edition, you will delve into the patterns and practices of the specific disciplines of clinical laboratory science, communication disorders, health administration, health information management, nursing, physical therapy, radiation therapy, and respiratory care. I believe you and your constituents will benefit from the richness of the presented perspective on specific healthcare services while recognizing the vital importance of collaboration.

Given that the healthcare disciplines are comprised of individuals who bring to the work environment their own professional culture, personality and attitudes, specific discipline knowledge, communication style, and scope of practice, it becomes even more critical to the overall complexity of the organization's function to achieve a successful collaboration.

Recognizing a term from our past, the healthcare "team," we now search for different words to describe the collaborative effort that is so critical to quality patient services. Whether we call it an interprofessional team, a participative management team, culture of accountability, team engagement, or integrative care, we know that for the various healthcare disciplines to interact successfully, they must function as one entity. This entity must then successfully influence the effectiveness of the organization that has the task of providing healthcare for patients.

After accomplishing many measures of success in the delivery of patient services this century, healthcare professionals are now poised to move into the 21st century with confidence, recognizing that our hospitals, driven by promising new technologies and skilled healthcare professionals, must work together in collaborative ways and strive for systematic and creative approaches in delivering healthcare services.

Ruth B. Welborn, PhD
Dean
College of Health Professions
Texas State University
San Marcos, Texas

Introduction to the Fourth Edition

Hospitals and medical centers are very complex institutions that treat thousands of patients, not yearly, but monthly. Some patients visit the hospital for routine tests or outpatient imaging services, some come to give birth, many face life-threatening emergencies, and some will not leave the institution alive—such is the daily routine of a modern medical center, whether it is in San Marcos, Texas; Shanghai, China; or Riyadh, Saudi Arabia.

This text is designed to simplify the complexity of the medical center by breaking it down into manageable portions. The reader will be guided not only through the medical, surgical, ancillary, and support services, but also the financial center that is responsible for the ABCs of accounting, billing, collecting, and the ever-important budget. The reader should be able to better understand the necessity of quality improvement, patient safety, and accreditation. For those students considering a career in healthcare, this text may provide inspiration to follow career paths into nursing, physical therapy, administration, finance, or medicine. The text attempts to be an all-encompassing examination of hospitals—what they are and how they work.

With the passage of the Health Care Reform Act on March 23, 2010, the American healthcare system underwent a dramatic shift to expand access to care for millions of otherwise uninsured Americans, while moving simultaneously to reduce the cost of health care.

This will also likely have a positive impact on the quality of health care delivered in the United States. On the downside, many seniors are bracing for cuts to Medicare, as are physicians and hospitals. Offsetting this may be increased insurance enrollments, as most citizens will be required to purchase health insurance.

These factors should not impact the fundamental mission of an acute-care facility: to provide health care to those in need. Physicians, clinicians, and administrators will have to work together to enhance quality and shorten the average length of stay while still managing to stay within the cost structure.

Part I

An Overview of Hospitals

CHAPTER 1

History of Hospitals and Health Care

Peggy Johnson

KEY TERMS

Hospital

Hippocrates

Almshouses

Pennsylvania Hospital

Florence Nightingale

Ignaz Semmelweis

American Medical
Association (AMA)

THE VERY EARLY DAYS

Health care, unquestionably, is a principal issue in the national consciousness of Americans. We are bombarded daily with debates over healthcare financing, new challenges and risks to health, the ethical implications of genome mapping, abortion rights, and various other dilemmas faced by both providers and patients. In the United States, 16% of our gross national product is consumed by health care, and with health care continuing to change at a breathtaking pace, the urgency of our healthcare dilemma can hardly be ignored. However, the problems of the system today have deep roots in the past. This chapter explores the diverse ways in which human beings have experienced sickness, and how hospitals and medical care have evolved over time. The history of our health culture helps us understand the problems, as well as the potential, of our healthcare systems today.

Hospitals date back to the beginning of civilization and medicine. According to medical anthropologists, they began as organized institutions more than 4000 years ago in Mesopotamia, and hospitals existed in Egypt and India even in antiquity. In the great river valleys of the world that were favorable for settlement, tribes became empires and civilizations rose and fell. Hospitals and medicine played a part in this world history, and have always had a relation to the political and economic affairs of society and the prevailing social norms of the day. After Christianity and Islam became widespread, hospitals were built in both Christian and Moslem countries (Chilliers & Retief, 2005).

Written accounts and archeological finds provide a window into the medical care of the time in the great civilizations of Egypt, China, Persia, Greece, and Rome (Risse, 1999). The historian Herodotus touted the Egyptians as a particularly healthy people with good health practices and gifted physicians. Early medical practices in Egypt and in many other ancient societies were integrated into religious practices, services, and ceremonies. Transcripts identifying certain religious deities with specific healing abilities dating back to 4000 BC. The temples of Greek and Roman gods, such as Saturn, and later of Asclepius in Asia Minor, were recognized as healing centers. These centers provided refuge for the sick and offered pleasant vistas, salty air, hot and cold baths, and prescribed medications such as salt, honey, and water from sacred springs. Around 100 BC, the Romans established hospitals (valetudinaria) for the treatment of their sick and injured soldiers. Providing care for the legions was of paramount importance, as the power of Rome depended on its great army (Risse, 1999).

Ancient Greek writings also tell of temples and healing places. Certain gods were named for their healing powers. Aelius Aristides, a wealthy Roman orator, who was reported going to a Greek temple to seek healing from the goddess Isis (Risse, 1999). **Hippocrates**, considered the father of medicine, advocated a rational, nonreligious approach to the practice of medicine. Hippocrates started the practice of auscultation (the act of listening to sounds of organs within the body), performed surgical operations, and kept detailed records of his patients in which he described diseases ranging from tuberculosis to ulcers (Risse, 1999). In the Asclepieion of Epidaurus, (Risse, 1999) three large marble boards that date to 350 BC preserve the names, case histories, complaints, and cures of about 70 patients who came to the temple with a healthcare need. These are reported to be among the first medical records. The surgeries listed in these records, such as lancing of an abdominal abscess or removal of foreign material, could have taken place while the patient was sedated with some soporific substance, such as opium, that was used at the time (Risse, 1999).

During the early days of Christianity in the Near East, sickness became a source of constant anxiety. Growing population densities and resultant sanitation issues in areas such as Rome and Mesopotamia were responsible for epidemics of infectious diseases that kept mortality rates high during this period (Chilliers & Retief, 2002). The rise of commerce with the Far East, over the Silk Road, brought people into frequent contact with foreign populations, and two separate disease pools—east and west—came together with grave consequences for the entire region. Many diseases, such as smallpox, measles, and plague, routinely devastated populations. The Byzantine Empire, for example, succumbed to famine and civil unrest brought about by extensive migrations from rural to urban centers, where both endemic and epidemic diseases decimated the cities (Chilliers & Retief, 2002).

As in Rome, the practice of medicine in Persia also became widespread. The Persians are credited with preserving the early Greek texts until the time of the Renaissance, and without their efforts, much would have been lost (Chilliers & Retief, 2002). Three kinds of medicine are described in a passage of the Vendidad, one of the surviving texts of the Zend-Avesta, found in the early 1700s: medicine by the knife (surgery), medicine by herbs, and medicine by divine words. According to the Vendidad, the best medicine was healing by divine words (Chilliers & Retief, 2002).

During the Middle Ages, the hospital movement grew to accommodate the Crusades, which began in 1096. Military hospitals sprang up for the wounded and weary crusaders along all the travelled roads. However, the most rapid growth in the number of hospitals in Europe occurred during the 12th and 13th centuries. In the 12th century in particular, religiously founded monastic hospitals flourished, and some became important teaching institutions (Risse, 1999). The Benedictines established the greatest number of monastic institutions—reportedly more than 2000. Hospitals were also established in Baghdad and Damascus during that time. The Arab hospitals were notable in that they admitted patients regardless of religious belief, race, or social order. Additionally, the Arab hospital system relied on resources from the community, all treatments were free of charge, and each member of society donated a portion of his or her wealth to support the institution (Risse, 1999).

The structure of hospital-like institutions began to change in the

Middle Ages as secular authorities began to support some type of institutional care. Hospitals served several functions during this time: they were almshouses for the poor, hostels for pilgrims, and institutions of learning for physicians in training. This gradual transfer of responsibility for institutional health care from the church to civil authorities continued in Europe after Henry VIII dissolved the monasteries in 1540. Monastic hospitals were gone in England by the late 1600s, which led the secular authorities to begin caring for the sick and injured in their communities. Toward the end of the 15th century, many towns and cities supported some type of institutionalized care. Reportedly, there were 200 such establishments at this time, indicating a growing social need in Britain (Risse, 1999; Starr, 1982). This was the beginning of the voluntary hospital movement. In France, the first such institution was probably established by the Huguenots around 1718 (Risse, 1999).

EARLY AMERICAN HOSPITALS: FROM THE FOUNDING OF THE NEW WORLD THROUGH WORLD WAR II (1500–1945)

Hernando Cortes built the first North American hospital in Mexico City in 1524, which is still standing. Near the middle of the 1600s, the French established a hospital in Canada in Quebec City. Jeanne Mance, a French noblewoman, built a hospital of ax-hewn logs on the island of Montreal in 1644 (Starr, 1982). The order of the Sisters of St. Joseph, now considered to be the oldest nursing group organized in North America, grew out of this endeavor. A hospital for soldiers on Manhattan Island, established in 1663, was the first hospital in the United States. **Almshouses** served as early hospitals in the United States, one of the first of which was established by William Penn in Philadelphia in 1713 (Starr, 1982).

The **Pennsylvania Hospital**, in Philadelphia, was the first incorporated hospital in America. The Pennsylvania Hospital was organized by Dr. Thomas Boyd to provide a place for Philadelphia physicians to treat their private patients. Benjamin Franklin helped Boyd obtain a charter from the crown in 1751 (Starr, 1982). In contrast, in 1769, New York City, with 300,000 residents, still had no hospital. Dr. John Jones formed the Society of New York Hospital and obtained a grant to build a hospital. During the Revolution, however, the New York Hospital fell into the hands of the British, who used it as a barracks and military hospital. Other early hospitals of historic interest include two marine hospitals (one in Boston, Massachusetts, and one in Norfolk, Virginia) that were established by the federal government in 1802 to provide care for sick servicemen (Starr, 1982). The first psychiatric hospital was established in Williamsburg, Virginia, in 1773. Massachusetts General Hospital in Boston, one of the pioneer hospitals of modern medicine, admitted its first patient, a 30-year-old soldier, in 1821.

Hospital systems in America developed in three distinct phases. The first, running roughly from 1751 to 1851, saw the formation of two kinds of institutions: voluntary hospitals operated by charitable boards and public hospitals descended from almshouses operated by municipalities. The second phase began about 1850, when particularistic (primarily religious or ethnic) and specialized hospitals became established. The third phase saw the development of profit-making hospitals operated by physicians, singly or in partnership, or corporations (Starr, 1982).

Americans were not inclined to seek care from hospitals during most of the early 19th century, and for more than a century to come, most Americans gave birth and endured illness and even surgery at home. The reasons for this were multiple: First, the country remained a largely rural society at this time, and few people had ever even seen a hospital. Second, the indirect cost of visiting a hospital could mean the loss of several days' work and perhaps the crops for that season. Hospitals also had a reputation, deservedly so, as death houses. Mortality rates in hospitals during this era were very high. Finally, during the Victorian era, when modesty and a desire for privacy prevailed, people preferred to be seen by their physician at home (Starr, 1982).

In the United States, the late 19th century was a period of economic expansion and rapid institutional development. Weber described the changing social structure as a general movement from communal to associative relations. After the industrial revolution, social structures changed and families were no longer able to provide care to family members as they had before. Families no longer lived primarily in large houses with many members; many had migrated to cities, had fewer children, and lived in smaller households. Households and communities gave up their functions to organizations, and these organizations also changed. Hospitals were first almshouses—unspecialized institutions that served general welfare functions and only incidentally cared for the sick. Almshouses metamorphosed into modern hospitals by first becoming more specialized in their function and then becoming more universal in their use (Starr, 1982).

Despite the fact that the number of institutions increased during the first half of the 19th century, this time stands out as a dark period in the history of hospitals. More surgeries were performed during this time than in any other period in the history of medicine. However, few of these surgeries were successful, and in contrast to earlier surgeons, who had at least attempted to keep wounds clean, physicians in this era considered the production and discharge of pus (suppuration) to be desirable and encouraged it. The mortality rates reflected the error of this belief (Starr, 1982). Surgeons wore the same operating gowns for months between washings, and the same bed linens served several patients. Gangrene, hemorrhage, and infections infested the wards of hospitals. Mortality rates from surgeries ran as high as 90%. To tolerate the stench of the wards, nurses used snuff and wore perfumed masks. By the time of the Civil War, however, hospitals had largely managed to overcome their reputation for squalor. The Union had established a system of over 130,000 beds by the last year of the war and treated over 1 million soldiers. Germ theory was not yet fully formulated, but the influence of **Florence Nightingale** made the system work better (Starr, 1982).

The contributions of Florence Nightingale during the mid-19th century are unfathomable in today's clean and modern healthcare setting. In the 1830s, Florence Nightingale went to Kaiserwerth, on the Rhine, to train as a nurse. She wrote disparagingly of her training, especially regarding the hygiene practices, and gained a reputation for delivering effective and efficient nursing care. In 1854, she was sent by the English government to improve the deplorable conditions of the care given to the sick and wounded soldiers of the Crimean War. The appalling conditions she found, including men lying in dirt and vermin, were quickly remedied. Florence Nightingale brought order and cleanliness to the practice of nursing. She organized kitchens, a laundry service, and departments for supplies, often using her own resources to fund her projects. Florence Nightingale brought an organized approach to the operation of hospitals and is considered by many to be the first true healthcare administrator. One of her major contributions was her use of statistics to track infections and determine the real cause of mortality in the Crimean War. This was one of the earliest uses of the scientific method to determine the cause of disease and develop effective treatment plans. Before many of the lifesaving innovations of that time had even been discovered, Florence Nightingale had decreased the incidence of disease and the ensuing mortality with her hygienic approach to nursing care (Starr, 1982).

Two developments brought about even more pronounced improvements. One was the professionalization of nursing. In 1873, three training schools were established in New York, New Haven, and Boston. The training of nurses and oversight of nursing in hospitals was taken up as a cause by upper-class women in New York. Some physicians opposed it, however, saying that educated nurses probably would not do as they were told. But the women prevailed and nursing became a profession. The other development was the advent of antiseptic surgery in 1867, led by Joseph Lister (Rosen, 1993). Like nursing, surgery enjoyed a tremendous rise in prestige in the late 1800s. The discovery of anesthesia made the practice of surgery much easier, and surgeries became slower, more careful, and safer endeavors. Surgery really began to take off in the 1890s and early 1900s, increasing in amount, scope, and daring. In 1883, the number of surgical patients exceeded that of medical patients for the first time in Boston hospitals. Hospitals also became more generally accepted and began to serve patients of different social classes. By the early 20th century, the occupational distribution of the adult patient population reflected that of the general population.

The introduction of the scientific method into medicine during this time was an important phase in the development of health care in this country and throughout the world. Louis Pasteur discovered bacteria while trying to help a friend determine why his beer was going bad before he could sell it. He further determined that it was also the cause of disease. In Europe, early infection control was achieved through the efforts of **Ignaz Semmelweis** of Vienna, Austria. Appalled at the high rate of mortality among postpartum women in his hospital, Semmelweis used the statistical data he gathered from medical students on the maternity ward to determine the cause of the infections. He boldly informed his colleagues that the high mortality rate from puerperal fever in maternity patients was due to infection transmitted by students who came from the dissecting room to take care of the patients on the maternity ward. The mortality rate was much lower for poorer women who were cared for by midwives, who practiced better hygiene. Semmelweis required the medical students to scrub their hands before seeing patients, and although he made enemies, he also lowered the mortality rate in the Lying-in Hospital's maternity ward. This was the beginning of work on germ theory, and along with the findings of Pasteur and others, the origin of modern bacteriology and clinical laboratories. Joseph Lister continued Pasteur's work. He noticed that broken bones over which the skin remained intact healed much faster and with fewer complications compared to fractures that were exposed. Lister theorized that some element that was introduced through the wound and then circulated within the body was responsible for the infections. By 1870, surgeons were following a protocol of spraying carbolic solution on both surgeons and patients, and in the operating rooms, resulting in fewer surgery-related infections. Two other important developments were the introduction of steam sterilization by Bergmann in 1886 and rubber gloves by Halstead in 1890 (Rosen, 1993).

The end of the 19th century also brought the discovery of anesthesia and antiseptics, two of the most significant influences on the development of modern surgical procedures. One of the final major achievements of the decade was the discovery of the x-ray in 1895. Additionally, hospitals began to care for patients with communicable diseases during this time. During the last decade of the century, the tubercle bacillus and malaria parasite were discovered, Pasteur vaccinated against anthrax, and Koch isolated the cholera and tetanus bacilli (Rosen, 1993).

The discoveries and events of the 19th century resulted in a great many hospitals being constructed in a short period of time. By the end of the century in the United States, there were 149 hospitals with a bed capacity of more than 35,000, and fewer than 10% of these were under any kind of government control (Starr, 1982). After 1900, the elite voluntary hospitals concentrated on acute care and had relatively closed medical staffs and the closest ties to universities. The municipal and county hospitals, usually the largest local institutions in terms of number of beds, cared for a full range of acute and chronic illnesses. The religious and ethnic hospitals were a mixed, intermediate group that rarely had endowments and consequently relied on patient fees. The profit-making hospitals were mainly surgical centers; they were usually small and had no ties to medical schools (Starr, 1982).

The **American Medical Association (AMA)** was founded in 1847 under the leadership of Dr. Nathan Smith. Additionally, during the 19th century, women were finally accepted as physicians after a considerable struggle. Also against considerable resistance, the AMA strove to raise the standards of medical education and professional competency during the early part of the 20th century. The Flexner Report, written by Abraham Flexner, a professional educator, was published in 1910 and proved to be a severe indictment of the system. Among the deficiencies Flexner wrote about were touted laboratories that did not exist, no disinfectant in dissecting rooms, libraries without books, alleged faculty members busily occupied in their private practices, and medical schools routinely waiving admission requirements for those who could pay. Flexner found a great discrepancy between medical science and medical education, and his report brought about great changes in medical education (Starr, 1982).

THE MODERN ERA: POST–WORLD WAR II TO THE PRESENT (1945–2010)

In the 20th century, two world wars ushered in major social, political, and technological changes in the United States. This marked the advent of interest in the financing of health care with the growth of insurance plans, such as Blue Cross and Blue Shield, in the nonprofit sector and many other for-profit insurance companies. The federal government also began to assume a larger role with regard to health care, as evidenced by the Hill-Burton Act and the establishment of research institutions such as the National Institutes of Health. By 1965, the implementation of Medicare and Medicaid established the principle that health care is a right, not a privilege (Starr, 1982).

During the 20th century, hospitals began to take on additional roles. Not only do modern hospitals provide care for the sick and ailing, and clinical education for the entire continuum of healthcare professionals, many also serve as an institution of health education for entire neighborhoods, communities, and regions (Starr, 1982). The hospital of today provides education for both professionals and laypersons, and conducts research in medical sciences from medical records, patients, and the community.

Beginning in the 1980s, restriction of growth and reorganization of the methods used to finance and deliver health care began to bring about a new era of medicine in the United States. Cost-containment policies and initiatives from Medicare and health insurance plans in general have resulted in diminishing reimbursements. Not only was there a decrease in the expansion of hospitals, there was also an increase in hospital failures and bed closings (Starr, 1982). The healthcare system began to emphasize outpatient rather than inpatient services, and to focus on expansion of ancillary medical facilities and freestanding outpatient centers.

Today, hospitals are just one among several components in the continuing evolution of organized delivery systems and the continuum of care. Some see the role of the hospital in the future continuing to change, with hospitals expected to serve only patients with complex problems (Starr, 1982). Many patients will probably be cared for at home or in other nonhospital settings. Many experts predict that hospitals will continue to downsize while still attempting to meet growing social needs and provide refuge for the poor and ailing.

SUMMARY

Early American hospitals were largely founded on the heritage of European hospitals. However, US hospitals developed rapidly and soon became quite different from their early counterparts. Hospitals began to care for the sick almost incidentally. The earliest hospitals were established for pilgrims, indigents, and plague victims. Later, they became institutions where people from all parts of society could come for diagnosis and recovery.

The hospital as an institution has become dynamic in nature; it exists to meet the needs of the people it serves. Today's hospitals continue to make history by reacting to the changing needs of society and providing better technologies, new services, and greater access.

CHAPTER REVIEW

1. According to medical anthropologists, where and when did hospitals begin?
2. Who is considered the father of medicine, and what was his approach to the practice of medicine?
3. List several functions of hospitals during the Middle Ages.
4. What is an almshouse?
5. When and where was the first hospital established in the United States, and what was its purpose?
6. What made the Pennsylvania Hospital different from previous hospitals?
7. Name the three phases in the development of hospital systems in America.
8. Why is Florence Nightingale important to the history of hospitals?
9. Discuss early infection-control efforts by Ignaz Semmelweis.
10. What is the AMA and why is it important?
11. What are some predictions regarding the role of hospitals?

REFERENCES

See page 350.

CHAPTER 2

Hospitals and Important Hospital Trends

Jim Summers and Donald J. Griffin

KEY TERMS

Average length of stay (ALOS)
Community hospitals
Specialty hospitals
Governmental

Outpatient visits
Proprietary hospitals
(for profit)

BACKGROUND

Hospitals are a vital part of society's infrastructure—as important as schools, the police department, or a dependable firefighting service. It is important to understand some macro information, such as the number of hospitals available, how hospitals are classified, the typical cost per day and per stay, and the **average length of stay (ALOS)** that might be expected.

Of equal importance are trends in hospital systems: Are hospitals increasing or decreasing in number, and are they becoming more or less profitable?

HOW WE CLASSIFY HOSPITALS

Hospitals may be classified in a number of different ways, such as by location (e.g., rural or **community hospitals**) or **specialty** (e.g., women's hospitals, orthopedic hospitals, cardiac hospitals, surgical hospitals, or,

Table 2-1. Number of Hospitals and Beds: 2009

	Hospitals	Beds
Federal	213	45,992
Nonfederal	5,602	905,053
Community	5,010	808,069
State and Land Government	1,105	130,531
Nongovernment not-for-profit	2,923	556,651
Investor Owned	982	120,887
Non Metropolitan	1,998	143,524
Metropolitan	3,012	664,545
US Total	**5,815**	**951,045**

Source: AHA Annual Survey Data for fiscal year 2008.

in the past, tuberculosis hospitals). Hospitals can also be classified by size, such as community-access hospitals (small, rural hospitals with fewer than 25 beds) or, at the other extreme, tertiary-care or academic medical centers that offer every specialty and subspecialty that is practiced in medicine (e.g., pediatric cardiology).

Hospitals may also be commonly classified as **governmental** or non-governmental. Examples of governmental entities would be the Veterans Administration (approximately 175 hospitals), the Indian Health Service, and military hospitals. When analyzing or comparing hospitals, such as a physician-owned orthopedic hospital and a government-owned military hospital, it is important to bear in mind the institutional differences between them (Table 2-1).

TRENDS IN GENERAL ACUTE-CARE COMMUNITY HOSPITALS

Trend 1: Downsizing, Mergers, and Closures

In the 1990s, the hospital industry in the United States underwent a host of consolidations and mergers, reflecting the fact that the system was "overbedded," with too many providers. Many hospitals had less

Table 2-2. Data for All AHA-Registered Hospitals in the United States

Year	1970	1980	1990	2000	2008
No. of Hosp.	7123	6965	6649	5810	5815
Beds (thous.)	1616	1365	1213	984	951
ALOS	****	7.6	7.2	5.8	5.5
Cost per day	****	$245	687	1149	1782
Cost per stay	****	$1851	4946	6649	9788

Source: AHA Hospital Statistics, 2009 Health Forum LLC.

than 50% occupancy and struggled to maintain enough revenue to operate efficiently. It was commonplace to see several hospitals in large metropolitan areas close, downsize, or merge with competitors, although this was not always bad. For example, in a metropolitan area with seven hospitals, three might battle to be the dominant purveyor of acute-care services. To avoid underutilization of the other hospitals, a common ownership could be established under which each hospital could specialize in a different field. For example, one might focus on cardiac care, the second on women's and obstetrics issues, and the third on general care (provided that this business arrangement would be allowed under antitrust statutes). (See Table 2-2 for a summary of data regarding American Hospital Association (AHA)-registered hospitals in the United States.)

In addition to the issue of surplus acute-care beds, another factor that resulted in mergers and downsizing was that physicians began to shift their focus from inpatient care to **outpatient** care in facilities in which they had partial ownership. Procedures that could be performed without an overnight stay in the hospital began to move to the forefront of many practices. These included procedures performed in outpatient surgery, outpatient imaging (CT, MRI, and PET), and even outpatient cancer treatment centers. This reduction in hospitals was also driven by improvements in medicine, tighter reimbursement policies, and better management. It is fair to say that the less sick benefited from the greater availability of outpatient services and less hospitalization. Together, these factors led to both fewer hospital admissions and shorter ALOS in American hospitals (Figure 2-1).

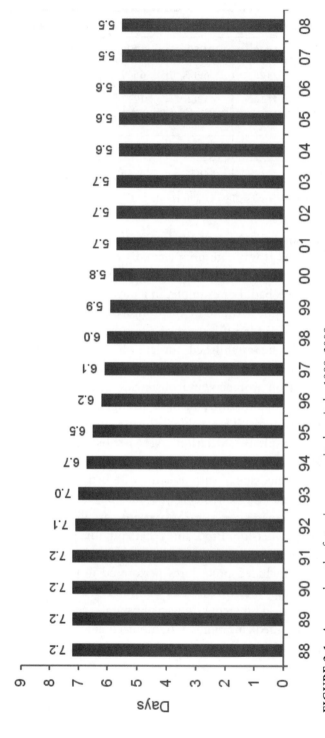

FIGURE 2-1. Average length of stay in community hospitals, 1988–2008.
Source: Avalere Health analysis of American Hospital Association Annual Survey data, 2008, for community hospitals.

This trend in hospital closures, admissions, and shorter ALOS will likely soon be reversed. As Americans age, the need for additional health care will increase, and in turn, more hospitals and physicians will be required. The country may now be at the bottom of a trough, and the number of hospitals and hospital beds can be expected to increase in the immediate future (2010–2025).

Trend 2: Tighter Profit Margins

The downsizing of hospitals has not resulted in lower hospital expenses. Because of the skyrocketing costs of technology (physicians want the latest and greatest MRI and CT scanners, and other hardware), the rising number of uninsured (before passage of the Patient Protection and Affordable Care Act in March 2010), the relatively low reimbursement rate of Medicare and Medicaid (which usually cover 40–50% of hospitalized patients), the trend is toward much tighter profit margins—if a profit is made at all. The future of many general acute-care facilities may be in jeopardy, while at the same time society will need more hospitals because of the aging baby boomers. The following bar graph illustrates an average hospital's payer mix. Please note that "private pay" in the chart represents nearly all payments other than Medicare and Medicaid, which in this case includes third-party insurance and self-pay patients (Figure 2-2).

This payer mix is of critical concern because of the currently low Medicare and Medicaid payment rates. In its annual survey, the AHA estimated that this payment structure has resulted in a $33 billion shortfall for all community hospitals in the United States (Figure 2-3). This downwardly negative payment structure is increasing negative operating costs and decreasing total profit margins (Figure 2-4). Stated another way, when operating revenues and expenses are plotted over time, we begin to see expenses exceeding revenues (Figure 2-5).

Trend 3: Increased Building of Specialty Hospitals

Specialty hospitals, which are frequently **proprietary** (for-profit) and physician-owned institutions, can be controversial. Instead of offering care to the entire general population, as traditionally done by acute-care hospitals, specialty hospitals appear to serve a favorable selection of patients and avoid charity care and emergency services. Critics also contend that physician ownership creates incentives that may inappropriately affect referrals and clinical behaviors.

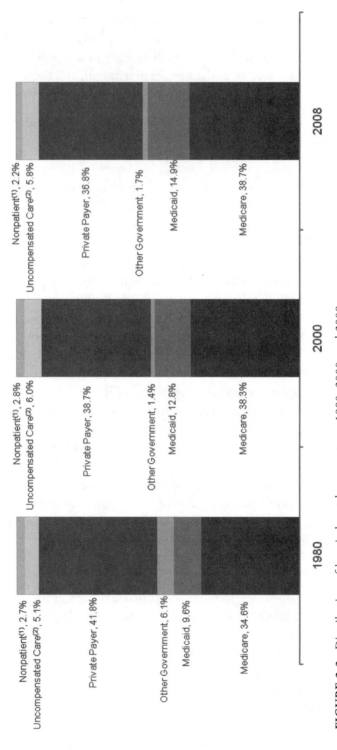

FIGURE 2-2. Distribution of hospital cost by payer type, 1980, 2000, and 2008.

Source: Avalere Health analysis of American Hospital Association Annual Survey data, 2008, for community hospitals.

(1) Nonpatient represents costs for cafeterias, parking lots, gift shops, and other nonpatient care operating services and are not attributed to any one payer.

(2) Uncompensated care represents bad debt expense and charity care, at cost.

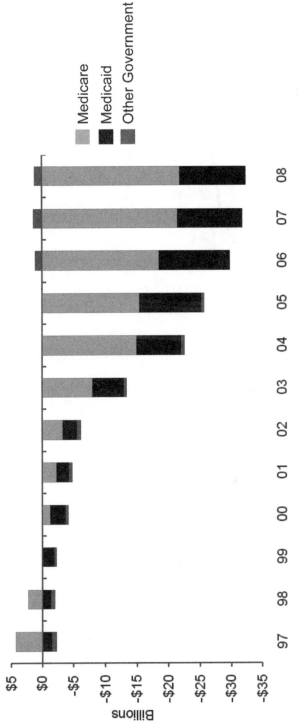

FIGURE 2-3. Hospital payment shortfall relative to costs for Medicare, Medicaid, and other government, 1997–2008.[1]
Source: Avalere Health analysis of American Hospital Association Annual Survey data, 2008, for community hospitals.
[1] Costs reflect a cap of 1.0 on the cost-to-charge ratio.

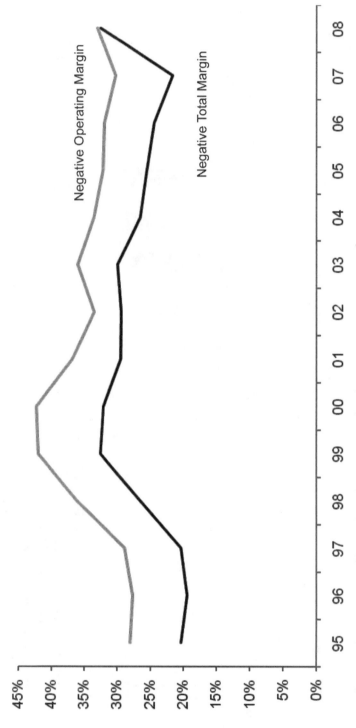

FIGURE 2-4. Percentage of hospitals with negative total and operating margins, 1995–2008.
Source: Avalere Health analysis of American Hospital Association Annual Survey data, 2008, for community hospitals.

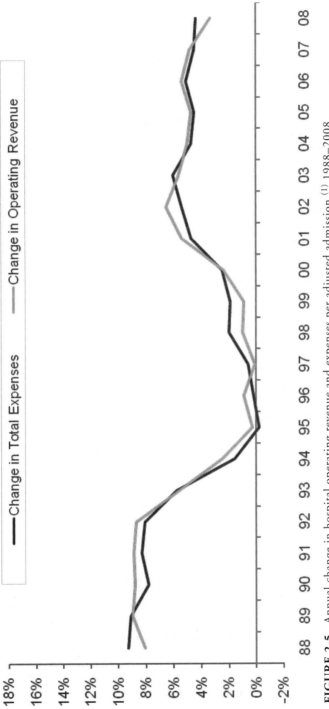

FIGURE 2-5. Annual change in hospital operating revenue and expenses per adjusted admission,[1] 1988–2008.

Source: Avalere Health analysis of American Hospital Association Annual Survey data, 2008, for community hospitals.

(1) An aggregate measure of workload reflecting the number of inpatient admissions, plus an estimate of the volume of outpatient services, expressed in units equivalent to an inpatient admission in terms of level of effort.

Advocates contend, however, that specialty hospitals can provide better and more efficient treatment for greater numbers of patients who need the same specialization of care.

For most health services, the Stark Law (or physician self-referral law) prohibits the referral of Medicare/Medicaid patients to facilities in which the physician has a financial interest; however, there is an important exception, termed the "whole-hospital exception." Physicians are permitted to refer patients if they have an ownership interest in the entire hospital and are also authorized to perform services there.

To address concerns about the negative effect of physician-owned hospitals on community hospitals, Congress established a moratorium from December 8, 2003, through June 7, 2005, to prohibit specialty hospitals from submitting claims for services as a result of physician-owner referrals. During this moratorium, the Department of Health and Human Services was charged with examining the overall impact of specialty hospitals.

As a result of the preceding study, the whole hospital exception to Stark will soon be a thing of the past. The Patient Protection and Affordable Care Act (commonly known as healthcare reform), signed into law March 23, 2010, along with modifications specified by the Health Care and Education Reconciliation Act of 2010 (commonly known as the amendment to healthcare reform), signed into law on March 30, 2010, will ban physician ownership of hospitals beginning in 2011. Unless they are repealed or amended, these acts should slow the construction of new specialty hospitals.

It is worth noting that physician-owned hospitals are exempt from Stark if they do not take Medicare reimbursement. In fact, many such specialty hospitals tend to treat well-insured, lower-acuity patients while avoiding Medicare, Medicaid, and uninsured patients.

Trend 4: Increasing Shortage of Nursing Personnel

Because of the increasing number of aging baby boomers, hospitals and the entire healthcare industry in general will need an increasing supply of nurses. Yet, just the opposite is predicted to occur. The majority of nurses today are in their mid 40s, and for every eight who leave the field, only five enter. This will lead to an ever-increasing demand for nurses while the supply curve moves downward. As a result, hospitals should expect higher increases in nursing salaries (Figure 2-6).

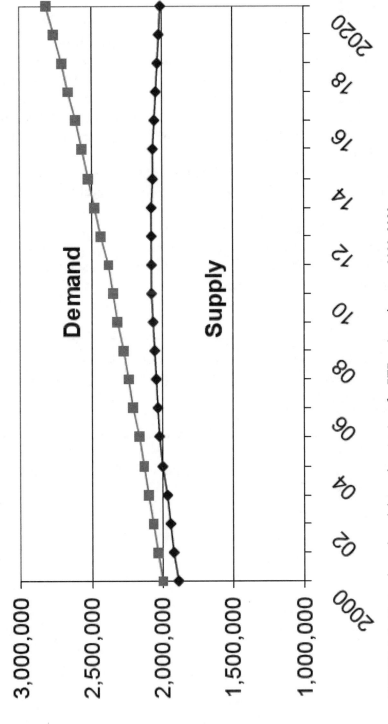

FIGURE 2-6. National supply and demand projections for FTE registered nurses: 2000–2020.
Source: Bureau of Health Professions, RN Supply and Demand Projections

SUMMARY

Although hospitals have declined in number, they are now better controlling the ALOS. Medicare and Medicaid expenses are exceeding revenues in most hospitals. Because of the negative economy, many Americans are without jobs and thus without health insurance. The healthcare industry and hospitals in particular have lost the support of employer-backed health insurance, which largely made up for the deficiencies of Medicare and Medicaid.

The Patient Protection and Affordable Care Act may serve to close this gap by mandating that most citizens purchase health insurance. However, this could be offset by cuts to the Medicare budget. As an interesting result of this legislation, physicians may be forced to divest themselves of ownership in specialty hospitals, allowing general acute-care facilities to regain their foothold in some areas of medicine that are more profitable.

CHAPTER REVIEW

1. What are five ways in which a hospital can be classified?
2. Has the number of US hospitals increased or decreased in the last 30 years? Why?
3. Why has the ALOS decreased in hospitals?
4. What are the likely effects of the healthcare reform bill that passed in March 2010?
5. Why was there an increase in the number of specialty hospitals? Why has this changed?

Part II
Leadership

CHAPTER 3

Organizational Structure, the Governing Body, and the CEO

Donald J. Griffin

KEY TERMS

Organizational structure
 (tall or flat)
Pyramid organization
Organizational theory
Span of control
Specialization
Board of directors
Board of trustees
Chief executive officer (CEO)
Chief operating officer (COO)
Team of three
Multihospital system

Appointing the medical staff
Fiduciary duty of the board of
 directors
American College of Healthcare
 Executives (ACHE)
Inside activities
Respondeat superior
Ex officio members
Outside activities
Networking
Chain of command

THEORIES OF ORGANIZATION, INTRODUCTION OF CONCEPTS

Introduction: Common Organizational Management Principles

Any organization may be viewed from a macro sense or a micro sense. For example, are we choosing to examine the entire Veterans Administration (VA) system, a single VA hospital, or a department within a VA hospital?

A hospital system may span across a nation or function within a single state or city. In the VA system, for example, there are approximately 175 hospitals, 400 clinics, and 126 nursing homes providing services to American veterans. The system is managed from a central office in Washington, DC; regional offices oversee several states, and local administrators supervise each hospital. This and many other hospital systems take on a pyramid **organizational structure** (Figure 3-1).

Efforts are being made to modernize the pyramid structure by making it flatter. Better organizational success can be achieved by expanding the scope of control to allow important decisions to be made at lower levels in

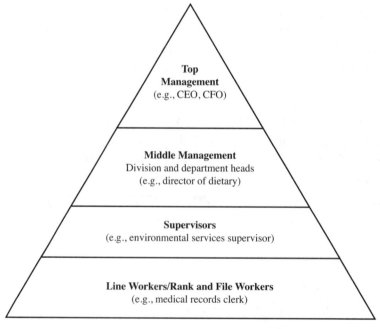

FIGURE 3-1. Pyramid organization.

the organization. For example, instead of the head of a department seeking the approval of an assistant administrator who oversees several departments, then the assistant administrator seeking the approval of a vice president (VP) who supervises a significant portion of the hospital, and then the VP discussing this with the chief executive officer (CEO), the decision can be made at the department level, provided the department stays within the previously approved budget.

For example, the imaging department may budget for an updated computed tomography (CT) scanner during the annual budget process. During the budget process, various CT models are discussed within the department, with input from members of the department (radiologists) who will directly use them, along with anticipated prices. After the board and chief hospital management approve the overall hospital budget, sometime during the next year, the imaging department will select a vendor, a final price, and a service contract. At the appropriate time, the department staff can act autonomously and initiate the transaction without being slowed down by red tape during the purchase, delivery, installation, and training period.

Hospitals also may use **organizational theory** to supervise personnel. According to the concept commonly known as "**span of control**," a manager can effectively and directly supervise a limited number of people (usually 8 to 10). This is especially true for the functional areas of housekeeping, dietary services, and nursing.

There is also specialization of labor within the organization of a hospital. **Specialization** refers to the ways in which a hospital organizes to identify specific tasks and to assign a job description and position number to each person. For example, a nurse's aide has a specific job that differs from that of a licensed vocational nurse (LVN, sometimes called a licensed practical nurse [LPN]), and an LVN differs from a registered nurse (RN), who in turn differs from a nurse practitioner or clinical nurse specialist.

Position numbers are assigned to each position so that the administrator can control the number of employees who are budgeted to work. If position #135 is an RN and the RN leaves the hospital's employment, only an RN may fill the vacant position #135.

In addition to the pyramid structure or the more modern, flatter structure discussed previously, organizational theory may be used to form teams (Figure 3-2). Such teams cut across department lines and are used for special projects, for limited time periods. For example, when a hospital is preparing for a Joint Commission survey, which usually occurs every 3 years, an

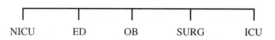

NICU   ED   OB   SURG   ICU

FIGURE 3-2. Product-line management (nursing).

intense effort is often made during the last 12–18 months before the survey. Teams are formed to focus on each standard of the survey. Teams may also be formed to study anticipated projects or product lines before the hospital commits large resources to them. For example, a team could be formed to brainstorm about new clinic locations and what each clinic would offer. Such a team might be comprised of personnel representing the physical therapy, pediatric, and OB/GYN departments in order to correctly anticipate the array of services needed to meet the needs of each clinic. Teams provide a useful tool because they foster cooperation, place authority in the hands of those who best know the processes involved, and can be disbanded and reformed for other projects when the need arises.

Product-line management is also very useful. Under this scheme, hospitals or divisions within the hospital are organized according to a specific product line. These categories may also be referred to as strategic business units. For example, a hospital might elect to organize around its surgical or obstetrical services or products within a formal department, such as nursing.

Line and Staff Functions

Line managers are usually viewed as supervisors who direct workers and sometimes have the authority to hire and fire, whereas staff members are usually assigned routine tasks they are expected to complete. Nurse managers have line authority, and floor nurses have staff functions.

ORGANIZATION CHART

In an overall view of a hospital, the **board of directors** (sometimes called the **board of trustees**) occupies the position at the top of the chart. The board hires and fires the **CEO** (sometimes called the executive director, administrator, or president), and also sets policy for the hospital. It is the final authority for the hospital and bears a fiduciary (greater-than-normal) responsibility for the people the hospital serves.

The CEO is responsible for the day-to-day operations of the facility and usually has some flexibility in managing it. The same general administrative hierarchical principles apply, whether the organization takes the form of a pyramid or a more modern, flatter organizational shape. Depending on the size of the organization, the administrator may be aided by associate administrators, assistant administrators, a **chief operating officer (COO)**, or, in a very small operation, an administrative assistant who reports to the administrator in an informal manner.

In a 100-bed hospital, one would expect to find a COO or a single assistant administrator. In a 200-bed operation, there may be a couple of assistant administrators. In addition to this, in nearly all cases, there is also a chief financial officer (CFO) and a chief nursing officer (sometimes called the director of nursing (DON) or VP of nursing). These senior staff personnel (COO, DON, and CFO) stand ready to oversee the hospital in the absence of the CEO. The number of senior staff personnel will vary with the size of the hospital, which is usually measured by the number of beds. (In counting beds, it is wise to understand what the hospital is claiming when it is speaking of its capabilities. The hospital may be licensed by the state for 342 beds, but it may only have set up 250 beds, and may only have an average daily census and personnel capable of caring for 150 patients. The remaining space may simply be used for storage.)

Just below the senior staff (COO, CFO, and DON) is the middle management group, which represents the departmental level of management. At the departmental level, generally four major types of functions are carried out: (1) nursing functions, (2) business or fiscal functions, (3) ancillary or professional services, and (4) support services. It is usual in a mid-sized hospital to have at least four distinctive administrative or functional groups that answer to the CEO or COO, with a VP responsible for each area (Figure 3-3).

Although an organization chart serves to portray formal lines of reporting, it certainly does not portray informal lines of authority and reporting. Many leaders may not be included in such a chart, yet they are the personnel to whom the rank and file turn in times of misunderstanding or confusion. Those in top- and mid-management positions would be wise to understand this structure and keep these people informed and close by when needed.

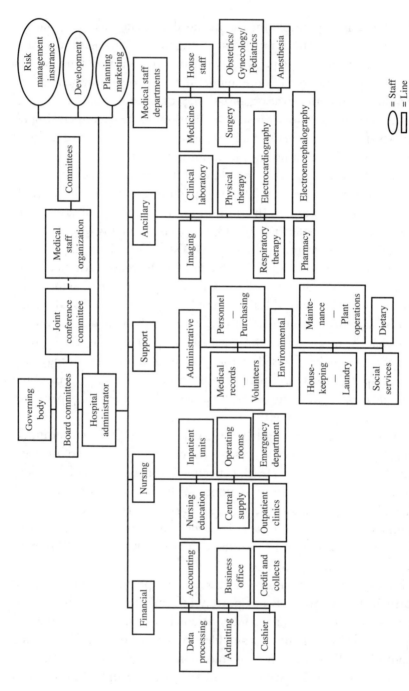

FIGURE 3-3. A typical hospital organization chart.

TEAM OF THREE—A VERY IMPORTANT CONCEPT

A complex acute-care medical center has three major sources of power: (1) the board of directors, (2) the CEO or administrator, and (3) the medical staff of the hospital. In an ideal world, these three would work in harmony to make the hospital the best it could be. In reality, this is too often not the case. Let us examine the power relationships among these groups.

Medical Staff

The activities of the medical staff significantly affect the management and governance of an institution. Physicians make daily decisions to admit patients, and depending on where they have admitting privileges, they can choose to send their patients to ABC Medical Center, MNO Medical Center, or XYZ Medical Center. If they believe ABC has better medical equipment, they may send their patients there. If, on a particular day, it is raining and the physician does not wish to drive across the city, the harsh and simple fact is that for that day, the physician may choose to have his or her patients admitted to the XYZ facility just because it is closer. The wise hospital administrator must understand that each physician is the hospital's customer, and the hospital must do everything it can to please that customer. The golden rule in hospital management is: Nothing happens until the physician admits the patient. A hospital would sit empty without the loyalty of its medical staff.

Usually, the medical staff can vote for members to serve on a hospital executive committee that also includes senior hospital management members (CEO and COO), or a joint conference committee comprised of board members, senior management executives, and elected physicians. In other instances, some hospital boards will allow one or two physicians to serve as board members.

Board of Directors

The board of directors may be elected by members of the community to oversee a local hospital or appointed by the corporation that owns the hospital, the county judge, or even the hospital CEO (and there are probably a host of other options).

In addition to hiring and firing the CEO, the board also has the important function of approving privileges for each physician. If Dr. Smith wishes to deliver babies, she must apply to the OB/GYN committee, the medical staff, the CEO, and finally the board of directors, who have the final say. These same board members may remove the privileges of any physician.

Chief Executive Officer

The CEO is responsible for the day-to-day management of the hospital. He or she can decide which product strategies to pursue, where to open clinics, and which marketing campaigns to launch—in short, affecting nearly everything the hospital does. It is up to the CEO to work in close harmony with both the board and the medical staff to maximize the efficiency of the hospital.

CORPORATE RESTRUCTURING OF THE HOSPITAL

Corporate restructuring, or the segmentation of certain hospital assets and functions into separate corporations, has become a popular strategy to help hospitals adapt to changes in regulations and reimbursements. The most prevalent form of corporate restructuring is when a hospital becomes a subsidiary of a parent holding company or foundation. Inpatient care usually remains the primary function of the hospital corporation, and nonprovider functions may be transferred to other corporations related to the hospital. The parent holding company and nonhospital subsidiaries are able to enter into less-restrictive joint ventures with physician groups and other healthcare providers than would be allowed by the traditional hospital structure. The traditional reasons for corporate restructuring include the optimization of third-party reimbursements, tax considerations, government regulations, flexibility, and diversification.

MULTIHOSPITAL SYSTEMS

An increasing number of freestanding hospitals are becoming part of a larger, **multihospital system**. In a multihospital system, two or more hospitals are managed, leased, or owned by a single institution. Some of the common advantages of multihospital systems include economies of scale in terms of management and purchasing, the ability to provide a wide spectrum of care, and increased access to capital markets.

ALLIANCES

Another development in the structuring of hospital systems is the creation of alliances. An alliance is a formal arrangement among several hospitals and/or hospital systems that establishes written rules for its members to follow. Unlike hospitals within a multihospital system, those in an alliance retain their autonomy. The advantage of an alliance is the development of a network of support among hospitals. For example, hospitals might join in an alliance to gain purchasing power or form a preferred provider organization to offer selected services to customers or patients at special rates. A disadvantage is that antitrust issues may arise from such alliances. Each hospital should consult with its legal counsel before it commits to an alliance.

THE GOVERNING BODY—A DEEPER DISCUSSION

Introduction

As we discussed in the previous section, the governing body (also referred to as the board of trustees, board of directors, or board of governors) is the organized entity that bears the ultimate responsibility for all decisions made within the hospital. The board essentially functions as the owner of the hospital and is accountable to the community. Board members are often elected by the community, just as school board members are elected. They hire and terminate the CEO/administrator and approve the privileges of all physicians.

The situation is slightly different in the case of for-profit companies that own many hospitals. Although the for-profit company has a corporate board at its central headquarters, each hospital within the company may have its own local governing board whose members are usually appointed by the local administrator (who is an employee of the for-profit company). This second board generally gives advice to help safeguard the community's best interests. This local board can only make recommendations (and can recommend to the company that the administrator be replaced, since he or she is an employee of the company and not of the local hospital; often the for-profit company will replace a valued administrator by simply transferring him or her to a different company hospital).

The trustees are ultimately responsible for managing the hospital's assets and setting policy. They assume a fiduciary responsibility (defined as a "greater than normal duty") similar to that of attorneys to their clients, or physicians to their patients). The courts have found that the governing body is responsible for all activities within the hospital. Members who serve on the governing body clearly have a significant responsibility.

Trustees are usually private citizens who often want to help their neighbors and community. One of the original reasons for selecting private citizens as hospital trustees was to secure financial support for the institution. By appointing local citizens who had some influence (and affluence), the hospital could guarantee a certain amount of contributions to underwrite its overall operations and care of the poor. Today, however, hospital boards frequently **appoint** individuals who have particular skills that can help the hospital; for example, they might be able to provide legal advice, accounting assistance, or business and management support. Modern hospitals have a multitude of legal and accreditation requirements. The board of trustees is required by law to watch over the hospital and its operations.

Nonprofit hospital trustees generally serve without pay; they are prohibited from profiting financially from their membership on the board of trustees. The rewards for being a trustee are the satisfaction of having delivered a service to others in the community, and the achievement of a certain level of status in the community. However, trustees have the additional burden of protecting the patients from all foreseeable and preventable harm, which they accomplish by approving the privileges of each medical staff member.

In part because of the scandals at Enron, Tyco, and other corporations, there is an increased sensitivity to board oversight and conflicts of interest. As part of a public service establishment, hospital trustees may be vulnerable to lawsuits and should ascertain whether the hospital carries director and officer (D&O) insurance on their behalf.

Hospitals are increasingly coming under public scrutiny. Some areas, including New York City and Washington, DC, have prohibited hospital trustees from doing business directly or indirectly with the hospitals in which they serve. More commonly, a state will require that trustees make full public disclosure of their business interests and dealings with the hospital they represent. Hospitals are well advised to comply fully with the procedures for disclosing conflicts of interest, even though it can be shown in many cases that overlapping trustee interests can actually work to the hospital's benefit. For example, a trustee might give an institution a favorable loan or expert advice on investments.

A Profile of the Governing Body

Just as hospitals vary considerably in size, purpose, and makeup, so do their boards. The average hospital board today has 17 members. Smaller hospital boards may have 8 or 9 members, and the larger hospital boards may have about 25 members. Typically, a board is predominantly composed of business executives, but it may also include members of the legal and accounting professions. Physicians sometimes serve as representatives of the medical staff, but they may or may not have voting power. Interest in and commitment to the hospital, followed by financial business skills, are the leading criteria for selecting trustees. Trustees are frequently chosen from among the more outstanding members of the community. It is common to find representatives with inherited wealth serving on boards. A more recent trend, however, has been to encourage community or consumer representation on boards. As to the age of a typical board member, we can generalize that about half are older than 50. The majority of board members have a business or healthcare background. Most often, the CEO of the hospital is a board member, but usually only a small percentage of boards will grant the CEO voting privileges.

The qualifications of a potential trustee must be carefully reviewed. Hospital trusteeship demands certain essential traits, including dedication to hospital business, management skills, involvement in the community, political influence in the community, and a cooperative attitude.

As mentioned earlier, in some areas of the country, hospital boards are similar to school boards in that board members are elected by the local citizenry. In rural areas and small towns, it is common to have an election every 2 years and elect a portion of the board. Civic-minded people usually run for the board, but often these people are not the most informed about hospital matters. An additional caveat is that the board members might see themselves as the boss of the CEO, instead of collectively acting with one voice. Horror stories abound among rural administrators, including tales of individual board members wandering the halls of the hospital, attempting to order employees to do certain tasks. It is the wise CEO who brings in an outside consultant for periodic board-member education, instilling a collective spirit within the board so that its members will act with one voice and stay within their agreed bounds of distant oversight.

Hospital boards typically meet 10 to 12 times a year, usually on a monthly basis. This is reasonable considering that a board might not meet during one of the summer months or during the holiday season. Board terms vary considerably, but the average term of membership is slightly in excess of 3 years, with a majority of hospitals stipulating no limit to the number of consecutive terms a board member may serve.

FUNCTIONS OF THE BOARD OF TRUSTEES

The basic function of the governing body is to protect and guide the hospital's mission in accordance with the institution's structure and the needs of the community. Since the board of trustees has an explicit or implicit obligation to act on behalf of the community's interest, it has a **fiduciary** responsibility to the community. This responsibility is founded upon trust and confidence, and involves (1) controlling the hospital and assuring the community that the hospital works properly, (2) ensuring that the hospital acts in a fiscally responsible manner, (3) appointing and removing members of the medical staff, and (4) appointing a capable CEO.

Hospital trustees help to set hospital policies. These policies are general written statements or understandings that guide or channel the thinking and actions of the medical staff and administrator in the decision-making process. The trustees' functions are summarized in Exhibit 3-1.

A hospital system may include a local board of trustees and a corporate board of the multihospital system. However, the local governing body retains primary responsibility for key medical staff relationships. The assumption of a role as a trustee in a multihospital system need not mean the loss of autonomy of the local hospital governing board.

Selection and Evaluation of the CEO

The trustees have an obligation to hire a competent CEO to oversee the day-to-day management of the hospital. One of the board's most important functions is to investigate and review the qualifications of a

Exhibit 3-1. Primary functions of the board of trustees.

Members of a board of directors or a board of trustees attain their positions in one of three ways. They are either elected by their fellow citizens (such as school board members or hospital district board members), are appointed by county officials (such as the county judge appointing county hospital board members), or are appointed by company officials, in the case of for-profit hospital companies appointing local citizens to their local hospital board. Most boards usually derive their authority and power from the hospital charter that created the hospital, or from state statutory regulations.

To encapsulate major points of the board's functions, it is nearly universally agreed that boards serve to:

- Interview, appoint, and sometimes discharge the chief executive officer (CEO).
- Engage in periodic strategic planning with the CEO and key medical and senior hospital staff members.
- Provide a mission statement that meets the needs of the hospital's target population. In this regard, the board should periodically discuss with the CEO his/her vision for the future and the board should assist in goal setting.
- Assist in providing a sound financial platform—this can be, but is certainly not limited to, a monthly review of key financial statements, a review of the annual budget, approval of spending for major capital equipment, approval of all hospital contracts, and approval of all insurance products.
- Approve all additions to and changes in the medical staff. The board also reviews and approves all changes to medical staff bylaws and standards. The Joint Commission carefully reviews this aspect to ensure the board is appropriately carrying out its oversight function.
- Be a liaison with the public to assist the public's understanding of the mission of hospital. Board members may be popular speakers for civic organizations and should represent the hospital when necessary.

Boards are often regulated by local, county, or state regulations. Members must be thoroughly familiar with open meeting laws and statutes that address conflict of interest issues. Wise hospital boards should insure coverage through director and officer insurance policies. As the guiding hand, board members are liable for potential litigation.

potential CEO, and decide which one to select. Hospitals are a big business, and trustees must seek executives who have strengths in planning, organizing, and controlling, as well as proven leadership skills. The board delegates to the CEO the authority and responsibility to manage the everyday operations of the hospital, but it retains the ultimate responsibility for everything that happens in the hospital. The relationship between the CEO and the governing board is primarily that of employee–employer, but not in the usual sense of the term. Since the hospital is a very special type of organization, the relationship between the CEO and the governing board is in fact similar to a partnership. Just as it is the responsibility of the governing board to hire the CEO, it must also discharge the CEO if necessary. Determining whether this is necessary can best be accomplished by having a contractual arrangement described in clearly understandable terms.

Relationship with the Medical Staff

The hospital medical staff operates under its own bylaws, rules, and regulations, but the physicians on the medical staff are accountable to the board of trustees for the professional care of their patients. The board of trustees is responsible for exercising care in appointing physicians to the staff. The medical staff carefully reviews a physician's application file, including credentials, references, and requested privileges. The medical staff then recommends to the board of trustees which privileges should be granted to the applicant. The trustees act upon these recommendations. The board can choose to grant the privileges, to request further information from the medical staff, or to reject the privileges outright.

The board of trustees is legally responsible for care provided in the hospital by attending physicians and hospital employees. In the case of *Darling v. Charleston Community Memorial Hospital,* the court pointed out that a board of trustees has a duty that may go beyond simple delegation of authority to the medical staff. In the Darling case, the court held that the hospital corporation was liable because it did not intervene through its employees to prevent damage that occurred to a patient through the negligence of one of the hospital's physicians. In another landmark case in 1973, the courts found in *Gonzales v. John J. Nork, MD, and Mercy General Hospital of Sacramento, California,* that a hospital owes the patient a duty of care. In this case, Dr. Nork performed 36 unnecessary operations over a 9-year period.

The court noted that the board of trustees has an obligation to purge the hospital of incompetent physicians. This case reconfirmed the board's corporate responsibility to ensure quality of care. It cannot be delegated.

The CEO and the chief/president of the medical staff also have major roles to play. Together with the board, they can develop and implement a quality-improvement program. The board's job is to monitor the program. This includes receiving monthly reports on the medical staff's performance as measured against standards, concurring with medical staff recommendations, or developing the board's own recommendations to improve quality in the institution.

The board of trustees generally delegates the hospital's daily medical affairs to the medical staff. The medical staff carries out these functions according to its own bylaws and regulations, but these bylaws and regulations are periodically reviewed and approved by the board. The board's joint conference committee includes representatives from the medical staff and administration, and serves as the main committee between the medical staff of the board and its administrator.

How Does the Board Operate?

The board of directors or trustees operates under the bylaws of the hospital. The bylaws spell out how a hospital board must operate to attain its objectives. Typical bylaws include a statement about the hospital's purpose and the responsibilities of the board. They also contain a statement of authority for the board to appoint the administrator and the medical staff. Additionally, bylaws outline how board members are appointed and for what period of time. Most bylaws indicate an elaborate committee structure. It is through these board-of-trustees committees that the governing board usually accomplishes its goals. This committee structure is frequently established along special functional lines. There is a remarkable consistency throughout the nation's hospitals in terms of board committee structure. Perhaps the reason for this consistency is the impetus for review of hospital bylaws and suggestions from The Joint Commission.

The most common committee is the executive committee, which is found in the vast majority of hospitals. Other examples would include a finance committee and a planning committee. Generally, recommendations made by the separate committees affect the governance, management, and administration of the hospital, as well as the hospital's medical staff.

It is the duty of the board to carefully select the members of these board committees. The caliber of the recommendations that emerge from these committees, and subsequently the caliber of the resulting board action are frequently a result of the quality of the committee assignments. By applying leadership skills and delegating management responsibilities, and working closely with these board committees, the CEO frequently can provide the ultimate key to success in all aspects of the hospital's operation.

Today, hospital boards usually operate like any other corporate board. Board members are accustomed to providing an independent voice. Clearly, hospital trustees are respected for their independence and their overview of the hospital. This is the result of an increasing need to make hospitals more efficient and competitive.

THE CHIEF EXECUTIVE OFFICER

Introduction

CEOs (also referred to as hospital administrators or presidents) come from many different backgrounds. At one time, they were likely to be chosen from the ranks of the nursing department. In many religion-based hospitals, it was common for the CEO to be selected from among members of the religious order or retired clergy. Some administrators worked their way up from the business office to become the hospital's CEO. It was also common in some hospitals for a retired executive or physician to assume the CEO position.

Such upward mobility through the ranks is not common today. CEOs are now products of universities. The first university course for hospital administrators started in the mid-1930s. After World War II, as the field of hospital administration became more and more complex, the demand for trained hospital administrators multiplied. One of the greatest influences on the advancement of hospital administration was the formation of the **American College of Health Care Executives (ACHE)** in 1933. The college encourages high standards of education and ethics, and only those administrators who meet the college's requirements are admitted as members. Today, a number of universities in the United States and Canada provide formal training of hospital administrators, and offer graduate and undergraduate degrees in hospital or healthcare administration.

A master's degree is the most widely accepted degree for a person applying for a position in health administration, and is required for the CEO position in most hospitals; usually the candidate will have a Master of Science in Healthcare Administration (MS-HA). Many people interested in healthcare administration choose instead to pursue a Master of Business Administration (MBA), Master of Public Administration (MPA), or Master of Public Health (MPH) degree. The formal training program for hospital administrators covers three general areas: (1) administrative and business theory, (2) the study of various components of healthcare services and medical care, and (3) the study of hospital functions, including organization and management within the hospital and the role of the hospital in the larger picture of healthcare delivery systems. The three basic types of skills developed in training are technical, social, and conceptual.

Historical Functions of the Administrator

The hospital CEO of the 1930s and 1940s chiefly conducted **inside activities**; that is, he or she dealt primarily with internal operations of the hospital. The administrator was concerned with matters that directly affected patients treated at the hospital. This involved bargaining with employees, developing proper benefit packages, and determining the best methods and techniques to manage the institution. However, beginning in the 1950s and continuing into 1970s, increasingly strong labor unions, third-party payers, and governmental agencies all began to significantly affect the hospital industry. During this period, the role of the administrator became a dual one, involving issues both inside and outside the hospital. More sophisticated and specialized management techniques were required to operate a hospital effectively, and the CEO became more involved in activities outside the hospital.

Today the CEO has to strike the proper balance between outside and inside activities. It is typical today for the CEO to delegate everyday hospital operations to the assistant administrator/COO, who often is also in charge of all the ancillary and support-services departments. The CEO might spend about 80% of his or her time outside the hospital visiting members of the medical staff in their offices, members of the board, or local government officials.

According to the ACHE, the governing authority must appoint a chief executive who is responsible for the performance of all functions of the institution and is accountable to the governing authority. The chief

executive, as the head of the organization, is responsible for all functions, including the medical staff, nursing division, patient support services, technical support, and general services support, which are necessary
to ensure the quality of patient care. In many cases, the CEO also leads
in recruiting new members of the medical staff.

Inside Activities of the CEO

The inside activities of the CEO include duties such as reviewing and
establishing hospital procedures, supervising hospital employees, overseeing fiscal activities, and maintaining internal relations. Traditionally, the CEO's job is to attend to those tasks that directly affect
patients. For example, it is the responsibility of the CEO to see that the
building and its facilities are in adequate order and the personnel are
qualified to fulfill their specific job requirements. Legally, the CEO
and hospital must answer for acts of employees under the principle of
"**respondeat superior**" (a Latin phrase meaning the master is responsible for the acts of the servant). Another traditional CEO function,
which is even more important today, is to serve as a liaison to the hospital's physicians. The administrator must keep both the physicians
and the governing board informed regarding the hospital and its plans.
Other important tasks include the recruitment of new medical staff and
retention of existing staff.

Generally, CEOs attend board meetings to communicate ideas,
thoughts, and policies that will aid the hospital. The CEO assigns the
responsibility of preparing annual budgets to the chief financial officer,
the director of nurses, and the assistant administrator. The budgets are
then presented by the CEO and approved or changed by the board of
trustees. This process includes identifying services that need to be offered, as well as equipment that must be purchased. Although the CFO
usually negotiates reimbursement rates with third-party insurance plans
(such as Blue Cross and Medicare) and prepares monthly financial
statements and statistical data to present to the board, the CEO should
always review these documents with the CFO before they are presented
to the board.

Maintaining a positive relationship and effective communication with
the hospital's governing body, medical staff, employees, and patients is
important. The official relationship between the CEO and governing

body is that of an employer and employee, but actually the CEO and board function as partners. The administrator represents the board in the institution's daily activities and must turn the board's wishes into administrative action. When administrators are members of the board, they hold the title of president of the institution and may serve as a liaison to the chairman of the board. CEOs can become active, with voting privileges, or act as **ex officio members** on strategic board committees, including nominating, bylaws, and planning committees. However, it is uncommon for the CEO to be chairman of the board.

The CEO should act in partnership not only with the board of trustees, but also with physicians and with other healthcare personnel in the institution. Under the best circumstances, the administrator will have a mutual understanding with, respect for, and trust in members of the medical staff. One of the key responsibilities of the CEO is to communicate with the hospital's medical staff. It is the CEO's job to see that the physicians have the proper tools in the right place at the right time to carry out their critical functions within the hospital.

Successful CEOs must be effective in keeping their medical staff members informed about organizational changes, board policies, and decisions that will affect them and their patients. Although hospital medical staff are ultimately answerable to the board and its management, they are also self-governing and have their own bylaws. The administrator should be sensitive to the medical staff's needs for self-governance and support. From time to time, tensions will naturally arise between the medical staff and administration. Frequently the sources of this conflict can be attributed to poor communication. The CEO must communicate effectively with the medical staff if the hospital is to function efficiently. Consequently, the CEO must always be available to medical personnel. It is a good idea for the CEO to attend the monthly medical staff meeting to foster good communications.

Many of the CEO's day-to-day challenges involve hospital employees. Employees must look to the CEO as their work leader. In this capacity, the CEO must keep employees informed about the critical role their services play in the successful operation of the hospital. This is easier to achieve with nurses and others who deliver direct patient care, but the CEO must continually inform all employees of their mission and importance. While managing employees at all levels, it is critical for the CEO to show objectivity, understanding, and fairness. The CEO must exercise the authority to employ, direct, discipline, and dismiss employees with these important principles in mind.

Finally, the CEO has a vital role in patient relations. The CEO must fulfill all legitimate patient requests for general comfort and care to assist in the patient's recovery. In dealing with patients, the CEO must also understand the needs of the patients' friends and relatives. It is important for the CEO to ensure that confidential patient information is protected.

Outside Activities of the CEO

The **outside activities** of today's CEO are numerous. They include periodically visiting all physicians in the community and encouraging them to use the hospital, relating information to the community about the hospital, building relationships with and lobbying government contacts, and participating in educational and planning activities. One of the roles of the modern administrator is to educate the community about hospital operations and healthcare matters. This is usually done through hospital publications and community lectures. It is the CEO's responsibility to present a positive image of the hospital. Public-relations duties are considered key outside activities, and the CEO must promote public understanding of hospital programs through the mass media.

One of the most valuable functions of today's CEO, together with the CFO, is to negotiate contracts with third-party payers (insurance companies) who pay the patients' bills. This is a time-consuming activity that requires a combination of management and negotiation skills. With the advent of Medicare in 1966, hospitals and government became more deeply intertwined. Today's CEO must stay on top of the latest government rules and regulations concerning funding, reimbursement, and planning issues. CEOs meet with governmental reimbursement agencies, planning bodies, and politicians to stay current and to lobby for the hospital's interests. CEOs may lobby on an individual basis, with area CEOs, or as part of regional or national groups through hospital associations.

Interacting with public vendors and other health administrators and agencies is vital to the CEO's mission. The CEO's job is to remain in close contact with the community that sponsors the hospital or healthcare institution. The CEO must realize that the institution has a responsibility to the public, and the public has a right to be informed. The CEO has to maintain high ethical principles in dealing with vendors, and be impartial and objective when representing the hospital in business transactions. Neither the institution nor the administrator can accept favors, commissions, unethical rebates, or gifts from vendors in exchange for doing business with a certain company.

Frequently, CEOs telephone each other or meet to gain additional information about a particular topic, insight, or problem, or just to discuss institutional plans and situations. This professional courtesy helps administrators broaden their own perspectives and strengthen their problem-solving abilities. This is referred to as **networking**. However, discussing pricing or agreeing as to which hospital will deliver which services is probably counterproductive, and possibly also in violation of antitrust laws.

Assistant Administrator or Vice President

One of the most important responsibilities of the CEO is to select and hire a competent administrative staff. The administrator's staff is given the responsibility of seeing that the hospital is run smoothly and efficiently. The assistant administrator or VP (sometimes referred to as the COO) is in charge of hospital operations and assists the CEO in coordinating all hospital activities, including support, ancillary, and fiscal services. Typically, there are assistant administrators or VPs in charge of all major functional areas in the hospital (Figure 3-4).

The administrative assistant is frequently involved in staff functions and is a junior member of the hospital's administrative team. The administrative assistant plans and participates in studies and programs that help the CEO in the hospital. Frequently, the administrative assistant will serve as a liaison between the hospital administrator and some of the other functioning hospital departments.

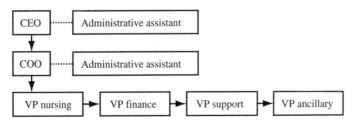

FIGURE 3-4. Typical organization of vice presidents.

THE FUTURE FOR CEOS

Although hospitals are not growing in number, they certainly are becoming much more complex. This has resulted in a middle management level in hospital administration, which means more management positions for healthcare administrators. Other changes in the healthcare industry are also leading to new jobs in hospital administration, such as VP of Regulatory Affairs and VP of Corporate Compliance. With respect to female hospital administrators, the future looks bright. A review of the number of students who are entering graduate programs in hospital administration shows nearly an equal number of men and women.

CHAPTER REVIEW

1. What is a **chain of command**?
2. Discuss the difference between line and staff functions.
3. What is a span of control?
4. What is product-line management?
5. What are some advantages of forming teams to undertake certain projects? What would be the disadvantages?
6. Discuss the concept of corporate restructuring. What are the pros and cons for a hospital?
7. You are the CEO of a 200-bed, free-standing hospital in a large city with 36 other hospitals. Discuss with your board members the pros and cons of becoming part of a multihospital system.
8. Discuss as an alternative the idea of joining an alliance.
9. What is meant by fiduciary?
10. How do not-for-profit and for-profit boards differ?
11. Why is director and officer insurance important?
12. What are five functions of the board of directors?
13. What is the importance of the board's bylaws?
14. Discuss the profile of a typical hospital board member. How might the person become a member of the board?
15. What relationship does the board of directors have with the medical staff? Discuss at least three important things the board does that directly affect the hospital's physicians.
16. What are some functions of the CEO?

17. What do we mean by activities outside the hospital?
18. What are some activities inside the hospital that should concern the CEO?
19. What is the typical function of the COO?
20. Discuss the term "respondeat superior." If an employee is sent to a local hardware store for plumbing parts, is the hospital liable for his or her traffic accidents while he or she is driving his or her own vehicle?
21. What are the steps involved in advancing within the ACHE?
22. Visit the ACHE website at http://www.ache.org and download the CEO employment contract that is available. Why is this an important document?
23. What are the typical rights and duties of an ex officio member of the board?

Part III

Accessing the Hospital

Part III

Keeping The Community

4

Doorways into the Hospital
Tina Fields

KEY TERMS

Federally Qualified Health
   Center (FQHC)
Hospital-based clinic
Admitting privilege
Preadmission workup
Advance directives
Proprietary clinic
Medical home
Sliding fee scale

Trauma
First responder
Emergency Medical Treatment
   and Active Labor Act
   (EMTALA)
Triage
Discharge plan
Golden hour
Diversion

INTRODUCTION

Patients usually have two general avenues by which they enter the hospital. They can self-refer or be referred to the hospital by a provider, but once they enter the doors of the hospital, the initial reception is similar. For patients who are not self-referred, the initial point of medical contact that begins the process of entering the hospital can take many forms, including physicians' offices, clinics, **Federally Qualified Health Centers (FQHCs)**, incarceration facilities, public health departments, and **hospital-based**

clinics. Depending on this initial point of entry, patients may enter the hospital through the emergency department or by going through the usual admission process. This chapter describes the patient's admission to the hospital and discusses key points along the way.

OBJECTIVES

By the end of this chapter, students should be able to:

1. Discuss the major avenues by which patients are admitted to a hospital.
2. Contrast hospital admission through a referral mechanism with emergency department admission.
3. Describe the general steps involved in entering a hospital.
4. Explain the importance of triage in the emergency department from the patient's viewpoint.
5. Explain the importance of the "golden hour" for emergency department personnel and patients.
6. Compare and contrast emergency departments and trauma departments.
7. Discuss the levels of trauma departments.

ENTERING THE HOSPITAL— PLANNED OR UNPLANNED

A planned entry into the hospital occurs when a medical provider refers a person to the hospital. The process begins with the patient going to the provider's office. The patient may initiate the process because of symptoms (e.g., headache, fever, or pain), for routine screenings (e.g., an annual physical, during which an abnormality is discovered), or because of a desire to have an elective medical procedure. When it has been established that the patient should go to the hospital, the provider will make initial arrangements for the person to be admitted to the hospital. Physicians have **admitting privileges** at certain hospitals, so the patient will generally be directed to go to a specific hospital. Although necessary admittance and elective admittance require similar **preadmission workups**, there is some variation in timing between the two. In elective admittance, the patient may visit the hospital's admitting office to complete admission forms, sign

advance directives, and arrange to have appropriate lab work before the actual day of admittance to the hospital. The information sought for pre-registration falls into three main areas: patient profile, guarantor (or person responsible for bill), and insurance (including any preauthorization requirements). If the patient has an illness necessitating immediate hospital admittance, the physician's office personnel will contact the hospital and send the patient directly to the hospital. Hospitals also provide a number of Medical Directive forms during admission, including Durable Power of Attorney for Healthcare Decisions (the patient appoints someone to make decisions should the patient be unable to do so), Do Not Resuscitate (specifies the conditions under which the patient does not want medical services provided), and Living Will (specifies the patient's wishes when faced with life-threatening illness) forms. During preadmission, patients will also be given a copy of the hospital's Patient's Bill of Rights and the Patient's List of Responsibilities, which describes what patients can expect while in the facility.

For planned admittances, patients may see their physicians at a number of specific clinic sites. Although clinic physicians have the same responsibility to provide care and refer patients to hospitals, the demographics of patients and their ability to pay may differ among the various clinic types. Most physicians are office-based, and these offices may contain a solo practice (one or two physicians, usually of a similar specialty, working together) or a group practice (a corporation consisting of numerous physicians of the same specialty or different specialties). Some physicians practice in **proprietary clinics** (i.e., clinics that are established according to a business plan with the goal of making money). A new type of proprietary clinic in many cities is the urgent (or emergency) clinic. These clinics are designed for nonappointments and to address medical situations that warrant expedient care with no waiting. People often use these clinics for minor emergencies or to see a physician during hours that are convenient for the patient. Proprietary clinics usually accept third-party payments as well as self-payments. Because they operate under a business plan, proprietary clinics do not accept nonpaying patients. Some hospitals have created hospital-based primary care centers to facilitate medical care for people who do not have a **medical home** and who are likely to inappropriately use the emergency department for minor illnesses. From a marketing standpoint, these hospital-based primary care centers may also be a source of hospital admissions.

Some physicians practice at FQHCs. FQHCs are federally funded clinics that emphasize primary care. In similarity to general community clinics, FQHCs serve as a medical home for people, although FQHCs usually have a **sliding fee scale** based on the current federal poverty guidelines. This means that people pay for services based on their income; although people are encouraged to pay for their needed services, FQHC guidelines allow patients to receive care regardless of their ability to pay. The social work department of the FQHC works with patients to identify paying mechanisms, such as Medicare, Medicaid, and Children's Health Insurance Program (CHIP), and can help them enroll in the appropriate program. Although FQHCs were once considered the medical home for people without health insurance, as more employers are decreasing the health insurance benefits offered to their employees, more people with insurance are seeking medical service at the FQHCs. Small FQHCs may offer limited primary care, whereas large FQHCs may offer several medical departments, including internal medicine for adults, pediatrics for children, obstetrics for pregnant women, and dentistry. Large FQHCs may be freestanding, meaning that they have an on-site pharmacy, laboratory, and limited x-ray capability.

People who are incarcerated in local jail facilities represent a unique population that may be referred to hospitals. Local incarceration facilities usually have agreements with local hospitals that allow inmates to be transferred to the hospital for extensive care. Most large jails have a medical director who oversees inmate health. Jails typically have limited medical staff (usually a mid-level provider and some support staff) on a 24/7 basis; however, large jails or prisons may have on-site medical clinics or limited hospital facilities. Because of the confined living arrangements, incarcerated people are subject to contagious diseases as well as **trauma**. Payment for medical services provided to incarcerated people is usually obtained from indigent funds (maintained by the county), but may also be made by other third-party sources. Because of the status of the incarcerated, hospitals and jail facilities must have policies and procedures in place to address transportation and treatment issues. Referral to the hospital is made through the medical director's admitting privilege and not through self-referral by the incarcerated.

Unplanned admissions to the hospital are generally associated with emergencies, and patients entering the emergency department usually have not been seen by their personal medical providers. In many cases, an unplanned admission begins when a **first responder** assesses a person's medical needs and provides a specific amount of medical care while transporting that person to an emergency department. In these situations, patients enter the hospital through the emergency department. Although similar forms and initial lab work are necessary in the emergency department, the timing/flow for capturing this information may vary depending on the level of the emergency. This is especially true when it comes to ascertaining ability to pay for services. Under the **Emergency Medical Treatment and Active Labor Act (EMTALA)**, patients who present at hospitals with emergency medical conditions must be seen regardless of their ability to pay (American College of Emergency Physicians, 2009). EMTALA was created to prevent hospitals or emergency departments from refusing to treat people who do not have the ability to pay for the services.

Although EMTALA was established to prevent "dumping" of patients, it also contributes to the crowded conditions at most emergency departments. People who do not have insurance or an established medical home often seek treatment for nonemergency conditions in the emergency department (Viccellio et al., 2009; Xu et al., 2009). In addition, there are no medical histories on file for people seeking treatment in the emergency department, so more tests must be performed to ensure an accurate diagnosis. These extra tests and procedures increase the cost of the visit. Thus, inappropriate use of the emergency department is a contributing factor to the crowded conditions, long wait times, and high cost of emergency medicine.

THE EMERGENCY DEPARTMENT

More people enter the hospital through the emergency department than by any other route. There are advantages and disadvantages of going to the emergency department. For people with life-threatening issues, the emergency department is the essential avenue. For people who do not have a medical home and who rely on the emergency department as a source of primary care, the emergency department can be a place of frustration and anger. Emergency departments treat ill and injured people; because there is a wide variation in degrees of sickness and injury, emergency departments rely on a triage mechanism to determine when patients are seen. People who have life-threatening illnesses are seen before other people. The **triage** protocol is an established policy based on scientific evidence and not on a patient's pain level or perception of illness. Often times, this creates friction within the emergency department, as patients waiting to be seen do not fully realize why other people are being seen before them (Moskop et al., 2008).

When patients initially enter the emergency department, they usually register. They are then assessed by the triage personnel for initial symptoms. Patients with severe trauma or life-threatening illnesses are placed at the top of the list, followed by patients with non-life-threatening illnesses. Some people who do not have medical homes will use the emergency department as a source of routine medical care (the type of care that should occur at the physician's office). These people are placed in the lowest position of the triage and thus usually have to wait a long time before they are seen by the physician. Some large city hospitals have established urgent care facilities adjacent to the emergency department, and people with non-life-threatening illnesses are given the option of going to the "urgicenter," which offers shorter wait times and less cost.

After patients are triaged in the emergency department, they then meet with a nurse who performs a written physical assessment. Patients will be asked questions about their allergies, medications, chronic illnesses, and medical history. Patients with life-threatening illnesses may be asked these questions while being wheeled to an examination department, whereas patients without life-threatening illnesses may answer these questions in an office setting. Women of childbearing age will be asked about their pregnancy status (this is required in case x-rays are to be ordered). Patients will be asked to describe their presenting problem and the severity of any pain they are experiencing. The nurse may ask numerous questions that may seem irrelevant to the presenting problem, but answers to these questions will be helpful when diagnostic procedures are ordered. Depending on the level of triage and the policies of the facility, patients may be asked about the form of their payment.

Once the initial diagnosis has been recorded, a physical evaluation will occur. Patients with non-life-threatening issues will put on a hospital gown and begin the physical assessment. Usually, the first step of the exam is to collect blood and urine specimens. Depending on the initial triage diagnosis, other tests (e.g., sonogram or x-ray) may also be administered. Initial physical tests are usually noninvasive and do not require written permission from the patient, although many hospitals have patients sign permission waivers during the written assessment. Invasive procedures, which require some type of equipment to be inserted into the body, require written permission and may also require hospital admission before they can be performed. Test determination is based on written and initial assessments, and the attending physician will determine specific tests as dictated by the patient's presenting signs.

After the initial tests are performed, the patient may be admitted to the hospital, may be treated and released, or may be transferred to a more appropriate hospital facility. A patient who is admitted to the hospital must wait in the emergency department until a bed becomes available in the hospital. Depending on many factors, the waiting time may be long (Vermeulen et al., 2009). This waiting period is often one of the main reasons for overcrowding in the emergency department. During this time, more information will be gathered from the patient, such as the name of the patient's primary physician and whether the patient has any advance directives.

Patients with minor illnesses may be treated and released. For such patients, the next step would be the development of a **discharge plan**. This would include instructions appropriate for the diagnosis, follow-up procedures, and prescriptions. The plan would also include what patients should do if their symptoms worsen after they return home. Upon completion of the discharge plan, patients would then meet with the discharge person, who is responsible for ascertaining financial arrangements for the visit.

Emergency departments must see patients, but the ability of an emergency department to provide the appropriate level of service varies among hospitals. For cases involving massive trauma or other life-threatening issues, a small hospital may not have either the equipment or the trained personnel to provide the necessary degree of care. In these situations, patients will be evaluated, stabilized, and then transferred to hospitals that are more sophisticated.

THE TRAUMA DEPARTMENT

According to the National Foundation for Trauma Care, all traumas are emergencies but not all emergencies are traumas: "Emergency departments and departments treat ill and injured people, while trauma centers handle the most severe, life-threatening blunt force and penetrating injuries" (http://www.traumafoundation.org). Trauma centers are classified by the

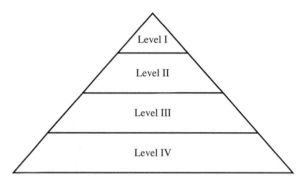

FIGURE 4-1. Trauma center model.

level of care provided (Centers for Disease Control and Prevention, 2009). As indicated in Figure 4-1, a Level IV trauma center provides initial evaluation and assessment, and 24-hour emergency coverage by a physician. Level IV trauma centers also have working relations with the nearest Level I, II, or III trauma centers so that patients with severe injuries can be readily transferred. Level III trauma centers offer continuous surgery coverage, have resuscitation and emergency surgery capabilities, and have standardized treatment protocols to address the care of patients who will be transferred to upper-tier trauma centers. Level II trauma centers provide comprehensive trauma care and are usually located in areas with no Level I trauma centers. Level I trauma centers are regional resource hospitals that are the core of the trauma care system. Level I trauma centers provide total care for every aspect of injury and usually serve as the point of care for the most severely injured patients. Level I trauma centers are usually associated with medical schools and teaching hospitals. These hospitals serve as referral sites for communities with less intensive trauma departments. Frequently, Level I trauma centers maintain air transport (either helicopters or jets) to fly patients from emergency departments or trauma sites to the Level I facility. Since Level I trauma centers usually are teaching facilities, they are staffed by both medical students and residents. Physicians in Level I trauma centers are board certified or may be pursuing a specialty that will allow them to become board certified in trauma surgery or a subspecialty.

The typical patient does not distinguish between emergency departments and trauma centers. However, emergency departments primarily treat ill and injured people, whereas trauma centers are charged with treating the

Table 4-1. Comparison of Emergency Department and Trauma Center by Type of Injury

Typical Patient Injuries Treated	
Emergency department	**Trauma center**
broken leg	multiple fractures
back sprain	paralysis
broken rib	punctured lung
laceration	stab wound
concussion	brain injury

Source: http://www.traumafoundation.org

most severe and most life-threatening cases. The National Trauma Foundation (http://www.traumafoundation.org) offers a comparison of emergency departments and trauma centers. As indicated in Table 4-1, emergency departments should be responsible for treating less complicated medical issues, and trauma centers should treat more complicated/complex issues.

Of course, if there is no trauma center in the vicinity, trauma patients usually are taken to the closest emergency department for stabilization. Sometimes, because of the severity of the trauma, victims are sent directly to a major trauma center. Frequently, transfer from the site of the traumatic occurrence to the higher-tier trauma center is coordinated through an air service (helicopters or planes that are designed and staffed to serve as mini emergency departments). These "life flight" services have contributed to saving many lives because they enable patients to receive the appropriate level of trauma care within the golden hour.

THE GOLDEN HOUR

The timing involved in the initial treatment of severely injured or ill patients is crucial. Emergency medicine/trauma departments refer to the first 60 minutes as the "**golden hour**." Research has demonstrated that if appropriate care is provided during this hour, the patient has a much greater chance of survival. To address this timing issue, the concept of the tiered trauma center model was created. According to this model, which was developed during the Vietnam War, trauma patients are initially seen by the closest facility and stabilized. If the diagnosis is beyond the capacity of the initial emergency department, the patient is transferred to the appropriate facility. About 10% of hospitals in the United States have some level of trauma capacity, and these 600 hospitals (http://www.traumafoundation.org) comprise the trauma center model.

COST OF RUNNING EMERGENCY DEPARTMENTS AND TRAUMA CENTERS

Today, not all hospitals have emergency departments, primarily because of the overhead costs associated with the emergency department. In the past, small hospitals were able to maintain an emergency department by having local doctors serve on a rotating basis. In 1979, emergency medicine became a recognized specialty for which physicians could seek board certification. Currently, emergency departments are staffed differently from most general hospital departments. Emergency physicians, nurses, and support staff must be in the emergency department throughout the day and night (24/7) regardless of the number of patients in the waiting room. Because personnel in the emergency department must be prepared to handle all medical conditions, they must be highly trained and have access to sophisticated medical equipment to facilitate diagnoses. Thus, the unit cost tends to be much greater for procedures done in the emergency department than elsewhere. The high costs of these procedures, along with the many people who do not pay for their emergency care, have contributed to most emergency departments being "in the red."

Because of the financial drain, many hospitals have closed their emergency departments, and the remaining emergency departments have become even more crowded. There are times when the emergency department is so crowded that the triage system is overwhelmed and even priority patients cannot be seen in an expedient manner. When this occurs, the hospital may use an approach known as "**diversion**." Hospital diversion requires intricate and real-time coordination between numerous emergency departments. Although diversion has a place in emergency care, it also leads to frustration and may lead to poorer patient outcomes (Olshaker, 2009).

SUMMARY

People enter the hospital through planned or unplanned routes. Planned entry usually is initiated at the medical provider's office, where the patient has been seen by the physician. If the diagnosis is serious, the physician may immediately refer the person to the hospital's admission office; for other procedures, a hospital admission may be scheduled. The first step in the hospital admission procedure is the preadmissions office, where the patient's information, including the payment mechanism, is gathered. The second step is the initial lab work. Unless the patient has been "handed off" to a hospitalist, the patient's primary care physician will be responsible for the medical care provided during the patient's hospital stay (see discussion of "Hospitalist" in Chapter 5).

The second avenue of entry into the hospital is through the emergency department. Sometimes a person may be too ill to wait for an appointment with his or her provider, and will go to the emergency department for more immediate treatment. People seeking treatment in the emergency department are assigned priority based on the severity of their initial assessment. Research in emergency medicine has shown that appropriate treatment within 60 minutes of an occurrence may greatly reduce the mortality rate for many diseases and traumas; for this reason, people with life-threatening issues are the first priority in the emergency department. For people who do not have life-threatening issues, the wait time in the emergency department may be long. Because many people who do not have medical homes or money for medical care use the emergency department as their primary source of care, emergency departments tend to be crowded.

Trauma centers and departments are geared more toward treating people who have been involved in accidents or traumatic situations. Just as not all hospitals have an emergency department, not all emergency departments have trauma departments. When severe trauma occurs, emergency department personnel may stabilize the patient and then transfer the patient to an appropriate trauma center for more elaborate care.

CHAPTER REVIEW

1. Discuss the difference between planned and unplanned entrance to the hospital.
2. What is triage? Why is it important in emergency departments?

3. What is the golden hour?
4. Discuss the meaning of the various levels of trauma centers.
5. How are trauma centers different from emergency departments?
6. How do the steps involved in hospital admission differ for emergency department (unplanned) and regular (planned) admittance?

REFERENCES

American College of Emergency Physicians. (2009). EMTALA and on-call responsibility for emergency department patients. Retrieved January 2010, from http://www.acep.org/PrintFriendly.aspx?id-29434

Centers for Disease Control and Prevention. (2009). Guidelines for field triage of injured patients. Recommendations of the National Expert Panel on Field Triage. *Morbidity and Mortality Weekly Report, 58*, 5.

Moskop, J. C., Sklar, D. P., Geiderman, J. M., Schears, R. M., & Bookman, K. J. (2009). Emergency department crowding, Part 1. Concepts, causes, and moral consequences. *Annals of Emergency Medicine, 53*, 605–611.

National Foundation for Trauma Care. (2009). *Trauma's golden hour.* Retrieved January 23, 2010 from http//:www.traumafoundation.org/restricted/tinymce/jscripts/tiny_mce/plugins/filemanager/files/about%20Trauma%20Care_Golden%20/tours.pdf

Olshaker, J. S. (2009). Managing emergency department overcrowding. *Emergency Medicine Clinics of North America, 27*, 593–603, viii.

Vermeulen, M. J., Ray, J. G., Bell, C., Cayen, B., Stukel, T. A., & Schull, M. J. (2009). Disequilibrium between admitted and discharged hospitalized patients affects emergency department length of stay. *Annals of Emergency Medicine, 54*, 794–804.

Viccellio, A., Santora, C., Singer, A. J., Thode, H. C., Jr., & Henry, M. C. (2009). The association between transfer of emergency department boarders to inpatient hallways and mortality: A 4-year experience. *Annals of Emergency Medicine, 54*, 487–491.

Xu, K. T., Nelson, B. K., & Berk, S. (2009). The changing profile of patients who used emergency department services in the United States: 1996 to 2005. *Annals of Emergency Medicine, 54*, 805–810.

Part IV

The Hospital Team

CHAPTER 5

The Medical Staff

Donald J. Griffin

KEY TERMS

Allied health staff

National Resident Matching
Program

American Medical Association
(AMA)

Approved residency program

Chief resident

Specialty boards

Medical staff bylaws

Appointment process

Clinical privileges

Categories of membership

Clinical department

Closed medical staff

Executive committee

Credentials committee

Reappointment

Hospitalist

National Practitioner
Data Bank

INTRODUCTION

The hospital medical staff is an organized body that may include physicians, dentists, podiatrists, nurse midwives, nurse practitioners, physician assistants, psychologists, and in some instances, **allied health staff** professionals who attend patients and participate in related clinical care duties.

The medical staff has the greatest impact on the quality and quantity of care given in the hospital. The medical staff is the heart of the hospital. Members of the medical staff have been authorized by the board of trustees to treat patients in the hospital and are accountable to the governing authority. They are accountable to the hospital for providing high-quality patient care through the application of ethical, clinical, and scientific procedures and practices. Though the governing body has the ultimate legal and moral responsibility for the hospital, including the quality of medical care, the board of trustees cannot practice medicine and depends on the members of the medical staff to admit patients, provide quality patient care, and partially police themselves.

The board of trustees appoints the medical staff. The staff formulates its own medical policies, rules, and regulations, and is responsible to the board for the quality of patient care. The medical staff is a disciplined, professional group made up of highly individualistic members who have their own unique approaches to medicine and organizational relationships. Therefore, the task of coordinating the efforts of the medical staff with those of the board of trustees, the administrator, and the rest of the hospital can be a challenging one.

BECOMING A PHYSICIAN

The training period to become a doctor is a long and arduous one. Usually, admission to medical school requires at least an undergraduate degree, with a concentration on courses in biology, chemistry, and other sciences, followed by the Medical College Admission Test (MCAT). To gain admission to an accredited 4-year college of medicine, applicants must score competitively on the MCAT.

After graduating from medical school, the newly graduated physician must complete a residency or postgraduate specialty training program in a hospital. The graduate does this by applying for the **National Resident Matching Program**, a program developed in 1951 by representatives from the American Association of Medical Colleges (AAMC), the **American Medical Association (AMA),** and various hospital associations. This group acts as a national clearinghouse to match the preferences of new graduates with the hospitals that are offering residencies.

The clearinghouse serves to give both the hospital and the medical students greater freedom of choice. Before the matching plan was implemented, graduating medical school students had to negotiate their own internships or residencies with individual hospitals. Since the students were notified by a specific date, it was often too late in the year to seek alternate internships if they were turned down. The matching plan allows more students to participate in residency programs approved by the Council of Education of the

AMA. Physicians used to spend the first year of postgraduate training in an internship. However, the internship category is no longer a part of AMA-approved programs, and the first year is now considered residency. The results of the matching plan are announced early each spring.

A hospital that has an **approved residency program** is more complex and perhaps more interesting than a hospital that does not offer such educational programs. The teaching hospital is essentially a living classroom. In teaching hospitals, the residents are referred to by their years of training. For example, a first-year resident is called a postgraduate year 1 resident, or PGY1. A PGY1 would be a low-ranking person on the resident (house staff) totem pole. He or she would be under the guidance of a senior resident, who in turn is under the guidance of the **chief resident** in a given specialty. The chief residents in each specialty have the supervisory, managerial, and teaching responsibilities in the program. Generally, these residents are not licensed physicians, though in many states, special temporary licenses are granted for a physician to practice within the institution that has an approved residency program. There was a time when residents worked for a meager stipend; now they receive respectable salaries for their efforts. Residents learn a great deal at the hospital, but they also give the hospital considerable patient services in return.

After physicians complete their hospital residency programs, many seek to become certified in their specialties. This may require further training. Certification, referred to as board certification, is under the jurisdiction of special boards such as the American Board of Surgery. The objective of **specialty boards** and associations is to upgrade the qualifications of specialists. These boards and associations have increased the length of time needed for training, developed subspecialties, and sponsored numerous continuing education programs and professional journals. After a physician passes rigorous examinations and demonstrates his or her abilities, certification by a specialty board is indeed recognition of professional competency. Fellowship in a specialty college is also meaningful peer recognition of competence.

There has been a movement toward recertification by specialty boards in an attempt to ensure that physicians will maintain an acceptable level of qualifications in their specialties. For instance, certification by the American Board of Surgery is valid for 10 years. Physicians may apply for recertification as long as they are active, hold privileges in a hospital accredited by The Joint Commission, and have received satisfactory evaluations by the medical director. Those who pass the examination given by the American Board of Surgery are recertified.

CONTINUING MEDICAL EDUCATION

Following appointment to the medical staff of the hospital, the physician is obligated to provide proof of participation in a program of continuing medical education (CME). The Joint Commission and all state medical organizations stipulate that the medical staff must participate in programs of continuing education. The scope and complexity of a physician's individual CME will be left up to that physician, but they must meet the needs of the hospital's in-house medical staff credentialing program. This usually varies depending on the resources at hand and the needs of the hospital, which are directly relevant to the type of patient care delivered at the hospital. The CME records of each staff member are documented and placed in that member's medical staff file.

ORGANIZED MEDICINE

In 1847, some 250 physicians, representing more than 40 medical societies and 28 colleges from 22 states, came together and founded the AMA. Pressure to establish the AMA stemmed from the poor quality of medical education in the United States, the very brisk traffic in patent medicines and secret remedies, and the questionable ethics of many physicians at that time. The people who founded the AMA believed that a national association of physicians was needed to lead the crusade for improved medical education and patient care. The founding objectives of the AMA were generally to promote the science and art of medicine to ensure better health for all people.

The AMA is involved in the legislative process and has become part of a strong hospital and medical lobby. In order to respond effectively to the regulatory and legal environment, the AMA has expanded its original mission to include the formulation of national healthcare policies.

MEDICAL STAFF ORGANIZATION

The internal organization of the medical staff varies from hospital to hospital. Complex university or teaching hospitals differ from the smaller community hospitals. As a result of The Joint Commission's efforts and its accreditation standards, however, the differences are less extensive today than in the past. The standards stipulate that there is to be a single organized medical staff that has overall responsibility for the quality of the professional services provided by individuals with clinical privileges, as well as accountability to the governing body.

Appointment to the medical staff is a formal process that is outlined in each hospital's **medical staff bylaws**, with encouragement for standardization from The Joint Commission. The following is a brief outline of a typical **appointment process** that a doctor must go through:

1. The applying physician completes a written application that includes information about his or her education, privileges at other hospitals, recommendations, years of practice, lawsuits, and so forth. The completed application is usually forwarded to the hospital chief executive officer (CEO).

2. The application is reviewed for completeness, all items are verified, and a check is made with the National Practitioner Data Bank (discussed later in this chapter). The application is then sent for screening to the head of the specific department or specialty (e.g., medicine or surgery) to which the physician is applying.

3. The application is then forwarded to the medical staff's credentials committee, which reviews the physician's qualifications and past professional performance. It is at this point that the credentials committee may request a meeting with the applicant.

4. The executive committee for the medical staff reviews and discusses the application. It sends its recommendation on to the hospital's governing body.

5. The board of trustees or one of its committees reviews the application. The board will accept, reject, or defer the application. If the application is questionable, requires more information, or needs discussion, it may be referred to the joint conference committee.

6. The CEO usually notifies the physician that the appointment has been approved or rejected. The notice letter sent to the physician also notes any limitations on privileges requested. In receiving approval, a physician is granted certain **clinical privileges** (procedures the doctor is permitted to perform within the hospital). This is called the individual's privilege delineation. The privilege delineation process is based on verifiable information made available to the credentials committee. A physician's current competence in his or her discipline is the crucial determinant for granting privileges. The privileges are recorded, and the record is kept on file in key places within the hospital, such as within the emergency department, in the operating theatre, and in the medical staff office.

Once a physician is admitted to the medical staff, he or she is appointed in two separate **categories of membership**: (1) a **clinical department**, such as surgery, obstetrics, pediatrics, or urology; and (2) status based on the extent of the physician's participation in the hospital. Staff membership status may be categorized as explained in Exhibit 5-1.

The organization of the hospital medical staff is divided into medical specialty departments and sections. For example, there may be departments of medicine, surgery, obstetrics and gynecology, and pediatrics. In

Exhibit 5-1. Status of medical staff membership.

Active or attending staff—These medical staff members have full rights and privileges. Each physician with this designation may be required to admit a certain number of patients each year or they lose active privileges. This will reduce the number of physicians who may wish to be on the medical staff of every hospital and not truly support the hospital.

Associate staff—Medical staff members have incomplete privileges and may be working toward active staff designation. They may have to be in this designation for a number of months while their colleagues evaluate their care, or they may have a limited number of admissions per month.

Provisional staff—These may be new staff members; there may be a probationary period associated with this . . . often they are supervised by other physicians for a certain number of cases.

Courtesy staff—A hospital may classify a physician as a courtesy staff member if that physician does not often admit patients to that hospital.

Consulting staff—These physicians do not admit patients, but rather they are called in to consult on particular patients who have been admitted by other physicians.

Temporary staff—These physicians are given privileges for a designated time, usually to treat one patient.

The above are general guidelines. The governing document for the hospital that will determine the level of medical staff membership is the medical staff bylaws—this document will be different for each hospital, determined by which medical staff members write the bylaws and what changes the board of directors or trustees makes to the document. Physicians should seek legal guidance, as many antitrust issues can arise.

larger hospitals, these departments may be further subdivided into sections. Each clinical department has a physician designated as chief or director who is the medical administrative head. This person is generally selected through a process outlined in the medical staff bylaws, which usually involves election by departmental members or appointment by the hospital board of trustees.

CLOSED AND OPEN MEDICAL STAFFS

Historically, individual hospitals have controlled their own admissions to their medical staff. A **closed medical staff** is one in which the medical staff closely monitors and restricts any new applicants to the medical staff or to a department of the medical staff. This is generally done with the concurrence of the hospital board of trustees. When a hospital does permit a closed medical staff, it is usually based on considerations related to the quality of and need for patient care within the hospital and the community. There may also be closed medical staffs within selected departments or sections in the hospital. Three notable examples are the imaging, emergency, and pathology departments. In these cases, the hospital signs a contractual agreement with a physician or a professional group to allow exclusive services in the department. The courts have generally found this to be a legal arrangement if such agreements are based on significant medical and administrative considerations. Closed medical staff issues are frequently addressed in the courts under federal antitrust laws. Additionally, since the Federal Trade Commission (FTC) has the power to establish rules and regulations defining unfair practices in this area, it is reasonable to assume that it will be a predominant enforcement agency for medical staff admissions in years to come. An open staff essentially admits all qualified physicians who meet the hospital's guidelines.

MEDICAL STAFF COMMITTEES

The Joint Commission standards dictate that the medical staff must develop bylaws to be self-governing, as well as to be accountable to the governing body. The medical staff conducts its business through committees. The committee chairpersons are either selected by members of the staff or appointed by the president of the staff.

One of the most important committees is the medical staff executive committee. Generally, the **executive committee** is composed of officers of the medical staff and a number of elected members from the staff. Typically, this committee meets monthly to conduct the business of the medical staff. The hospital CEO usually attends. The medical executive committee coordinates various committees and establishes rules that affect the different clinical departments of the staff. The credentials committee, medical records committee, tissue committee, medical audit committee, and medical quality improvement committee are other key committees of the staff. The **credentials committee** has the responsibility to review the qualifications of new physicians applying for membership. This committee also reviews the credentials of medical staff members who must be reappointed. **Reappointments** are usually made once a year or every other year. The review is conducted to ensure that the reapplying physician has attended committee meetings, has not been involved in lawsuits, is getting on well with his or her peers and the hospital employees, and has renewed his or her medical insurance coverage and renewed training certificates (e.g., for CPR). The credentials committee may also investigate allegations of misconduct or breaches of ethics among the members of the medical staff. This committee reports directly to the executive committee.

Usually, a medical quality improvement committee is the principal instrument for reviewing quality improvement matters (e.g., patient and surgical outcomes, number of cesarean sections, etc.). It also reviews the quantity and quality of patient records as written by physicians, nurses, or other associated health professionals in the hospital. It also serves to monitor physicians who have delinquent medical records. This committee generally works closely with the hospital's medical records administrator.

An efficient medical audit committee and a well-functioning tissue committee traditionally have been key instruments for assessing quality. The tissue committee, which is comprised of practicing surgeons and a member of the hospital pathology department, provides a vehicle to confirm the diagnosis for surgical cases and acts as a control against unnecessary surgery. The committee reviews all surgical cases to determine, based on a review of tissue taken from the patient, whether the surgery was necessary. Tissue removed during an operation is forwarded to the pathology laboratory for postoperative diagnosis and review.

THE MEDICAL DIRECTOR

The medical staff will sometimes elect a part-time medical director, or the hospital may have employ one full-time or part-time. Generally, the medical director is a top-level management employee. If the medical director works part-time in that position, he or she may also see patients, and therefore, could be a member of the medical staff. The medical director's role is to evaluate clinical performance and to enforce hospital policies related to quality care. However, as in other management jobs, the role may be expanded to include other activities. This person can be an excellent liaison between the administrator and the medical staff, being able to speak doctor to doctor.

THE HOSPITALIST

A phenomenon of the last 10 years has been the addition of a hospitalist to the medical staff. The **hospitalist** is usually an internal medicine specialist who makes daily rounds and visits every patient in the hospital. The advantages to this are many. By limiting his or her practice to the hospital, the hospitalist clearly can understand the inner workings of the hospital better than physicians who also have an office practice and must spend precious time driving back and forth daily to see their patients. The hospitalist can take over the care of other physicians' patients, allowing those physicians to maximize their office time, or contact physicians to report the condition of their hospitalized patients. This person can help minimize the time a patient spends in the hospital by seeing each patient more frequently and by better understanding the services each department in the hospital delivers, as well as the personality of each specialized employee (e.g., respiratory, laboratory, and imaging technicians). The hospitalist adds efficiency.

ALLIED HEALTH PERSONNEL

There continues to be an increasing number of nonphysicians applying for clinical privileges in hospitals, including (but not limited to) podiatrists, chiropractors, physician assistants, nurse practitioners, nurse midwives, and psychologists. By applying for medical staff privileges, some of these groups have raised the question of how they fit into the hospital medical staff.

Historically, with the backing of laws and regulations, hospitals have usually excluded these groups from practicing within the hospital. Generally, state regulations regarding nurse practitioners and physician assistants indicate that a physician must supervise their work. The AMA agrees with the American Hospital Association on this issue and believes that full medical staff privileges should be restricted to physicians and dentists. The Joint Commission has been somewhat more liberal with regard to podiatrists, and has delineated what it believes a podiatrist can do within a hospital. The Joint Commission permits other duly licensed healthcare professionals to practice in hospitals under the supervision of a practitioner who has clinical privileges. The case law on the privilege question is not clear, and it is reasonable to assume that each individual issue may be decided based on state statutes and license practice laws within each state.

LEGAL RESTRICTIONS ON PHYSICIANS

Today, physicians are legally and professionally restricted in their practice of medicine and in their commercial ventures. A physician's professional conduct is also monitored closely. The Health Care Quality Improvement Act of 1986 set up a **National Practitioner Data Bank** (initiated in 1990) to prevent physicians, as well as other healthcare professionals, from hiding acts of malpractice and professional misbehavior by moving to other states. Sources of data include hospitals, malpractice insurers, and state licensing boards. Hospitals must check the data bank during the credentialing process.

A Final Word Regarding Physicians

The administrator should never forget that nothing happens in a hospital unless physicians admit patients. Without patients, the beds sit empty and the hospital employees are idle. Physicians are one of the hospital's most important resources.

CHAPTER REVIEW

1. What are some items that are typically reviewed by the credentials committee?
2. Who appoints members of the medical staff?

3. Discuss the appointment procedure involved in becoming a medical staff member at a typical hospital.
4. What are the two typical categories of medical staff membership and the six levels of admitting privileges?
5. What is the difference between a closed medical staff and an open medical staff?
6. List and discuss five medical staff committees.
7. What are the typical functions of the medical director?
8. What is a hospitalist and what role does he or she play?
9. What is the National Practitioner Data Bank?
10. Discuss the process of becoming a physician, beginning with college.
11. Discuss five types of allied health personnel and their roles in the health community.

CHAPTER 6

Physician Extenders
Divya Pandurangadu

KEY TERMS

Physician assistant (PA)
Dr. Eugene A. Stead
Obstetrics and gynecology
Nurse practitioner (NP)

Holistic outlook
Midwifery
Direct-entry midwife (DEM)

INTRODUCTION

The growing need for healthcare professionals has created a niche for mid-level professionals such as physician assistants (PAs), nurse practitioners (NPs), and midwives. The allied health profession is a field on the rise due to the shortage of physicians in rural and inner city areas. These individuals are trained to perform routine medical procedures under the indirect supervision of a physician. They are able to work independently to treat and diagnose patients and refer to the supervising physician or surgeon as needed.

HISTORY OF PHYSICIAN ASSISTANTS

PAs, in contrast to what the title claims, are not necessarily an aide to a physician; more often, **PAs** serve as an extension of the healthcare team in providing routine care to patients, including conducting physical exams, diagnosing and treating illnesses, ordering and interpreting tests, performing rudimentary surgical procedures, and prescribing medicine. The PA profession was created during the 1960s by **Dr. Eugene A. Stead** (Duke University Medical Center, Durham, North Carolina) to address the shortage of primary care physicians in the United States. Dr. Stead saw this as an opportunity to create an experimental 2-year program made up of former Navy corpsmen with experience in health care as candidates. In 1965, the first four PA students enrolled in the newly founded PA curriculum at Duke University and set the foundation for what is now one of the fastest growing healthcare occupations.

SPECIALTIES

As a licensed healthcare professional, a PA may enter into a broad range of specialties. Essentially, anywhere a physician is found, a PA also has the opportunity to work. This can include private practice, outpatient clinics, university hospitals, and health maintenance organizations (HMOs). In private practice, PAs spend a large amount of time working directly with a physician to provide patient care, perform laboratory work, and handle paperwork. In this setting, physicians can spend more time dealing with patients in urgent situations while the PA tends to patients with more routine ailments. As for outpatient clinics, the supervising physician can either be onsite at the same location as the PA or can be contacted through telecommunication, with periodic site visits. In rural or inner city communities, PAs are often the only available primary care providers. PAs carry the majority of the workload in these locations, and the physician is only a phone call away if any challenging situations occur. The patients seen by the PA embrace their provider and appreciate the invaluable services offered at a convenient location (Hytrek, 2010). According to the US National Library of Medicine, about 30% of PAs practice in areas with populations of 50,000 or less, improving the distribution of healthcare providers throughout the general area (Vorvick, 2009). In addition to dealing with patients, PAs who work in HMO settings or for a large medical corporation may also be responsible for assigning other PAs to the physician they will be supporting. In university hospitals, a PA may have a wide range of responsibilities that, in addition to assisting the physician, can include research and instruction (Princeton Review, 2010).

The scope of a PA practice is not limited to the primary care field. At the present time, roughly half of the practicing PAs work in primary medical care, which includes family medicine, internal medicine, pediatrics, and **obstetrics and gynecology**. Other PAs work in fields such as general surgery, surgical subspecialties, emergency medicine, dermatology, psychiatry, radiology, and pathology (Princeton Review, 2010).

WHAT IS A NURSE PRACTITIONER?

NPs are similar to PAs in that they also work under the supervision of a physician and treat both physical and mental conditions. An **NP** is a registered nurse who has earned a master's or doctoral degree in advanced nursing education, and has been trained in a specific field. NPs focus on individualized care and may work with individuals of all ages depending on the scope of their practice. NPs focus not only on the condition of the patient, but also on how the illness will affect the rest of the patient's life and his or her family. In addition to treating patients, NPs are responsible for educating patients and teaching wellness and prevention. This **holistic outlook** can help patients achieve the emotional and spiritual well-being to manage their condition outside of the healthcare setting (Women's Health Channel, 2009).

RESPONSIBILITIES OF THE NURSE PRACTITIONER

The duties of an NP are also comparable to those of a PA. In addition to collaborating with physicians and other healthcare providers, NPs treat and diagnose patients with diseases and injuries. They monitor patients with chronic conditions and teach them how to manage their conditions. Physical examinations and diagnostic studies, such as x-rays, EKGs, and lab tests, may be conducted by NPs. They also have the ability to prescribe medication, make referrals for rehabilitation, and provide prenatal care and family planning services. NPs provide cost-effective care in all states and can work in a wide array of institutions, including community health clinics, urgent care centers, HMOs, home healthcare agencies, women's health centers, nursing homes, physician offices, school/university clinics, and Veterans Administration facilities (Women's Health Channel, 2009).

WHAT IS A MIDWIFE?

NPs working in obstetrics and gynecology can also provide specialized care in the field of midwifery. Midwives are healthcare professionals who provide prenatal care to expectant mothers, care for the infant during the birthing process, and assist both the infant and the mother with postpartum care. Midwives offer their services during normal pregnancies and deliveries, and if any complications arise throughout the process, they can call upon an obstetrician or physician. The foundation of care is centered on safety, achieved by noninterventional means. This can include refraining from the use of pain medication, and using noninvasive procedures to reduce the risk of complications during labor and delivery. Having a midwife present during the birthing process can help lessen the duration of labor, the need for pain medication, the use of forceps and other operative devices, and the prospect of a cesarean section (Women's Health Channel, 2007).

Types of Midwives

In the **midwifery** field, there are different types of midwives based on training and education. A **direct-entry midwife (DEM)** can gain the necessary skills by serving an apprenticeship with a midwife or physician, completing an independent study, receiving training in the community, and/or attending a midwifery school. DEMs are centered on experience-based training, and the majority provide assistance during at-home deliveries. DEMs also have the option to become a certified midwife (CM) through the North American Registry of Midwives. This requires a baccalaureate degree and completion of a national certification examination. CMs have the ability to work independently in medical clinics or hospitals. Nurse-midwives are another type of midwife. Nurse-midwives are registered nurses who have completed an accredited midwifery program and become a certified nurse-midwife (CNM). CNMs are able to prescribe medication as well as provide a broad range of care. This can consist of preconception care, prenatal care, gynecological exams, labor and delivery, and care after labor. Nurse-midwives work with physicians, especially when complications arise during pregnancy. By encouraging the active participation of the expectant mothers and open lines of communication, nurse-midwives assist in making the transition from labor to delivery as smooth as possible (Women's Health Channel, 2007).

Mid-level healthcare professionals hold the key to equalizing the shortage of healthcare professionals. PAs and NPs can reduce the burden of physicians by providing primary care, and midwives can provide a natural-care alternative in the field of gynecology and obstetrics.

CHAPTER REVIEW

1. What is the history behind the PA profession?
2. What is the role of the PA in the healthcare field?
3. How does a healthcare facility benefit from having an NP?
4. What are some key differences between a PA and an NP?
5. List some of the services provided by a midwife.
6. What are some differences between an NP and a midwife?

REFERENCES

Hytrek, N. (2010). *Rural clinics rely on midlevel providers.* Retrieved March 3, 2010, from http://www.siouxcityjournal.com/lifestyles/leisure/article_c73678ee-8381-5ff1-96f2-23502c642913.html

Princeton Review. (2010). *Physician assistant.* Retrieved March 1, 2010, from http://www.princetonreview.com/Careers.aspx?cid5181

Vorvick, L. J. (2009). *Physician assistant profession (PA).* Retrieved March 5, 2010, from http://www.nlm.nih.gov/medlineplus/ency/article/001935.html

Women's Health Channel. (2007). *What is a midwife?* Retrieved March 11, 2010, from http://www.womenshealthchannel.com/midwife.shtml

Women's Health Channel. (2009). *What is a nurse practitioner?* Retrieved March 5, 2010, from http://www.womenshealthchannel.com/nursepractitioner.shtml

CHAPTER 7

Nursing Services

Cheryl Rowder

KEY TERMS

American Nurses
  Association (ANA)
Nursing degrees
Certified registered nurse
  anesthetist (CRNA)
Quality assurance (QA)
Wound-care nurse

Nursing informatics specialist
Case management in nursing
Nursing standards
Nurse staffing
Scheduling
Tall organizational model
Flat organizational model

INTRODUCTION

Inpatients and outpatients should receive quality, courteous, and considerate care from skilled, understanding personnel. The primary department required to meet this goal is the nursing service department. Nurses comprise the single largest healthcare professional group in the United States.

EARLY TRADITIONS

Both individuals (e.g., Florence Nightingale) and institutions (e.g., the Roman Catholic Church and the military) influenced the early history of nursing. Perhaps the best-known person associated with the history of nursing is Nightingale, whose work during the Crimean War gave nursing a more respectable image. She became known as the mother of modern nursing. After the war, in 1859, Nightingale founded the Florence Nightingale Nursing School in connection with St. Thomas Hospital in London.

Records of schools for training American nurses can be traced as far back as 1798. However, American schools that embodied the principles of Florence Nightingale's school in London were established much later. The first such school was the New England Hospital for Women and Children, founded in Boston in 1872. The Bellevue Hospital School of Nursing in New York City and the Massachusetts General Hospital School of Nursing in Boston followed in 1873.

NURSING EDUCATION

After World War II, changes in the well-established Nightingale nursing education model began to be implemented. Registered nurses (RNs) were typically trained in the hospital setting in what were called diploma programs. This training focused on clinical skills, with nurses functioning in the role of handmaiden to the physician. An acute shortage of professional RNs led to the development of the licensed practical nurse (LPN) and licensed vocational nurse (LVN). These positions required half the training time of an RN, but they were also limited in their scope of practice. Because of the scarcity of RNs, the numbers of nurses' aides and unlicensed assistive personnel continued to rise to meet patient-care needs.

Meanwhile, educational programs for RNs also changed, especially in the 1960s, with the presentation of a position paper by the **American Nurses Association (ANA)** that promoted an orderly transition from hospital-based nursing education to nursing education at colleges or universities. During this time, the 2- to 3-year hospital-diploma nursing education programs began to be phased out due to pressure on hospitals from the ANA to require a baccalaureate degree (4 years) from a college/ university or an associate degree (2 years) from a community college. Educational programs have continued to evolve. Today, nursing programs include sophisticated technologies to enhance reality through simulation.

Nursing Degrees

There is a continuing debate about 2-year associate degree nurses (ADNs) versus 4-year baccalaureate degree nurses (BSNs) in terms of the entry level for nursing practice. Several studies have compared patient outcomes after care by nurses at each level. Aiken et al. (2008) concluded that hospitals with higher proportions of BSNs had a 4% decrease in patient risk of death. This level of education, therefore, is necessary not only to ensure quality patient care, but also to promote evidence-based practice where practice is guided by the most current research. The ability to interpret research and incorporate it into practice is only taught in baccalaureate programs. Furthermore, nurses now have opportunities to extend their education beyond a baccalaureate degree.

Nurses can now choose from a variety of education/experience combinations. RNs can earn an advanced degree that requires a minimum of 2 years of academic work. The advanced practice nurse (APN) is defined as "a registered professional nurse who is prepared for advanced nursing practice by virtue of knowledge and skills obtained through a post-basic or advanced educational program of study, [and] acts independently and/or in collaboration with other health care professionals in the delivery of health care services" (O'Keefe, 2001, p. 529).

The role of the clinical nurse specialist (CNS) has been replaced in recent years by that of the registered nurse practitioner (RNP), who holds a degree that requires advanced health assessment and advanced pharmacology. These advanced practice registered nurse (APRN) roles differ significantly. The CNS was originally intended to be a hospital-based nurse who brought special knowledge to a group of nursing units involved in the care of a specific patient population. A CNS degree included five major roles: educator, researcher, administrator, clinical knowledge expert, and resource to nurses. This degree required approximately 36 credit hours to complete. Generally, a CNS was considered the resource person for specified areas such as cardiac care or intensive care. With credentialing, a CNS could gain prescriptive ability and relieve the physician from writing routine orders and prescriptions.

A nurse practitioner (NP) has a more advanced clinical focus than a CNS. This degree requires approximately 54 credit hours and includes advanced pharmacology and assessment skills, along with many more hours of clinical practice prior to graduation. APNs can be delegated by a physician to prescribe medications under agreed-upon protocols. The APRN may function independently in providing wellness training and specialized nursing services directly to patient and groups of patients.

The APRN should not be confused with the physician assistant (PA), who has received a total of 2 years of medical training and whose license is totally dependent upon supervision by a physician.

A PhD in nursing usually requires more than 7 years of academic work beyond the baccalaureate degree, interspersed with practical experience. This degree is typically focused on research practice. A similar degree is the doctorate in nursing (DNP), which has recently evolved with a strong clinical focus and is especially appealing to APRNs. These programs are relatively new and may require different courses for their completion.

During the mid-1990s, master's programs offered various tracts, such as advanced knowledge as an educator, administrator, or CNS. Typically, nursing students in a master's program would choose their major area of study based on their preference for maternal/child health, psychology, or medical/surgical nursing. This study format was almost completely replaced by NP programs in the late 1990s. However, the need for knowledgeable resource nurses led to the recent creation of the clinical nurse leader (CNL) degree, which replaces the CNS degree with an additional focus on leadership skills.

With additional training, nurses with advanced degrees may also work as nurse midwives or nurse anesthetists. **Certified registered nurse anesthetists (CRNAs)** are in demand in high-population areas and must function with at least one physician anesthesiologist on hand. Typically, CRNAs handle cases that are not thought to be complex or to involve unstable patients. This position is extremely popular because it is lucrative and offers regular work hours and few weekend shifts. It is a very competitive field, as few schools in the country offer this program. Admission requirements include competitive scores in advanced pathophysiology as well as at least 2 years of critical-care experience.

All RNs and LVNs must be licensed by the state board of nursing in the state where they will be practicing. The states have similar licensure eligibility requirements, and licensure is based on passing a national examination for RNs and LVNs. RNs have a compact that allows RNs registered in participating states to also be licensed in other compact states. Each board of nursing is responsible for suspending and revoking licenses. A nurse can renew a license by simply completing the required continuing education and paying a small fee, if it is done before the original license expires.

There are two large and influential national professional nursing association groups. The ANA, founded in 1896, is a federation of 54 constituent associations, including those in the 50 states, the District of Columbia, and Puerto Rico. As the encompassing professional organization for RNs, the ANA promotes policy and legislation on healthcare and nursing issues, establishes standards for nursing, and publishes the *Code of Ethics for Nurses*. There are numerous specialty nursing organizations. Another influential nursing association is the National League for Nursing (NLN), founded in 1951. It is primarily concerned with promoting standards and innovation in nursing education. The NLN's membership is composed of RNs, practical nurses, nurses' aides, doctors, and hospital administrators—all of whom have a professional interest in nursing.

Nursing Roles

RNs are utilized in almost every department of the hospital. The various roles they fill require either specialized training or mentorship. Some roles involve patient treatments and others include administration or **quality assurance (QA)**.

The position of house supervisor is an administrative one. Work begins during the afternoon shift and continues through the night, and the house supervisor is responsible for making decisions about any issue that may arise during the night or when the administrative staff is not on duty. Additionally, this nurse is responsible for assessing the upcoming shift to determine whether additional staff nurses are needed, and how the staff can best be utilized to meet the patients' care needs.

Wound-care nurses have special knowledge related to skin integrity issues. Recently, Medicare declared that treatment for any skin integrity issue that occurred during a hospital stay would not be reimbursed. This fact alone increased this nurse's importance, as well as the importance of a thorough assessment of the patient on admission. If a skin integrity issue is documented on admission, Medicare will pay for the care of this issue during the patient's inpatient stay. If it is not documented on admission but is assessed later during the patient's stay, the hospital will pay for care related to that skin integrity issue. High-risk patients being admitted from nursing care units outside of the hospital must be carefully monitored. The wound-care nurse is the resource for information about the latest products available for various skin care issues, as well as for educating the staff on the use of specialized equipment.

The knowledge of infection-control nurses has gained in importance with the increase in known cases of methicillin-resistant *Staphylococcus aureus* (MRSA). To control the spread of infection, these nurses must ensure that proper contact precautions are maintained until a patient's infection status is known. In many hospitals today, infection is assumed until proven otherwise. Contact precautions, such as donning gloves and gowns before entering a patient's room, are in place for all people who expect to touch the patient. These precautions remain until the patient is found to be negative. For MRSA, this is accomplished by collection and laboratory examination of two nasal swabs. If the results are negative, the contact precautions are suspended. Contact precaution signs indicate the necessity of using the gowns and gloves provided in the infection control cabinet (usually red or yellow) near the patient's door. When in doubt, all visitors and hospital personnel should ask a nurse whether they need to use gowns and gloves before entering a room that has such a cabinet by the door.

QA nurses may work in concert with infection control nurses. The QA department acts in a manner similar to that employed by the Centers for Disease Control and Prevention (CDC). It is responsible for collecting data on identified benchmark conditions that have been identified as indicators of quality of care. For instance, a sudden rise in postoperative infection rates will raise a red flag for the QA department to investigate this trend to ascertain any cause or link that can be corrected. Often, nurses are hired for this position because of their strong assessment skills and knowledge of clinical conditions and indicators.

A new specialty is the **nursing informatics specialist**, who brings special technological skills in the patient-care arena. These skills include developing and implementing electronic medical records, patient monitoring equipment, and simulations for education and competency validation of the staff. Additionally, this specialist may assist in designing new and innovative patient-care areas and programs using evolving technologies to improve care and contain costs.

Ancillary Help

Several forms of ancillary helpers have come into vogue to ensure that adequate staff can be maintained during an influx of patients or when a number of personnel are out sick. Per diem nurses may be hired to work in one particular unit or trained to float to any unit in the hospital that needs their services. They are utilized on an as-needed basis and may be called off or called in depending on the census of the unit where they work. Such nurses do not receive benefits, but they are able to dictate their schedules. They are similar to part-time nurses except that part-time nurses must work 20 hours per week and may not be able to control their own schedule. Part-time nurses may receive benefits, but they will be more costly than those offered to full-time nurses.

A traveling nurse is a special category of nurse, and is similar to a temporary full-time agency nurse. These nurses accept long-term work placements that are not permanent assignments for a particular unit of a hospital. For instance, they might agree to work for 6 months on the cardiac floor of a particular hospital in Boston, Massachusetts. When the 6 months are over, they may agree to continue if they are needed or they may travel to another location. This type of nursing is especially attractive to young single people or those who wish to see some other parts of the world.

Agency nurses are employees of a private agency. Their credentials are maintained by the agency, which sometimes is responsible for their vacation pay. Although these nurses appear to make relatively higher salaries, it should be remembered that they either function as independent contractors who must withhold their own income taxes, or they are paid directly by the agency, which then withholds the taxes. Sometimes these nurses choose to work in particular units in certain hospitals where they become familiar with the routines. Even so, they are often given a lighter patient load because they are not considered regular staff. These nurses are only brought in on an as-needed basis for one shift when no other staffing options are available.

A large number of nursing employees serve as nurses' aides, orderlies, and technicians. Nurses' aides provide basic patient care, such as giving bed baths and checking vital signs and blood sugar levels. They do not conduct any patient assessments or administer medications. These auxiliary nursing personnel commonly go through at least a hospital orientation training program before assuming their nursing duties with patients. Some states require a formal training program for nurses' aides. They do not need to be graduates of a formal education program, nor are they licensed. They can, however, be certified. The graduate nurse, staff nurse, or nurse manager generally assigns duties to the certified nursing assistant (nurses' aide).

Nauman
Nurse working
now the[?] Msrei[?]

Many of the individual nursing units in larger acute-care settings have a host of clerical functions to be performed. Unit clerks or ward clerks assigned to the nursing unit handle the enormous quantity of administrative work, such as coordinating reports, orders, and prescription orders for patients, answering telephones, directing visitors, helping with hospital requisitions for patients and supplies, and performing a multitude of other duties. These clerks usually work directly under the supervision of a nurse manager. In smaller facilities, these duties may also be performed by the charge nurse. Charge nurses generally carry a lighter patient workload so that they can be free to coordinate patient movements, communicate with physicians, and perform clerical duties such as entering medical orders and transferring and admitting patients.

MODES OF NURSING CARE DELIVERY

Organizational structures today are moving away from "tall" hierarchical structures with formal channels of communication and moving toward "flat" organizations with collaborative teams, with a concomitant change in focus from product- to customer-centered care. This shift, along with the shortage of nurses, has been accompanied by an increase in outpatient care, self-care of chronic illness, and use of medical technologies, including electronic medical records (Coddington et al., 2000).

Today there are several commonly used modes of nursing delivery: (1) case nursing, (2) functional nursing, (3) team nursing, (4) primary care nursing, (5) modular (or district) nursing, (6) case management, (7) collaborative practice, and (8) differentiated practice.

Case Nursing

The case method of nursing is one of the earliest forms of nursing care. In this system, the nurse or case manager individually plans and administers the care of a patient on a one-to-one basis. The case method was popular in the 1980s and persists in some institutions today. With this method, the patient has a different nurse each shift. This method can provide better results than team nursing, but it may not be as effective as primary nursing, where the patient's care is totally planned by one nurse. In case nursing, a specialized nurse, the patient-care coordinator, supervises and evaluates the care given in any particular unit. Historically, the case method revolved around the physician's orders. Currently, case management has been introduced to provide coordinated care using a multidisciplinary approach.

Functional Nursing

Starting in the 1920s and continuing into the 1950s, nurses became aware of studies about the functional division of labor in industry, as exemplified by the assembly line approach to manufacturing used by Henry Ford and other industrialists. Nurses then applied these time and motion studies to their own discipline. Essentially, functional nursing uses a pyramid organization to look at the division of labor. Under such an arrangement, the technical aspects of each nursing staff member's job are identified, and based on his or her technical expertise, each unit member is given specific functions or tasks to perform in the unit. For example, one nurse might administer medications, another might perform all treatments, a third might take each patient's temperature and blood pressure, and a fourth might prepare patients for surgery or imaging. All nurses would give baths, make beds, and try to meet the patient's psychological and emotional needs. The simpler tasks would be given to the less trained nursing personnel and the more complex tasks would go to the RNs. This method requires fewer RNs, but it may lead to dissatisfaction resulting from the repetitive nature of conducting one set of tasks.

Team Nursing

Team nursing began around the time of World War II, when there was a growing shortage of RNs. In the absence of RNs, hospitals had to use technicians, vocational nurses, and nurses' aides. Frequently, the less trained nursing personnel were put under the supervision of a more highly trained RN, who was called the team leader. A team would be asked to provide care to a group of patients in the nursing unit. Ideally, the team leader would be the best prepared person and could be expected to help the team formulate and carry out nursing care plans for every patient assigned to the team. Team nursing fits well into the pyramid structure of the hospital organization. By 2000, the team system had become popular and included elaborate team planning meetings that involved all health-care providers involved in an inpatient's care. From this format evolved the nursing care plan, which identifies present and future problems that might be faced by a patient. These team meetings add to work satisfaction, but team nursing as a whole can be expensive because it requires more personnel.

Primary Care Nursing

Primary care nursing has some of the characteristics of the case method of nursing, in that one RN is assigned to each patient. However, in contrast to the case method of nursing, the nurse assigned to the patient is not responsible for only one shift of work. The primary care nurse is responsible for the patient's care for 24 hours a day, 7 days a week. The primary care nurse must assess a patient's nursing needs, collaborate with other health professionals, including the physician, and formulate a plan of nursing care for which he or she is held accountable.

The primary care nurse attends to all of the patient's custodial care needs, such as bathing and feeding, as well as the patient's skilled care needs, such as administering medications. The primary care nurse may delegate certain responsibilities for executing the nursing care plan on other shifts, but the delegation is accomplished by means of other nursing care plans, including written notes and recordings. The plan is never carried out through a supervisor or third party; thus, an important element of primary care nursing is the triple A nurse. The triple A nurse is autonomous, has authority, and is held accountable for the nursing care of the patient.

Modular (or District) Nursing

Modular (or district) nursing is a form of both team nursing and primary nursing. Smaller teams care for the patient. An RN, with the assistance of a team, delivers care to as large a group of patients as possible. The RN functions as the coordinator of care. Sometimes the same team will be assigned to the same patient rooms in a unit that experiences longer patient stays.

Case Management

Psychiatry and social work provided the model for **case management in nursing**. This method was initially utilized in community nursing and was introduced into inpatient settings in the 1980s. This specialized nurse coordinates the care of an episode of illness for a patient and their family. This work includes evaluating and monitoring services from the time of admission to the hospital to post discharge. Living arrangements, social services, and all required elements of care after the hospital stay are evaluated and coordinated. This system includes interdisciplinary team meetings to assess the quality of care, which may be guided by critical paths for particular outcomes.

Collaborative Practice

The American Medical Association and the ANA used funds from the W. K. Kellogg Foundation to establish a National Joint Practice Committee in 1972. The committee examined the effects of collaboration between physicians and nurses on such issues as nurse satisfaction and quality of care, and concluded that collaboration was beneficial. Collaboration gained in importance in the 1990s as health care moved from inpatient settings to outpatient and community settings. With this came the development of the NP role, visiting-nurse organizations, and methods to classify patient diagnoses as established by the North American Nursing Diagnosis Association (NANDA).

Differentiated Practice

The differentiated practice method of assigning workloads to nurses takes into account their credentials and levels of education. Nurses with graduate or bachelor degrees are assigned care and planning for patients who require more complex care, whereas nurses with a 2-year associate's degree are assigned patients who require less complex care in less structured settings. The educational level of the nurses may influence the strategy chosen for staffing. For instance, team nursing requires fewer RNs. Modular and primary nursing systems require a greater number of RNs, but have been found to result in greater nurse satisfaction, more personalized care, less turnover, and fewer negative outcomes for patients.

TERMS AND STANDARDS

An understanding of precisely which nursing standard was utilized when the nursing department's budget and staffing schedule was established is an important element in a nursing service. A nursing standard or norm is defined as the amount of time and resources that is needed or considered desirable for each patient in a 24-hour period in order to give the type of care that is judged appropriate. The American Hospital Association and the ANA identified various **nursing standards** as early as 1950. To ensure that the standards are being met, nursing managers might ask the following questions: Is the ratio of RNs to other personnel in the department appropriate to the patient's needs? Are there too many or too few licensed practical nurses for the situation? Is there another way to assign duties to improve budgetary performance? Financial managers should know that when nursing service expenses are low or below budget, a detailed look at the nursing staff patterns may be required. The following possibilities must be considered: (1) nonnursing assistive personnel were utilized in place of RN staff nurses, (2) nurses were attached to some other cost center and were used in place of regular staff nurses, (3) inadequate information was available at the time the budget was established, (4) the department was unable to fill all budgeted positions, and (5) the on-duty nursing staff is carrying an unfair load. To analyze all of these specific circumstances, a financial manager must have an understanding of certain nursing definitions and terms that are widely accepted in the nursing service area. The patient must be able to rely on a reasonable standard of care, which means that the hospital must meet regulatory requirements and professional standards.

STAFFING

Nurse staffing is accomplished by determining how many full-time equivalent (FTE) nursing personnel from each skill class (e.g., RNs, LPNs, and nurses' aides) are needed to properly operate each nursing unit. Given the variety of levels of nursing care required by different populations of patients, and the large labor needs of a nursing unit, staffing is a challenge for a nursing department. The key to determining the number of staff and the qualifications needed is to use patient acuity systems and nurse competence and expertise, guided by staffing policies. In Texas, by law, staffing plans are established by the nurse staffing advisory committee. An initial consideration is whether staffing will be handled by one central office or delegated to each separate unit. Guidelines must also be established to determine how many weeks will be scheduled at one time. If hospitals tend to vary in the number of inpatients (census), the decision to staff for the minimum number of patients with additional numbers of prn (for *pro re nata*, meaning "as needed" or "for the existing occasion") employees may be attractive. This avoids the need to cancel full-time staff when the patient census decreases. A disadvantage is that when the census is at maximum capacity, it may be difficult to have adequate staffing. In this instance, hospitals may use float nurses, part-time nursing pool personnel, and agency contract nurses in addition to the hospital's full-time nursing staff to meet patient-care needs.

Hospitals may choose to use patient acuity systems to classify patients according to care categories and to quantify the nursing expertise and effort required. Generally, a patient's physical, technical, psychological, social, and teaching requirements are assessed in determining acuity levels. A common type of classification system is to create a list of critical indicators or condition indicators, such as sensory deficit, oxygen therapy, and wound care, that are separately rated and then summed up to determine the patient's care category. Care categories include routine care, moderate care, complete care, and continuous care. The nursing department quantifies the total nursing care time required for each patient-care category. Many patient acuity systems are computerized. Daily, weekly, and seasonal variations must be considered in the staffing arrangements.

NURSE STAFFING ISSUES

Changes in the labor force in most areas of the nation have resulted in a shortage of RNs as well as other allied health professionals. Because hospitals are a labor-intensive industry, staff shortages can have a major impact on their operation. Hospitals are meeting this challenging labor issue by implementing creative strategies such as giving bonuses, using clinical career ladders to motivate and reward nurses involved in direct patient care, allowing nurses to budget for their unit, broadening job responsibilities and autonomy, providing in-service training, and offering child daycare services. Staffing issues will be a challenge for many years because (1) the average age of a nurse in the United States is above 40 years; (2) for every eight nurses who leave the field, only five enter; and (3) the baby-boom population is aging and will be in increasing need of care.

In an effort to improve staff retention, hospitals have instituted programs to bring recognition to their institutions and make them a desirable place to work. One of the first such programs was initiated in 1982–1983. The ANA sponsored a study to identify hospitals that reported high nurse retention rates, high job satisfaction, and quality patient care. The fellows of the American Academy of Nursing chose a selection of hospitals that met those high standards. Over the next two decades, this program evolved in form from the original Magnet Hospitals to the American Nurses

Credentialing Center (ANCC)'s Magnet Recognition Program. The developers of the program originally identified 14 "forces of magnetism": quality nursing leadership, organizational structure, management style, personnel policies and programs, professional models of care, quality of care, quality improvement, consultation and resources, autonomy, the community and the hospital, nurses as teachers, the image of nursing, interdisciplinary relationships, and professional development (ANCC, 2005). These measures brought recognition to hospitals, increased awareness of nursing contributions, encouraged a competitive marketing edge, enhanced relationships, and increased nursing staff satisfaction and productivity (ANCC, 2005). However, these measures were difficult for small or rural hospitals to achieve; furthermore, they were driven from the top down and did not always reflect the needs of the very population of direct-care nurses the program wished to attract.

The Texas Nurses Association (TNA) developed the Nurse-Friendly program to address the concerns of direct-care nurses. The program was geared to smaller or rural hospitals with the goal of enhancing nurse retention and quality of care (Meraviglia et al., 2008). The developers of this project identified 12 criteria that they considered essential for a positive work environment, including a safe environment, no tolerance of nurse abuse, facilitation of leadership competency among direct-care supervisors and middle management, recognition of nurses, professional development, the presence of a qualified chief nursing officer, competency-based orientation, performance improvement, and a balance between life inside and outside the workplace. The program required a hospital to receive a positive rating from direct-care nurses as determined by a secret ballot. After 30 small or rural hospitals enrolled in the program, it was found that these measures "improved nurses' perception of their workplace, creating a positive practice setting" (Meraviglia et al., p. 312). The TNA Nurse-Friendly program was purchased by the ANCC and renamed Pursuit of Excellence; it is marketed globally along with the Magnet program to hospitals of all sizes.

SCHEDULING

Once the nursing leadership or (in Texas) the Nurse Staffing Advisory Committee agrees on a staffing plan for each unit, and the nursing administration determines the type of nursing modalities that are best suited for the hospital, the challenge is then to schedule nursing personnel so that patients will receive the necessary care at the time they require it. Nurse **scheduling** is defined as determining when each member of the nursing staff will be on duty and on which shift each will work. Scheduling should take into account weekends, the length of an individual's work assignments, and nurses' requests for vacations or time off. Scheduling is typically done for a period of 4 or 6 weeks, and is frequently tailored to each individual nursing unit. There are four commonly used approaches to nurse scheduling, which are described as traditional, cyclical, computer-aided traditional, and self-scheduling.

Traditional Scheduling

In traditional scheduling, the nurse schedulers initiate each work period (e.g., a week or a month). If the hospital is organized in a decentralized manner, the nurse manager makes the scheduling decisions by looking at the roster of personnel who are available to work on specified dates and for certain durations. A great deal of responsibility is placed in the nurse manager's hands to ensure the quality and quantity of coverage in the nursing unit. The major advantage of this traditional approach is flexibility. Nurse schedulers can adjust quickly to changes in the environment of the patient-care unit. Some disadvantages of traditional scheduling include spottiness in coverage at certain times and uneven quality of coverage. Unless the policies of the nursing administration provide for some elasticity in the process, uneven staffing could also lead to maximum personnel cost or, at the other extreme, minimum patient care.

Cyclical Scheduling

Cyclical scheduling is a system that covers a certain period of time, perhaps 1 or 3 months. This block of time is the cycle or scheduling period. Once a nurse agrees to a definite period, the scheduling in the cycle simply repeats itself period after period. The advantage of cyclical scheduling is that it provides even coverage and better quality staffing for each nursing unit. Special requests would interfere with the coverage, which could affect the quality of staffing. The major disadvantage to cyclical scheduling is that it is inflexible compared to the traditional system and cannot adjust rapidly to changes in the nursing unit environment. The ability to adjust is important, since change characterizes so many nursing units. Cyclical scheduling seems to work best in an environment where the numbers and needs of patients are fairly constant, and the nurses are stable and do not rotate between shifts. New nurses can be hired into any open cyclical slot with very little difficulty.

Computer-Aided Traditional Scheduling

In the third approach to scheduling, a computer is mathematically programmed to assist in the traditional method of scheduling. This system provides more flexibility and reduces the operating costs involved in calculating and working with the schedule. To some extent, a computer centralizes the scheduling process. If the mathematical models are properly used, a computer can produce high-quality schedules. The system will also facilitate the incorporation of standard personnel policies into the schedule, and these policies can be applied uniformly in all nursing units. It can also add more stability to the entire nursing department. The advantages of computerized scheduling are most dramatically apparent in situations where nurses rotate frequently among shifts and the nursing environment is subject to persistent change. Computer-aided, centralized schedules minimize the time spent preparing and maintaining schedules.

Self-Scheduling

The self-scheduling system is coordinated by staff nurses and based on scheduling policies and procedures. Nurses can sign up for shifts on a grid or computer during a specified time period. Staff members are responsible for negotiating for time off. Allowing nurses to negotiate their schedules improves morale and allows the manager to function in a more supportive and less supervisory manner. This scheduling technique has resulted in improved nurse retention and job satisfaction.

Rotating Work Shifts Versus Permanent Shifts

Some hospitals choose to schedule straight shifts; in other words, nurses are hired for the day shift, evening shift, or night shift. At times, a new graduate will need to begin on the night shift and wait until a day shift becomes available, particularly if the hospital has few night nurses. This system has the disadvantage of decreasing movement among departments, as nurses may not want to start over on the night shift in a different unit. To avoid this situation, some hospitals enforce rotating shifts so that all nursing personnel will have equal shifts divided among day, evening, and night shifts. Although this may seem fair, it is extremely difficult for staff members who must constantly adjust their sleep and work patterns to accommodate these varying shifts.

Weekend Alternative

The weekend-alternative arrangement was developed by Baylor Hospital in Dallas, Texas, and consequently was labeled the Baylor Plan. The purpose of the plan is to ensure weekend coverage for nursing shifts. According to this arrangement, nurses can work two 12-hour day shifts on the weekend, resulting in 36 hours of pay, or two 12-hour night shifts, resulting in 40 hours of pay. This plan tends to improve staff morale by providing more time off on the weekends, but it may also result in higher budgets for staff.

DEPARTMENT ORGANIZATION

Two general methods are used to organize the work of health professionals in an acute-care hospital. Each method is centered on a function (specialized work to be performed) or a program (output to be achieved). A functional organization revolves around the work or services to be performed, such as nursing, radiation therapy, or environmental services. In this system, healthcare professionals report to a specific supervisor for their specialty area (e.g., a respiratory therapist would report to the manager of respiratory therapy). This organizational form enhances relationships within a specialty area and can be cost-effective while promoting professional growth. However, this form of organization discourages collaboration and coordination among specialties and may fragment care.

Organization by program in an acute-care hospital divides up work for a particular service or disease process, such as diabetes, women's services, or elderly services. This multidisciplinary approach is useful for integrating care; however, patients who require services from several programs may find it difficult to navigate the system. This form has the added burden of ensuring professional standards throughout one cadre of professionals. Additionally, duplication of services in separate programs can lead to inefficiency.

Approximately 40–50% of all hospital employees work in the nursing department. The nursing department's organization is a reflection of the overall organizational structure of the hospital. The shape of this organizational structure may be influenced in part by the size and complexity of the institution. Generally, the decision-making and power positions will be arranged in either a "tall" shape with many layers of managers between the chief executive officer (CEO) of the hospital, the director of nurses, and the direct-care providers, or a "flat" shape with fewer levels between the director of the hospital and the care provider. Each of these organizational structures provides advantages and disadvantages. Stresses on the system can cause institutions to seek a change in the overall structure as they try to correct situations that are deemed critical to stakeholders.

The nursing department may be organized in a pyramid fashion, very much like the hospital with a **tall organizational model**. In this model, the primary responsibility for nursing functions rests with the director of the nursing department or division. The director may be referred to as the director of nurses (DON), the chief nursing officer (CNO), the chief nursing executive, or (more commonly now) the vice president (VP) of nursing. DONs are usually selected because of their management abilities; they are often RNs with advanced degrees (sometimes in the specific discipline of nursing service administration). The director may have one or two assistant directors to aid in the management of the department. The title of supervisor is frequently given to the RN who supervises or directs the activities of two or more nursing units. Another RN often conducts patient education.

The nursing department can also be organized along geographical lines in a **flat organizational model**. In this model, the nursing departments responsible for patient care are decentralized to a specific location in the hospital called a nursing unit or patient-care unit. Certain responsibilities and functions required to operate a nursing unit are assigned to a nurse manager. A nurse manager supervises the personnel in a patient-care unit. This person may also be referred to by other titles, such as patient-care manager, and is responsible ensuring for the quality of nursing care in the unit (medical/surgical, OB, ICU, ED, etc.), controlling supplies, and scheduling the staff's work hours. Usually, the nurse manager is assisted by a group of staff nurses who are assigned specific responsibilities for the nursing care of patients in the patient-care unit.

THE PATIENT-CARE UNIT

As noted previously, hospital nursing departments may be organized in a decentralized fashion into patient-care units or nursing units. Patient-care units vary in size. They may be very small, with 8- to 10-bed units for specialized care, or (rarely) they may contain as many as 60 to 70 beds. Perhaps the most common size is between 20 and 40 beds per unit. Nursing units generally operate in three shifts to cover a 24-hour period. They usually operate as a day shift from 7:00 a.m. to 3:00 p.m. The evening shift, or evening tour, runs from 3:00 p.m. to 11:00 p.m., and the night shift runs from 11:00 p.m. to 7:00 a.m. Some units operate on two 12-hour shifts, 7:00 a.m. to 7:00 p.m. This model has the advantage of facilitating coordination of care with fewer changes of personnel, and is generally preferred in critical-care or emergency departments.

In the past, rooms were generally semiprivate and accommodated two patients. This has changed recently with competition among many acute-care settings. Now, acute-care settings are planning their designs around patients' preferences for private or single-bed rooms. In competitive situations, acute-care hospitals are now seeking to attract patients by providing amenities such as modern flat-screen televisions and choice of meal times. Most hospital units include rooms that are designed and reserved for patients with illnesses that warrant isolation. Units dedicated to respiratory disease may also have a negative pressure room designed to eliminate any outflow of air and are reserved for potential or actual patients with tuberculosis.

The size of the patient-care unit and the distribution of single- and multi-bed rooms are considered before a unit is built. Consideration is given to the cost of construction of the unit, the duplication of equipment, and how much nursing service time will be required to staff the unit. If the unit is spacious and rooms are distributed at a distance from the central nursing point, the staff must continually travel to reach patients and supplies. Although the unit may look pleasing, it may not work efficiently. Regardless of whether a rectangular or circular configuration is used, it is imperative that unstable patients or patients at risk of falling can be seen from the nursing station. Usually, the patient rooms are cubicles with a separate bathroom. In semiprivate rooms, curtains are situated to provide privacy when needed.

Private or semiprivate rooms vary in size depending on usage. For example, an inpatient rehabilitation unit will need extra space to accommodate wheelchairs and walkers. Likewise, the bathrooms in such units are configured according to state regulations regarding accessibility for handicapped persons.

Other Components and Technology in the Patient-Care Unit

One of the fundamental areas in a patient-care unit is the nurses' station, which tends to be the focal point of administrative activity. The nurses' station is normally where patients' charts are kept. It is centrally located for all the activities of the entire nursing unit. Generally, an area is designated for physicians to examine records and write orders. With the increase of computerized documentation, this area may have computers dedicated to physician use. A quiet area may also be provided for physicians to dictate notes on a patient's condition.

The nursing unit will also contain a medication room. The dispensing of medications has changed dramatically in recent years. In an attempt to decrease medication errors, hospitals are now commonly using unit dosing. With this method, each unit of medication is separately packaged and usually has a bar code such as those seen in grocery stores. In larger hospitals, nurses use a computerized system to administer medications. A computer is first used to scan the patient's ID bracelet, and each medication is then scanned before it is given to the patient. The computer alerts the nurse if the medication must be adjusted because the unit dose in the hospital's formulary is different from what has been ordered. This may require the nurse to halve or double the amount of medication given. The computer will also alert the nurse if the wrong medication has been scanned for that patient, or if a dose has been missed by showing the time of a dose in red on the computer screen. The computer can also request the nurse to verify a required laboratory result before administering a medication, or to verify a patient's pain information before administering a pain medication. The computer may be located permanently in the patient's room or it may be on a rolling cart. When used properly, such computers can decrease medication errors and thus improve the safety and quality of care. They also allow the nursing staff to access online references and medication information to improve patient teaching. The nurse may also document the care of a patient, patient assessments, and current orders for a patient.

In larger hospitals, medications are stored in a pyxis, a computerized machine that dispenses unit-dose medications. This storage unit is located in a secure, separate room that may or may not also contain clean supplies, instruments, and equipment. The positioning and storage of scheduled medications for each patient varies from hospital to hospital. In some hospitals, locked cabinets in each patient's room contain scheduled medications for that patient, whereas other hospitals store all scheduled and prn medications in a pyxis. Still others use rolling computer cabinets that contain locked drawers for each patient room in a hallway. This particular configuration may reflect how nursing is delivered in the hospital. If one nurse is designated the medication nurse for a team of patients, a locked rolling cabinet saves time and allows the nurse to deliver many medications to many patients. Additionally, a separate room in the nursing unit is set aside for used or dirty items. Hazardous waste is also stored in the dirty utility room.

Usually, there is a small pantry or sometimes even a kitchen in the patient-care unit for use by patients and their visitors. There is a nurses' lounge where nurses take breaks, eat meals, receive in-service training, and give change-of-shift reports. Other rooms that might be found in nursing units are a common toilet/bath area for visitors, a consultation room where physicians can meet with the patients' families, and treatment rooms. Some units may also have a pleasant place for visitors to sit down with the patients outside of their rooms.

SPECIAL-CARE UNITS

Special-care units have developed with increased technology and modern medical advances. Over the last decade, special-care units have multiplied and matured. The sophisticated modern hospital that functions under a program form of organization may have a variety of special-care facilities to manage and maintain patients with special illnesses and injuries. These facilities may include intensive-care units for medicine and surgery, special cardiac-care units, kidney dialysis centers, inpatient psychiatric units, inpatient alcohol and drug addiction units, inpatient rehabilitation units, obstetrics units, pediatric units, and skilled nursing facilities for long-term care. A special unit need not be based in the hospital; it may be constituted as a hospital home-care program or a hospice.

Intensive Care Units

The most common type of special care unit in the hospital is the general medical/surgical intensive care unit (ICU). ICUs were established to meet the clinical needs of hospitalized patients and their physicians. Critically ill patients who are in a precarious clinical state and require intense supervision are cared for in the ICU. ICUs handle both surgical and medical cases, including patients in shock, stroke victims, or persons with heart failure, serious infection, respiratory distress, or neurological disease. When the hospital's resources are marshalled in one specific area, as in a program organizational structure, it is much easier to provide efficient, high-quality care across the specialties required to care for critically ill patients. In addition to their sophisticated equipment and instrumentation, ICUs rely on a highly concentrated nursing staff. Sometimes there is one nurse to each patient. These nursing personnel generally receive specialty critical care training at the hospital, and may have experience in medical and surgical nursing care.

Some hospitals further segregate their ICUs into specialty units based on the specific type of acute care needed. Examples include the cardiac critical care unit (CCU), neurological intensive care unit (NICU), thoracic intensive care unit (TICU), and surgical intensive care unit (SICU). The CCU handles cardiac patients who are being treated medically. The NICU is for patients who require treatment of the brain or nervous system. Patients who have had surgery above the diaphragm (cardiac or pulmonary) are cared for in the TICU, whereas those who have had surgery below the diaphragm (abdominal) are kept in the SICU. Each of these specialty areas contains the particular equipment and trained personnel required to assist these patients toward recovery. Smaller hospitals may have all of these populations housed in one area, requiring the nurses to have a broader area of expertise.

A special offshoot of the ICU is the neonatal intensive care unit (also referred to as NICU, not to be confused with neurological intensive care unit), which specializes in the management of critical health problems in newborns. Caring for the critically ill newborn requires a specially trained nurse and physician. NICUs have had great success in caring for premature infants. In an effort to resist duplication of services, large metropolitan areas with several children's hospitals may choose to allocate specialty services within neonatal care to each hospital (i.e., children who require special respiratory support may go to one children's hospital in the area to receive treatment, while those who require special facial surgery may go to a different hospital that has the necessary equipment and specialized staff).

Coronary Care Units

Today, nearly all medical/surgical hospitals in the United States have some CCU capacities. The CCUs do for cardiac patients what the ICUs do for severe medical and surgical patients. The CCU has had a dramatic impact on saving lives. Patients likely to require the services of a CCU are those who have had or are having a heart attack or a cardiac arrhythmia. Often these patients will have arrived in this unit after undergoing a cardiac catheterization, and a nurse may have to safely remove a remaining catheter from the patient's femoral artery. This requires an extended period of care by the nurse to ensure that the patient does not bleed from the site. The predominant care given in this unit, however, is based on medication rather than surgery. Some of the patients may be on specialized equipment, such as a balloon pump or cardiac assist device, prior to a planned surgery. These machines are temporarily inserted near the exit of the artery of the heart to help a weak heart pump adequately until the patient can be taken to surgery.

Some very large hospitals further divide this population into acute cardiac patients and those who are not acute but require special monitoring. These monitoring units are called "step-down" units because although they involve close monitoring, they do not require the special one-to-one or one-to-two ratio of care for a patient who is critically ill.

Hospitals with ICUs or CCUs usually have a cardiologist and pulmonologist who routinely admit patients to these units. If the institution is a large teaching hospital associated with a medical school, these physicians may be employed full time as attending physicians (in charge of teaching residents and interns). Private-pay physicians in these facilities manage their patients in collaboration with a specialist.

The nurses' role in these units requires that they be well trained to monitor and interpret changes in a patient's condition. Under critical circumstances, the nurse may have to diagnose and provide immediate care to the patient. Nurses in these units are generally certified in advanced cardiac life support (ACLS) and can attempt to resuscitate a patient requiring such action. One of the primary objectives of the CCU staff is to detect early signs of impending cardiac distress so that it can be treated before cardiac arrest takes place.

Thoracic Intensive Care Unit

Patients admitted to the TICU have had either cardiac or pulmonary surgery. The protocols for their care include activities such as infusing blood that was lost during cardiac surgery into the patient. These patients have been placed on a ventilator to assist their breathing during surgery and come to the unit still being assisted by the ventilator. Certain parameters must be met before this machine is discontinued. The nurses in this unit must be familiar with these parameters and alert the physician when the patient is ready to have the ventilator removed. TICU nurses generally work as a team when a new patient is admitted, as this is a critical time and there are many activities to perform to ensure that the patient is stabilized. Various types of specialized equipment, such as chest tubes for drainage, are common in this unit and require specialized knowledge for safe handling.

Neurological Intensive Care Unit

Patients admitted to the NICU have typically had a disruption in their neurological system (e.g., due to brain or spine injury, or brain surgery). These patients require special monitoring of cardiac and vital signs, such as the internal cranial pressure (ICP). Nurses in this area must know how to interpret changes in these signs and understand the standard of care required by these acute patients. They must also be familiar with the special needs of spinal cord injury patients. Specialized equipment, including beds and mechanical lifts, may also be housed here, and the staff must know how to ensure their proper functioning.

Surgical Intensive Care Unit

Patients who have had abdominal surgery and are unstable or require close surveillance may be sent to the SICU. Nurses focus on postoperative conditions that require monitoring of returning bowel sounds and stability of vital signs. They must be familiar with the latest wound vacuum machines, which continually remove purulent material, as well as the specialized dressings that are required in this unit.

Nonacute Special Care Units

Some special care units are not intended for life-threatening situations, although all units must be prepared for such an event. An example of a nonacute special care unit is a renal dialysis center. These centers have increased in number over the last decade. They provide artificial kidney support for patients whose kidneys have stopped functioning properly. These units may also serve patients who suffer from similar underlying disease processes such as diabetes. This may require special education and support. Additionally, as with any patient with a chronic illness, people on dialysis may require special emotional and/or financial support.

Special care units also include psychiatric units and inpatient alcohol- and drug-related units, although these services are currently declining. On the rise now are specialty units dedicated to rehabilitation. It is recognized that these units may provide the measures needed by a patient prior to discharge that will allow them to return to their homes. Admission to these units is dictated by reimbursement. Post-orthopedic surgery patients, stroke victims, and people with general deconditioning may be referred to these units. The patients must be able to tolerate 3 hours of rehabilitation per day. Nurses in these units are specifically trained to assess and care for rehabilitation patients and collaborate with physical, occupational, and speech therapists. This specialized care is intended to prevent the necessity of transferring the patient to a long-term care facility.

Typical areas of a hospital may be viewed at the following website: http://www.osha.gov/SLTC/etools/hospital/index.html

TELEMONITORING AND BEDSIDE TERMINALS

Along with burgeoning technological innovations and the use of patient acuity levels, telemonitoring equipment, bedside terminals, and auto- mated clinical records are also being used by nurses. The type of tele- monitoring equipment used may vary from hospital to hospital depending on the complexity of the unit, the needs of the patients, and the resources of the hospital. This equipment can be used for routine evaluations of blood pressure, pulse, respiration, and temperature, as well as other physical and physiological conditions. In the ICU, it is important to have built-in alarm systems that will warn the staff about critical changes in a patient's condition. Cardiac monitoring equipment may include visual readouts of cardiac rhythms at the patient's bedside, heart-rate meters with audio and visual alarms, pacemakers with automatic or manual controls, and electrocardiograph recordings. At the nurses' station, there is usually a central panel that includes heart-rate meters with audio and visual alarms.

Unlike telemonitoring equipment, bedside terminals require interac- tion with the nursing staff. Nurses directly enter and retrieve patients' clinical data, such as vital signs, lab results, and medications given, using bedside computer terminals. This is an efficient and accurate way to capture data at the source or point of care. Ideally, the bedside terminals will be integrated with the hospital's information system. This facilitates communication between nurses and other allied health professionals, and results in more responsive patient care. Bedside terminals also produce an automated clinical record. This is a substitute for the traditional patient chart. The patient's clinical data become part of an integrated system and can be easily accessed by nurses, physicians, and allied health professionals.

In the 21st century, the nursing service is undergoing rapid changes centered on interprofessional collaboration and communication, increased safety awareness, activities to improve performance, standards of care, and evidence-based practice. Issues involving staff retention and efficient orientation and transition to practice for new nurses will continue to be a challenge.

CHAPTER REVIEW

1. Name three educational paths to becoming an RN.
2. List three different types of nurses.
3. What are two ways in which nursing staffs may be organized in a hospital?
4. Describe several types of special patient-care units.
5. Describe four modes of nursing delivery.
6. What are three commonly used approaches for nurse scheduling?
7. How do nurses utilize bedside terminals?
8. Describe several methods hospitals use to cope with the nursing shortage.
9. You are the CEO of a 100-bed hospital, and 219 of your 450 employees are nurses. You have an average daily census of 75 inpatients. Because of a flu epidemic, vacation leave, and a large bus wreck, you are experiencing both a spike in the census (you now have 94 patients) and a shortage of nurses (you now have 191 nurses). What do you plan to do to make sure you have a full complement of nurses today and can meet patient safety requirements?
10. Discuss the pros and cons of staffing the nursing department based on acuity of illness.

REFERENCES

Aiken, L., Clarke, S. P., Sloane, D. M., Lake, E. T., & Cheney, T. (2008). Effects of hospital care environment on patient mortality and nurse outcomes. *Journal of Nursing Administration, 38*, 223–229.

American Nurses Credentialing Center. (2005). *Magnet Recognition Program® application manual (2005 ed.).* Silver Spring, MD: American Nurses Credentialing Center.

Coddington, D. C., Fischer, E. A., Morre, K. D., et al. (2000). *Beyond managed care: How consumers and technology are changing the future of health care.* San Francisco: Jossey-Bass.

O'Keefe, M. (2001). *Nursing practice and the law: Avoiding malpractice and other legal risks.* Philadelphia: F. A. Davis.

Meraviglia, M., Grobe, S. J., Tabone, S., et al. (2008). Nurse-friendly hospital project enhancing nurse retention and quality of care. *Journal of Nursing Care Quality, 23*, 305–313.

CHAPTER 8

Older Patients in the Hospital—Geriatrics

Yvonne Lozano

KEY TERMS

Geriatrics

Memory care center

Arthritis treatment center

Hospice unit

Pain management program

Geriatric psychiatry

Geriatric care management

Skilled nursing facility

THE FIELD OF AGING

The increasing presence of older adults in hospitals is not surprising to anyone in the field of health care. This is consistent with the growing aging population in the United States and around the world. "Compared with younger adults, older Americans use a disproportionately larger share of health care services provided by physicians, nurses, pharmacists, physical therapists, and other practitioners. While people older than age 65 represent 12 percent of the U.S. population, this group consumes one-third of healthcare services and occupies one-half of all physician time" (O'Neil & Barry, 2002, p. 13). It is apparent that many people working in the field of health care will soon be required to have formal training in geriatrics.

SERVICES TO THE ELDERLY

Hospital administrators must be mindful of the fact that elderly patients will require additional services to assist them in the process of healing. Providing services that meet the specific needs of geriatric patients can reduce their length of stay in the hospital. These services can include geriatric case management, transportation, and physical or occupational therapy. The geriatric case manager plays an important role in the hospital setting. Although hospitals usually have nurse and social-work care managers on staff, these managers may not have had formal training in the field of **geriatrics**. Hospitals can benefit from hiring individuals who have been specially trained to deal with the elderly and have the knowledge base to understand and evaluate the special needs of this population.

UNDERSTANDING AGING

In the hospital setting, it is important to understand how aging is individualized and specific to each patient. For example, a 45-year-old person with severe arthritis may have a functional age of 88 years, whereas an 88-year-old person in good health may have a functional age of 55 years. On many occasions, a frail older adult may exhibit symptoms and/or additional conditions unrelated to the original admission criteria. These may include complicated symptoms of dementia, delirium, poor vision, hearing loss, mental illness, elder abuse, and placement issues.

ROLE OF THE HOSPITAL/STAFF

In a perfect world, the family of inpatient geriatric patients would be available to provide added care for the patient. This would allow the hospital staff to rely on family members as mediators between the patient and the medical staff. In reality, however, members of the nursing staff (primarily nurse's aides and medical technicians) bear the major responsibility for geriatric care, and they may not be appropriately trained in geriatric issues. The nursing staff may complain of time constraints that prevent them from giving their patients the extra attention necessary to provide quality of care. In this situation, hospitals should provide competency training in the field of geriatrics to provide added support to the staff. Some staff members may find it difficult to spend additional time with geriatric patients because of their lack of specialized training in this field.

Hospitals can benefit by providing competency training to reflect the patient population they serve. In addition, job descriptions should reflect geriatric education, including continuing education and work experience specifically with older adults.

SPECIALIZED DEPARTMENTS: A MULTIDISCIPLINARY APPROACH

Hiring staff with no formal training in the field of geriatrics can negatively impact direct patient care. In addition to hiring staff with formal training in geriatrics, some hospitals have developed geriatric departments that focus on the needs of the older patients. These departments can provide a variety of services for older adults, ranging from transportation to social events. The hospital may offer a memory care center, arthritis treatment center, hospice (including a bereavement support program), pain-management program, palliative care, geriatric psychiatry, geriatric care managers, eye institute, and wound-management services. Some of these specialized units are described as follows:

Memory care centers are designed to meet the growing need for appropriate geriatric assessment, treatment, and support for memory-impaired individuals and their families.

Arthritis treatment centers provide clinical care, education, training, support, and research for geriatric patients experiencing any form of arthritis.

Hospice units are designed specifically to provide an interdisciplinary team care approach to facilitate advance care planning, end-of-life care, clinical services, bereavement support, and palliative care.

Pain management programs are designed to provide specialized care to older patients suffering from chronic pain.

A **geriatric psychiatry** department can provide comprehensive treatment for older adults with mental illness. Mental illness is not a normal part of aging. Many older adults can experience some type of mental illness, such as depression, as a result of dementia or stroke. This department can provide geriatric assessments, family support, didactic therapy, and medicinal support.

Senior programs are designed to meet the social and educational needs of older patients. These programs may offer a variety of educational courses, exercise classes, phone support, support groups, dance classes, income tax assistance, field trips, and even annual cruise events.

Transportation services are available for individuals who have difficulty arranging transportation on their own (for nonemergency appointments).

Geriatric care management programs can provide personal care services in the patient's home that are not covered by Medicare or private insurance.

Skilled nursing facilities are designed to provide skilled nursing to patients on a short-term basis. Because they are part of the hospital complex, they enable access to a variety of hospital services.

To prepare for the upcoming demographic realities of the aging population in the United States, hospitals must take action in providing expert services that will meet the specialized needs of older patients. Hospitals must assure the communities they serve that qualified personnel have been hired to provide services to older patients, and they have established programs within their facility to provide quality care to an often-overlooked segment of the population.

CHAPTER REVIEW

1. Identify four types of departments a hospital can develop to meet the specialized needs of older adult patients.
2. What percentage of healthcare services are used by people older than age 65?
3. List four hospital services that benefit geriatric patients.
4. Give examples of conditions that may be unrelated to the original admission criteria for a geriatric patient.
5. Which members of the hospital staff usually bear the major burden of geriatric care?
6. Discuss how hospital geriatric departments can focus on the needs of the elder patient.
7. Define hospice unit.

REFERENCES

O'Neill, G., & Barry, P. P. (2002). Training physicians in geriatric care: Responding to critical need. *Public Policy and Aging Report, 13*, 1–21.

Part V
Key Ancillary Services

CHAPTER 9

The Clinical Laboratory and the Pathologist

Thomas L. Patterson

> ### KEY TERMS
>
> Anatomical pathology
> Clinical pathology
> Clinical Laboratory
>   Improvements Act (CLIA)
> Clinical laboratory accreditation
> Proficiency testing
>
> Medical laboratory scientist
>   (MLS)
> Medical laboratory
>   technician (MLT)
> Quality improvement
> Molecular diagnostics

INTRODUCTION

Clinical laboratory science has rapidly evolved since the 1600s, when physicians tasted urine for sweetness to determine whether a patient had diabetes. A great leap forward occurred in 1876 when Robert Koch, a German physician, experimented with the bacteria that cause anthrax. He had to grow these infectious microorganisms very carefully in a crude laboratory as he carried out his experiments. Koch concluded that infectious disease is caused not by dark powers, but by microscopic organisms that are passed from animal to animal, animal to person, or person to person. His work was instrumental in the development of the germ theory of disease.

With objective scientific inquiry leading mankind out of the dark age of superstition, hexes, and curses, the body of medical knowledge has exploded.

The clinical laboratory is no exception. A century ago, the attending physician would perform the very few clinical laboratory tests that were available at the time. Today, there are hundreds and hundreds of tests on the menu, and clinical laboratory science has grown into a respected profession.

STRUCTURE AND FUNCTION OF THE CLINICAL LABORATORY

The standard clinical laboratory includes two basic divisions: **anatomical pathology** and **clinical pathology**. The anatomical division is overseen by a medical doctor or osteopathic physician who has graduated from an accredited academic program and is board certified in pathology. The pathologist and his or her staff examine tissue and exfoliated cell samples collected from patients. The pathologist also performs autopsies to determine the cause and manner of death. The support staff assists with autopsies and prepares tissues and cells for microscopic examination by the pathologist.

In most cases, the clinical pathology division is also under the technical direction of the pathologist. This division is divided into functional sections or departments. For example, the hematology staff examines blood cells, the urinalysis staff analyzes urine samples, the clinical chemistry staff measures various analytes in plasma and serum, the coagulation staff examines the clotting properties of blood, the microbiology staff isolates and identifies microorganisms collected from patients, and the immunology staff analyzes the immune response of patients or uses immunological methods to measure other analytes. Technicians in the blood bank type patients' blood, select appropriate blood units, and prepare blood components for transfusion. Staff in the phlebotomy section collect blood samples from patients, although in some healthcare organizations, this responsibility is shared with the nursing staff.

CLINICAL LABORATORY CERTIFICATION

Any laboratory that tests human samples to aid in the diagnosis or treatment of disease must be certified by the Department of Health and Human Services. In 1988, Congress passed the **Clinical Laboratory Improvements Act (CLIA)** to establish minimum standards for clinical laboratories. This act was passed in response to several incidents in which Papanicolaou (Pap) smears were misread or mixed up, resulting in the misdiagnosis of many patients.

CLIA established minimum educational and experience requirements for all clinical laboratory personnel. CLIA also clearly defined testing categories according to their level of complexity. Tests that are very simple to perform and require little to no specimen preparation are classified as waived tests. An example would be a simple blood glucose test that diabetics use to monitor their blood sugar. Waived tests can be performed by persons who have not had formal training in laboratory science. Moderately complex tests require some specimen preparation and some expertise in laboratory science. Persons with at least a 2-year degree in laboratory science are authorized to perform this level of testing. Highly complex tests that require more elaborate specimen preparation and interpretation of results must be performed by a laboratory professional with at least a bachelor's degree. Healthcare providers who use microscopic analysis in their office or clinic to aid in diagnosis must be certified for provider-performed microscopy. Laboratories can obtain an initial temporary registration certificate that is good for 2 years. During this time, the laboratory must complete a formal application and must be inspected to ensure compliance with CLIA. After a successful inspection report is achieved, the laboratory is granted a certificate of compliance. The certificate must be renewed every 2 years.

Blood collection organizations and blood banks are regulated by the Food and Drug Administration. These facilities are inspected to ensure that their blood and blood products are safe, pure, free of infectious disease, and effective in treating the diseases or conditions for which they are intended.

CLINICAL LABORATORY ACCREDITATION

Accreditation shows that a clinical laboratory has met the stringent standards of the accrediting agency. Clinical laboratories can be accredited by various nongovernmental accrediting organizations. Accrediting agencies differ from governmental agencies in that they do not have enforcement powers and can only withdraw accreditation if a laboratory fails to comply with the accreditation standards. Many clinical laboratories are accredited by the College of American Pathologists (CAP). After an application for accreditation is submitted, a team of representatives from the accrediting agency inspects the laboratory. The lead inspector or auditor submits a report that identifies any discrepancies found during the inspection. Discrepancies must be corrected and proof of correction must be submitted to the agency. The clinical laboratory receives accreditation if the corrections are acceptable to the agency. The Joint Commission, formerly known as the Joint Commission for Accreditation of Healthcare Organizations (JCAHO), can accredit clinical laboratories as well as other activities and operations of a medical treatment facility. Hospital blood banks can also be accredited by the AABB, formally known as the American Association of Blood Banks.

PROFICIENCY TESTING

CLIA requires clinical laboratories that perform moderately complex or highly complex testing to be enrolled in an approved external proficiency-testing program. Samples are sent to each participating laboratory on a regular basis. A sample is sent for each type of test the laboratory performs. The laboratory tests the proficiency samples and submits the results to the program for evaluation. The proficiency samples must be analyzed in exactly the same way patient samples are analyzed. The results from all participating laboratories are reviewed and laboratories that fail to report the correct results are notified. The laboratory must submit a corrective action response to the proficiency program. Multiple failures in testing the same analyte may result in the laboratory temporarily losing the authorization to perform the test in question. **Proficiency testing** ensures that clinical laboratories are producing accurate and timely results.

PERSONNEL

There are several different personnel positions in the clinical laboratory. The medical director or laboratory director must be a physician (i.e., a graduate from an accredited medical school or osteopathic college of medicine) or have a doctorate in a physical or biological science. Physicians must be board certified in pathology if they are to perform tissue and cell examinations or autopsies. The director must have a PhD and be certified by the American Board of Microbiology, American Board of Clinical Chemistry, or American Board of Bioanalysis. The director is responsible for the overall operation and administration of the anatomical and clinical divisions of the clinical laboratory.

The technical consultant is responsible for overseeing tests in the clinical division or department. The technical consultant can be a qualified physician or a PhD scientist, but is usually a clinical laboratory scientist (CLS) with a master of science or bachelor of science degree in clinical laboratory science. The technical consultant may have a slightly different official title on the laboratory's organizational chart, such as lead technician, department supervisor, or laboratory manager.

The term "medical technologist" (MT) is an older one that gradually became replaced by the CLS title. Today, however, the title that is most often used for this position is **medical laboratory scientist (MLS)**. The MT or MLS must have a bachelor's degree in clinical laboratory science and must have passed a national certification examination. The two main organizations that grant certification are the American Society for Clinical Pathology (ASCP) and the National Certification Agency. These two organizations recently signed a letter of intent to combine their separate certification examinations into one national examination. The MLS can perform any test in the laboratory, regardless of the complexity. In some states, the MLS must be licensed by the state to work in the laboratory. The MLS who wishes to specialize in one area of the laboratory can do so after receiving additional training and successfully passing a special certification examination.

American Medical Technologists (AMT) is another certification agency. The educational requirements of this agency are not as stringent as those of the ASCP. A bachelor's degree is required, but some laboratory experience may be substituted for part of the educational requirement. Many clinical laboratories will hire an MT who has received either ASCP or AMT certification.

Most clinical laboratories also employ a **medical laboratory technician (MLT)**. This position requires a 2-year associate degree in an accredited program and certification by passing a national certification examination. The MLT generally does not perform tests of high complexity. According to CLIA, enlisted personnel who have successfully completed military clinical laboratory training are equivalent to an MLT with an associate degree.

The phlebotomist is trained to draw blood specimens from patients for laboratory analysis. Phlebotomy training can be obtained at a technical school or on the job. Several different organizations offer certification tests for phlebotomists.

The laboratory assistant supports the activities of the clinical laboratory by washing glassware, cleaning the area, inventorying supplies, and filing reports. The laboratory assistant is usually trained on the job and no certification or specific education is required.

In the anatomical division of the laboratory, the histologic technician cuts, stains, and mounts tissues on slides for review by the pathologist. The technician must have graduated from an approved program and must have passed a certification test. The cytologic technologist examines exfoliated cells for disease and forwards questionable samples to the pathologist for review. Like the histological technician, the cytologic technologist must have graduated from an approved program and must have passed a certification examination. A fairly new position in the anatomical division is the pathology assistant, who assists the pathologist on autopsy cases and other anatomic pathology procedures. This also requires successful completion of a special academic program and a certification process.

QUALITY IMPROVEMENT

Clinical laboratories are required to have a **quality improvement** system in place that promotes the highest standards of quality regarding patient test results, employee qualifications, management, training, and services provided to the patient and physician. Laboratory tests must be timely and accurate, as clinical laboratory results play a critical role in the diagnosis of many disease states.

A formal quality improvement program must be clearly defined and in place. It must include a description of how the laboratory is organized, what equipment and manpower resources are necessary, how the equipment is maintained and monitored, how suppliers and vendors are qualified, how processes are controlled, how documents and records are maintained, how deviations and nonconformance issues are resolved, and how performance is assessed.

In addition, the quality improvement program must ensure continuous process improvement. Outcomes must be continuously monitored and evaluated so that opportunities for improvement can be identified. A plan of action must be implemented, and improvements must be documented.

A key facet of the quality improvement program is quality control. By adhering to a stringent quality-control program, laboratory staff can verify that a laboratory test is as accurate as possible. A sample or samples of known values (controls) are tested along with patient samples. Errors in the analytical process are detected when the control values do not fall within a narrow acceptable range. Control values falling outside the acceptable range indicate that there is an analytical error with the test system, and there may be a problem with the accuracy of the patient test results. Patient test results cannot be released until they are verified by acceptable quality-control results. Records of all quality-control activities must be available for inspection by auditors from accrediting or certifying agencies.

THE FUTURE OF THE CLINICAL LABORATORY

Like other fields of medicine, the clinical laboratory is evolving rapidly. Many new tests are being developed in the areas of molecular diagnostics and bio-markers. In the **molecular diagnostics** approach, a patient sample is searched for specific RNA/DNA base sequences or other regulatory molecules associated with cell functions. Analysis at the molecular level can detect disease and even the potential to develop a specific disease in the future.

Molecular diagnostics can detect the activation of some oncogenes (i.e., genes that can cause cells to divide in an uncontrolled manner). It can also detect the loss of function of various tumor-suppressor genes and DNA repair genes. Test systems are currently available to detect BRCA1 and BRCA2, two genes that are associated with increased potential for development of breast cancer in women.

The polymerase chain reaction (PCR) test is becoming commonplace in clinical reference laboratories. This is a molecular diagnostics test that searches for a specific DNA or RNA base sequence to detect the presence of a species bacteria or virus in a patient sample. This type of test can greatly reduce the time it takes to get results, which can significantly improve patient care. The standard method in clinical microbiology is to culture bacteria for a period of days to sometimes weeks in an incubator, and then spend another day or two identifying the organism so that the correct antibiotic treatment can be initiated. As the efficiency of PCR testing is increased and the cost is gradually reduced through research and development, PCR tests will also become commonplace in the hospital laboratory.

Biomarkers are molecules that can be detected in a person's blood to confirm a diagnosis or, in many cases, predict the risk of disease in the near future. One exciting area of research is inflammatory biomarkers. A good example of a recently discovered inflammatory biomarker is lipoprotein-associated phospholipase A_2. This molecule is produced by specific white blood cells that are associated with atherosclerotic plaque in the wall of an artery that feeds the heart muscle. Rupture of the plaque cap is a serious and sometimes life-threatening event. Increased levels of this biomarker are suggestive that the lining over the top of the atherosclerotic plaque has the immediate potential to rupture. Various treatments are available to help prevent this when it is detected. It is clear that the clinical laboratory will begin to play a more significant role in preventing disease as these new areas of testing are further developed and implemented.

THE PROFESSIONAL LABORATORIAN

It is apparent that the professional laboratorian must be a highly educated and skilled individual. Today's laboratorian must have a thorough knowledge of quality improvement, medical ethics, biology, microbiology, parasitology, chemistry, biochemistry, anatomy, physiology, pathology, and now molecular biology. It must be noted that the current 4-year curriculum for clinical laboratory science is completely full. As this field continues to grow, the amount of education required to be a functional CLS may have to be extended beyond the 4-year bachelor's degree program to a master of science degree. In any case, the clinical laboratory will continue to provide physicians and healthcare professionals with reliable and accurate results so that patients can be diagnosed, treated, and monitored to achieve the best outcome possible.

CHAPTER REVIEW

1. Compare the functions of the two main divisions of the clinical laboratory.
2. Discuss the educational requirements of the various personnel in a clinical laboratory.
3. Explain why accreditation of the clinical laboratory is important.
4. Discuss why the Clinical Laboratory Improvement Act of 1988 was implemented by Congress.
5. Explain external proficiency testing and why it is a requirement for clinical laboratories.
6. Describe the purpose of quality improvement in the clinical laboratory.
7. Define molecular diagnostics.

CHAPTER 10

Diagnostic Imaging and Therapeutic Radiology Departments

Megan Trad

INTRODUCTION

Diagnostic imaging and therapeutic radiology departments offer a wide array of services to patients, ranging from an initial diagnosis of injury or disease to treatment for diseases such as cancer. The umbrella of radiologic services covers all specialties that use ionizing (and in some cases nonionizing) radiation to view and treat internal anatomy, and each will be discussed in detail throughout this chapter. Ionizing radiation has been in use since 1895, when William Roentgen first discovered the x-ray. Today, the uses of radiation are ever increasing and technological advances are allowing for more accurate and prompt treatment of patients, holding out the hope for a cure for many suffering from a variety of cancers and debilitating diseases.

MISSION OF THE DEPARTMENT

Each department within a hospital will have a mission statement that defines the services it hopes to render to its patients. In the diagnostic imaging and therapeutic radiology departments, the goal is to provide patients with high-quality, cost-effective imaging and therapeutic services to aid in the diagnosis and treatment of disease. It is important to educate patients about the procedure they are about to undergo, including its risks and benefits, before they receive ionizing radiation of any type.

Patient education is vitally important because of the potential risks associated with exposure to ionizing radiation, such as genetic damage and the development of cancer. Because of the potential risks associated with ionizing radiation, employees in this field must undergo extensive training in radiation safety and protection, for their own safety as well as that of the patients. Radiation personnel are guided by the **principle of ALARA** (as low as reasonably achievable), which in this case means that measures should be taken to deliver the lowest level of exposure to the patient while still gaining the intended result.

DIAGNOSTIC IMAGING DEPARTMENT

A visit to the diagnostic imaging department is often one of the first experiences a patient will have in the hospital setting because diagnostic imaging can give the treating physician great insight into what is truly wrong with the patient. The art of **diagnostic imaging** is used to reveal, diagnose, and examine what is ailing the patient and determine the proper treatment. Diagnostic imaging currently encompasses a large variety of modalities, each of which requires a unique set of skills from the people performing the procedure and the physicians interpreting the images.

What Are Diagnostic X-Rays?

Radiography, or the use of diagnostic x-rays, is the most commonly thought of procedure in the imaging department, as it was the first imaging modality available in modern medicine and is now widely used throughout the world. With radiography or traditional x-ray, the output will be a two-dimensional black and white image, or radiograph, of the body part under investigation, and patients should receive a relatively low dose of radiation. Patients often come into a hospital not knowing exactly what is wrong with them, but they have a general idea about where they are having pain. X-rays may be used to detect bone fractures, find foreign objects in the body, or just examine the internal anatomy. The most common type of x-ray exam is chest radiography.

Fluoroscopy is also used in the diagnostic imaging department. This technique is similar to radiography, but instead of taking a snapshot of the anatomy, it uses a continuous flow of x-rays to visualize the anatomy in real time. The results can be used to visualize functioning organs to look for abnormalities or to assist in a variety of medical procedures, such as image-guided biopsies or the placement of pacemakers in the heart.

Radiologists

The radiologist specializes in interpreting images of the body produced by modalities such as x-rays, computed tomography (CT) scans, and ultrasound. These images can be used to diagnose diseases and help other healthcare professionals decide which course of treatment to follow. The radiologist is a medical doctor who has completed medical school and a 4-year residency in diagnostic radiology. He or she is in charge of interpreting the results of the diagnostic imaging exam, and thus is ultimately responsible for the accurate diagnosis of an injury or disease.

Radiologic Technologists

The personnel who are in charge of performing diagnostic imaging examinations are called **radiologic technologists**. They are specially trained so that they can accurately obtain the medical image requested by the attending physician or the radiologist. The radiologic technologist must position the patient in such a way as to obtain a high-quality image while exposing the patient to the least amount of radiation possible, and must also provide empathetic and compassionate care to the patient.

The educational requirements for radiologic technologists include anatomy and physiology, patient care, patient communication, radiation safety and protection, and medical law, just to name a few. After completing their education, students must pass a credentialing examination administered by the American Registry of Radiologic Technologists in order to be certified and licensed to perform radiography procedures. A licensed and credentialed radiographer will display the initials RT (R) after his or her name, indicating that he or she is a registered radiologic technologist in radiography. Many radiologic technologists go on to seek certification in other specialized areas of diagnostic and therapeutic radiology, such as CT, magnetic resonance imaging (MRI), nuclear medicine (NM), mammography (M), or radiation therapy (T).

SPECIALTIES WITHIN THE DIAGNOSTIC IMAGING DEPARTMENT

Innovations in x-ray techniques have played a huge role in the advancement of medicine and the ability to diagnose disease early and accurately. The clearer and more precise an image is, the easier it is for the physician to find the problem and prescribe treatment before irreversible damage is done. With each new imaging modality, there must also be trained radiologists to interpret the images, as well as technologists to perform the exam or produce the image. Radiologists who choose to specialize in a specific modality must spend extra time in training and learning to read the specific type of images produced by that modality. Technologists are required to go to school and pass a credentialing examination for each specialty they wish to perform.

Computed Tomography (CT)

CT scans provide a three-dimensional view inside the body. In contrast to traditional x-ray machines, CT scanners produce multiple x-rays from a variety of angles at the same point in the body. A computer then processes these x-rays to produce a detailed image that allows physicians to see the patient's anatomy from many different directions, and to identify a disease or injury that might go undetected by traditional x-ray imaging.

CT scans quickly generate many images for the physician to review. To increase the clarity of the images, the patient must lie very still during the procedure, and radiation protection protocols should be strictly followed because CT scans use ionizing radiation to produce the images. Contrast agents are sometimes necessary to enhance the anatomy on the scan. CT scans are commonly performed on the abdomen, chest, and pelvis.

Magnetic Resonance Imaging (MRI)

MRI is a fairly new imaging technique that was first used in the late 1970s. Unlike other diagnostic imaging modalities, MRI scans do not use ionizing radiation to produce images; instead, images are produced by means of a powerful magnet that interacts with different molecules in the body. Like CT scans, MRI produces a variety of images that allow physicians to see the body in three-dimensional views. However, MRI provides a far superior contrast between soft tissues in the body, which makes it an ideal tool for brain, musculoskeletal, and oncologic scans.

Nuclear Medicine

In the field of **nuclear medicine**, also known as scintigraphy, radioactive materials are used to diagnose and treat disease. In nuclear medicine procedures, radioactive isotopes are combined with chemical compounds or pharmaceuticals to form radiopharmaceuticals. These radiopharmaceuticals are administered internally (orally or intravenously injected) and differ according to which organ or body part is under investigation. Differences in the way the patient's body reacts to the substance, as opposed to a body with no disease or injury, can reveal underlying physiologic and metabolic processes.

OTHER SPECIALTIES OF DIAGNOSTIC IMAGING

There are many other specialties within the diagnostic imaging department, and to discuss them all would be beyond the scope of this chapter. However, three commonly used modalities that should be mentioned are mammography, ultrasound, and interventional radiology. Mammography is a diagnostic screening procedure that is used to examine the breast, and has had great results in decreasing the mortality rates of breast cancer patients. Ultrasound is another nonionizing form of radiation that is used routinely in obstetrics. Interventional radiology provides guidance during minimally invasive procedures so that physicians can see what they are doing inside the patient's body.

Therapeutic Radiology

Therapeutic radiology, also known as radiation oncology or radiation therapy, is used to treat or cure cancer with high-energy radiation. Radiation therapy is one of the three main treatment modalities for cancer patients alongside surgery and chemotherapy. Patients may be treated with radiation therapy alone or with any combination of these treatment modalities.

Radiation therapy delivers high doses of radiation to the specific body part that is inflicted with cancer. The radiation will then interact with the cells of the body and prevent the cancer cells from multiplying by causing damage to the DNA. The main goal of radiation therapy is to deliver a high enough dose of radiation to control the tumor while sparing as much of the surrounding normal tissue as possible from the radiation. Radiation therapy is most commonly administered externally through the use of a linear accelerator machine that delivers the dose. The radiation may also be administered internally through a procedure called brachytherapy.

Radiation therapy is given throughout a course of treatment that usually lasts several weeks. Because such a high dose of radiation is being delivered, the entire dose prescribed must be broken down into smaller doses delivered over a length of time. Patients will come in on a daily basis and receive a small amount of radiation, and continue to come in until they have completed their entire treatment regime as prescribed by the radiation oncologist. Breaking a high dose of radiation into smaller daily doses gives the normal tissue time to recover or repair itself. Cancerous cells, on the other hand, find it harder to overcome the radiation damage and will die or cease to continue growing.

Radiation Oncologists

The **radiation oncologist** is the physician in charge of prescribing a regimen of radiation to the cancer patient. The radiation oncologist first consults with the patient and other physicians regarding the extent of the disease and the goals for the treatment. After reviewing any previous diagnostic studies and ordering further diagnostic procedures if necessary, he or she will then determine how much radiation should be delivered and how the prescription will be carried out. These physicians oversee the patients throughout their entire course of treatment, checking on the patients' progress and taking measures to alleviate side effects that may be accruing due to the treatment. Radiation oncologists also continue to see their patients after the regimen is completed to look for possible recurrence of disease or late side effects from the radiation treatment.

Radiation Therapists

Radiation therapists are the individuals who carry out the course of treatment as prescribed by the radiation oncologist. The radiation therapist works closely with the radiation oncologist, as well as many other members of the cancer care team, to ensure that the patient is properly educated about the procedure and there will be a continuum of care throughout the patients' treatment schedule. The radiation therapist's job is to follow the prescription laid out by the oncologist as to how much radiation should be delivered, and to offer advice on how to most effectively treat the patient. The radiation therapist sees the patient every day during the prescribed treatment regimen to ensure that the radiation is being accurately delivered, as well as to provide emotional support to the patient.

SUMMARY

The diagnostic imaging and therapeutic radiology departments are vital components of the healthcare system and treatment of patients. Diagnostic imaging is often one of the first steps in identifying what is ailing a patient who has entered the hospital. A variety of imaging options are available to physicians depending on which body part is being investigated and the degree of sensitivity that is needed to ensure an accurate diagnosis. Basic x-rays are often taken to look for a broken bone or the cause of certain symptoms, such as difficulty breathing. If a patient comes in with a head injury and internal bleeding is suspected, the physician may order a CT scan to aid in a rapid diagnosis and prevent further injury.

Radiation oncology comes into play when a patient is diagnosed with cancer and cannot be treated with surgery alone. Radiation oncology offers a localized treatment option that has shown results in curing patients of cancer, or alleviating symptoms caused by the progression of the disease, by using high-energy ionizing radiation to destroy cancerous cells.

Many other individuals contribute to the fields of diagnostic imaging and therapeutic radiology, including nurses, patient-care coordinators, and healthcare administrators. The use of radioactive material is overseen by the Nuclear Regulatory Committee (NRC). Radiation protection guidelines and recommendations are provided by the National Council on Radiation Protection and Measurement (NCRP) and the International Commission on Radiological Protection (ICRP).

The use of ionizing and nonionizing radiation is an important part of the diagnosis and treatment of patients throughout the world, but there are always risks associated with this approach. It is important for hospitals to constantly monitor and evaluate the diagnostic and therapeutic equipment being used, and to ensure that qualified and competent personnel are administering the treatments or examinations, and skilled radiologists or radiation oncologists are reading the results and overseeing all procedures.

CHAPTER REVIEW

1. What are some risks associated with exposure to ionizing radiation?
2. Discuss the art of diagnostic imaging.
3. What is the most common procedure in the imaging department and what are some of its uses?
4. What is fluoroscopy and what is its use?
5. Discuss the role of a radiologist.
6. What is CT used for?
7. What is the advantage of MRI over CT?
8. Define nuclear medicine.
9. Name three specialties of the imaging department other than those mentioned in this review.
10. Therapeutic radiology is also known as _____ or _____.
11. What does a radiation therapist do?

CHAPTER 11

Physical Therapy

Jason Hardage

KEY TERMS

Physiotherapy
Physical therapist (PT)
Ambulation
Bed mobility
Transfer

Physical therapist assistant
  (PTA)
Physiological reserves
Functional independence
Comorbidity

INTRODUCTION

Physical therapy (also known as **physiotherapy**) is "a dynamic profession with an established theoretical and scientific base and widespread clinical applications in the restoration, maintenance, and promotion of optimal physical function" (American Physical Therapy Association, 2003, p. 13). According to the *Guide to Physical Therapist Practice* (American Physical Therapy Association, 2003), physical therapists (PTs) perform the following functions:

Diagnose and manage movement dysfunction and enhance physical and functional abilities.

Restore, maintain, and promote not only optimal physical function but optimal well-being and fitness and optimal quality of life as it relates to movement and health.

Prevent the onset, symptoms, and progression of impairments, functional limitations, and disabilities that may result from diseases, disorders, conditions, or injuries.

In essence, **PTs** are experts in restoring and improving mobility in people's lives (American Physical Therapy Association, 2010a). They play a key role in caring for many patients in the hospital setting whose mobility has been affected by an incident such as joint replacement surgery, stroke, or amputation. The PT must perform a skilled assessment of the patient's functional status (i.e., how much assistance the patient needs to perform basic tasks such as **ambulation** and **bed mobility**). The patient may have other medical precautions to consider (see the glossary in Table 11-1). For instance, a patient who has undergone orthopedic surgery may be under medical orders to reduce the amount of weight he or she places on the surgical limb (partial weightbearing) or to place no weight at all on the surgical limb (nonweightbearing). A patient who has undergone heart surgery requiring a sternotomy (i.e., an operation involving separation of the sternum or breastbone) may be told to limit upper-body activity while the sternum heals. Many patients in the hospital setting have had lines (e.g., intravenous lines) or tubes (e.g., urinary catheters) inserted that must be properly managed when the patient moves. In addition, patients who require hospitalization often have multiple comorbidities that must be considered in their care and recovery. Many of these patients have chronic

Table 11-1. Glossary

Ambulation: The act of moving from one location to another. Examples include walking and propelling a wheelchair.
Bed mobility: The act of repositioning oneself in bed. Examples include rolling, moving toward the head of the bed, and moving from a supine position to a side-lying or sitting position.
Comorbidity: A medical diagnosis (i.e., disease, disorder, or condition) that a patient has in addition to the primary medical diagnosis.
Functional independence: The ability to care for oneself without routine assistance from others.
Physiologic reserves: Levels of health and fitness based on components such as muscle strength, muscle endurance, and cardiovascular/pulmonary fitness, above those that are needed for routine day-to-day function. Reserves give the individual a measure of protection against losses due to illness or injury.
Transfer: The act of moving from one support surface to another support surface. Examples include bed-to-bedside-commode transfers, bed-to-wheelchair transfers, wheelchair-to-toilet transfers, and sit-to-stand transfers.

conditions (e.g., diabetes) for which there is no cure, making long-term management the goal. PTs who work in acute-care settings are experts in providing services to such medically complex patients.

HISTORICAL PERSPECTIVE

Many interesting changes in hospital care have occurred over time; however, two are particularly salient for PTs. In the past, patients were often subjected to long hospital stays and lengthy periods of bedrest (i.e., restricted activity), and were discharged home only when they were essentially fully recovered. Hospital stays are typically much shorter now, as patients are moved to other settings within the continuum of care (e.g., inpatient rehabilitation centers, skilled nursing facilities, home health agencies, or outpatient facilities). Also, there is now a large body of evidence supporting the health benefits of early mobilization, as opposed to bedrest, for patients with a wide variety of conditions. PTs apply this body of knowledge in clinical care and contribute to it by conducting research.

SERVICES PROVIDED BY THE PHYSICAL THERAPY DEPARTMENT

The main service that is provided by the physical therapy department is patient care. PTs often work in concert with other rehabilitation professionals, including occupational therapists and speech therapists. Because of the complex nature of health care, particularly in the hospital environment, PTs must communicate and coordinate not only with other rehabilitation providers but also with physicians, nurses, and other members of the healthcare team (e.g., respiratory therapists, medical social workers, and case managers). Such communication and coordination ensures that each member of the healthcare team has a complete picture of the patient's status, which in turn ensures that the patient will receive optimal care.

In addition to patient care, PTs often provide staff training in such things as proper body mechanics for back safety during heavy-lifting tasks, and proper techniques for performing patient **transfers**. PTs may also participate in teams to manage clinical outcomes for particular types of patient problems or diagnoses (e.g., a fall or stroke), or participate in clinical outcomes research. Finally, PTs may fill roles other than patient care, such as administration, research, community education, and consultation.

PERSONNEL

The physical therapy department is staffed by PTs and support personnel, including **PT assistants (PTAs)** and aides. PTs are licensed professionals who provide physical therapy services and supervise the support personnel. PTAs are licensed providers who "provide selected physical therapy interventions under the direction and supervision of the physical therapist" (American Physical Therapy Association, 2003, p. 14). Aides are unlicensed support staff members who perform "designated and supervised routine tasks related to physical therapy services" (Federation of State Boards of Physical Therapy, 2006, p. 4) such as preparing patients and patient-treatment areas. Typically, the director of the physical therapy department is a PT. Sometimes a hospital will have a combined rehabilitation services department, in which case the director may be a PT, an occupational therapist, or a speech therapist.

Requirements for Education and Licensure

PTs are highly educated professionals. Most entry-level PT education programs offer a clinical doctorate degree (i.e., doctor of physical therapy [DPT]), which generally takes 3 years to complete. This level of education parallels that of other healthcare professions, including clinical psychology, optometry, pharmacy, and medicine. Other healthcare professions, including occupational therapy, audiology, and nursing, offer a clinical doctorate as well.

The admissions requirements for entry-level PT education programs typically include a bachelor's degree and completion of specified prerequisite coursework in the sciences and social sciences. The curriculum includes supervised clinical experience in a variety of clinical settings. After graduation, the student must pass the National Physical Therapy Examination for Physical Therapists (Federation of State Boards of Physical Therapy, 2010a) to become a licensed PT. Only then can he or she practice as a PT.

PTAs must complete a 2-year associate's degree program that includes supervised clinical experience. Upon graduation, they are eligible to sit for the National Physical Therapy Examination for Physical Therapist Assistants (Federation of State Boards of Physical Therapy, 2010a) to become a licensed PTA. In most states, PTAs are licensed, certified, or registered (American Physical Therapy Association, 2010b). The Commission on Accreditation in Physical Therapy Education is the accrediting body that works to ensure quality education for PTs and PTAs.

After they receive their initial license, licensees must renew their license periodically, typically every 2 years. Most jurisdictions have a mechanism in place to ensure continuing competence; therefore, to renew their licenses, licensees must fulfill the specific requirements of the jurisdiction or jurisdictions in which they practice (Federation of State Boards of Physical Therapy, 2010b). Commonly, the licensee is required to complete a certain number of hours of continuing education from an approved provider.

Compliance and Accreditation Issues

Licensed personnel (i.e., PTs and PTAs) must practice in accordance with the respective practice acts of the state or states in which they practice. The physical therapy department supports the hospital in achieving and maintaining accreditation by The Joint Commission (The Joint Commission, 2010).

HOW THE PATIENT IS AFFECTED

The patient participates in physical therapy services to improve his or her mobility, function, and health. In addition to overcoming the debilitating effects of a specific condition or procedure, such as surgery, patients benefit from early mobilization to minimize secondary complications caused by inactivity. These complications can include general deconditioning, pneumonia, and joint contractures. The effects of general deconditioning, in which the patient loses muscle strength and endurance and cardiovascular/pulmonary fitness, can be significant, especially for older adults or adults with disabilities who may have been only marginally functionally independent before they were hospitalized. Such individuals have few **physiologic reserves** upon which to draw when they must be hospitalized for a major illness or injury. Thus, continued physical activity, including therapeutic exercise, can be a critical determinant of the patient's physical function and **functional independence** as he or she recovers.

Depending on patients' medical diagnoses, they may require services in the fields of orthopedics, neurology, general medical care, or wound care. Amputees comprise another common patient population. Although diabetes is not usually the primary reason for a physical therapy consultation, PTs often work with people who have diabetes as **comorbidity**. Specialty services include oncology, vestibular rehabilitation, transplant medicine, and the neonatal intensive care unit. PTs may also work in children's hospitals that specialize in any of these areas.

Patients are generally seen once or twice a day for sessions lasting from approximately 15 to 60 minutes as dictated by the patient's needs, medical status, and activity tolerance. Table 11-2 lists the locations of delivery of physical therapy services in the hospital setting. These services are typically provided at bedside (i.e., in the patient's room) or in a central physical therapy or rehabilitation services gym. Bedside treatment sessions are employed for patients who are unable to leave their rooms for medical reasons, or for those who would be exhausted by the process of being transported to the gym. For these patients, the PT will simply bring any portable equipment that might be needed, such as a walker (used to help patients walk with support) or portable standing frame (used to help patients assume a standing position). Gym treatment sessions can provide access to equipment that is not portable, such as high-low (i.e., adjustable height) mat tables (used for practicing basic mobility tasks and exercise), parallel bars (used for practicing standing, walking, and balancing activities), and steps with rails (used for practicing the ability to ascend and descend steps).

Scheduling for therapy sessions can be challenging not only because the patient may need to receive care from multiple members of the healthcare team, but also because of the inherent unpredictability of the patient's personal needs and health status. At times, patients may be out of their room because they are undergoing a test or procedure or participating in other services, such as occupational therapy or speech therapy, or they may be unavailable due to toileting, bathing, or bedside tests or procedures.

The physical therapy episode of care begins with an initial examination and evaluation by the PT, followed by interventions that may be provided by the PT or by the PTA under the PT's supervision. Common types of

Table 11-2. Locations of Delivery of Physical Therapy Services in the Hospital Setting

1. Patient's room/bedside (including medical and surgical intensive care units).
2. Physical therapy gym (may be combined with other rehabilitation services, such as occupational therapy).
3. Short stay/ambulatory care centers (e.g., for crutch training).
4. Satellite rehabilitation gyms (e.g., for patients in specialized units).

This table is meant to be representative, not exhaustive.

interventions include bed mobility training, transfer training, gait training, other types of functional activities (e.g., balance training), therapeutic exercise, patient/family education, procurement and fitting of appropriate adaptive equipment, wound care, and the application of various physical agents such as thermal modalities and electrical stimulation. Services are typically initiated by the physician when the patient is medically stable and are continued until the patient is discharged from the hospital to his or her home or another care setting.

The patient also benefits from any professional recommendations the PT might make. For example, the PT can identify patients with a high risk of falling and recommend measures to reduce falls; recommend specific types of durable medical equipment, including assistive devices (e.g., walkers, canes, and wheelchairs); and make recommendations related to the patient's discharge disposition (i.e., the appropriate setting to which the patient will be discharged). The discharge disposition ranges from the home setting to other settings in the continuum of care. For example, a patient who is recovering from a stroke may benefit from receiving additional care from a home health agency or in an inpatient rehabilitation setting, skilled nursing facility, or outpatient rehabilitation clinic—or he or she may not need any additional care at all. The discharge disposition is a multifaceted consideration that requires input from the entire healthcare team. Frequently, a medical social worker will assist in finding the optimal facility for the patient, considering his or her financial resources, preferences, and other relevant factors.

For all patients, the PT must carefully document his or her findings, the treatments provided, and the patient's response to those treatments in the patient's medical record. This activity is important for multiple reasons, including communication and coordination with other members of the healthcare team and fulfillment of legal and regulatory standards.

SPECIAL CONSIDERATIONS

There are a number of special considerations that inform a PT's practice in the hospital setting. For example, hospitals vary greatly in terms of size (e.g., the small rural hospital versus the large urban medical center), mission (e.g., the for-profit hospital, the not-for-profit hospital, and the academic medical center), and clinical focus (e.g., the Level I trauma center versus the Level III trauma center, and the full-service medical center versus the specialty hospital), and the work of the PT varies accordingly. Some PTs who work in a hospital setting consider themselves to be generalists, whereas others consider themselves to be specialists in a defined area of clinical practice. Currently, there are eight areas of clinical practice in which PTs may become board certified through the American Board of Physical Therapy Specialties of the American Physical Therapy Association: cardio-vascular/pulmonary, clinical electrophysiologic, geriatric, neurologic, orthopedic, pediatric, sports, and women's health.

In addition to board certification, PTs may have other advanced credentials, including postprofessional degrees such as a PhD (in physical therapy or a related area of study) or a Doctor of Science in Physical Therapy (DScPT), residency or fellowship training in a defined area of clinical practice, or multidisciplinary certifications. For example, a PT may apply to sit for the examination to become a certified wound specialist (CWS) through the American Academy of Wound Management, or a certified hand therapist (CHT) through the Hand Therapy Certification Commission.

For all patients, the PT's role includes an assessment of the patient's functional status and skilled monitoring of the patient's medical status (e.g., vital signs) before, during, and after treatment. In the hospital setting, PTs are highly involved in the clinical decision-making process. They must use their skills to decide how best to apply common treatments such as bed mobility, transfer, ambulation, and therapeutic exercises in patients with various medical conditions and comorbidities. In the case of high-acuity patients, these skills come into play regardless of the specific setting in which the patient is being seen. The term "acute care" is not actually synonymous with

Table 11-3. Major Documents That Guide Physical Therapist Practice

1. State practice acts.
2. American Physical Therapy Association. (2003). *Guide to physical therapist practice* (2nd ed., Rev.). Alexandria, VA: American Physical Therapy Association.
3. American Physical Therapy Association. (2010). *Code of ethics for the physical therapist.* (http://www.apta.org/AM/Template.cfm?Section=Ethics_and_Legal_Issues1&Template=/CM/ContentDisplay.cfm&ContentID=63686)
4. American Physical Therapy Association. (2010). Vision 2020. (http://www.apta.org/AM/Template.cfm?Section=Vision_20201&Template=/TaggedPage/TaggedPageDisplay.cfm&TPLID=285&ContentID=32061)

Table 11-4. Resources for Additional Information

• American Physical Therapy Association (www.apta.org)
• Designations in physical therapy (http://www.apta.org/AM/Template.cfm?Section=Certification2&CONTENTID=64594&TEMPLATE=/CM/ContentDisplay.cfm)
• Understanding physical therapy degrees, designators, and other credentials (http://www.apta.org/AM/Template.cfm?Section=Certification2&TEMPLATE=/CM/ContentDisplay.cfm&CONTENTID=44754)
• Acute Care Section of the American Physical Therapy Association (http://www.acutept.org)
• Federation of State Boards of Physical Therapy (http://www.fsbpt.org)
• Kigin, C. (2009). A systems view of physical therapy care: Shifting to a new paradigm for the profession. *Physical Therapy, 89,* 1117–1119.
• Jette, D. U., Brown, R., Collette, N., Friant, W., & Graves, L. (2009). Physical therapists' management of patients in the acute care setting: An observational study. *Physical Therapy, 89,* 1158–1181.

the term "hospital," because acute care can be rendered in many settings. For example, a homebound patient who is receiving home health physical therapy may be acutely ill. Serving the medically complex patient in hospitals and other settings is a role that many PTs relish.

To learn more about physical therapy, see Table 11-3 for major documents that guide PT practice, and Table 11-4 for resources for additional information.

CHAPTER REVIEW

1. What is the primary domain of expertise of the PT?
2. What are some possible medical complications of patients served by PTs in the hospital setting?
3. What are some examples of major changes that have occurred over time in the nature of hospital care?
4. In addition to patient care, what other functions do PTs serve? How might each of these contribute to patient care or public health?
5. Discuss the differences among the roles of PT, PTA, and physical therapy aide. How can each of these members of the healthcare team be used to the greatest advantage within the healthcare system?

6. What are the education and licensure requirements for a PT and PTA?
7. How often and for how long are patients usually seen by PTs in the hospital setting?
8. What are some examples of scheduling challenges that patients and PTs encounter in the hospital setting?
9. What are some examples of interventions that PTs provide in the hospital setting?
10. What advanced credentials might a PT hold? How might they benefit the PT? How might they benefit the public?

REFERENCES

American Physical Therapy Association. (2003). *Guide to physical therapist practice* (2nd ed., Rev.). Alexandria, VA: American Physical Therapy Association.

American Physical Therapy Association. (2010a). Branding the physical therapist. Retrieved March 10, 2010, from http://www.apta.org/AM/Template.cfm?Section=Brand_Beat&Template=/MembersOnly.cfm&NavMenuID=3095&ContentID=54963&DirectListComboInd=D

American Physical Therapy Association. (2010b). The physical therapist assistant. Retrieved March 10, 2010, from http://www.apta.org/AM/Template.cfm?Section=News_and_Info&TEMPLATE=/CM/HTMLDisplay.cfm&CONTENTID=33206

Federation of State Boards of Physical Therapy. (2006). *The Model Practice Act for Physical Therapy: A tool for public protection and legislative change* (4th ed.). Alexandria, VA: Federation of State Boards of Physical Therapy.

Federation of State Boards of Physical Therapy. (2010a). *National physical therapy examination program.* Retrieved March 10, 2010, from https://www.fsbpt.org/ForCandidatesAndLicensees/NPTE/index.asp

Federation of State Boards of Physical Therapy. (2010b). *Continuing competence.* Retrieved March 10, 2010, from https://www.fsbpt.org/ForCandidatesAndLicensees/ContinuingCompetence/index.asp

The Joint Commission. *Hospitals.* Retrieved March 10, 2010, from http://www.jointcommission.org/AccreditationPrograms/Hospitals/

CHAPTER 12

The Respiratory Therapy Department

S. Gregory Marshall

KEY TERMS

Evidence-based patient care

Advanced cardiac life support
   (ACLS)

Oximetry

Product line

Scope of practice

Incentive spirometry (IS)

Mechanical ventilation

Respiratory care practitioner
   (RCP)

Certified respiratory therapist
   (CRT)

Registered respiratory therapist
   (RRT)

Arterial blood gas

Therapist-driven protocols

INTRODUCTION

The American healthcare system is somewhat responsible for the evolution
of the respiratory care profession and the establishment of the department
of respiratory therapy readily found in our healthcare facilities today.
Advancements in Western medical technologies during the 1950s led to
the expansion of respiratory modalities and therapies, resulting in internal
and external recruitment efforts by hospitals to meet the growing need for
qualified respiratory therapists. Stories abound of many healthcare workers
who were enticed to become on-the-job trainees for this emerging profession

some 60 years ago, but the need for specific training programs and management in this field soon became apparent. Although the majority of contemporary European healthcare models do not include a respiratory therapy department or respiratory practitioner in their delivery system, comprehensive healthcare models abroad do include identifiable respiratory modalities managed by other healthcare personnel. Of interest, as a direct result of studies indicating more successful patient outcomes when respiratory therapists are utilized, other countries are showing a trend toward increased development of respiratory therapy departments.

In the United States, all accredited healthcare facilities are required to include credentialed, qualified, and properly trained respiratory therapists as part of their key ancillary services. The vast majority of respiratory therapy departments are identified as centralized units within the organizational structure of the hospital; however, some respiratory therapy units are decentralized according to service areas provided throughout the facility. Regardless of the configuration used, the delivery of all respiratory therapy-related patient care and diagnostic services should be consistent. Although the departmental nomenclature common to most facilities is "respiratory therapy," other terms, such as cardiopulmonary services, respiratory care, or pulmonary services, may be substituted to more descriptively reflect the types of services offered within a particular unit.

In general, the mission of the respiratory therapy department is to provide a continuum of **evidence-based patient care** within an integrated delivery system, documented by patient outcomes. The central focus of respiratory care services should be the patient or client. Respiratory practitioners directly assist physicians and other members of the healthcare team in determining the most appropriate care or diagnostics to be delivered. The mission statement should challenge the department staff to practice professionalism, keep up with the latest information and innovations, and ensure patient/client satisfaction in the delivery of all diagnostic and therapeutic services. By definition through national and state respiratory care practice acts, respiratory therapists are educated to provide diagnostic and therapeutic treatments to patients requiring cardiopulmonary intervention. Because the respiratory therapist must perform both diagnostic tests and therapeutic treatments in consultation with physicians, department mission statements should also include elements encouraging leadership, team participation, continuing education, and advanced professional credentialing. Ideally, the mission statement should be developed by the staff and management to reflect current and prospective respiratory care services in a patient-focused manner.

Traditionally, the function of the respiratory therapy department has been defined by two major service areas: general care and critical care. General care refers to therapy provided to the general medical/surgical areas of the hospital and includes services such as oxygen therapy, treatment modalities, and specific oxygen monitoring diagnostics. Critical-care services include advanced interventions provided in critical-care units, such as mechanical ventilator implementation and management, **advanced cardiac life support (ACLS)**, **oximetry**, and specialty diagnostics (e.g., bronchoscopy). With the technological advancement of diagnostics and services, these two areas of service can now be reclassified into five major **product lines**: (1) therapy modalities, (2) oxygen therapy, (3) ventilator management, (4) physiological monitoring, and (5) specialized procedures and diagnostics.

The specific services offered in each area of service or product line represent different areas of expertise of the respiratory therapist (Exhibit 12-1). As noted previously, respiratory therapists' dual role in providing both diagnostic services and therapeutic treatments in consultation with physicians places them in a unique situation. With progressive technological developments comes a greater responsibility to maintain expertise and acquire advanced training to achieve favorable patient outcomes. In a large healthcare facility that offers a variety of services, respiratory therapists will likely be assigned to specific service areas to ensure that a particular product line is provided by staff with advanced clinical expertise. Smaller facilities that offer fewer services may require all therapists to function equally well in all service areas without designated personnel assignments.

The **scope of practice** for respiratory therapists is defined at the national level by the American Association for Respiratory Care (AARC). On the state level, the scope of practice is defined by each state's requirements for licensure. Although the scope of practice may vary somewhat from state to state, the AARC maintains a national standard for practicing respiratory practitioners by identifying current and expanded scope-of-practice elements (Exhibit 12-2).

Staffing of the respiratory therapy department is directly related to the mission of the healthcare facility and the services it offers. Understandably, facilities that provide a larger variety of services and specialty diagnostics will require a larger and more diversified staff. The Joint Commission's requirements for hospital accreditation require the director/manager of the

Exhibit 12-1. Product lines/areas of service.

Treatment Modalities
- Small volume nebulizer (SVN) therapy
- Metered dose inhaler (MDI) therapy
- Intermittent positive pressure breathing (IPPB)
- **Incentive spirometry (IS)**
- Chest physiotherapy (CPT)
- Ultrasonic nebulizer (USN) therapy
- Intrapulmonary percussive ventilation (IPV) therapy
- Positive expiratory pressure (PEP)
- Constant positive airway pressure (CPAP)

Oxygen Therapy
- Routine O_2 therapy with/without humidification
- Aerosol therapy
- O_2 transport
- Hyperbaric (HBO) therapy

Ventilator Management
- Adult critical care
- Pediatric critical care
- Neonatal critical care
- Emergency department
- Noninvasive (noninvasive positive airway pressure [NIPAP], bilevel positive airway pressure [BiPAP])

Physiologic Monitoring and Diagnostics
- ABG procurement and analysis
- Pulmonary function testing
- Pulse oximetry (SpO$_2$)
- Capnography (ETCO$_2$)
- Exercise and metabolic studies
- Cardiac stress testing
- SvO$_2$
- Cardiac monitoring
- Cardiomuscular monitoring
- Polysomnogram (sleep study)

Specialized Procedures
- Transport (air/land)
- Cardiopulmonary resuscitation (CPR)
- Airway care
- Specialty procedures related to subspecialties

Exhibit 12-2. Respiratory therapy scope of practice.

1. **Mechanical ventilation**, management/adjustment of vent settings, life-support systems, iNO/specialty gases used with mechanical ventilation
2. Cardiodiagnostic, hemodynamic monitoring, invasive/noninvasive cardiopulmonary monitoring, critical-care monitoring, critical therapeutics, ECG (electrocardiogram), Holter monitoring, cardiac monitoring, arterial line, indwelling catheters
3. Traditional/current therapies (O_2 therapy, aerosol therapy, humidity therapy, etc.)
4. Airway care, airway management, intubation
5. Pulmonary function testing
6. Treatment assessment, outcome assessment
7. Home care
8. CPR, resuscitation (basic clinical skills [BCS], advanced cardiac life support [ACLS], neonatal advanced life support [NALS], pediatric advanced life support [PALS] certifications)
9. Respiratory care of the neonatal and pediatric patient, perinatal pediatrics
10. Acid-base balance, blood gas analysis, arterial puncture, automated lab analysis
11. Rehabilitation, cardiopulmonary, pulmonary rehabilitation
12. Patient education, family counseling, and education techniques (AE-C [asthma educator-certified] certification)
13. Therapist-driven protocols
14. Health promotion, disease prevention, health teaching
15. Smoking cessation, nicotine intervention
16. Hyperbaric oxygenation, hyperbaric medicine
17. ECMO (extracorporeal membrane oxygenation) and other life-support techniques
18. Management
19. Discharge planning
20. Sleep studies, sleep lab, sleep disorders, sleep apnea, sleep study intervention
21. Research
22. Medication administration, medication delivery via aerosols
23. Stress testing, exercise testing, exercise physiology assessment
24. Alternative-care delivery, long-term care, subacute care, hospice care, physician office, clinical practice
25. Bronchoscopy, bronchoscopy assistance
26. Infection control, cleaning, sterilization
27. Electrolyte analysis, blood lab, stat lab
28. Geriatrics

(continues)

Exhibit 12-2. *(continued)*

29. Quality improvement, performance assessment/improvement, quality assessment
30. Case management
31. EEG (electroencephalogram), neurodiagnostics
32. Computerization, information management, informatics
33. Transport, trauma in-flight specialist
34. Metabolic measurements
35. ACLS, NALS, PALS
36. Mechanical cardiac support
37. Ethics, ethical decision making
38. Teaching other healthcare providers, being part of a healthcare team, managing other healthcare professionals
39. Patient-focused care, evidence-based medical practices
40. Technology assessment
41. Charting and medical record-keeping

respiratory therapy department to be nationally credentialed and state licensed as a **respiratory care practitioner (RCP)**. All staff personnel in the department must be minimally licensed by the state and/or hold a national credential before they can provide patient care.

The staffing structure that can best facilitate departmental efficiency is one that takes into account the relationship among the service unit, revenue, total costs, personnel costs, and medical supply costs. Staff productivity must be balanced with performance standards and proficiency reviews to comply with the operational standards of the healthcare facility and its mission to the community. Documentation regarding patient outcomes can readily be utilized to support the addition of staff or reorganization of the department's staffing structure, since a facility with numerous specialty units (e.g., pediatric intensive care, neonatal intensive care, transplant intensive care, surgical/trauma adult intensive care, and pulmonary intensive care) will require a larger and more specialized staff.

Many facilities justify their staff size according to productivity units performed and documented by the therapist. The methodology for assigning weights and values to these procedures varies greatly among institutions, but using some means of measuring productivity to validate the addition or deletion of staff seems to be consistent nationwide. For example, if a facility has identified 60 productivity units as a reasonable workload for a therapist during a 12-hour shift, the mean number of productivity units ordered per month divided by 60 units should substantiate the number of staff therapists needed to provide appropriate therapy and diagnostics for all physician-ordered services. As with many other departments, the ebb and flow of patient admissions and discharges, as well as the types of patients admitted, can directly affect the workload activity level of the respiratory therapy department. Although the facility census may be high, if the number of pulmonary-related admissions has declined, the productivity of the department will be decreased. As a general rule, the winter season ushers in the largest number of pulmonary-related admissions, since in addition to seasonal flu complications, cold weather can exacerbate most pulmonary disorders.

Typically, the respiratory therapy director designates a day-shift supervisor and a night-shift supervisor to schedule staff, make daily patient assignments, and evaluate the therapies that have been delivered. Most respiratory therapy departments are required to submit patient charges on a daily basis, and many will designate a staff member to complete and submit all charges for services rendered. Such staff members are not required to have respiratory credentials; they may also serve as an administrative assistant to the director, and often handle the scheduling of outpatient appointments for diagnostic services. They may also manage the day-to-day operations of the department when physicians or other units make special requests for equipment or services.

Because of the high volume of disposable equipment and respiratory therapy equipment that must be sterilized, reassembled, and properly packaged for storage, many departments also employ an equipment tech. This individual does not have direct contact with patients and is not required to be a credential/licensed therapist, but is responsible for cleaning and maintaining all departmental equipment. In cooperation with the biomedical department of the hospital, the equipment tech ensures that all equipment is in proper working order and has met all facility requirements regarding quality assurance and maintenance.

The number of therapists needed to deliver respiratory-care modalities and diagnostic services is linked to the size of the facility. A recent study of respiratory-care manpower issues surveyed 51 hospitals classified according to size (small, ≤200 beds; medium, 201–499 beds; and large, >500 beds). According to the study, the administrators' preferred number of beds per RCP was 9.445/1.0, whereas the actual bed/RCP ratio reported was 10.75/1.0. The ratio of one RCP per 10 beds appears to be fairly representative of the current situation in US hospitals, which is consistent with the findings of this study.

In the contiguous United States, RCPs must be credentialed and licensed before they can deliver patient care. All therapists must complete an accredited educational program and sit for national board exams, in contrast to other healthcare providers, such as nurses, physicians, and physical therapists, who are only required to sit for state board exams. The national credentialing process permits respiratory therapists to be recognized in Canada, Europe, and all 50 states of the United States. State licensing of healthcare providers permits patient care only in the state where the licensing exam was taken, unless reciprocity agreements have been established between the states in question.

In similarity to nursing, there are three strata of respiratory therapy related to length of education and training. Individuals who have completed a 1-year respiratory therapist (RT) program in a community college are eligible to sit for the **certified respiratory therapist (CRT)** exam administered by the National Board for Respiratory Care (NBRC). Once the national credentialing exam is successfully completed, the therapist must apply for a state license and become an RCP before he or she can provide patient care. The entry-level credential for patient care in respiratory therapy is a CRT credential with an RCP state license. Hospitals that employ therapists without these specific qualifications are in violation of state law, and services rendered to patients are not financially covered by third-party agencies. However, hospitals will often assign therapists with only a CRT credential to limited-skill areas that require less expertise because they can be paid a lower wage than a therapist with advanced credentials. The CRT level of training and expertise is analogous to that of a licensed vocational nurse (LVN) or licensed practical nurse (LPN).

Echoing the registered nurse model of education, individuals seeking to earn a **registered respiratory therapist (RRT)** national credential must attend either a 2-year associate degree program or a 4-year baccalaureate degree program. Upon completion of such a program, they must sit for the NBRC national board exam and complete the CRT entry-level exam, the RRT written board exam, and the RRT clinical simulation exam before earning the RRT credential. Once they have successfully completed all three national board exams, they must also obtain a state RCP license before they can directly provide patient care.

Although the AARC and NBRC are considering recommending a transition from associate degree programs to baccalaureate degree programs, the manpower issues involved in providing respiratory care today make such a change unfeasible. Currently, there are 375 accredited RRT associate degree programs in the United States and only five remaining 1-year CRT programs. All 1-year programs are slated to be closed within the next 5 years. Nationally, there are 53 RRT baccalaureate degree programs and three master's degree programs available, with three more graduate programs in progress. As in the nursing field, the workforce of the respiratory therapy profession is very dependent at this point on individuals with associate degrees. Fewer than 15% of the 140,000 respiratory therapists in the United States possess a bachelor's degree. Current staffing efforts depend heavily on all CRTs and both levels of RRTs to meet patient-care demands.

Subspecialty credentials in respiratory therapy have emerged as a way of recognizing advanced skills, and many hospitals now require additional specialty credentials to qualify for assignment to a specialty area. The NBRC and AARC elected to recognize both CRT and RRT therapists as qualified to sit for specialty examinations based on clinical experience and/ or additional education. The NBRC offers examinations in the following subspecialties: neonatal-pediatric specialist (NPS), certified pulmonary function technologist (CPFT), registered pulmonary function technologist (RPFT), and sleep disorders specialist (SDS). Plans to offer a critical care specialty (CCS) credential are under way, but this specialty will only be offered to therapists with an RRT credential. Therapists who have passed a specialty exam are designated by their highest respiratory therapy credential hyphenated with the specialty credential. For example, the credential of CRT-NPS denotes that the individual is a certified respiratory therapist who is also a neonatal-pediatric specialist. An individual with the RRT-SDS credential is a registered respiratory therapist with a specialty credential as a sleep disorder specialist. Other specialty credentials, such as asthma educator–certified (AE-C, for individuals who are specially trained to provide asthma education) and registered polysomnographic technologist (RPSGT, for individuals who are nationally credentialed to conduct polysomnographic studies or sleep studies), can be obtained in addition to those offered by the NBRC.

Respiratory therapists must maintain their licenses and credentials by earning continued education credits (CEUs). The CEU requirements vary among the states, but they range between 12 and 20 credits annually. Although CEUs can be obtained in a number of ways, the RT department director should make a deliberate effort to provide continuing education opportunities for all therapists to ensure that they maintain their credentials and licenses, and meet the standards of The Joint Commission. Lack of compliance in maintaining credentials and licenses will result in significant fines and penalties levied against the hospital by state and national agencies on a per-day basis. The department director must confirm the license/credential status of all staff members and maintain records of their CEUs.

Because the respiratory therapy department provides both diagnostics and therapeutic treatments, the patient flow through the unit is quite unique. As a rule, patients visit the department on an outpatient basis when provided with a physician order for a diagnostic test (e.g., a pulmonary function test, **arterial blood gas** procurement/analysis, exercise or stress test, or bronchoscopy), hyperbaric oxygen therapy, patient/family education for asthma, smoking cessation, home care, or some other form of outpatient service. All diagnostic procedures, whether inpatient or outpatient, require a physician's order to initiate testing. Outpatients are usually admitted through the hospital's outpatient admission office and diagnostic tests are usually scheduled through the department and the physician's office; however, some patients will present unscheduled and unannounced with physician orders in hand.

The therapist assigned to the specific diagnostic area receives the patient, processes the outpatient admission section relevant to the respiratory therapy department, conducts the diagnostic test according to facility and departmental policies and procedures, and assists the patient to either return to outpatient admissions or proceed to the next diagnostic area scheduled for the patient. All diagnostic test results are sent to the appropriate physician for interpretation, and the physician's office is responsible for communicating all test results to the patient. Patients are not provided with data from diagnostic tests and are instructed to contact the physician's office for testing results and follow-up.

The procedure for in-house diagnostic testing depends on the type of diagnostic test ordered and the patient's current condition. Thanks to technological advancements that are bringing diagnostics to a point-of-care proximity, some procedures can be performed at the patient's bedside; however, some procedures require the patient to be transported to the department unit or specific diagnostic area. Before any in-house diagnostic tests are performed, the patient's condition should be evaluated to determine whether accurate results can be obtained without compromising the patient's safety. Inpatient diagnostics follow the same policy and procedure pathway of providing the results of the diagnostic test to the ordering physician on a timely basis. Tests that are ordered for immediate processing (STAT tests) are given priority over other regularly scheduled tests. Test specimens are either processed in the respiratory therapy department or transported to the appropriate laboratory for analysis. All diagnostic test results are entered into the patient's personal medical records for review by physicians and other members of the healthcare team.

The most comprehensive role of the respiratory therapist involves the product lines or areas of service clustered around therapeutic treatments. This array of modalities, therapies, and monitoring techniques is found in most every area of the hospital. Therapists are routinely active in emergency departments, adult intensive care units, pediatric intensive care units, neonatal intensive care units, delivery rooms, postoperative recovery rooms, cardiac catheterization laboratories, outpatient clinics, pulmonary rehabilitation units, subacute and set-down units, transplant specialty units, burn units, and polysomnography or sleep centers. In each of these specialty areas, the physician's order is primarily the event that initiates therapy.

After the therapist arrives at the patient-care area, he or she reviews the physician's orders, reviews the patient's medical chart for any contraindications or hazards associated with the patient's condition and the therapy requested, and obtains any ordered medication or equipment needed for the procedure. The therapist discusses the treatment with the patient, including why the doctor ordered it, and its benefits and expected therapeutic outcomes; administers the ordered treatment to the patient; assesses the patient for any expected or unexpected response; charts the procedure in the patient's medical chart; and notifies appropriate personnel. If the therapist assesses a specific need for advanced therapy or modification of the therapy, the patient's physician or nurse may be consulted. Patient charges for the therapy are generated through the respiratory therapy department or the specific patient unit. The healthcare team should respect the autonomy of the therapist within the guidelines of the hospital's policies and protocols.

Due to the nature of the types of therapy offered by the respiratory therapist, emergency patient situations may require immediate diagnostic and therapeutic intervention in the absence of the patient's physician or a physician order. When a state of emergency is identified, the healthcare team is trained to respond to the patient's immediate needs regardless of the presence of a physician. The respiratory therapist is a key member of this first-response team. This level of autonomy is a critical part of the educational process for all respiratory therapists, who must learn to exercise clinical judgment in an emergency situation. **Therapist-driven protocols** should be part of a hospital's policies and procedures. These agreed-upon protocols provide legal coverage for therapists and nurses who must address life-threatening conditions. They are very specific and outline a course of actions to be followed according to a branching-logic, decision-tree type of process. By allowing therapists to use their training and skills to appropriately respond to a life-threatening situation when time is a critical factor and no physician is present, such protocols can result in many lives being saved.

As part of the first-response team in the hospital, many therapists receive basic life support (BLS) training, and most therapists are also required to receive advanced cardiac life support (ACLS) certification. Under the provisions of ACLS certification, a healthcare team member is qualified to conduct advanced life-support protocols on patients experiencing cardiopulmonary arrest in the absence of a physician. ACLS-trained team members must be able to oversee and manage a resuscitation team during a cardiopulmonary arrest sequence, including initiating endotracheal intubation, administering cardiac medications, interpreting cardiac activity, and, if necessary, administering external cardiac defibrillation "shock" treatment. All ACLS-certified therapists who possess the leadership abilities and critical-thinking skills required to lead a full-arrest resuscitation are a credit to their healthcare team and institution.

A respiratory therapist's level of skill and clinical role are often strongly associated with his or her level of education. In similarity to nursing, RRT therapists must demonstrate proficiency in all areas of service and product lines in their field, regardless of whether they have received an associate degree or a baccalaureate degree. However, the RRT who has earned a baccalaureate degree has had additional opportunities to receive advanced training in critical thinking and leadership. In an attempt to recognize the value of an advanced degree and reward additional education, hospitals have developed professional career ladders, or tracks, that can lead a staff member to management and leadership roles within a department. Most directors of respiratory therapy departments have earned a bachelor's degree as well as the advanced RRT credential and license, and many have also obtained a graduate degree. The value of an advanced degree may not be evident at the time of hiring, considering that associate-degree and baccalaureate-degree RRT therapists are hired at the same hourly wage, but the opportunities for advancement certainly favor the advanced-degree therapist. Although at present there are no plans to implement an entry-level master's degree in respiratory care, the emphasis on completion of the bachelor's degree at some point in the therapist's career is certainly supported by hospitals' continuing-education goals and recommendations.

Finally, the role of the respiratory therapist and the department of respiratory therapy is one of providing support to the physician. Respiratory therapists receive a considerable amount of education in the proper selection of therapeutic modalities based on patient assessment and diagnostic test results; thus, they can serve as an extension to the physician in monitoring and treating cardiopulmonary diseases and conditions. If embraced as such by the physician, therapist autonomy can enhance and advance patient care, and studies have shown that the services of a respiratory therapist can decrease the average length of stay for patients in the intensive-care unit. The scope of practice for respiratory therapists stipulates that they answer directly to the physician, as do nurses, when caring for their patients. Like nurses, therapists take verbal orders directly from the physician and serve an important function in communicating patient status and therapeutic options to the physician. Working as part of a healthcare team, respiratory therapists provide an approach to care for patients with cardiopulmonary diseases and conditions that is comprehensive and supportive of evidence-based medical practices.

CHAPTER REVIEW

1. Describe the two traditional areas of service provided by respiratory therapists.
2. Discuss how these two areas of service have been reclassified into five major product lines.
3. Describe what is meant by the term "scope of practice."
4. Discuss the typical characteristics of an RT staff in a large healthcare facility with multiple specialty services.
5. Discuss the differences between a CRT and an RRT therapist with regard to education and clinical roles.
6. Discuss the subspecialty credentials and the purpose of obtaining such credentials.

7. Describe the typical patient flow for an outpatient requiring diagnostic services.
8. Describe the typical patient flow for an inpatient requiring therapeutic services.
9. Discuss the role of therapist-driven protocols in the healthcare setting.
10. Two respiratory therapists—one with an associate's degree and one with a bachelor's degree—are candidates for a job in the respiratory therapy department. Discuss what impact their education might have on their future employment.

REFERENCES

Chilliers, L. & Retief, G. (2005). The evolution of hospitals from antiquity to the Renaissance. *Acta Theologica Supplementum*, Vol. 7 (2005).

Chilliers, L. & Retief, G. (2002). The evolution of the hospital from antiquity to the end of the middle ages. *Curationis*. 2002 Nov;25(4):60-6.

Risse, G. (1999). *Mending Bodies, Saving Souls: A History of Hospitals*. New York. Oxford Press.

Rosen, G. (1993). *A History of Public Health*. Baltimore, Maryland. The Johns Hopkins University Press.

Starr, P. (1982). *The Social Transformation of American Medicine*. Printed in the United States.

CHAPTER 13

Speech-Language Pathologists

Jana Proff and Valarie B. Fleming

KEY TERMS

Communication disorder

Swallowing disorder

Aphasia

Cleft palate

Stroke

Otolaryngology

Rapport

Standardized test

Modified barium swallow study
  (MBSS)

Endoscopic

Videofluoroscopy

The primary role of the speech-language pathologist (SLP) in the hospital setting is to diagnose and treat patients with communication or swallowing disorders (American Speech-Language-Hearing Association [ASHA], 2007). A **communication disorder** is an inability to receive, send, manage, or understand verbal, nonverbal, or graphic messages. A **swallowing disorder** is any impairment in the ability to suck, chew, or move food and liquids from the mouth to the stomach. SLPs provide the highest standards of care to all patients, including using best practices for assessment and evidence-based treatment techniques. The SLP also has an obligation to act as a patient advocate to make sure the patients' needs are being met and they have access to any applicable services to maximize their safety and recovery. To ensure that patients receive necessary services, the public and other healthcare professionals must be educated as to the role of the SLP. Patients may be underserved or undiagnosed simply due to a lack of awareness about the scope of practice for SLPs in the hospital system.

The typical training of an SLP involves a wide variety of courses and experiences (ASHA, 2009). High school students who are interested in becoming an SLP should take courses in basic sciences (i.e., biology and physics), social sciences, English, and mathematics. Undergraduate college course work in communication sciences and disorders includes classes in anatomy, biology, human development, linguistics, mathematics, phonetics, psychology, physical science, physiology, and social/behavioral sciences.

Graduate studies are required for certification in speech-language pathology. Students should enroll in programs that are accredited by the Council on Academic Accreditation in Audiology and Speech-Language Pathology (CAA), and acquire the necessary knowledge and skills required to meet certification standards. Once they have earned a graduate degree in communication sciences and disorders, they are eligible to apply for certification. Certification requires the completion of a graduate degree and a supervised clinical fellowship (CF), and a passing score on a national examination. Once the SLP has successfully completed these steps, he or she can apply for a certificate of clinical competence (CCC).

In addition to meeting national certification requirements, SLPs must comply with their state's regulatory (licensure) standards to practice. Typically, the requirements for state licensure or teacher certification are similar or even identical to the requirements for the CCC. To maintain the CCC, SLPs must submit documentation to verify 30 professional development hours every 3 years, abide by ASHA's code of ethics, and pay an annual certification fee. The requirements to maintain state licensure and/or teacher certification vary by state, but are often similar to the requirements for maintenance of the CCC.

SLPs assess and treat a variety of communication disorders, including speech disorders, **aphasia** (difficulty understanding or using language), voice disorders, cognitive impairment, and swallowing disorders. Patients range in age from newborn to the very elderly. Premature babies and infants with feeding or swallowing issues may be referred to the SLP. Many major medical centers also have cleft-palate teams. As a part of these teams, SLPs evaluate and treat the speech and feeding issues of infants and children with **cleft palates**. SLPs see adult patients with various diagnoses, including **stroke**, traumatic brain injury, or brain tumor. Often, these patients present with changes in their speaking and listening abilities and critical-thinking skills that are directly related to their diagnoses. Patients with progressive diseases such as dementia, Parkinson's disease, and amyotrophic lateral sclerosis (ALS) are also evaluated and treated by SLPs. As the symptoms of these diseases worsen and begin to impact speech clarity and swallowing safety, the SLP can offer treatment, guidance, and support.

SLPs are a part of a dynamic team that offers treatment and support to patients in hospital settings. In some hospitals, the speech-language pathology department may operate as an independent unit, whereas in others it may exist within a broader department of rehabilitation services. Even when they function as an independent department, SLPs are still members of a multidisciplinary team of healthcare professionals who work together to provide comprehensive patient care in the hospital setting. Other team members may include physical therapists, occupational therapists, and respiratory therapists. All members of the multidisciplinary team work collaboratively to address the needs of patients with multiple areas of deficit.

Staffing within the speech-language pathology department can vary greatly from hospital to hospital depending on the size and location of the hospital, and the hospital's designation as a Level I–IV trauma center. In Level I or II trauma centers in major metropolitan areas, a team of SLPs with diverse specialties may have to manage a large patient caseload. A team leader or coordinator may manage the scheduling and assign patients based on the team members' different areas of expertise. For example, one person might have more experience with swallowing assessments in adults, and another might have more experience with pediatric patients. SLPs who specialize in voice disorders may work closely with (or even within) the **otolaryngology** department. Cognitive rehabilitation and aphasia treatment may be other areas of expertise for SLPs operating within a larger department. SLPs with doctoral degrees may also have research laboratories in major trauma centers. They may use these facilities to investigate possible causes of communication and swallowing disorders, or to research the efficacy of different treatment techniques and outcomes in terms of evidence-based practice.

In contrast, the speech-language pathology team in a smaller hospital may consist of one or two individuals who will be called upon to see all patients across the age and disorder spectrum. Some smaller or rural hospitals may not have an on-staff SLP and will solely contract services as needed for patient care. Regardless of the hospital's size or designation, however, SLPs will need to communicate with members of a larger team of health professionals, including nurses and physicians, to ensure that all patients with deficits receive the services they need.

Within the hospital system, a patient can receive SLP services only with a physician's referral. Nurses or other therapists may notice symptoms of speech or swallowing disorders and suggest a referral, but a doctor's referral is required to initiate an SLP consultation. Once the SLP receives the referral, he or she will first check the patient's chart and examine the patient's medical history, including allergies and possible reasons for the referral. When possible, the SLP may also speak with the patient's nurse or other therapists to learn more about the patient's current condition and obtain a clearer picture of how speech–language pathology might help.

After reviewing the chart, the SLP enters the patient's room to begin an interview. During the interview, the SLP introduces himself or herself and explains why the patient was referred for a speech or swallowing consultation. It is important to build **rapport** with the patient during the interview and ascertain his or her perception of the problem. The interview also allows the SLP to assess the patient's communication and cognitive skills in conversation.

When interviewing the patient, the SLP makes judgments regarding the types of assessment that would be most appropriate and the specific materials needed to best reveal that particular person's strengths and weaknesses. Most assessments begin with a motor speech examination. This examination is to assess the structures of the speech and swallowing system, which may have impaired functioning due to neurological damage. The SLP systematically evaluates the face muscles, lips, tongue, jaw, palate, and larynx for symmetry, sensation, range of motion, and strength. After the motor speech examination is completed, the SLP performs a specific speech, language, cognitive, or swallowing assessment as indicated in the referral.

Speech and language assessments may include a **standardized test** and/ or nonstandardized speech and language measures. Any evaluation should be structured to include performance measures for a wide variety of communication tasks, such as answering "yes/no" questions, following directions, naming objects, and describing pictures. The speech and language examination may also include an assessment of the patient's reading and writing abilities. If the patient's ability to communicate is severely impaired, the SLP may also evaluate the patient's ability to use alternative forms of communication such as gesturing or pointing to pictures on a communication board. A good speech and language assessment should reveal the patient's communication strengths and weaknesses, enabling the SLP to promptly set goals for therapy and teach the staff and the patient's family how to best facilitate communication. Treatment may include daily sessions focused on improving communication skills through various language stimulation tasks or functional communication activities.

Occasionally, patients may experience changes in their communication abilities due to a decline in cognition. The resultant communication disorder is called a cognitive-communication disorder and is commonly seen in patients with traumatic brain injury or dementia. In a cognitive evaluation, the SLP will examine multiple areas of thinking, including attention, orientation, memory, organization, sequencing, and basic problem-solving and reasoning abilities. Patients with mild impairments may also perform higher-level cognitive tasks that require analyses of more-complex information. The information gleaned from a cognitive assessment can give the staff and the patient's caregivers critical insight into the patient's ability to safely perform activities of daily living. This vital information is needed to both minimize the patient's risk of falling while in the hospital and to make plans for discharge from the hospital. Sometimes, modifications to the patient's room or home may be all that is necessary for the patient to function independently and successfully. Other patients may need full-time supervision or assistance, and the SLP works as part of a team in deciding what plan will best keep the patients and their caregivers safe. Treatment for cognitive-communication disorders often focuses on compensating for reduced cognitive functioning, as well as rehabilitating the attention, memory, and executive function skills needed for successful communication. For patients with a progressive disease, such as Alzheimer's disease, treatment may be focused more on managing behaviors and retaining skills for as long as possible.

Perhaps the most common type of evaluation performed by SLPs in a hospital setting is a swallowing assessment. Swallowing assessments include bedside swallow evaluations and instrumental assessments such as a **modified barium swallow study (MBSS)** or **endoscopic** assessment of swallowing function (ASHA, 2001). Most swallowing consults will begin with a bedside swallowing evaluation. A bedside swallow evaluation allows the SLP to assess the patient's ability to swallow food and liquid of different consistencies in the comfort of the patient's own room. Most often, this can be done while the patient consumes a meal; however, if the patient has not been cleared for a meal yet due to choking concerns, the SLP may give the patient substances of various consistencies. The SLP will be looking, listening, and feeling for any signs of swallowing difficulty before, during, and after each bite and sip. Pureed foods, such as pudding or yogurt; soft-consistency foods that are easy to chew, such as canned peaches; and semisolid foods such as meat and vegetables may all be evaluated in terms of safety, efficiency, and dietary need. The SLP also observes while the patient drinks a thin or thick liquid to determine whether the patient is experiencing any delay in swallowing or difficulty managing the liquid in his or her mouth. Such difficulties could put the patient at risk for liquids entering the airway and resulting in pneumonia.

Sometimes a bedside swallow evaluation will reveal the need for a more in-depth look at the patient's swallowing mechanism through instrumental assessment. In this case, an MBSS or endoscopic assessment may be ordered, depending on the hospital's resources and the SLP's training. The MBSS is the most common instrumental assessment of swallowing, as most hospitals already have the necessary equipment within the radiology department. This test is essentially similar to a bedside swallow evaluation, but it is performed during videofluoroscopy with aid of a radiologist. With the use of **videofluoroscopy**, swallowing motions can be observed, and areas of the throat and airway that are not visible during the bedside swallow evaluation can be examined. To perform an endoscopic assessment, SLPs need special training and certification in passing a flexible endoscope (a narrow tube with a video camera on the end) through a patient's nose. Typically, endoscopic assessments can only be performed in larger hospitals with an on-site otolaryngology department or funds for the necessary equipment.

No matter which type of swallowing assessment is used, the SLP's goal is to make safe and appropriate dietary recommendations for the patient. The most critical part of the SLP's job is to educate the patient, caregiver, and staff. Ensuring that diet recommendations and feeding techniques are followed may require posting of swallowing precautions, frequent training, and vigilant monitoring. Patients may put their lives at stake by eating or drinking something that could enter their airway or lungs. It can be difficult for some patients to achieve a balance between preventing choking and aspiration-related pneumonia while maintaining adequate nutrition and hydration. It is the SLP's role to educate patients and their caregivers to make this as manageable as possible. Treatment of swallowing disorders involves a combination of compensatory strategies for safe swallowing as well as therapeutic tasks aimed at improving the act of swallowing.

Whether an evaluation is for speech and language, cognition, or swallowing, its main purpose is to identify a patient's needs. Often a patient may be referred to a physician, such as an otolaryngologist, neurologist, or gastroenterologist, or to a registered dietician or occupational therapist. If a patient requires further speech-language pathology intervention, treatment goals and the frequency of treatment will be established based on the assessment results. Typically, patients are seen on a daily basis in the acute-care setting until they are discharged from either speech services or the hospital. Patients who need continued speech services after they are discharged from the hospital can be seen by an SLP at home or in long-term acute-care centers, skilled nursing facilities, home health agencies, and outpatient clinics.

SLPs strive to improve their patients' quality of life by managing and treating difficulties in speaking, thinking, and swallowing. Such difficulties can severely impact people's daily lives and how they define themselves. Talking with loved ones, reading a favorite magazine, drinking a hot cup of coffee—these are all activities that can make life more enjoyable and can be devastated by communication and swallowing disorders. By identifying and treating these disorders, and working together with patients, caregivers, and other members of the healthcare team, SLPs can help their patients live the fullest lives possible.

CHAPTER REVIEW

1. Define the terms "communication disorder" and "swallowing disorder."
2. Explain the differences between major trauma centers and smaller or rural hospitals in staffing of SLPs.
3. Describe the process involved in choosing an appropriate assessment for a new patient in the hospital system after the doctor's referral has been received.
4. Why is a cognitive-communication assessment important for ensuring patient safety within the hospital and for discharge planning?
5. Name the consistencies used for a swallowing assessment and give an example of each.
6. What is the most critical part of the swallowing assessment and treatment process, and why?

REFERENCES

American Speech-Language-Hearing Association. (2001). *Roles of speech-language pathologists in swallowing and feeding disorders: Technical report.* Retrieved September 9, 2010, from www.asha.org/policy

American Speech-Language-Hearing Association. (2007). *Scope of practice in speech-language pathology.* Retrieved September 9, 2010, from www.asha.org/policy

American Speech-Language-Hearing Association. (2009). *2005 Standards and implementation procedures for the certificate of clinical competence in speech-language pathology.* Retrieved October 26, 2009, from http://www.asha.org/certification/slp_standards.htm

CHAPTER 14

The Pharmacy

Polly Griffin

KEY TERMS

Compounding drugs
Telepharmacy
Pharmacy technicians
Pharmacy and therapeutics
   (P&T) committee

Unit dose system
Robotic pharmacists
Generic drugs

INTRODUCTION

The hospital pharmacy is responsible for dispensing and **compounding drugs** (i.e., mixing drugs to fit the needs of a particular patient) and other diagnostic and therapeutic chemical substances that are used in the hospital. The hospital pharmacy is almost always found within the premises of the hospital and may include outpatient services as well as inpatient services. The pharmacy might also sell items to the public, but this practice is generally discouraged and varies according to state law. As with all areas of a hospital, patient safety is of paramount importance in the pharmacy department and will be discussed later in this chapter.

   Some hospitals have a decentralized pharmacy system, with one main pharmacy and satellite pharmacies in each nursing unit of the hospital. In larger hospitals, the emergency department may also have pharmacy services.

FUNCTION OF THE PHARMACY

Hospital pharmacies serve different functions, some of which are listed as follows:

- Inpatient/outpatient pharmacy
- Dispensing facilities
  - Dispensing system
  - Medication counseling
  - Inventory/stock management
- Production pharmacy
- Pharmaceutical preparation activities
- Pharmacy procurement and supply
- Service facilities
  - Procurement and supply system
  - Inventory/stock management
  - Storage procedures

Often, very small (usually rural) hospitals will not have a regular pharmacy department. As an alternative, the hospital may purchase items from a local pharmacist and maintain only a limited supply of pharmaceuticals under supervised security. It is sometimes difficult to recruit pharmacists to work in rural areas. Some small community hospitals may contract with a pharmacist from a retail pharmacy, but this often proves to be an unsatisfactory association because he or she is not a hospital pharmacist.

TELEPHARMACY

Telepharmacy is a relatively new concept that offers 24-hour pharmacy coverage for small hospitals. The process is rather simple: A physician writes an order for a medication. A nurse enters the order into a computer and a pharmacist at a contracting hospital then reviews the order, ensures there are no drug interactions, and authenticates the order by computer. After the order is approved, a nurse can dispense the medication. If the hospital has a medication-dispensing device, the nurse can retrieve it from that.

THE PHARMACY STAFF

In most hospitals, a full-time pharmacist is available to supervise and coordinate the activities of pharmacy assistants, pharmacy technicians, and other staff. **Pharmacy technicians** assist the pharmacist in prepackaging drugs, controlling inventory, distributing floor stock items, and other activities that do not require professional judgment. Pharmacy technicians may be trained on the job or in a hospital-based program. Currently, with pharmacists in short supply, many hospitals contract with an outside pharmacy company to supply personnel and manage the department.

The pharmacist oversees or personally performs inpatient and/or outpatient pharmacy services, and the preparation of a wide range of sterile products for the medical facility. Hospital policy dictates whether the pharmacist is allowed to compound certain solutions or drugs. For quality assurance and financial reasons, most hospitals prefer to purchase preprepared drugs and solutions, whether for injection or intravenous (IV) administration.

The pharmacist is responsible for providing pharmaceutical services in accordance with the policies and procedures of the hospital and accepted pharmacy practice. The duties of the pharmacist include interpreting medication orders written by physicians, providing information and consultative advice to prescribing doctors regarding the contraindications and side effects of drugs, selecting drugs, compounding drugs, and dispensing appropriate medications. Hospital pharmacists are also responsible for the special preparation of IVs, nutritional solutions, chemotherapeutic agents, and radioactive medications. Pharmacists may be involved in medication counseling for cardiac rehabilitation or cancer patients. Some hospital pharmacists are allowed privileges that include assessing patients and adjusting medications accordingly. Hospital pharmacists may work rotating shifts, including evenings, weekends, and holidays.

PHARMACIST EDUCATION

Pharmacists who are trained in the United States must earn a PharmD. degree from an accredited college or school of pharmacy. Before being admitted to a PharmD program, the applicant must have completed at least 2 years of studies, including courses in mathematics, chemistry, biology, and physics. While completing the 4-year program, students are allowed to practice with licensed pharmacists before moving on to the 1- to 2-year residency program required for hospital pharmacists. Students must pass all examinations required by the state in which they plan to practice before they are granted a license.

PHARMACY AND THERAPEUTICS COMMITTEE

The **pharmacy and therapeutics (P&T) committee** serves as a liaison between the pharmacy and the medical staff, and oversees the medical aspects of the hospital pharmacy's activities. Members usually include physicians, a pharmacist, a nurse, and an administrator. Although the P&T committee recommends the standard drugs to be dispensed in the hospital, in the vast majority of hospitals, it is the pharmacist's responsibility to select the brand or supplier of drugs dispensed for all medication orders and prescriptions, unless a specific notation to the contrary is made by the prescriber.

A key duty of the P&T committee is to develop a formulary of acceptable drugs. The formulary contains a list of drugs that are approved by the medical staff and available for use within the hospital. Recommended dosages, contraindications, warnings, and pharmacology are described in the formulary. Other functions of the committee include educating the medical staff about new drugs when they become available, reviewing drug reactions and studies, participating in quality-improvement programs, and establishing cost-effective drug therapies.

DRUG DISTRIBUTION SYSTEM

Once they are received in the hospital or pharmacy, drugs and supplies are distributed to the nursing units for administration to patients. Inpatients receive the majority of drugs dispensed by the pharmacy. Generally, these drugs fall into one of three categories:

- Items sent to the nursing units for floor stock inventory. These are items regularly stored in the unit and not charged to patients directly. Examples of such nonchargeable items include rubbing compounds, antiseptics for wounds, and bandages.
- Patient-chargeable stock items kept in the nursing unit. These include disposable enema packs and other disposable external preparations.
- Common prescription drugs that are dispensed and charged only upon receipt of a prescription by a physician. This category of prescription drugs represents the vast majority of drugs used and accounts for the greatest costs in the pharmacy.

A common method for dispensing medication to patients is the **unit dose system**. The pharmacy either packages the medication or purchases prepackaged medications in specific dosages. The former method allows for better control and less waste of the drugs, but it entails the additional cost of packaging them. Under the unit dose system, a 24-hour supply of medications is dispensed to each nursing unit. The medications are kept in patient drawers in the nursing unit's medication cart. The drawers are combined into cassettes, and cassettes are exchanged by the pharmacy at a designated time every day. The unit dose system offers greater convenience and efficiency for the hospital pharmacist, nurses, and patients, and reduces preparation and distribution errors.

Very modern hospitals have automated dispensing methods and equipment, such as state-of-the-art "**robotic pharmacists**" that deliver medications from the central pharmacy to patient rooms for dispensing by the nursing staff. The typical robot can speed up the process of issuing medication to patients by using its three robotically controlled arms to fill a tray for a medication round in just 3 minutes. Although all of the medications are double-checked by humans, the use of such robots can reduce prescription errors and give the nursing staff more time to spend interacting with patients.

A common problem in hospital pharmacies is the number of calls received daily from nursing services asking when their medications will be delivered. Sometimes this occurs because a medication request has been misplaced, resulting in frustration for both the nursing and pharmacy staffs. Some hospital pharmacies are currently using a wireless tracking system with a barcode scanner that records, in real time, the preparation of a medication and its location in the distribution process from the pharmacy to the nursing delivery site. With this system, STAT orders and high-cost drugs can be prioritized, nurses can view the order status, and fewer phone calls to the pharmacy can result in increased productivity for both the pharmacists and hospital staff.

The pharmacy department is also responsible for preparing and distributing IV solutions or parenteral feeding products, including nutritional substances and chemotherapeutic agents. The timing of preparation and delivery is crucial, since some solutions are stable for only a short period of time. A sterile environment is critical for these drug preparations; therefore, a laminar flow hood (a special cabinet designed to prevent contamination) is considered a necessary piece of equipment for pharmacies that prepare such solutions.

MEDICATION DISPENSING ERRORS

Medication error is one of the most commonplace problems involving patient safety and security in a hospital. To reduce dispensing errors that can be potentially harmful to patients, hospital pharmacies make a great effort to apply the medical industry's five rights of medications: (1) the right patient, (2) the right drug, (3) the right time, (4) the right dose, and (5) the right route of administration.

The National Coordinating Council for Medication Error Reporting and Prevention defines a medication error as "any preventable event that may cause or lead to inappropriate medication use or patient harm while the medication is in the control of the healthcare professional, patient, or consumer. Such events may be related to professional practice, healthcare products, procedures, and systems, including prescribing; order communication; product labeling, packaging, and nomenclature; compounding; dispensing; distribution; administration; education; monitoring; and use" (http://www.nccmerp.org/aboutMedErrors.html).

Many hospital patients do not tell their doctors about other medications they are taking, or whether they have allergies or drug reactions to certain medications. This makes it difficult for the doctor and hospital pharmacist to prescribe the correct medication and/or dosage. In addition, a doctor may have poor handwriting or may confuse drugs with similar names, medications may be mislabeled, patients may have the same name or similar names, and environmental conditions in the hospital pharmacy, such as noise, may cause a distraction. All of these factors can lead to medication errors.

In 2004, the Food and Drug Administration (FDA) issued a rule requiring bar codes on the labels of thousands of human drugs and biological products in an effort to prevent medication errors and reduce the costs of health care. This system has been very effective in helping doctors, nurses, and hospitals give patients the right drugs at the right dosage. The FDA routinely gives hospitals and other medical facilities information about new drugs, FDA safety notifications and product recalls, and on other ways to protect patients while using medical products.

Some hospital pharmacies subscribe to Web-based software programs to assist pharmacists in identifying possible problems with their patients, and, as discussed previously, robots are also a "prescription" for reducing errors.

CONTROL OF NARCOTICS AND BARBITURATES

The hospital must exercise strict control over the dispensing of narcotics and barbiturates. These drugs must be kept under security in both the pharmacy (usually in a large safe) and the nursing units (usually in very limited doses). Thorough and adequate records must be kept for narcotics and barbiturates. At the change of each nursing shift, a narcotics and barbiturates count is taken. The use and maintenance of narcotics in the hospital must comply with strict state and federal laws, and hospitals should be aware that both state and federal agencies conduct surprise inspections. Some hospitals use narcotic cameras that allow recordings to be viewed in case of missing or unlogged narcotics.

When ordering a narcotic, physicians must note their narcotic license number on the prescription. When a telephone order is given to a nurse for narcotics, the nurse taking the order must place a written signature and number on the patient's medical record within 48 hours. Most hospitals have established policies mandating that the physician must reorder narcotics after a certain length of time. Narcotic drugs are carefully defined and regulated by a host of state and federal laws. By knowing the pharmacy staff, conducting surveillance and audits, and investigating discrepancies in a timely manner, hospital staff can help keep narcotics under control.

GENERIC VERSUS BRAND-NAME DRUGS

The federal government and other agencies are encouraging the use of **generic drugs** simply because they cost less than brand-name drugs. Generic equivalents are made according to the same strict FDA standards as brand-name drugs and therefore have the same quality, strength, purity, and stability as their more costly equivalents. A drug's generic name is the scientific (nonproprietary) name by which the drug is known, based on its chemical substance and irrespective of the manufacturer. Manufacturers assign a brand name or trade name, followed by a registered trademark. Brand names are generally capitalized, whereas generic names are written in lowercase. Not every brand-name drug has a generic equivalent. When a pharmaceutical company develops a new drug, it is issued a drug patent. Such patents, which are usually in effect for about 11 years, prevent anyone else from making or selling the patented drug, and protect the original developer. When the patent expires, other drug companies can start testing, manufacturing, and (after it is approved by the FDA) selling a generic version of the drug.

It is quite costly to produce a drug. Under the Drug Price Competition and Patent Term Restoration Act of 1984, also known as the Hatch-Waxman Act, generic drug companies do not have to repeat expensive clinical trials. Because generic drug makers do not develop a drug from origination, it costs less to market the drug; therefore, generic drugs are almost always less expensive than brand-name drugs. Generic drug makers must show that their product performs in the same way as the brand-name drug and is as safe and effective.

SELLING DRUGS TO HOSPITALS

A discussion about hospital pharmacies and the sale of drugs would not be complete without mention of the drug detail people, or pharmaceutical service representatives, employed by the major drug manufacturing companies. These individuals provide a valuable service, particularly to the physicians who order the drugs. The detail people assist the hospital pharmacists and physicians in purchasing and procuring quality drugs through analysis and selection, in addition to reinforcing the use of existing drugs. By providing market research and feedback on the pharmaceuticals, drug representatives can save the purchaser a great deal of time. Hospitals buy the vast majority of their drugs through group-purchasing, supply-chain arrangements that allow them to receive volume discounts, and some hospitals acquire drugs from the company that contracts to manage the pharmacy.

SECURITY OF DRUGS

Controlled substances present a problem for hospitals, and it must be remembered that the pharmacy is not the only storage area for narcotics. The emergency department, cardiac-catheterization lab, surgery, and even outpatient areas may contain narcotic cabinets. Too often, nurses, physicians, and other health professionals have substance-abuse problems and attempt to divert drugs for their own purpose. Conducting a thorough and accurate medication count with each shift change, coupled with random drug screenings, should help control this problem. Local, state, and federal laws (e.g., the Drug-Free Workplace Act of 1988) prohibit the unlawful use, possession, consumption, or distribution of illegal drugs or alcohol, and anyone found misappropriating drugs must be reported immediately to both law enforcement officials and the appropriate professional board. Because drug abuse is a potential security, safety, and health problem, most hospitals have some form of assistance program that offers counseling and support services for employees struggling with substance abuse.

QUALITY IMPROVEMENT

A hospital's quality improvement program for pharmaceutical services must establish policies and procedures for the preparation and distribution of drugs and parenteral products such as feeding formula. The pharmacist should be active in developing criteria and standards for the use of drugs in the hospital. Drug misuse needs to be identified and corrective measures need to be proposed.

One of the specific tasks of a quality-improvement program is to identify drug usage according to drug type. Statistics can indicate what percentages of patients are receiving certain types of drugs during hospitalization. Such a program can also be used to examine drug usage according to diagnosis. In the past, patient diagnoses were reviewed to determine whether any drugs were being used in the presence of a contraindicating medical problem (e.g., steroids used in the presence of a peptic ulcer). This procedure has largely been replaced by computer software that can spot contraindications and misuse of pharmacy products.

SUMMARY

In this chapter we have established the roles of the hospital pharmacy and pharmacist, and how critical they are to the success of a hospital. Pharmacists are experts in dispensing and compounding drugs, and can determine how certain medications will affect individual patients. The entire hospital healthcare team relies on the pharmacist to provide correct advice on drug selection, administration, and levels of dosage. New developments in the drug distribution system, such as the use of wireless tracking systems, tele-pharmacy, and robotic pharmacists, are increasing operational efficiency and decreasing preparation times and distribution errors.

CHAPTER REVIEW

1. Name some of the responsibilities of a pharmacist.
2. What is drug compounding?
3. Define telepharmacy.
4. What is the function of the P&T committee?
5. What are the five rights of medications?
6. What are some different ways of dispensing drugs to inpatients?
7. Why do hospital personnel count controlled substances at every shift change?
8. What is the Hatch-Waxman Act and why is it important?

REFERENCES

National Coordinating Council for Medication Error Reporting and Prevention. (n.d.). *About Medication Errors.* Retrieved September 9, 2010, from http://www.nccmerp.org/aboutMedErrors.html

Part VI

Patient Support Services

CHAPTER 15

Hospital Essentials

Tondra Moore

KEY TERMS

Receptionist
Telecommunications
    department
Codes
Dietary services

Pastoral services
Patient transportation
Interpreters
Volunteers

INTRODUCTION

As the healthcare industry is becoming more consumer-oriented, hospitals are increasingly focusing on customer satisfaction levels and the quality of service provided. This paradigm shift has caused many facilities to take another look at their patient-support departments and their functions. In many instances, hospitals have strategically integrated patient-support services into their plans for improving the quality of care. Patient-support staff are typically frontline employees for an organization and play a vital role in engendering a positive relationship between the patient and the hospital.

RECEPTION

Typically, when patients first enter the hospital (unless they are admitted through the emergency department), their first contact is with the receptionist. The **receptionist** often acts as a gatekeeper to the facility. As the gatekeeper, this individual plays a crucial role in either establishing or sabotaging a rapport between the patient and the organization. Yes, I did mention sabotage. If the receptionist for the hospital is unfriendly or unprofessional, the patient may perceive that this attitude will be pervasive throughout the hospital. Therefore, it is vital for the receptionist to embody the mission and values of the organization, and for hospitals to use great care in hiring individuals for this position.

The role of the receptionist is twofold: he or she must provide clear, concise directions to all visitors and patients, and give all visitors and patients a positive first impression of the hospital. Although the latter may seem trivial to some, remember that an organization has only one opportunity to make a positive first impression. This first impression can influence a patient's decision to continue care in the facility or refer others to it, and what level of satisfaction will be reported based on the services rendered. In the United States, the role of the receptionist is often overlooked, and individuals in this position are not provided the proper training commensurate with their importance in the patient-care continuum. In fact, very little research has been conducted on the role of the receptionist within the hospital. It should be standard practice for this individual to be monitored by hospital management to ensure that the organization is being properly represented.

Typically, the primary mission of the receptionist is to provide excellent customer service to patients and visitors to the hospital. As the gatekeeper, this individual is also responsible for maintaining up-to-date information in order to properly direct patients or visitors. The receptionist may also serve as the first line of defense against acts of violence or situations involving imminent danger. Because the receptionist area is usually located at the main entrance of the hospital, the receptionist must be vigilant and aware of anyone who is entering the building—not only to greet them, but also to alert the security staff in case of danger. This is not to imply that the receptionist carries any legal liability if he or she fails to screen someone properly; it is simply to emphasize that the receptionist should be alert and vigilant. The role of the receptionist will become even more important as organizations expand in terms of both size and the number of services provided. With so many organizations expanding and having multiple points of entry, some facilities may require more staff to fill receptionist positions.

The job of receptionist is an entry-level position at most hospitals and typically requires no licensure or certification. Many facilities consider a high school diploma or equivalent adequate education for this position. For most organizations, this standard is acceptable; however, in some facilities, the receptionist might be required to conduct some emergency department triage or facilitate patient load distribution, in which case a minimal level of health-related education is required for the position. This education may be offered as in-service training, as there are currently no formal training programs for receptionists. Considering that the patient satisfaction score is used as a measure of quality of care, it is important for receptionists to be included in any hospital's strategic plan for improvement. Therefore, although the current standards are minimal, the industry may begin to require more training and a higher base of education for this position.

Some hospital administrators may overlook the role of the receptionist; however, they should remember that in today's consumer-driven market, no employee should be undervalued—especially those who have a high level of patient impact.

TELECOMMUNICATIONS

The **telecommunications department's** role is closely related to that of the receptionist in that it is the first point of contact for people calling the hospital. The telecommunications department varies in size according to the size of the facility; however, regardless of size, it plays a vital role. This department usually manages a large and intricate switchboard that connects callers to the hospital departments, offices, physicians, staff, and patient rooms. It is important to ensure that callers are properly routed and the process is as seamless as possible, since communication plays a vital role in the quality of care received by patients.

Another duty of the telecommunications department is to broadcast codes that alert the physicians and staff about various events. These **codes** may be related to the status of a patient, imminent danger, or any matter that requires immediate attention. The telecommunications office broadcasts these codes and typically maintains the official hospital record. As these codes are relied upon to provide a timely response, this function of the telecommunications office is also intricately woven into the patient care continuum. The department may also be responsible for contacting physicians regarding emergent patient needs. Because this could be a matter of life or death for the patient, it is imperative to handle such calls in an efficient and professional manner.

Despite its importance to the organization, the skills and education required to join the telecommunications department are typically similar to those of a receptionist. This position is considered an entry-level one and does not require much advanced education or training. However, just as with the receptionists, this may change as the consumer-driven aspect of health care becomes more pervasive. Therefore, it is important to be aware of the operations that occur within this department.

DIETARY SERVICES

The **dietary services** department is vitally important in facilities that provide inpatient care, because it is primarily responsible for planning and providing the nutritional components of a patient-care plan. Because dietary requirements can seriously affect the condition of a patient, it is necessary for a highly trained individual to oversee this process. In hospitals, registered dieticians are responsible for this task. However, since this department also usually offers additional services to the staff, as well as patients' families and friends, additional staff members are often required. Today, as dietary services increase their efforts to deliver meals that are not only nutritionally sound but also palatable, the need for additional staff will continue to expand.

As mentioned previously, a registered dietician plans the meals and ensures that the nutritional needs of the patients are being met. However, the dietary-services department may also include chefs, cooks, and servers. Depending on the type of facility, there may be several registered dieticians or chefs on staff. The composition of the staff usually reflects the size of the hospital and the services it offers; for example, a hospital with a cafeteria must have more servers on staff. However, since the patients' nutritional needs are dictated by science, their basic nutritional needs must be met regardless of the type of facility or the qualifications of the staff.

The educational and training requirements of the staff vary according to their position within this department. Registered dieticians must maintain licensure, which requires at minimum a bachelor's degree and successful completion of a national test. Chefs or cooks may have formal culinary training, but depending on the type of facility, usually only a high school diploma or equivalent, along with some experience, is required. Servers are typically only required to have a high school diploma or equivalent. However, all staff must receive training in food handling and safety. Although there is no uniform training program for this department, there are several industry-accepted training courses that can be conducted in-house or online. The specific level of training is not mandated by any accrediting or licensure organization; however, some degree of training is required.

It is important to note that this department is usually inspected by the local or state health department to ensure that the hospital is conforming to all relevant codes and ordinances. Because the failure to meet proper standards could be costly to the organization, most hospital dietary-services departments are very vigilant. In addition to local inspections, the department must also comply with standards established by the accrediting body. These standards apply to any dietary service provided throughout the facility. In other words, the dietary staff is responsible for ensuring that any nutrition delivered to the patients by nondietary staff in the units is properly maintained according to the standards.

Because patients receiving inpatient care usually have no other means of meeting their daily nutritional needs, the dietary-services department plays an integral role in the care of the patients. The dietary-services department comes into contact with all patients admitted to the facility. Preparing nutritionally sound meals for the entire census of patients, as well as those with special dietary needs, is a great feat. The staff must not only know how to cook in mass quantities, they must also be able to prepare special meals (e.g., low-sodium, sugar-free, gluten-free, or liquid). This department must be well organized because meals are typically provided three times a day for inpatients and visitors, which means that as one meal is being served, another is being prepared.

The dietary-services department serves a vital function within the hospital because, regardless of the illness or injury involved, any patient who is admitted will come in contact with it and depend on it for basic sustenance.

PASTORAL SERVICES

The **pastoral services** department provides religious or spiritual guidance and counsel to patients and their families. Regardless of the type of hospital, pastoral services are provided. If the hospital has a religious affiliation, the services may be more heavily concentrated on that particular religion. Nevertheless, all facilities today aim to provide multidenominational pastoral services to any patient. The pastoral-services department is usually very small; however, if the hospital is affiliated with a particular religious institution, it may have a slightly larger department. According to the Bureau of Labor Statistics, in 2008, more than 10,500 clergy were employed by a health-related organization, and almost 6000 of these were employed in hospitals.

The mission of this department is to meet the spiritual and religious needs of the patients and their families. In the past, facilities often tried to employ clergy who could provide services to individuals with a specific religious affiliation. However, there has been a move toward providing hospital-based clergy who can perform multidenominational services. The clergy may be employed by the hospital or may offer their services on a volunteer basis. Their employment status is usually dependent on the type and size of the organization. They are usually required to be ordained in their particular religion, and may have to receive some training in counseling.

The pastoral-services department can play a vital role in caring for patients and their families. The need for services tends to increase as the severity of the patient's condition increases. Patients who are expected to expire, have been admitted as a result of an accident, or are about to undergo a risky procedure tend to have the most immediate need of pastoral services. Regardless of the severity of the illness or situation, though, all patients and family members can call upon this department in times of need. However, it may sometimes be difficult for a department with a small staff or volunteer clergy to meet their needs, and therefore many patients rely on their personal clergy for such services.

Pastoral services, especially staff clergy, also have a role in ensuring that the hospital staff is sensitive to the needs of religious patients and their families. For example, the pastoral-services department may conduct or participate in training sessions for hospital staff to address the religious requirements of patients currently admitted to the facility. This may include conducting research into religious requirements or restrictions, or securing an area for different religious groups to practice their religion. For instance, Muslim family members might be provided a place in which they can say their daily prayers. This does not mean that the hospital must construct any special religious edifices or accommodate religious needs that might endanger the patient.

Quite simply, the role of pastoral services is to provide the faith-based services needed by patients and their families. In difficult times, individuals often find solace in their religious beliefs or practices. Members of the pastoral-services department are dedicated to helping fulfill the needs of patients and their families in such critical moments.

PATIENT TRANSPORTATION SERVICES

The **patient transportation** services department provides several vital services for patients. Many patients who present in hospitals are immobilized or have impaired mobility. To reduce the number of potential injuries, hospitals employ special staff to ensure that such patients can travel throughout the facility. Faced with increasing liability and decreasing funds, however, hospitals are reluctant to offer any transportation services outside of the facility.

Because hospitals can be held financially responsible for injuries that occur within their facilities, most will employ a dedicated staff to transport patients throughout the facility when they need to undergo tests or procedures, and even when they are leaving the hospital. It is simply more cost-effective to have a dedicated staff making sure that all patients travel safely throughout and from the facility. Patients sometimes do not understand why they must use patient transportation services if they have full mobile capacity; however, it can quite simply be explained as an effort to increase patient safety. Because a slip-and-fall within a hospital is a very serious occurrence, the staff must make a concerted effort to reduce the likelihood of one occurring.

Staff members in this department are not required to possess any education beyond a high school diploma or its equivalent. Depending on the services offered by the facility, they may be required to have a state-issued driver's license and a clean driving record. Additional in-service training may be offered to instill and reinforce certain safety measures and procedures. For instance, if a patient is being transported to an area that has a large magnet or contains harmful radiation, it is imperative to educate the patient transporter about proper procedures within that area. Also, because patients are also transported for procedures and surgeries, the staff must receive formal in-service training regarding the proper protocols for establishing patient identity and adhering to patient privacy laws.

Although the importance of the patient transportation department may sometimes be overlooked, this department plays a valuable role in helping to shield the hospital from potential legal liabilities and ensuring good customer service in the continuum of patient care. The sight of patients wandering helplessly through a facility does not positively reflect upon the level of care provided by that facility. Therefore, it is imperative that professional staff be employed to ensure safe transportation for all patients throughout the hospital.

PATIENT REPRESENTATIVES

Patient representatives are dedicated to ensuring that patients know their rights within the hospital system, and that those rights are protected. These individuals make sure that patients understand consent forms, living wills, and power-of-attorney forms, and assist them in completing any necessary documents. Since practices vary among facilities, patient representatives must be well versed in the practices of the particular hospital where they are employed. This position is not as common as it used to be, as many of its tasks have been integrated into other departments.

Traditionally, the primary role of the patient representative was to preserve the rights of the patient. This was particularly important when the medical staff were not fully aware of the legal and ethical regulations that had been established to protect patients. Since these same regulations also serve to protect the hospital, resulting in more hospital staff education, the patient representative has become more of a patient advocate. This role becomes particularly important when the patient representative has to remind those making treatment decisions about the patients' documented wishes. As the result of laws such as Health Insurance Portability and Accountability Act (HIPAA), hospitals now educate and train their clinical staff about potential violations of laws and regulations in an effort to reduce liability, thereby decreasing the responsibilities of the patient advocate.

However, cases may still arise in which the patient's wishes are not being respected; in these cases, the patient representative serves as the voice of the patient.

INTERPRETERS

Patients with communication barriers, due to physical or language limitations, may also receive disparate care in the hospital system. With the population served by US hospitals becoming extremely diverse, it is important for all hospitals to establish a communication method for all patients and their providers. This is no small task, considering the variety of different languages spoken by patients presenting to the hospital. In an effort to shrink the communication divide, hospitals are increasingly providing interpreters.

Interpreters attempt to create a verbal communication bridge between the patient and the provider. In some areas of the United States, communication divide is large for patients who do not speak English, as many facilities are not able to recruit and retain multilingual staff. This issue is not as complex for hospitals that have the capacity to build a strong base of multilingual staff and hire adequate interpreter services. Nevertheless, it is a major concern if patients cannot effectively explain why they are presenting at the hospital, or describe the symptoms they are experiencing. To address this problem, some hospitals hire multilingual staff and/or interpreters, or pay for a telephone-based interpreting service. Although demand is increasing dramatically, interpreters are rarely employed full time in hospitals. The basic requirements for interpreters are to speak more than one language and have a high school diploma. With interpreters privately contracting with many facilities, the price and quality of their services vary and can be unpredictable. This also means that quality of care may be affected.

Nevertheless, interpreters are often the only recourse for patients who are unable to interact with their physician. When a patient is unable to communicate with the hospital staff, anxiety levels rise for both the patient and the provider. The patient may become agitated or frustrated because of the lack of relief. The provider may become aggravated by his or her inability to ascertain what should be done to give the patient relief. In these situations, interpreters provide an invaluable service to the hospital.

VOLUNTEER SERVICES

Although the patient-services department employs many different types of employees, hospitals also rely on unpaid **volunteers** to provide vital services for patients. The roles of these volunteers vary depending on the facility. In some facilities, volunteers have direct access to patients, whereas in others they may simply play a role in providing ancillary support to the hospital. Regardless of the manner in which the services are provided, the roles are equally important.

The variation in volunteers also reflects the different types of people volunteering. In the past, the typical image of a hospital volunteer was that of a candy striper. Today, volunteers provide a variety of services, including fund-raising and quality-improvement efforts. Sometimes their primary role is simply to give patients individual attention. Volunteerism is usually based on a personal desire to "give back" to an institution. This may be because a hospital has treated the volunteer or a family member. Sometimes volunteers become active because they want to support a particular type of facility, such as children's or cancer hospitals. Regardless of the genesis of their desire to volunteer, however, hospital volunteers usually provide much-needed compassion for patients, and help the hospital achieve positive customer satisfaction levels.

Because patient safety has been pushed to the forefront, many facilities have structured volunteer programs, ranging from student groups to church groups, to address this issue. These facilities often do a preliminary screening of the volunteers and conduct a minimal level of training to ensure that volunteers do not inadvertently endanger a patient or violate any patient rights. Because this is not a paid position, it is filled by a wide variety of individuals. This variety allows the needs of many different patients to be met when paid employees of the hospital are unable to meet those needs.

When patients interact with individuals they know are uncompensated for their time and efforts, they often feel a level of gratitude and appreciation that enhances their perception of the quality of care delivered by the facility. In turn, volunteers often report that they receive a great deal of satisfaction from volunteering and appreciation for their efforts. Any type of facility can benefit from volunteer services as long as it makes sure that the services are well organized and coordinated to ensure patient safety and satisfaction.

SUMMARY

Patient-support departments encompass many different areas, but they all focus on improving patient satisfaction and quality of care. All of these departments have direct patient contact and are involved in the patient care continuum. Their staff members must understand their role in providing the highest level of care to patients. Although patient-support staff may be some of the least-compensated employees in the hospital, they play an integral role in ensuring patient loyalty and securing patient safety. Without the members of the patient-services departments, hospitals would not be able to provide adequate inpatient care.

CHAPTER REVIEW

1. What hospital employee is typically the first point of contact for a patient? Why is this employee important for the image of the hospital?
2. What are "codes" in a hospital, and what department is responsible for broadcasting them?
3. Explain the function of dietary services.
4. Does a hospital dietician have to be registered or licensed? Why or why not?
5. What is the role of the pastoral-services department?
6. Why are hospitals reluctant to provide transportation services outside the facility?
7. How important are patient privacy laws in the transporting of patients?
8. What service is provided by a patient representative? Discuss patient's documented wishes and the role of the patient representative.
9. Discuss the importance of language interpreters in a hospital.
10. Why do volunteers need screening and training?

CHAPTER 16

The Social Services Department

Andrew T. Marks, Rosamaria Murillo, and Betsy Wisner

KEY TERMS

Medical social workers
Situational factors
Advocacy

"Person-in-environment"
  perspective
Case management
Patient empowerment

INTRODUCTION

The roots of the social services departments found in healthcare facilities today can be traced to almshouses in the 1700s. Social services departments as we know them now formally began in 1905, and their initial development is attributed to Dr. Richard Cabot of Massachusetts General Hospital. Cabot believed that a patient's personal difficulties are often part of the cause, as opposed to the result, of their medical illness (Dziegielewski, 2004; Griffin, 2006; Hubschman, 1983). By addressing these difficulties, the social service worker can help ensure that the patient receives the appropriate medical care. Modeled on the "friendly visitor" approach to client care, the first **medical social workers** typically were trained as nurses whose primary role was to be sympathetic to the plight of their patients. In 1907, Ida

191

Cannon became the first medical social worker hired by Dr. Cabot (Hubschman). Cannon was a nurse by training and had studied psychology and sociology, which gave her insight into both the medical and psychosocial issues of her patients. Dr. Cabot envisioned the role of the social services worker as (1) reporting to the physician about domestic and social conditions faced by patients, (2) helping patients to comply with their doctors' orders, and (3) providing a link between the hospital and community resources and organizations (Hubschman).

The development of formal specialized training in social work at the School of Philanthropy in New York City in 1898 and the creation of the American Association of Hospital Social Workers in 1918 formalized the role of the social services department and the medical social worker in medical settings (Dziegielewski, 2004). In most healthcare settings, including hospitals, social workers are integral members of the treatment team and work with all departments in the healthcare facility. In addition to the hospital setting, medical social workers also work in community health centers, outpatient clinics, long-term care facilities, and hospice.

THE SOCIAL SERVICES DEPARTMENT AND FUNCTIONS OF MEDICAL SOCIAL WORKERS

Although once the main role of the medical social worker was to report to the physician and assess medical compliance, today these workers are integral members of the healthcare team in hospitals and other healthcare settings. Depending on the type of facility or system, social work services may be requested by the medical team and/or by patients.

Hospitals and other healthcare settings often have a social work department. Within this system, medical social workers are supervised by a credentialed social worker, who often is the manager or director of the social work department. Some hospitals and healthcare facilities include the director of the social work department within the system's administrative team. In other hospital systems, the medical social worker may report to the heads of specific departments, such as the administrator of the psychiatry department. In smaller hospitals or healthcare centers, or in long-term care facilities, medical social workers may be the only social workers at the agency. In this case, the agency's administrator generally supervises the medical social workers.

The functions of medical social workers vary depending on the type of medical facility they are working in. In general, medical social workers serve as case managers, advocates, clinicians, consultants to multidisciplinary teams, and educators. In each of these categories, social workers perform a variety of tasks, as listed below:

Case Manager
- Assess and identify patient needs, and the services and resources available to address those needs.
- Work with patients and their families, physicians, and the interdisciplinary team to move the patient through the phases of care. This role may include discharge, transitional planning, and utilization of services.
- Determine patients' eligibility for financial assistance and other services or equipment.
- Inform patients about services available as part of discharge planning, and help them access these services.
- Act as a liaison among the patient, hospital, and community to coordinate services.

Advocate
- Advocate for patients/clients within different systems and levels.
- Ensure that patients are treated with dignity and respect, which helps them return to the highest possible level of self-care.
- Identify gaps in services and resources, and encourage the development of hospital or community resources or programs to meet the needs of patients.

Clinician
- Identify goals and objectives related to biopsychosocial, spiritual, cultural, financial, and **situational factors** that may impede rehabilitation or access to services.
- Assess for child or elderly abuse or neglect issues, and ensure mandatory reporting.
- Provide direct counseling to assist patients and/or their families in adjusting to loss, illness, the results of illness, and/or problems related to health interventions needed or received.
- Assess and treat the mental health and emotional status of patients, and assess the potential need for specialized hospitalization or treatment.

- Identify suicidal symptomology, substance abuse issues, and related need for either inpatient or outpatient services.

Consultant
- Consult with hospital staff to determine the utilization and appropriateness of social services.
- Participate in the utilization review process to ensure that appropriate resources and staff are being allocated for patient care and to meet hospital standards.
- Participate in hospital ethics committees and investigations regarding patient care.

Educator
- Inform the treatment team about patients' social or emotional conditions and the potential impact these factors might have on their successful recovery.
- Educate patients and families about wellness, improved health status, and prevention related to patient needs from the "person-in-environment" perspective.
- Assist patients in understanding their diagnosis and its implications, determining their adaptive needs, and addressing the resulting emotional impact of the diagnosis on the patients and/or families.
- Provide in-service training to other hospital departments, volunteers, students, and the community regarding the social work profession (Dziegielewski, 2004; Griffin, 2006; Scesny, 1991).

COMPLIANCE AND REGULATION ISSUES: LICENSURE, EDUCATION, AND TRAINING OF MEDICAL SOCIAL WORKERS

Licensure

Each state, as well as the District of Columbia, has its own requirements for licensure, certification, or registration for social work practice and professional titles (Bureau of Labor Statistics, 2010). Additionally, there is no specific, nationally recognized credential for medical social workers; therefore, social workers in hospitals and other healthcare settings are trained and regulated in the same manner as other social work professionals according to the laws of their particular state.

Common licenses held by medical social workers are the licensed baccalaureate social worker (LBSW) and licensed master social worker (LMSW). Each of these levels of licensure requires jurisdictional application and successful completion of a national examination. Clinical social service functions are typically provided by a licensed clinical social worker (LCSW) who has been licensed at the LMSW level for a certain period of time (generally 2 years) and has practiced under the supervision of an LCSW. To obtain this clinical credential, the social worker must pass an additional national examination. In addition, most licensure provisions require continuing education as part of the renewal process to ensure continued competency to practice social work. Social work licensing is an important issue because, depending on the type of services rendered, insurance providers might require certification and/or licensing in order to reimburse for services rendered in a hospital setting.

Although no national medical social work credential is available at this time, there are several professional associations and organizations, such as the Society for Social Work Leadership in Healthcare (http://www.sswlhc.org/), that provide opportunities for social workers to participate in healthcare-specific social work, continuing education and training, and networking. In addition, the National Association of Social Workers (NASW) provides voluntary credentialing for medical social workers in select healthcare settings. In Texas, the Certified Social Worker in Health Care (C-SWHC) specialty credential acknowledges medical social workers who are NASW members, have met the licensing criteria, and have completed 3000 hours of postmaster's degree paid work experience under acceptable supervision. This credential is for members of the NASW who desire recognition for their professional efforts. No test or examination is required for this credential.

Education

Most medical social workers are educated at the graduate level and have received a master's degree in social work (MSW). Social services provided in the areas of trauma, renal disease, oncology, mental health assessment, and the emergency department require more advanced social work skills and abilities, indicating the need for master's level education training, licensure, and ongoing training in health, behavioral health, and healthcare policies and systems. Some baccalaureate level social workers (BSW) serve in areas such as discharge planning, rehabilitative services, bariatric procedures, patient education, and **advocacy**. Although licensure is specific to each jurisdiction, it typically reflects the formal education (master's or baccalaureate) received by the medical social worker at a university or through a program of social work recognized by the Council on Social Work Education (CSWE).

Training and Ongoing Professional Development

An important minimal competency expectation of medical social workers is to be informally educated through self-directed or continuing education activities regarding medical conditions, treatment modalities, and medical terminology. As part of the treatment team, medical social workers should be knowledgeable about a wide variety of general medical information and have a rudimentary understanding of medical terms and treatments. To be able to advocate effectively for patient care, medical social workers must be able to understand the medical terms used in patient charts and treatment team discussions and rounds. In addition, they must have sensitivity to and competency in issues regarding cultural diversity. Medical social workers are often required to be knowledgeable about cultural implications and how they can influence treatment, and to be able to discuss such issues in an informed manner with the healthcare team and patients.

SOCIAL SERVICES AND PATIENT CARE

Medical social workers approach patients with the "**person-in-environment**" **perspective**. This means that they view patients as part of an environmental system that encompasses all relationships and influences concerning the individual and his or her physical and social environment.

According to Zimmerman and Dabelko (2007), medical treatment facilities have traditionally made a distinction between curing and caring. Curing encompasses efforts made to correct an underlying medical condition. In contrast, caring refers to the act of providing supportive assistance to (1) promote healthy growth and development, (2) sustain function, (3) relieve distress over a temporary problem, and (4) maximize comfort and function when a problem is permanent or even terminal (Zimmerman & Dabelko).

In the continuum of patient care, members of the medical staff, such as physicians and nurses, focus primarily on the physical requirements for improvement, whereas medical social workers focus more on the social and emotional needs of the patients and/or their families in relation to the medical condition. This symbiosis between the medical and social services teams gives patients a greater opportunity to become better informed consumers of medical care and more involved participants in the treatment process. As patients and their families become more informed consumers of health care, through the use of the Internet and other media, members of the treatment team must be prepared to work together to ensure that they can offer a holistic view of treatment.

SUMMARY

The model of social services in hospitals and other healthcare facilities has transformed, over the past several hundred years, from an emphasis on patients' needs in the healthcare setting to a patient-focused model in which medical social workers serve as integral members of healthcare teams designed to provide efficient, competent, and ethical medical services to patients. The contemporary distinction between curing and caring helps to orient the social worker toward providing patient opportunities for a continuum of care ranging from healthy growth to appropriate palliative care.

As licensed professionals, medical social workers are likely to have master's degrees, are expected to engage in professional development, and may work toward specialty certification. Highly trained social workers can partner with other professionals to provide comprehensive patient care.

The particular roles of medical social workers vary according to the unique settings in which they work; however, they generally include **case management**, advocacy, clinical, consultation, and educational services. In each of these roles, the social worker's goal is to **empower patients**, provide quality patient services, and ensure that patients' health, psychological, social, and spiritual needs are being met.

Clearly, the roles and opportunities for medical social workers will continue to evolve as our healthcare systems continue to change. However, one thing is certain: Medical social workers will continue to offer crucial services to patients in a variety of settings.

CHAPTER REVIEW

1. What was an initial motivation for implementing the medical social services department?
2. What was the original model of the social services department?
3. What are the educational and licensure requirements for medical social workers?

4. Describe the five major functions of today's medical social worker.
5. How are social work departments organized in medical facilities today?
6. Describe the difference between curing and caring.
7. The first medical social workers were trained as:
    a. Psychologists
    b. Social workers
    c. Nurses
    d. None of the above
8. Initially, the tasks of medical social workers included:
    a. Advocating for patients
    b. Educating and linking patients to services
    c. Informing the doctor about the patient's psychological status and providing therapy
    d. Informing the physician about the domestic and social conditions faced by patients, and helping patients to comply with their doctors' orders
9. In most of today's medical facilities, social workers:
    a. Work across all departments and are an integral part of interdisciplinary teams
    b. Work in the social services and psychology departments
    c. Educate physicians about community resources
    d. Develop healthcare policy
10. Medical social workers may be supervised by:
    a. Credentialed social workers
    b. The director of the social work department
    c. Heads of specific departments or administrators
    d. All of the above

REFERENCES

Bureau of Labor Statistics, 2010. U.S. Department of Labor. (2010). *Occupational outlook handbook 2010–2011*. Retrieved February 22, 2010, from http://www.bls.gov/oco/ocos060.htm

Dziegielewski, S. F. (2004). *The changing face of health care social work*. New York: Springer

Griffin, D. (2006). *Hospitals: What they are and how they work*. Sudbury, MA: Jones and Bartlett.

Hubschman, L. (1983). *Hospital social work practice*. New York: Praeger Publishers.

Scesny, A. M. (1991). *Essentials for directors of social work programs in health care.* Chicago, IL: American Hospital Association.

Zimmerman, J., & Dabelko, H. I. (2007). Collaborative models of patient care: New opportunities for hospital social workers. *Social Work in Health Care, 44,* 33–47.

SUGGESTED READINGS

Auerbach, C., Mason, S. E., & LaPorte, H. H. (2007). Evidence that supports the value of social work in hospitals. *Social Work in Health Care, 44,* 17–32.

Carlton, T. O., Falck, H. S., & Berkman, B. (1985). The use of theoretical constructs and research data to establish a base for clinical social work in health settings. *Social Work in Health Care, 10,* 27–40.

Chung, W., Edgar-Smith S., Palmer, R. B., Bartholomew, E., & Delambo, D. (2008). Psychiatric rehospitalization of children and adolescents: Implications for social work intervention. *Child & Adolescent Social Work Journal, 25,* 483–496.

Craig, R. W. (2007). A day in the life of a hospital social worker: Presenting our role through the personal narrative. *Qualitative Social Work, 6,* 431–446.

Fadiman, A. (1997). *The spirit catches you and you fall down.* New York: Farrar, Straus and Giroux.

Farmer, P. (2005). *Pathologies of power.* Berkeley, CA: University of California Press.

Giles, R., Hart, C., & Swancott, J. (2007). Clinical priorities: Strengthening social work practice in health. *Australian Social Work, 60,* 147–165.

Mason, S. E., & Auerbach, C. (2009). Factors related to admissions to a psychiatry unit from a medical emergency room: The role of social work. *Social Work in Mental Health, 7,* 429–441.

Mizrahi, T., & Berger, C. S. (2005). A longitudinal look at social work leadership in hospitals: The impact of a changing health care system. *Health & Social Work, 30,* 155–165.

Palusci, V. J., Cox, E. O., Shatz, E. M., & Schultze, J. M. (2006). Urgent medical assessment after child sexual abuse. *Child Abuse & Neglect, 30,* 367–380.

Praglin, L. J. (2007). Ida Cannon, Ethel Cohen, and early medical social work in Boston: The foundations of a model of culturally competent social service. *Social Service Review, 81,* 27–45.

Schneiderman, J. U., Waugaman, W. R., & Flynn, M. S. (2008). Nurse social work practitioner: A new professional for health care settings. *Health & Social Work, 33,* 149–154.

CHAPTER 17

Health Information Management

Susan H. Fenton, Tiankai Wang, Jacqueline Moczygemba, Danette Myers, and Sue Biedermann

KEY TERMS

Storage of information
Health information
   management (HIM)
Clinical Modification
Patient record
Record ownership

Custodian of records
Health Insurance Portability and
   Accountability Act (HIPAA)
Average length of stay
Discharge summary
Confidentiality

INTRODUCTION

Information plays a vital role in today's healthcare systems. According to Dr. Daniel Masys of Vanderbilt Medical Center, "From a business-process viewpoint, the health care industry performs only two kinds of actions: medical procedures . . . and the acquisition, use, communication, and **storage of information**" (Masys, 2002). The department that is generally responsible for maintaining patient information in an efficient, legal, and confidential manner is the **health information management (HIM)** department.

Traditionally, paper or manual records (or charts) have been the standard, and in some places, they remain so today. However, the American Recovery and Reinvestment Act (ARRA) of 2009 mandated rewards for providers and hospitals that can demonstrate "meaningful use" of an electronic health record (EHR). It also stipulated penalties for hospitals and providers that have not demonstrated this capability by 2015 (US Government, 2009). The use of EHRs is anticipated to accelerate rapidly over the next several years, with paper records becoming obsolete.

In addition, on October 1, 2013, the US healthcare industry will begin to use the International Classification of Diseases, 10th edition, **Clinical Modification** (ICD-10-CM) for all diagnostic coding. This change will impact all healthcare providers, payers, researchers, and others who are currently using ICD-9-CM data.

HIM departments are undergoing tectonic shifts that promise to ripple throughout the entire healthcare industry.

PURPOSE OF THE PATIENT RECORD

The main purpose of maintaining a **patient record** is to document the course of the patient's illness and treatment. However, patient care is not the only focus. In addition, patient records are used to:

- support clinical decision making and communication among clinicians;
- document the services provided to patients in support of reimbursement;
- provide information to evaluate the quality and efficacy of care delivered;
- provide information in support of medical research and education;
- facilitate the operational management of the organization; and
- provide information as required by local, state, and national laws (Reynolds & Bowman, 2010)

Content of the Patient Record

Although the content of the patient record can vary among providers, both inpatient and outpatient records usually include the following information:

Patient demographics (name, address, phone number, date of birth, etc.)
History and physical reports

- Clinician notes (physician or nurse)
- Laboratory tests
- X-rays and scans

- Procedure or operative notes
- Discharge summary (usually only for inpatients)

The Joint Commission, the Centers for Medicare and Medicaid Services (CMS), and state governments all promulgate standards and requirements for maintaining patient record content. For example, these standards require the discharge summary to be dictated within 24 hours after a patient is discharged from the hospital. Providers (especially physicians) who do not comply with these standards can lose their admitting privileges at the hospital. A provider who regularly fails to comply with documentation requirements can even be sanctioned by licensing or other regulatory boards.

Patient *Record Ownership*

Hospitals often refer to the patient health records as "their" records. Although hospitals do create and maintain the patient record, and are responsible for keeping it confidential, technically they do not "own" the record. It is a generally accepted legal tenet that the information in the patient health record actually belongs to the person it is about—the patient. The hospital actually only owns the medium (e.g., paper or computer drive) that contains the patient record.

The Patient Record as a Legal Document

The patient record is a hospital business record. This means that it is a legal document created according to hospital policies and procedures during the course of care. Hospital patient records can be used in various types of legal proceedings, including medical malpractice suits against the hospital or other providers, civil suits involving the injury of a person subsequently treated by hospital, and criminal cases such as driving under the influence. Usually the director of the HIM department, or another supervisor in the department, serves as the hospital's designated **custodian of records**. This person is responsible for receiving and responding to all subpoenas duces tecum, deposition requests, and court orders for patient health records. If asked to testify in court, the custodian of records only offers testimony regarding the hospital's policies and procedures for creating and maintaining patient records, as well as the extent to which the requested records were created and maintained in compliance with those policies and procedures. The custodian of records is not qualified to testify about the care that is documented in the record, and should never do so. The custodian of records often works very closely with the hospital risk manager and attorney when records are subpoenaed or ordered for a court case.

It is important for organizations to determine the contents of their patient records for legal purposes in accordance with their policies and procedures. This is termed the designated standards organization (DSO) and is required by the **Health Insurance Portability and Accountability Act (HIPAA)** of 1996 (US Government, 1996). With the advent of email and other electronic forms of communication, in addition to internal hospital communications, quality-assurance documents (e.g., incident reports and medical staff peer reviews), and other operational management documents, it can sometimes be difficult to ascertain which information belongs in the patient record and which does not when the facility has not determined the DSO. Documents that are included in the DSO can more easily be obtained (or discovered) and admitted into evidence in civil and criminal court cases. Records of a more sensitive nature, such as incident reports, are sometimes sought by parties in a court case; however, the hospital attorney may try to prevent their admission as evidence on the grounds that they are not routinely used in the delivery of care to patients.

As a legal document, the patient record is regulated on both federal and state levels. It is important for the custodian of records to be familiar with all such laws and regulations that are applicable to his or her facility.

PRIVACY, CONFIDENTIALITY, AND SECURITY

Healthcare providers must ensure that a patient's medical information remains private and secure. In this case, "private" means that the patient has the right to designate who can have access to the information, and "secure" means that the information is safe from unauthorized or accidental alteration or destruction. Patients share their private health information with providers believing that it will remain confidential.

Although there is no constitutional right to privacy, HIPAA did establish minimal privacy and security requirements for healthcare providers, insurers, and claims clearinghouses that handle protected health information (PHI). These organizations are called covered entities (CEs). PHI includes all information that can be found or accessed via data elements that might identify an individual. CEs and any business that works with or for a CE (a business associate (BA)) is required to keep PHI confidential. They may use PHI for treatment, payment for services, or treatment payment and operations (TPO). Patients seeking treatment must first be given a notice of privacy practices, and they must sign a form acknowledging that they received the notice. Generally, any disclosure of patient information must be authorized by the patient. Employees, volunteers, students, and others who work with or for CEs and BAs are required to undergo annual training regarding PHI privacy and security requirements.

In 2009, ARRA updated HIPAA to incorporate the technological shifts that have occurred in the 13 years since the original law was enacted. ARRA includes provisions that make BAs subject to the same requirements and penalties as CEs, and new requirements for breach notification. A breach is the unauthorized acquisition, access, use, or disclosure of PHI that might compromise the security or privacy of such information, except where an unauthorized person to whom such information is disclosed would not reasonably have been able to retain such information. The advent of computerized patient databases and EHRs has brought an increase in breaches. Breaches must be reported to the Department of Health and Human Services regularly. Breaches involving the information of 500 or more persons must be reported immediately and must be publicized in the media so that people can know whether their information is at risk. ARRA also established new security regulations that require CEs and BAs to use specific methods and technologies to secure PHI. These regulations will now be updated on an annual basis, requiring organizations to have an annual update process.

Many states also have laws addressing health information privacy and security. When the state law ensures greater privacy protections or gives individuals better access to their information than HIPAA, the state law has precedence. Conversely, when HIPAA ensures greater privacy protections or greater individual access than state law, HIPAA has precedence. The increasing electronic sharing of data among organizations and across the nation has highlighted the many differences in state health information privacy and security laws and regulations. A national project, known as the Health Information Security and Privacy Collaboration (HISPC), has compiled information on these differences and is working on reconciling them (Dimitropoulos, 2007).

HIM and information technology personnel must stay abreast of federal and state laws regarding health information privacy and security to ensure that their organizations are in compliance.

THE HIM DEPARTMENT

The size, staffing, and organization of the HIM department can vary widely depending on the healthcare organization's purpose and size. Regardless of the number of employees, however, most HIM departments support the following functions:

- Maintaining the master patient index (MPI)
- Hospital statistics reporting
- Transcription
- Abstracting
- Coding
- Patient record completion
- Release of information
- Patient record storage and archiving

Each of these functions will be discussed in greater detail in the following sections.

Master Patient Index

The MPI is the means by which the hospital establishes one permanent record for each patient treated. The MPI usually includes the patient's name, date of birth, gender, Social Security number, and patient record number, as well as other relevant information.

When a person is admitted to the hospital for care, admissions personnel will try to access that person's MPI. If the person was previously treated in that hospital, his or her information will be stored under the same patient record number so that previous records can be easily accessed by clinicians and others for continuity of care.

The correct identification of patients is very important for the quality of care. If the MPI is not correctly maintained, a patient with a severe drug allergy and a name similar to that of another patient with no such allergy could potentially receive a life-threatening dose of medication. The HIM department must regularly check the MPI for duplicate records and perform other procedures to ensure that it is maintained in a quality fashion.

Hospital Statistics Reporting

All hospitals must maintain and report administrative, clinical activity, and public health statistics. The HIM department is usually responsible for maintaining and reporting these statistics for various internal and external purposes, as summarized below.

Standard administrative acute-care statistics:

- Inpatient census—a list of all persons occupying a hospital bed at a certain time each day. The hospital census is usually conducted every day at midnight.
- Inpatient bed occupancy rate—the percentage of official hospital beds that are occupied by hospital inpatients for a given period of time.
- Bed turnover rate—the number of times each hospital bed changes occupants over a period of time; used to measure hospital utilization.
- **Average length of stay**—the mean number of days a patient stays in the hospital. It is calculated by totaling all of the patient lengths of stays (in days) and dividing the total by the number of patients discharged. It is also used as a measure of hospital utilization.

Standard clinical acute-care statistics:

- Hospital death or mortality rate—the number of patients who die in the hospital.
- Hospital acquired infection (HAI) rate, or nosocomial infection rate—the number of infections identified as having begun while the patient was in the hospital divided by the total number of discharges from the hospital; used as an indicator of care quality.
- Postoperative infection rate—the percentage of patients who acquired an infection as the result of a surgical procedure.

Standard public health statistics that must be reported to federal, state, and local authorities include births, deaths, and certain infectious diseases (e.g., HIV and tuberculosis).

The reporting of hospital statistics has been made easier with the widespread use of computers in hospitals. However, HIM departments will make it a policy to check the statistical computations, especially when software used in the hospital is upgraded.

Patient Record Completion

The HIM department is tasked with ensuring the completeness and accuracy of the patient health record. This is accomplished through a variety of activities, including the transcribing and editing of various clinical reports, and incomplete-record control.

In an effort to document patient care efficiently and accurately, many physicians will choose to dictate certain reports, including the history and physical report, operative report, and **discharge summary**. This is usually done via a dictation system maintained by the HIM department or via voice recognition (VR) software.

If the traditional dictation system is used, HIM will be responsible for ensuring that the documents are accurately typed or transcribed and placed into the record. The transcription can be done by hospital employees or, as if often the case, outsourced to a contract transcription company. In either case, all dictated documents must be carefully tracked to ensure they are typed and placed into the correct patient health record in a timely fashion. Copies of these documents are also often sent to the physician's office or to a consulting or referring physician.

Hospitals that use the newer VR software also often employ transcriptionists as document editors. This is done to ensure that the software has correctly understood not only the sound but also the context of the dictated words. For example, it is not uncommon for VR software to confuse words such as "won" and "one."

Incomplete-record control is a very important HIM function. The custodian of records can use this process to determine whether the patient health record is being maintained in accordance with hospital policies and procedures. For both electronic and manual systems, the process generally occurs as follows:

1. The patient record is delivered to the HIM department when the patient is discharged from the hospital.
2. A discharge analyst clerk will check the patient record for completeness, using criteria specified in hospital and medical staff policies and procedures.
3. Missing or incomplete components will be noted and the responsible clinician notified; examples include a missing discharge summary from the attending physician, a missing surgical report from the surgeon, and nurses' notes that are not signed.

4. The clinicians will be notified regularly until the components are completed.

Incomplete-record reports are delivered to medical staff and administration leaders on a regular basis. Clinicians who do not complete their records, especially habitual offenders, may be sanctioned by the facility, licensing boards, or other professional organizations. Accrediting and other regulatory organizations often review the accuracy and completeness of patient records. Given the importance of patient information for health care and other functions, complete and accurate patient records are considered to be a reflection of the quality of care provided by the hospital.

Abstracting and Coding

The functions of coding and abstracting are generally performed together, although in some larger hospitals they are considered separate processes. Abstracting is the process of compiling pertinent information extracted from the patient record and entering it into a computerized data set. Abstracting is done to facilitate hospital data reporting.

Coding involves the assignment of ICD-9-CM (soon to be ICD-10-CM) or current procedural terminology (CPT) codes to diagnoses and procedures, though other classifications can be utilized. The 1996 HIPAA law designates the code sets and guidelines that must be used in the United States. Historically, coding was primarily used to indicate the cause of death on death certificates. However, coding is now also used to facilitate claims submitted for reimbursement from third-party insurance and other payers, quality measurements, research, and the design of healthcare and reimbursement policies.

Coders are HIM professionals who have the experience and training to accurately assign the required codes according to government and payer guidelines. The American Health Information Management Association and the American Academy of Professional Coders administer coder credentialing programs, and individuals who have been credentialed by these organizations must also adhere to their ethical guidelines for coding practice.

Failure to accurately assign codes can have extremely negative consequences for hospitals and their administrative leaders. The Department of Justice can bring charges of fraud and/or abuse if it can be determined that incorrect codes were assigned with the intention to deceive or misrepresent the care delivered, with the knowledge that the deception could result in additional reimbursement or other unearned benefit. The CMS and other third-party payers regularly monitor and data-mine their claims databases in an effort to minimize fraud and abuse.

The processes of coding and abstracting give structure to otherwise unstructured or free text healthcare data, enabling the data to be utilized for a wide variety of purposes.

Release of Information

The HIM staff is responsible for ensuring that all laws and regulations are followed when a patient's record or copies of that record are released to anyone for any purpose. This requires a thorough understanding of the HIPAA rules and regulations, as well as any applicable state privacy laws and regulations.

The release-of-information process usually begins with the receipt of a request for copies of the patient record from the patient, a payer, a provider, or another individual who wants the information for some purpose. HIM personnel must review each request to determine whether the requestor has the right to receive the PHI being requested, which information is actually required, and whether all required authorizations are present. The hospital custodian of records often supervises the release of information. Release-of-information procedures are meant to protect patients' privacy and the **confidentiality** of patient–provider communications.

PATIENT RECORD STORAGE AND ARCHIVING

The HIM department is responsible for establishing control measures to ensure that patient records can be located efficiently, are maintained for the required retention periods, and can only be accessed by authorized individuals.

Active or current paper patient records are maintained in file rooms. These large storage rooms are often located in the basement or on the ground floor of the hospital due to the enormous weight of the records. Records are filed according to a medical record numbering system. Clerks receive requests for medical records from all over the hospital. When the records are pulled from the shelf, an outguide is used to mark the place of the record and the department that requested the record. Records should always be stored in a secure location to limit access to PHI. Hospitals often do not have adequate storage room for all of their patient records. Files that are inactive but cannot be destroyed yet, in accordance with state record retention laws, can be scanned to computer disks or stored in off-site long-term storage facilities.

Active EHRs are stored on readily accessible, high-capacity disk drives. The continuing decrease in the cost of electronic storage combined with the ever-increasing demand for data make it likely that EHRs will remain in accessible computer storage past the time required by state regulations. The use of EHRs is tracked by means of computerized audit logs. Whenever an EHR is created, accessed or viewed, modified, deleted, or printed, that activity is recorded in the audit log. Often a hospital will assign the responsibility for monitoring audit logs to a particular staff member or members. Suspicious or illegal activity can result in disciplinary action.

States enact record retention laws to ensure that patients who believe they have harmed by a healthcare provider have adequate time to file a claim and access information to back up that claim. For example, some states require adult patient records to be maintained for 10 years from the last date of activity, and records of minors to be maintained for 10 years from the last date of activity or to the age of majority plus an additional 2 years, whichever is greater.

Safe, secure, and accessible information is necessary for the delivery of high-quality longitudinal patient care.

SUMMARY

The HIM department is responsible for ensuring that the right patient information is available to the right provider at the right time, in compliance with all applicable laws, rules, and regulations.

CHAPTER REVIEW

1. What is the purpose of the American Recovery and Reinvestment Act (ARRA) of 2009 as it applies to hospitals?
2. What is the main purpose of maintaining a patient record? List additional purposes.
3. What are some data that may be included in patient records?
4. Explain the patient record as a legal document.

5. Why must a medical provider secure patient authorization prior to releasing any information?
6. Discuss HIPAA and its importance.
7. What are some functions of the HIM department?
8. List some standard administrative acute-care statistics.
9. What is the purpose of coding?

REFERENCES

Dimitropoulos, L. (2007). *Privacy and security solutions for interoperable health information exchange: Nationwide summary.* Retrieved April 4, 2009, from http://www.rti.org/pubs/nationwide_execsumm.pdf

Masys, D. R. (2002). Effects of current and future information technologies on the health care workforce. *Health Affairs, 21,* 33–41.

Reynolds, R., & Bowman, E. (2010). Paper-based and hybrid health records. In K. M. LaTour & S. E. Maki, *Health information management: Concepts, principles, and practice* (3rd ed., pp. 189–228). Chicago, IL: AHIMA.

US Government. (1996). *Health Insurance Portability and Accountability Act of 1996.* Public Law 104-191.45 CFR 164.514(a).

US Government. (2009). *American Recovery and Reinvestment Act of 2009.* Retrieved March 2, 2009, from http://frwebgate.access.gpo.gov/cgi-bin/getdoc.cgi?dbname5111_cong_bills&docid5f:h1enr.pdf

Part VII

Facilities Support and Security

Supporting the Medical Center—Materials Management, Environmental Services, Laundry, Maintenance, Parking, Biomedical Engineering, and Contract Services

Donald J. Griffin

KEY TERMS

Centralized purchasing
Group purchasing
Centralized requisitions
Par levels
Environmental services

Sanitation specialist
Executive housekeeper
Infectious waste
Laundry manager
Maintenance

> Preventive maintenance
> Work order
> Power plant
> Biomedical engineering
>
> Biomedical equipment
> specialists
> Contract services

INTRODUCTION

This chapter will examine the departments of materials management, environmental services (housekeeping), laundry, maintenance, plant engineering, parking, biomedical engineering, and contract services.

MATERIALS MANAGEMENT DEPARTMENT

Materials management is the management and control of goods and supplies, services, and equipment from acquisition to disposition. It involves the centralization of procurement, processing, inventory control, receiving, and distribution. Effective materials management ensures that quality goods, services, and equipment are obtained at the lowest costs, and that inventories are monitored and controlled.

Purchasing Section

The hospital purchasing section or department is usually under the direction of a purchasing agent or a materials manager. The purchasing agent has to determine what, when, and how much to purchase for hospital inventories, and to seek out appropriate vendors for supplies. A key objective is to acquire quality products at the lowest price possible, and the purchasing agent must negotiate or evaluate bids to achieve this objective.

Before suitable bids can be obtained, the specifications for each product must be established, preferably in writing. One of the side benefits a hospital realizes from competitive bidding is that the purchasing agent and department heads requesting an item have to give more thought to the item, its usage, and the standards they require for the item. When the price of an item is used as the main determinant, issues involving service and the cost of service contracts can arise. If the product needs repair, the purchasing agent must demand that the sales and service representatives for the vendor arrive quickly to repair the equipment or come in to discuss the product and its characteristics with the users. Service is a factor that must be weighed along with price in competitive bidding. Competitive bids surely can be successful economic tools for the purchasing department and the hospital.

Centralized Purchasing

It is believed that **centralized purchasing** can lead to efficient operations and cost containment in hospitals. Purchasing for the entire hospital is handled by a single purchasing department, resulting in savings through consolidation of departmental needs and a reduction in the number of employees involved in the process. Further, centralized purchasing provides the means for strengthening the purchasing department and establishing clear purchasing policies.

Shared Purchasing

The concept of shared purchasing power, or **group purchasing**, is not new to hospitals. Over the years, hospitals have experimented with various cooperative arrangements to reduce their costs. Group purchasing can be as simple as two hospitals deciding to combine certain purchasing activities in order to obtain lower prices for goods and/or services. However, each hospital should review all pertinent anticompetition regulations before committing to such an arrangement. The issue should also be referred to the hospital's attorney.

Leasing

Hospitals frequently lease capital equipment instead of purchasing it. Leasing allows administrators to obtain equipment without having the needed cash on hand. There are two types of leases: financial and operating. A financial lease usually dictates that the term of lease will be no longer than approximately 80% of the expected useful life of the asset. Under an operating lease, the lessee may cancel the contract with due notice. Highly technical medical equipment that soon may be obsolete is usually acquired in this manner.

Receiving Section

The receiving section ensures that the correct number and type of supplies and equipment are properly received. It is responsible for checking the condition of the items and notifying the accounting department that they have been received. The accounting department is responsible for scheduling payment to vendors. Supervision of these receiving functions generally falls to the purchasing agent or personnel in the purchasing section.

Inventories and Inventory Management

Savings result when inventory levels are reduced so that both money and space can be used for other purchases. The objective is to reduce inventories to the lowest level possible without running out of items. Table 18-1 highlights some effective management tools for inventory control.

Storage and Warehousing

The majority of a hospital's inventory is kept in the main hospital warehouse. Items may be distributed via **centralized requisitions**, par-level systems, or exchange carts. The use of requisitions is a traditional system whereby individual departments or patient-care units determine when and how much to order. In the par-level system, personnel from the central supply department go to each appropriate hospital department or patient-care unit and count supplies, write up orders, obtain supplies, and bring them back to the unit. Supplies are brought up to standard or

Table 18-1. Typical Inventory Management Tools

Tool	Formula	Description	Purpose
Inventory turnover	Annual dollar value of items; average inventory	Determine how fast items are moving, on average; value inventory turnover should be 123/year.	Identify obsolete, slow-moving, or excess items.
Economic order quantity (EOQ)	The square root of the equation (annual usage 323 order cost) (annual carrying cost of the unit)	Determine optimal order quantities for items (annual usage of each item in dollars; determine dollar costs of placing purchase orders, holding or carrying costs, and average inventory on hand).	Make economic goals and efficient par levels for each inventory item.
ABC analysis		Classify entire inventory into three categories based on yearly dollar usage of items (A5, high dollar usage; B5, middle dollar usage; C5, low dollar usage).	Determine percentage of costs spent on percentage of inventory.

"**par level**." A variation of the par-level system is to distribute supplies on a movable cart. According to a designated schedule, depleted carts are exchanged with full carts. This is called an exchange cart system.

ENVIRONMENTAL SERVICES DEPARTMENT

Not long ago, **environmental services** (or housekeeping services, as they were known then) were the responsibility of the nursing service department. As nurses received more medical training and their duties shifted, the need arose for a separate functional area of environmental services. The department has two principal functions: to keep the hospital clean and to control the linen supply.

Keeping a hospital clean is challenging. Part of the problem is that a hospital is an active place that is open 24 hours a day, every day of the year. High-traffic areas need special attention to prevent a negative image of the entire hospital and to contain infections.

There is more to cleaning a hospital than simply making sure that each room and floor are cleaned properly—why cleaning is done is just as important as what is done. Ensuring a clean facility for hospital patients, visitors, and the medical staff has several benefits: it creates a positive public relations image, it can have a good psychological effect on patients and visitors, and, most importantly, it can reduce the possibility of infection.

Staffing the Environmental Services Department

The environmental services department is a labor-intensive department. It uses modern, up-to-date equipment, but the job of cleaning the patient rooms, corridors, offices, and lobbies of the hospital falls to the labor force, made up primarily of **sanitation specialists**. The administrative head of the department is the **executive housekeeper**, chief housekeeper, or director of housekeeping. The organization of this department is conventional in that it is based on a hierarchical principle, with the chief housekeeper at the top, just above one or two assistants who supervise the sanitation specialists.

Rank among the sanitation specialists is based on a traditional division of labor. Some are assigned light cleaning, dusting, and mopping of floors. Others do heavy housekeeping and furniture moving. These people are the front line of the environmental services department and are generally assigned to divisions, sections, or units in the hospital. A nursing unit may have one regularly assigned person, with additional staff working the evening shift or on weekends. These key people have an impact on patients in several ways. The results of their work (that is, a clean nursing unit or patient bedroom) have both public-relations and psychological effects. The sanitation specialists' approach, professionalism, attitude, and personality directly affect each patient, since they come in daily contact with patients while cleaning their rooms. A cheerful, well-informed, and polite employee, the product of a good guest relations program, can add much to the total image of the hospital.

Infectious and Hazardous Waste Removal

Hospitals today treat every patient according to the concept of universal precautions, that is, they recognize that all patients have the potential to spread serious infectious diseases, including HIV and hepatitis A, B, and C. The housekeeping department must assume that every patient is infectious, and properly disinfect all patients' rooms and remove infectious or hazardous wastes. Working with the infection control committee, the housekeeping staff may be assigned to disinfect a given area or room using special bacterial solutions and certain techniques (e.g., misting) that have proved to be effective. **Infectious wastes** are always placed in specially marked red bags and double-bagged. Incineration is the most efficient and cost-effective way to dispose of infectious wastes, although the laws and regulations regarding acceptable waste removal vary from state to state. Housekeepers must always wear gloves and watch for discarded needles in trash cans. Needle-sticks can be life-threatening because of the possibility of infection.

The removal of hazardous wastes, such as chemotherapy drugs and radioactive materials (e.g., radionuclides used in the imaging department) is regulated by local, state, and federal agencies. Many state laws concerning hazardous waste follow federal Environmental Protection Agency (EPA) guidelines. The environmental services department must keep informed about changes in these regulations. Hospitals may have on-site removal mechanisms, such as incinerators, or they may contract with outside firms to provide waste removal services. Hospitals can be held liable for the unsafe or ineffective disposal of hazardous or infectious wastes (e.g., tissue removed during surgery, discarded blood products, and patient specimens) produced in their facilities.

LAUNDRY DEPARTMENT

Hospitals often have their own hospital laundry, operated on the hospital grounds or in the hospital itself, or they may contract out their laundry services. A typical hospital laundry will have areas set aside for receiving and sorting soiled linen. Other functional areas of the laundry are the washing room and the clean-linen processing room, which has large tables for sorting, tumblers for drying, and machines for pressing. In addition to the linen processing room, the laundry will also have a linen and pack preparation room where the clean linen is put on shelves for storage or placed directly into decentralized linen carts. Administrators and **laundry managers** are continually seeking new and improved types of automated equipment to save time.

The head of the laundry department is the laundry manager. The laundry manager must possess skills in dealing with people and should understand laundry equipment and the technical aspects of laundering, including proper cleaning solutions. The exact number of personnel required to operate a hospital laundry will vary with the number of beds in the hospital. If the laundry is responsible for retrieving soiled linens, distributing the linens, and packing certain sterile instruments, the number of personnel will increase.

The hospital must first determine the quantity of linens needed for the facility. The usual standard is to have six complete sets of linen for each occupied bed. According to government studies, these six sets should be used as follows: one set on the patient's bed, one set en route to the laundry, one set being processed in the laundry, one set at the nursing unit ready to be used, and two sets in active storage for weekends or emergency use.

The hospital laundry serves many areas of the hospital in addition to patient-care units. The operating room uses a vast supply of clean linens. The delivery room and imaging department need gowns and drapes. The hospital's central medical supply (or central sterile supply), where all of the sterile packs and instruments are wrapped, is a big user of linen. The environmental services department is also a principal customer of the laundry department.

Linen Control and Distribution

A traditional and chronic problem facing hospitals is effective linen control. Patient care, employee morale, and economic hospital operations can all be negatively affected if the right amount of linen is not available at the right time.

One way to control the supply of linens is to establish regular operating levels, or par levels. The par level is the amount of linen inventory that is required for a specific period in a certain area. In a patient-care unit, par levels are usually planned on a daily or weekly basis. Another means of controlling supplies, and especially to guard against theft, is to ensure that all hospital linens are properly marked. Marking linens with the hospital name or a symbol woven or stamped onto the items is a very effective way to minimize loss. Decals can also be used for this purpose. It is common for hospitals to use different-colored linens in different departments. For example, the operating room may use green, maternity may use light blue or pink, and medical/surgical patient-care units may use patterned linens.

Two different methods are used to distribute linen to the nursing units. Clean linen for the day should be on the nursing floor no later than the start of the first shift (7:00 AM). Distribution is handled in a centralized fashion, such that one or more large linen carts are regularly rotated around the nursing units from floor to floor. In a decentralized system, each patient-care unit is supplied with its own separate linen cart. The patient-care unit may have a small supply of emergency linens on the floor, with the bulk of the linens kept in supervised and/or locked linen carts.

MAINTENANCE DEPARTMENT

A department in the hospital that is often unseen by patients and visitors is the **maintenance** department. This is especially true in modern hospitals. It is difficult to imagine that there would be much maintenance involved in repairing equipment, buildings, or grounds in a new facility. Yet when one looks at some older hospitals, the role that maintenance has in keeping the hospital operating properly becomes apparent. Hospital equipment and buildings were once relatively simple. With the increasing complexity of hospital facilities and equipment, the role of maintenance has become more complex and an additional burden has been placed on the maintenance department of the hospital.

Functions

The traditional primary function of the maintenance department is to maintain the buildings and machinery of the hospital. This includes the hot water and steam plant, plumbing, waste disposal systems, and the hospital's electrical power system (including emergency power systems). This department also maintains and repairs hospital furniture, as well as interior and exterior walls. Additionally, the department may be responsible for landscaping and maintaining the grounds, including snow removal.

Preventive maintenance is work done on a regular basis to keep the hospital in a good state of repair and to keep machinery and equipment from breaking down. It includes scheduled inspections, maintenance, minor adjustments, and standard repairs. Record keeping is a critical component of an adequate preventive maintenance program; records should include the purchase date of each item, major repairs done on equipment, and inspection reports.

A key document in maintenance control is the **work order**, which is used to plan, estimate, schedule, and control labor. Examples of items on a work order include the date when service is requested, the date it is needed, the work order number, the equipment and/or materials required, the estimated number of hours required to complete the job, a brief job description, and the name of the supervisor of the department requesting the service.

Some hospitals use computerized preventive maintenance programs as well as automated systems to process work orders. This enables the maintenance department to respond quickly and more efficiently to complaints and requests.

Contract maintenance is the use of outside maintenance experts to repair hospital equipment. This is usually done for large, complex pieces of equipment, such as elevators. However, with hospitals becoming more complex and having to rely on esoteric clinical equipment, outside maintenance specialists are increasingly being called upon to supplement the regular maintenance staff. Outside experts usually service imaging equipment. The cost of such repairs can rightfully be included in the cost of hospital maintenance, even though they may show up as a direct expense in the clinical department.

The maintenance department may also be in charge of hospital renovations. Due to the high costs of new construction, renovations have become common practice for hospitals. However, a renovation can be just as expensive as new construction when there is inadequate management, planning, and staffing. The maintenance department must also be concerned with energy conservation because hospitals are in operation 7 days a week and use energy-intensive machines such as sterilizing units in the central sterile supply, and computed tomography (CT) and MRI units in the imaging department.

PLANT ENGINEERING

The plant engineering department is responsible for operating the hospital's **power plant** or boiler room section. This department is primarily concerned with the production and transmission of heat, cool air, power, and light, and the hospital's medical vacuum system.

Many hospitals generate some of the energy used for critical functions within the hospital, including steam for heating systems, hot water, and sterilizing. In addition, it is common for hospitals with laundries to generate their own energy for that function. The engineering department, through its power plants, may be involved in cogeneration of steam and electricity. Standby electrical systems for emergency power are also this department's responsibility. Most power plants have a standardized chiller or air-conditioning capabilities.

The hospital boiler room is supervised by a boiler engineer. Many states and cities have licensure laws that require boiler engineers to undergo examinations by a board or some other qualified group. After passing the qualification examinations, the boiler engineer receives an operating license. This license must be posted in the hospital's power plant as proof of the individual's qualifications. The engineering license primarily covers boiler operations, refrigeration, and the fundamentals of other activities related to the power plant.

PARKING FACILITIES

All hospitals need parking facilities. It may fall to the maintenance department to operate and maintain the parking facilities. Convenient, safe, and adequate parking can be a big marketing plus for any hospital. Adequate parking facilities can also be helpful in recruiting medical staff and employees. For hospitals in high-crime areas, a well-lighted, secure parking facility is necessary to retain qualified staff. The most acute need for parking usually occurs during the half-hour overlap time before the change of the day shift (7:00 AM to 3:30 PM) and the half-hour overlap time before the evening shift (3:00 PM to 11:30 PM).

There are generally three types of parking areas: surface or on-ground parking, multilevel or above-ground parking, and subterranean or below-ground parking. Surface parking is the least costly, and subterranean parking is the most costly. The enormous growth in outpatient activity has put a tremendous strain on hospitals to provide sufficient parking spaces. It is especially crucial for urban hospitals, which tend to be land-locked, to provide adequate parking areas. As a result, multilevel parking garages have become popular.

BIOMEDICAL ENGINEERING DEPARTMENT

Biomedical engineering (also referred to as clinical engineering) involves functions related to medical equipment. Medical (or clinical) equipment includes diagnostic equipment (e.g., devices used to measure physiological parameters), clinical laboratory equipment, devices that apply radiant energy to the body, and various types of equipment for therapeutic treatment, resuscitation, prosthesis, physical therapy, surgical support, and patient monitoring.

Functions

The biomedical engineers are responsible for certain tasks, which can be categorized by levels. Level I tasks entail the repair of equipment and related documentation of the repair history and costs. Level II tasks deal with preventive maintenance, including electrical safety checks, new-equipment checks, and preuse preparation of equipment. Level III tasks involve management and design, and specifically deal with planning, purchasing, installation, hazard notification, and safety-committee support.

Equipment Maintenance

A hospital must adequately maintain all biomedical equipment because the proper functioning of this equipment has a direct bearing on patient care and safety. To ensure that the equipment is properly maintained, hospitals can (1) establish an in-house program; (2) contract with a single commercial vendor to provide services; (3) participate in a shared service arrangement with other hospitals; or (4) use a combination of vendors, manufacturers, representatives, and dealers. The fourth approach is the most exact, but also the most expensive.

Staff

Support personnel who are responsible for working on biomedical equipment are referred to as **biomedical equipment specialists**. There are two recognized levels of specialists. The first level is that of operation specialist. This individual has little formal training but may have received a great deal of on-the-job training in the hospital, and is responsible for setting up, checking, and operating the biomedical equipment. The second level involves a more technically oriented specialist with specific biomedical equipment training. This individual is trained to construct and repair complex, specialized equipment. The Association for the Advancement of Medical Instrumentation (AAMI) represents and certifies clinical engineers and biomedical equipment specialists.

CONTRACT SERVICES

All facilities-support services tend to lend themselves to contract management. Whether a hospital decides to use a **contract service** exclusively or in-house staff depends on the following factors: quality of service, availability of in-house personnel with the necessary knowledge and skills, availability of in-house equipment, licensing requirements, cost-effectiveness, legal issues, and the need to expand services. Such contracts may include housekeeping, dietary, pharmacy, and physical therapy services. The hospital may contract for a complete turnkey operation, with vendors bringing in their own cleaning or cooking equipment, or it may simply hire a supervisor to train employees in better techniques and work methods. Often a rural hospital may have trouble recruiting a pharmacist, dietician, or physical therapist, and contract services provide a good, if sometimes costly, solution.

CHAPTER REVIEW

1. What is the function of the materials management department?
2. What does the purchasing agent do?
3. Describe competitive bidding, centralized purchasing, and shared purchasing.
4. Discuss several contract services in which a hospital might engage, and give examples.
5. Discuss par levels and why they are important.

19

Safeguarding the Hospital

Attila J. Hertelendy

KEY TERMS

Environment of care
Security assessment
Security management plan
Surveillance systems
National Incident Management
   System (NIMS)

Fire safety
Emergency preparedness
Incident command system
   (ICS)

INTRODUCTION

Hospitals are not immune from safety and security risks, which can affect all healthcare workers, visitors, and patients. Planning and careful adherence to established standards to identify and mitigate these risks play an important role in a hospital's ability to prevent and effectively respond to potential incidents.

Most hospitals that are accredited by The Joint Commission are familiar with the detailed standards contained in the Comprehensive Accreditation Manual for Hospitals (CAMH). Each standard has one or more elements of performance (EPs). This chapter focuses on three areas designated by The Joint Commission as comprising the **environment of care:** general safety, security, and fire safety. A fourth topic that is considered in this chapter is emergency management. Accreditation standards in this field began to change in 2008, and the nomenclature related to job titles in hospitals has changed accordingly. Some hospitals have combined the roles of safety and security under one department or supervisor. In addition, some hospitals have created new administrative roles in emergency preparedness.

SECURITY

Hospital security is a unique challenge. Many hospitals promote accessibility and are open 24 hours a day, 7 days a week; indeed, for many years hospitals have focused more on providing open and friendly access to the public, rather than security. Patients and visitors alike have grown accustomed to coming and going as they please. In many healthcare facilities, this practice inherently creates potentially significant security risks. In light of the various threats faced by hospitals today, an open door policy is not considered feasible for most facilities. Safety procedures and policies should be enacted to control access to the facility, which requires that individuals and groups coming and going from the hospital be identified. Preventing access to unauthorized individuals is a prerequisite for hospital security efforts. Hospitals should begin a review of their security by conducting a security assessment.

Security Assessment

Performing a **security assessment** enables a facility to take the first steps toward protecting its patients, staff, and visitors by identifying the inherent strengths and weaknesses in its infrastructure protection and security practices. Ideally, the assessment should aid administrators in analyzing procedures, policies, and protocols. Findings from the analysis should be evaluated and written recommendations should be made to mitigate the threats and vulnerabilities found. Security, much like emergency management, is a systems concept that requires ongoing training, surveillance, and prompt identification of problems. A successful security program requires a long-term commitment from senior hospital administrators. Another feature that the security assessment is designed to identify are deficiencies related to hazards and unsafe practices. New guidelines require hospitals to document security issues and provide corrective actions. A comprehensive self-assessment can help a facility comply with the standards set by The Joint Commission and the Centers for Medicare and Medicaid (CMS). Hospitals may approach a hospital security assessment in a number of ways. One method is to utilize an outside healthcare security expert who has the appropriate industry credentials and professional certifications, as well as experience in evaluating hospital security programs. The hospital security assessment should begin in the parking lot and continue all the way to the roof of the building.

Security Management Plan

Once the security assessment has been completed and security threats and vulnerabilities have been assessed and identified, a **security management plan** should be developed. The written security management plan is intended to provide a proactive approach to protecting patients, visitors, staff, and the facility. The plan should address areas that are unique and may require additional security protection. Specific policies and procedures pertinent to security-sensitive areas should be identified. This may necessitate specific policies that address access control, information security, patient privacy, visitation, and identification procedures. Examples of some security-sensitive areas are listed below:

- Pharmacy
- Labor and delivery rooms
- Pediatrics department
- Emergency department
- Psychiatry department
- Nuclear medicine department
- Radiation therapy department
- Medical records
- Information services
- Operating rooms
- Food services

Access Control

The security management plan should specifically address access control, or how patients, visitors, and staff gain access to the facility. Authorized persons of course must be allowed to enter and exit the hospital; however, security breaches in this area have certainly contributed to many problems in hospitals. Everyone who enters or exits the hospital should be appropriately identified. Exit points should also be monitored and controlled. This is particularly important for curtailing potential crimes, such as infant abduction, theft, and rape, since the perpetrator might enter the building under false pretenses and elude capture by using an unauthorized exit. Uncontrolled exits also encourage patients to leave the hospital against medical advice, exposing the hospital to potential liability for abandoning a patient. The National Fire Protection Association (NFPA) Standard for Health Care Facilities permits door-locking devices with delayed egress in clinical areas that may require special security measures. The delayed-egress device is engineered to lock and sound an alarm for 15 seconds before allowing an individual to exit. In the event of a fire, the delayed-egress locking system has an override function controlled by the master fire protection system. The fire alarm protection system will automatically unlock all emergency exits in the event of a fire. Delayed-egress doors provide an additional measure of security and act as a deterrent to a potential terrorist or criminal intent on targeting the facility. Most hospitals have signage that directs patients and visitors to specific entrances for public access. Staff members usually use separate, controlled-access entrances and must show identification to gain entrance or egress. All visitors should be identified. In most hospitals, visitors are required to sign in and produce identification. They are subsequently issued a temporary visitors identification badge that must be worn and be clearly visible. Hospital staff should be trained to deny access to anyone who is unable to produce hospital identification. Suspicious persons should be immediately reported to security personnel.

Emergency Department Protection

One of the most vulnerable areas with regard to the risk of violence in the hospital is the emergency department. Hospital emergency departments often treat patients who have the potential to become violent. Numerous reports in the literature cite nurses and other medical personnel as the victims of assault, and a number of homicides have occurred in emergency departments. The potential of mass violence due to a terror attack is a distinct possibility as well, and hospitals are becoming increasingly vulnerable. In the nation's busiest hospitals, patients and visitors trying to gain access to the emergency department are often found to be illegally in possession of knives or handguns. Such threats require a proactive assessment of a hospital's vulnerabilities. Many hospitals now require patients, family, and visitors to go through a metal detector at the entrance of the emergency department to screen for persons attempting to bring in unauthorized weapons or suspicious items. Failure to adequately secure the emergency department exposes a healthcare facility to significant liability.

Surveillance

In many hospitals, a thorough security assessment will reveal outdated security technology. The closed-circuit television (CCTV) **surveillance system** may use old black-and-white analog cameras that are obsolete and do not have recording capabilities. Further investigation may reveal that the cameras are not positioned correctly, or are not working at all. Hospitals should consider placing their security assets in a central location to facilitate monitoring, recording, and dispatching of security services to sentinel events in the hospital.

Modern technology should serve as a focal point in providing state-of-the-art security services at healthcare facilities. Outdated CCTV surveillance systems should be replaced with digital surveillance equipment capable of digital recording and archiving. The system should be integrated with access control throughout the hospital and the information technology (IT) infrastructure. Cameras should be installed according to the recommendations of the security analyst, and in areas defined in the security management plan as security-sensitive locations. The Federal Emergency Management Agency (FEMA) offers programs to help hospitals assess critical infrastructure vulnerabilities, and may be able to provide assistance in conducting threat and vulnerability analyses.

Identification

The **National Incident Management System (NIMS)** provides the framework for mandatory identification of employees. Many hospitals are not compliant in this regard and are using outdated technology, such as laminated ID badges that often do not include the employee's picture. These types of unsophisticated IDs can be easily reproduced at a local photocopy shop and significantly compromise security efforts. Every hospital employee, including physicians, should be required to wear a tamper-proof ID badge, facing forward, that at minimum displays the person's first and last name, title, department (if applicable), and the hospital's name and logo. For tamper-proof ID badges, computerized photo-imaging systems can be used to implant the image into the PVC card. Hospitals may also incorporate a bar code or smart chip into the card to serve human-resources functions as well as to restrict access to certain locations. The consequences of failure to adequately implement and maintain appropriate identification measures can be severe. Hospitals have been sued in situations where a perpetrator pretending to be a new employee gained access to a nursery and abducted an infant. In these cases, photo IDs were not routinely worn by staff.

Infant and Patient Protection

New technologies are on the market to aid hospitals in tracking patients. Currently they are mostly being used to address the problem of wandering patients and the threat of infant abductions. Hospitals should consider implementing state of the art security devices for women's health centers and pediatric/newborn units. This can include electronic tracking and monitoring using dedicated CCTV systems.

Information Technology Security

Hospitals that store any type of patient records electronically must ensure that the data are safeguarded. The Health Insurance Portability and Accountability Act (HIPAA) requires all hospitals to safeguard patient confidentiality and privacy. Computer and IT security requires a secure network and data transmission to meet this goal. Continuous assessment of the IT network through real-time monitoring and auditing as part of the security assessment will help validate IT security policies and procedures.

GENERAL SAFETY

Hospitals can be unsafe places to work. Safety statistics compiled by the US government indicate that the injury rate in medical care facilities is higher than that in many other industries. The vast majority of preventable injuries in hospitals result from slips, trips, or falls, or from using incorrect lifting techniques, especially when lifting patients. Therefore, hospital staff must exercise great care in protecting themselves and ensuring a safe environment for anyone who enters the hospital, and to identify any hazardous or unsafe conditions. All levels of the organizational staff, functional managers, supervisors, and employees must be vigilant in the performance of their jobs to eliminate practices or conditions that could result in injury to patients, visitors, or employees, or damage or loss of property.

Throughout the United States, the Occupational Health and Safety Administration (OSHA) defines and regulates safety practices in industry. Each hospital is required to establish some type of a safety management program. Policies and procedures should be based on experience and compliance with both state and federal regulations.

A qualified individual, often referred to as the safety officer or director, should be designated by the chief executive officer and charged with the responsibility to develop, implement, and monitor a safety management program. A safety committee, including representatives of administration, clinical services, and support services, should be established to analyze identified safety management issues and recommend actions to resolve them. The safety officer should then work with the appropriate staff to implement those recommendations and monitor their effectiveness.

In accordance with most standards, such as those established by The Joint Commission, the safety management plan must describe how the hospital will provide a physical environment that is free of hazards, and manage staff activities to reduce the risk of injury. In addition, the safety management plan must establish a staff orientation and education program to address safety issues, program performance, and provisions for monitoring and periodic reviews.

FIRE SAFETY

The NFPA has published guidelines for **fire safety** in various healthcare facilities, including hospitals, such as NFPA 101 (Life Safety Code) and NFPA 99 (Standard for Health Care Facilities). Hospitals present a unique set of problems relating to the evacuation and movement of people, especially high-risk patients. These problems are often exacerbated due to the physical layout of the hospital, which may have multiple stories. A guiding principle of fire protection in healthcare facilities is known as sheltering in place. Current fire engineering standards and building construction codes stipulate that facilities must provide a means for patients to remain safe. This can be achieved by ensuring that corridor walls have been constructed properly, fire barriers have been erected, and fire detection and suppression systems have been installed. For some patient population groups, such as those in the intensive care unit, cardiac care units, or surgical operating rooms, the shelter-in-place approach may be necessary due to the potential complications and risks involved in moving a patient in critical condition. Patients in hospitals are presumed to be incapable of evacuating themselves. Their safety depends on several factors. Supervisors should ensure that staff members are trained in basic fire-suppression methods, such as the use of portable fire extinguishers. In addition, they should be made aware of the fire safety plan and participate in fire drills to ensure compliance in the event of an emergency. Supervisors who are responsible for fire safety will need to verify the adequacy of built-in fire detection and alarm systems. Along with fire inspection and maintenance logs, fire safety plans should be reviewed and updated on a regular basis.

EMERGENCY MANAGEMENT

Floods, power failures, and pandemic diseases are just a few of the possible situations that can threaten the continuity of patient care and hospital services, and pose a significant risk to staff and patients. An isolated emergency can result in a temporary disruption in services, but multiple emergencies occurring at the same time may impair a hospital's ability to provide care, treatment, and services for a prolonged period of time. Both natural and man-made disasters can create situations in which the resources of the community and the hospital are quickly overwhelmed, as demonstrated in recent disasters such as hurricane Katrina in 2005 and the Haiti earthquake in 2010.

Standards that address **emergency preparedness** have been revised to reflect an "all-hazards" approach. This approach broadens the context of disaster planning to include preparedness efforts that facilitate flexible and effective responses, and addresses the variety, intensity, and duration of disasters that can affect a single organization, multiple organizations, or an entire community. Standards such as those promoted by The Joint Commission also stress the importance of planning and preparing for situations in which traditional protective organizations, such as fire and police departments, are unable to respond.

Several different documents are available that outline the procedures by which hospitals can meet emergency management standards. One such document is NFPA Standard 1600, Recommended Practice for Disaster/Emergency Management. FEMA also provides the umbrella framework for emergency management in the United States. Its cornerstone concept, termed comprehensive emergency management (CEM), is an integrated approach for organizing various programs and activities. The hallmark of these activities is the life cycle, which is visualized as a circle comprised of the four phases of emergency management: mitigation, preparedness, response, and recovery. The integrated emergency management system (IEMS) provides a mechanism by which CEM can be implemented. The IEMS includes program development, planning, orientation for organizing groups, and resources for functions that are generic to all hazards, and promotes a philosophy of inclusiveness for all disaster-relevant resources and groups.

The terrorist attacks of September 11, 2001, resulted in the formation of the NIMS. A federal mandate requires all private, tribal, and governmental entities to be compliant with NIMS and understand how it functions. NIMS was designed to be applied nationally, at all jurisdictional levels and across functional disciplines, to further improve the effectiveness of emergency-response activities within the construct of an all-hazards approach. This national approach improves coordination and cooperation between public and private entities in a variety of domestic incident management activities, resulting in increased interoperability and compatibility, and less duplication of services. Hospitals and healthcare systems in most jurisdictions are required to adopt NIMS. Hospitals are also encouraged to develop emergency operations plans (EOPs) that are structured to be NIMS-compliant. FEMA provides detailed implementation guides for hospitals, as well as "crosswalks," or templates, for developing EOPs. Hospital emergency management directors can also receive guidance and support from their local county and state emergency preparedness officials. At a minimum, hospitals that adopt NIMS and strive to be compliant should consider the following suggested components:

Organizational Adoption

Hospitals should adopt NIMS at the organizational level, which includes all functional areas of the hospital. This would include such areas as materials and logistics, and relationships with vendors and third-party entities. Many hospitals also encourage their stakeholders and communities to adopt NIMS, and in many cases will only do business with vendors and other stakeholders who have done so.

Command and Management

The **incident command system (ICS)** should be used to manage both emergencies and planned events in compliance with ICS organizational structures, doctrine, policies, and procedures as defined in NIMS. Hospitals should remain consistent in using ICS, which requires the use of common communication plans and coordinated incident action plans.

Multiagency Coordination System

Hospitals are not stand-alone entities. Organizational support and coordination of emergency and incident management are aided by the development of relationships and formalized partnerships with EOCs at the hospital, local incident command posts (ICPs), and local and state EOCs.

Public Information Systems

Hospitals should have a public information system that ensures the timely and accurate dissemination of information in a state of emergency. This is optimally done by establishing a joint information center.

Preparedness Planning

Hospitals should develop a system in which they can track NIMS implementation on a yearly basis as part of their emergency management program. Not only is this essential for ensuring NIMS compliance, it is also required for hospitals that are accredited by The Joint Commission. In addition to tracking, hospitals should set aside funds or obtain funding from local, state, or federal entities for hospital emergency preparedness activities. As part of their quality improvement and compliance initiatives, hospitals should also update their plans and documents to incorporate NIMS components and policies regarding training, response, planning, mutual-aid agreements, and evaluation methods.

Preparedness Training

Local, state, and federal emergency management agencies sponsor several types of courses that are either required or recommended for hospital personnel. Hospital training records should track the completion of programs by individuals who are likely to assume an incident command position as detailed in the hospital's emergency management plan. FEMA provides specific guidance as to which courses employees and management personnel should take. At a minimum, organizations should consider the following courses: IS-700 (NIMS: An Introduction), IS-800 (NRP: An Introduction), and ICS-100 and ICS-200.

Preparedness Exercises

Hospitals should incorporate NIMS/ICS guidelines into their preparedness training and exercises. This is commonly referred to as "exercising the plan." Preparedness exercises should be scaled in levels of complexity and participation, and focus on particular scenarios that encompass an all-hazards approach. These exercises should involve a broad spectrum of organizations across multiple disciplines, including local, state, federal, tribal, and private organizations. Postreview of training and exercises should encompass a method by which participants are provided feedback. Areas of improvement should be identified and incorporated into preparedness response plans and procedures. This is a critical step that is often done infrequently or not at all. The only way to ensure that the EOP reflects operational reality, and that staff members are competent and trained in their respective roles, is to test the plan.

Resource Management

Logistics and materials management are essential components of hospital operations. A resource inventory of equipment and supplies that support emergency preparedness should be documented in the emergency management plan. Whenever possible, purchasing of equipment and supplies should conform to NIMS standards to ensure interoperability of response equipment and communications and data systems with other agencies and partners.

Communications

Hospitals tend to use their own particular jargon. The NIMS recommends the use of plain English in all communications. Technical and medical terminology unique to the hospital environment should be avoided. EOPs and exercises should emphasize the use of plain English by entities involved in emergency response or incident planning.

SUMMARY

Community stakeholders who utilize hospital services are increasingly evaluating healthcare centers not only for the level and quality of medical care they offer, but also in terms of security and safety issues. It behooves hospital administrators to take a proactive approach in implementing and adhering to regulations mandated by local, state, and federal authorities. This can be accomplished by maintaining adequate staff, controlling access to facilities (e.g., by identifying visitors, patients, and staff), ensuring that the hospital is using the latest security technology, and participating in training exercises. In addition, hospitals should take advantage of the opportunities afforded by state, local, and federal emergency management agencies. These agencies can provide inexpensive access to tools and training programs, and assistance with designing emergency preparedness plans, exercises, and evaluations.

CHAPTER REVIEW

1. Why is fire safety so important for a hospital? What are some precautions a hospital facility should take to detect and contain fires?
2. What are the elements of a general safety program?
3. What are two ways to categorize disasters?
4. What makes hospital security a unique challenge?

Part VIII

Administrative Services and Issues

Human Resources Department, Risk Management, Legal Services, and Corporate Compliance

Donald J. Griffin

KEY TERMS

Position control plan
Orientation
Full-time equivalent
  employees (FTEs)
Employee assistance
  program (EAP)
Employment Retirement
  Income Security Act (ERISA)
Americans with Disabilities
  Act (ADA)
Equal Employment Opportunity
  Commission (EEOC)

Civil Rights Act of 1964
Health Insurance Portability and
  Accountability Act (HIPAA)
Pregnancy Discrimination
  Act (PDA)
Sexual harassment
Risk management
Tort
Respondeat superior
Corporate compliance

INTRODUCTION

Nearly every hospital has an organized human resources department (previously referred to as the personnel department). This is a very important department when one considers that labor usually accounts for more than 50% of the cost of operating a hospital. This department oversees the maintenance of personnel records and benefits, and its members often guide or consult with top management personnel. The role of the human resources department is becoming increasingly important because of the responsibilities and legal requirements being placed on hospitals by federal and state governments and other regulatory agencies.

FUNCTIONS OF THE HUMAN RESOURCES DEPARTMENT

The human resources department coordinates the processes involved in hiring personnel, and assists departments in their recruiting needs. The department's activities generally are divided into at least three functional areas: (1) attracting, interviewing, and hiring employees; (2) maintaining employees' records and programs after they are hired; and (3) ensuring that the hospital complies with applicable legal regulations. Some particular functions are listed below:

- Maintaining a **position control plan**
- Job analysis
- Creating job descriptions
- Recruitment
- Arranging interviews
- Conducting **orientation** programs
- Motivation and job enrichment
- Dealing with troubled employees

Maintaining a Position Control Plan

The position control plan is a management tool that allows the hospital to control the number of **full-time equivalent employees (FTEs)** on the payroll in accordance with what was budgeted. A full-time equivalent is the number of hours a full-time employee would work in a given year—2080 hours per year, which includes paid vacations or other paid time off. It is the human resources department's responsibility to maintain the master employee file and the employee-position control files.

Job Analysis

Before an employee is recruited, selected, interviewed, and hired by the hospital, the human resources department will perform a job analysis. This analysis examines the tasks and functions to be performed by the employee, the conditions under which the employee will be working, and the training and skills that are required to perform the job.

Creating Job Descriptions

After the job analysis is completed, a job description is written. Job description specifications vary among hospitals. Generally, they include the job title, the department to which the employee will be assigned, an outline of the tasks and duties to be performed, any equipment or special tools to be used, and the name of the individual who will be supervising the position.

Recruitment

Usually advertisements to announce job opportunities are placed in newspapers, trade journals, or magazines that are most likely to attract qualified candidates. Previous applications are also reviewed. The human resources department may also post vacancies on the hospital's website and review applications received through the site. Potential employees are subsequently invited for an interview.

Arranging Interviews

After human resources employees have interviewed and selected the best applicants for a job, interviews are arranged with the appropriate department head or supervisor. After the interviews have been conducted, a candidate is selected and an offer is made. The human resources department does not ordinarily make the final selection; it should act only in an advisory capacity to assist the department director in filling the vacancy.

Conducting Orientation Programs

Orientation has two basic purposes. First, it allows the new employee to get background information about the hospital and its functions, and to see how he or she can contribute to the hospital's overall mission. The orientation should begin to make new employees feel like they are a real part of the hospital family. Second, the new employee's benefits, including life insurance, dental insurance, and healthcare insurance, are explained and written information is distributed. Hospital policies will also be explained, and parking stickers and a hospital handbook are issued. Sometimes hospitals assign a temporary buddy to each new employee. Hospitals use different techniques for orienting employees, but most include an orientation lecture and a general tour of the hospital.

Motivation and Job Enrichment

Once the employee is hired, the task of retaining, motivating, and making the employee feel like he or she is part of the organization begins.

One of the measures that hospitals use to evaluate employee morale and retention is the turnover rate. This is calculated by dividing the number of employees who voluntarily separated or were fired in a given month by the number of authorized FTEs in the hospital. Turnover rates should be calculated every month, and management personnel should review a graph depicting trends by department.

Dealing with Troubled Employees

Another responsibility of the human resources department is to work with troubled or problematic employees. Individuals with substance abuse problems should be referred to appropriate treatment centers. This is handled through the **employee assistance program (EAP)**. The department also handles grievances concerning employee–employer relations. The human resources department also conducts disciplinary workshops so that rank and file department directors can take a unified approach with regard to warnings, write-ups, and discharges, in compliance with employment and labor laws.

SALARIES, WAGES, AND BENEFITS

The human resources department is responsible for developing, maintaining, and monitoring a wage and salary program. This process includes four main steps:

1. Analyze each position and determine the skills and education required for the position.
2. Place each position in a group classification based on its relative importance to the hospital.

3. Assign a salary range to each classification.
4. Rate employees according to a designated system.

Often the human resources department will review areawide wage and salary surveys conducted by hospital councils.

Hospitals traditionally have offered benefits in addition to salary in order to recruit and retain personnel. These benefits may include life insurance, group hospitalization, pension plans, parking, paid vacations, and educational assistance. Some hospitals offer a cafeteria plan for benefits, which allows employees to select their own fringe benefits.

EMPLOYEE PERFORMANCE APPRAISAL

The human resources department guides and supports department directors in rating employees. The rating process may involve a supervisor completing a form or writing a report. Employee performance appraisals should reflect an employee's knowledge, skills, behavior, attitudes, and overall contribution to the organization. Employee performance appraisal systems are very specific to each institution.

IMPORTANT LAWS, ACTS, AND ISSUES

A skilled human resources director needs to have a solid understanding of the law and regulatory environment. Management and human resources personnel must ensure that the hospital stays in full compliance with all applicable statutes and regulations, and must be familiar with a veritable alphabet soup of acts (e.g., Family and Medical Leave Act [FMLA], **Employment Retirement Income Security Act [ERISA]**, and **Americans with Disabilities Act [ADA]**) and agencies (e.g., **Equal Employment Opportunity Commission [EEOC]** and Occupational Health and Safety Administration [OSHA]). Some key regulations are discussed here.

Equal Employment Opportunity Commission

In 1972, the EEOC was established by an amendment to Title VII of the **Civil Rights Act of 1964**, which prohibits private employers and state and local governments from discriminating against an employee based on age, race, color, religion, sex, or national origin. The EEOC website can be accessed at http://www.eeoc.gov.

Americans with Disabilities Act of 1990

Unlike employees experiencing discrimination problems due to their color, age, sex, religion, or national origin, Americans with disabilities had no legal recourse even after the EEOC was established. This changed in 1990 when Congress passed the Americans with Disabilities Act (ADA), which prohibits discrimination based on disability in hiring, promotion, or other provisions of employment. Employers must try to make reasonable accommodations for disabled employees.

Employment Retirement Income Security Act

The Employment Retirement Income Security Act (ERISA), passed in 1974, was designed to ensure that employee benefit and pension plans conform to minimum standards in private industry. Because this plan preempts state law covering employee benefit plans, many employers choose to become self-insured in order to opt out of state-mandated benefit plans.

Fair Labor Standards Act

The Fair Labor Standards Act (FLSA) sets minimum wages and maximum employment hours for employees; executive and professional employees are exempt. Although this federal law applies throughout the United States, each hospital should also be familiar with its own state laws, as they may vary.

Equal Pay Act of 1963

In 1963, Congress amended the FLSA to mandate equal pay for equal work. This was done in an attempt to end discrimination based on sex.

Health Insurance Portability and Accountability Act

From a human-resources perspective, the **Health Insurance Portability and Accountability Act (HIPAA)** is important because it limits health-insurance exclusions for preexisting health conditions. HIPAA is discussed more thoroughly in Chapter 19.

Nursing and Other Professional Licenses

A common function of human resources is to ensure that all employees' and applicants' licenses are current. Applicants and employees should provide the department with a copy of the license, and human resources personnel should also check with the licensing board to see that the license is active and has not been suspended.

Polygraph Protection Act

The Polygraph Protection Act prohibits employers from making employees submit to polygraph tests. There are exceptions for employees in certain industries, such as those in which personnel handle top-secret information. There is also a limited exception for situations involving the theft of or access to controlled substances, which could mean requiring a nurse or pharmacist to take a polygraph. In such cases, the wise administrator would seek advice from legal counsel before moving forward and should be forewarned about the negative effect on rank-and-file employees who would probably view this as very heavy-handed management. A better approach would be to contact the local police department and the pharmacy board and/or nursing board, and invite them to investigate the disappearance of the controlled substance.

Pregnancy Discrimination Act

The **Pregnancy Discrimination Act (PDA)** protects pregnant women from being discriminated against or discharged because of their pregnancy.

Random Drug Screens, Criminal Background Checks, and References

Hospitals today commonly use random drug screens, criminal background checks, and reference checks to safeguard the workplace and avoid negligence lawsuits. Most states have statutes mandating random testing of employees for drugs and alcohol. It is wise to have a written, posted policy, and to ensure that each employee signs a form agreeing to random testing. It is also wise to administer tests to all new employees as a condition for employment, to administer further tests on a random basis, and to also test for cause, such as when an employee exhibits erratic behavior or is involved in an accident. Criminal background checks by an outside agency and job references are commonly required as a condition for employment.

Sexual Harassment

In 1980, the EEOC issued guidelines expanding the EEO Act, which prohibits **sexual harassment** whether it is meant as a hostile act or with a quid pro quo (Latin for "something for something") intent. A hostile work environment is created when an individual is subjected to unwelcome sexual advances, and that employee may be reluctant to go to work. A quid pro quo situation arises when a person in a position of power, such as a boss or supervisor, suggests that an employee be awarded a raise or promotion in exchange for sexual favors, or will be fired if the sexual favors are denied. Employers can be fined or face private lawsuits if sexual harassment is conducted in the workplace. The employer has an absolute duty to conduct educational meetings and display posters informing employees of their right to be free of harassment.

Workers' Compensation

Every state has laws that mandate compensation for people who are injured on the job. The specific regulations, the covered amount of time off the job, and the amount of compensation and benefits vary from state to state.

HOSPITALS AND UNIONS

In 1936, the American Federation of Labor and Congress of Industrial Organizations (AFL-CIO) initiated a campaign to organize nonprofessional healthcare workers, including dietary, maintenance, and housekeeping personnel. In 1947, the Taft-Hartley Act, or Labor-Management Relations Act, was passed. This law denied employees of nonprofit hospitals the right to organize. On July 26, 1974, Congress passed Public Law 93-360, which removed the nonprofit-hospital exception from the Taft-Hartley Act. The National Labor Relations Board (NLRB) recognizes four divisions of labor in hospitals: (1) registered nurses; (2) all other professionals, including interns, residents, and medical staff physicians; (3) service and maintenance employees, including business office employees; and (4) technical workers, including licensed practical nurses. Not surprisingly, hospital management has been opposed to the concept of labor organization in hospitals. Until 1991, the key battleground was the size and nature of bargaining units. This dispute ended in April of that year when the US Supreme Court upheld the NLRB's guidelines allowing up to eight bargaining units for hospital workers.

OCCUPATIONAL LICENSURE

The ever-increasing application of new medical and scientific technologies requires skilled personnel. These personnel are usually licensed, and it is the function of the human resources department to keep abreast of all employees' licenses and ensure that they are still active.

RISK MANAGEMENT, LEGAL SERVICES, AND CORPORATE COMPLIANCE RISK MANAGEMENT

Risk management is an early warning system for identifying and avoiding potential liabilities resulting from the actions of patients, visitors, and employees. The primary function of the risk management department is to coordinate and implement loss prevention and corrective activities throughout the hospital. It also receives, evaluates, and maintains confidential reports on incidents and/or accidents that have occurred in the hospital. These incident reports are a key component in risk management's efforts to identify and minimize risk situations.

The Team Approach to Risk Management

Although a particular individual may be designated as the hospital risk manager, a team approach is essential for effective risk management. In addition to the risk manager, team members may include administrators, members of the governing body, physicians, professional staff, an in-house attorney (if the hospital employs one), other employees, a lawyer on retainer, and insurance consultants.

Risk management should be integrated with the hospital's traditional quality improvement committees, such as those focusing on utilization reviews, quality improvement, safety and loss control, and infection control.

Risk Management and Quality Improvement

Even though risk management and quality improvement are separate areas with independent functions, some of these functions overlap. For instance, the primary purpose of risk management is to protect the hospital's assets, whereas the fundamental reason for quality improvement is to protect patients. The risk management team seeks to identify all risk exposures, whereas quality-improvement programs measure care against standards. Risk management is apt to be a prospective activity, and quality improvement is largely a retrospective activity. Despite their differences, however, it is clear that one function serves the other in ensuring a safe hospital environment.

MEDICAL MALPRACTICE

Risk management has proven to be a beneficial tool for hospitals in the prevention of medical malpractice suits. By detecting substandard practices and correcting them, hospitals can avoid many situations that might lead to malpractice claims. In addition, discussing incidents with patients and their families can often avert litigation. Risk management also helps to ensure that physicians and healthcare professionals are practicing according to acceptable standards.

Overview of Malpractice (Tort Law)

The phenomenon of medical malpractice suits began to flourish in the early 1960s and is continuing to grow. In 1973, the Department of Health, Education, and Welfare conducted a thorough study of medical malpractice, and noted the following in its report:

> Medical malpractice has been defined as an injury to a patient caused by a health care provider's negligence; a malpractice claim is an allegation with or without foundation that an injury was caused by negligence; injury implies either physical or mental harm that occurs in the course of medical care whether or not it is caused by negligence; compensation requires proof of both an injury and professional negligence.

A **tort** is a legal term meaning a civil wrong or harm for which the remedy is the awarding of money to compensate the victim for the damages incurred. Medical malpractice cases allege breaches of tort law. To win a malpractice suit, the plaintiff (the individual suing the hospital) must prove that (1) the provider of care (the physician or hospital) owed a duty to the patient (e.g., to do no harm); (2) the duty was breached (harm was done); (3) the plaintiff incurred damage of some sort; and (4) the damage resulted directly from the breach.

DEFENSIVE MEDICINE

Although only an estimated 3–8% of physicians are sued annually as a direct result of medical malpractice, there has been an alarming increase in the tendency of physicians to practice defensive medicine. Defensive medicine is generally thought of as unnecessary tests or procedures done to ward off lawsuits. The costs for additional tests performed to protect the physician are staggering.

HOSPITAL LIABILITY FOR PHYSICIANS' ACTS

It is important to recognize that in some cases a hospital may be held liable for a physician's negligent acts. This most frequently occurs when the hospital permits an incompetent or unqualified physician to treat a patient. The hospital can be held liable even if the physician is not employed by the hospital. The institution is not held liable for the negligent act that caused harm to the patient, but it is held liable for its own negligence in permitting the physician to treat the patient. It is argued that a physician's incompetence should be known to hospital authorities. These cases generally involve negligent credentialing (i.e., the hospital granted privileges to an incompetent physician) or a physician who was allowed to practice while under the influence of drugs or alcohol.

Respondeat Superior

Under the doctrine of **respondeat superior** (the master is liable for the actions of the servant), the traditional view is that the employer (hospital) can be sued if an employee harms a patient, visitor, or guest. However, the courts have expanded this to include apparent employees. For example, if a contract physician who is not a hospital employee is working in the emergency department and harms a patient, the patient may sue both the physician and the hospital if the physician appears to be an employee. Hospitals can avoid this problem by requiring nonemployee physicians in the emergency department to wear name tags showing their company name (such as "1st Rate Emergency Physician, Dr. Thomas") and posting signs in the emergency department stating that the physicians on duty are a contract group and are not hospital employees.

ENDING MEDICAL ERRORS

Errors do not have to happen. Simple safety measures, such as one nurse preparing a medication and another nurse checking it, can avoid many problems. By storing heparin and insulin (which are similar in appearance) in different areas, hospitals can prevent mistakes made in administering these drugs.

It is believed that the use of computers in healthcare fields could eliminate as many as 2 million drug interactions and 190,000 hospitalizations each year. Many medication errors could be eliminated simply by using electronic drug orders. This would eliminate problems due to bad handwriting, reading errors, and similar medication names, and the all-too-frequent problem of misunderstanding the pronunciations of certain medications.

Even without computers, some medication errors can be eliminated or reduced through better training of caregivers. For example, if caregivers are taught to use a zero before any number less than one (e.g., 0.5 instead of .5) there will be less chance for error. Conversely, they should not use a zero after a number greater than one (e.g., 2 instead of 2.0). On written orders, print rather than script will lessen the chance for mistakes.

Problems in the ordering and administration of medications can also arise because of the involvement of different caregivers and the number of steps involved in prescribing a medication. A physician writes the order, the pharmacy fills the prescription, and nurses administer the medication. In many hospitals, however, there are approximately 20 steps in this process. Many medication errors that can occur during this lengthy process could be eliminated simply by having the physician type the medication name, dose amount, frequency of administration, and duration.

Adverse drug reactions (which are very different from medication errors) can stem from errors such as overdosing the patient or interactions between medications. Adverse reactions also include side effects. The use of computer software in the pharmacy could eliminate these problems, since the computer can be programmed to alert the pharmacist and physician as to possible drug reactions.

Newly approved medications or the off-label use of medications (i.e., the use of medications in a manner not originally intended by the drug manufacturer) can also cause problems. Many drugs that have been taken off the market were removed in the first year of their use. Physicians must become familiar with new medications and promptly report any unusual side effects that were not described by the drug manufacturers. Physicians may report the problem directly to the pharmaceutical company or (less frequently) submit a risk form to the Food and Drug Administration.

Nurses must take care at all times. For example, suppose Patient A asks to transfer to another room because Patient B is snoring loudly. Sometime during the night, Patient C is admitted into Patient A's original room. The nurses change shift at 7:00 AM. The medication nurse walks in and administers insulin to Patient C, not knowing that Patient A was moved. Insulin can be fatal if given to a nondiabetic patient. Many hospital systems are experimenting with bar-coded wristbands that must be swiped by a wand connected to a laptop carried by the nurse. This device will give an audible warning if the patient is about to get the wrong medicine.

US VERSUS EUROPEAN OPERATING ROOMS

Another area of concern regarding patient safety is surgery. Most European operating rooms (ORs) tend to be larger than ORs in the United States, often by about 100 square feet, allowing much more room for the surgery team to maneuver. These larger rooms also have space to accommodate induction and early recovery. It is anticipated that all surgery rooms in the future will have monitors and cameras that can be viewed by all members of the surgery team and operated remotely if necessary. It is anticipated that many of the cables that now clutter the room will be eliminated by wireless technology. The need for surface-to-surface transfers will be eliminated by using the OR table as a combination transporter and tabletop. This technique has been available for 30 years and is popular in Europe, but is not often seen in the United States. As US hospitals renovate their facilities, however, surgery suites likely will be updated. Another innovation for patient safety is the use of bar-coded or radiofrequency armbands that sound an alarm if the wrong patient is brought into surgery. To prevent surgeons from operating on the wrong body part, many hospitals now require surgeons to sign their name with a felt-tip pen on the correct area of the patient's body. This heightens the awareness of both the surgeon and the OR crew.

ADDITIONAL LEGAL ISSUES

The hospital attorney serves as the tip of the spear in warding off medical malpractice suits. He or she should constantly build awareness among the physicians and nurses about ways to ensure best practices in medicine, and review all patient, visitor, and employee incident reports.

In addition to risk management issues, the hospital attorney is also responsible for ensuring the legality of all hospital contracts, and he or she should review and initial all contracts before they are officially signed. The hospital attorney should work with human resources to ensure that all federal, state, and local employment laws are followed. This can include Title VII, FMLA, ERISA, ADA, HIPAA, Emergency Medical Treatment and Active Labor Act (EMTALA), the PDA, and a host of other laws previously discussed in the human resources chapter. The hospital attorney is also responsible for vetting all real estate transactions.

CORPORATE COMPLIANCE

Most hospitals today have a **corporate compliance** officer who is charged with ensuring that the hospital is in compliance with all federal, state, and local laws. At a minimum, effective compliance programs should include the following components:

- A hotline employees can use to contact the compliance officer if they suspect or know of any wrongdoing.
- Periodic corporate compliance training for all employees, and orientation training for new employees.
- Posters in employee areas to remind everyone of the importance of compliance procedures.
- Audits conducted internally and/or by outside accounting firms to uncover potential fraud or abuse.
- Random testing of employees to ensure compliance with drug laws.
- Change-of-shift drug inventories to discourage drug theft.

CHAPTER REVIEW

1. Describe a position control plan. Why is it important?
2. What is an EAP?
3. What are two forms of sexual harassment?
4. What does Title VII of the 1964 Civil Rights Act cover?
5. Why are drug screens and criminal background checks important in preemployment screening?
6. Can management require employees to undergo polygraph examinations?
7. What are some of the duties of the hospital attorney?
8. Why is a corporate compliance plan important?
9. What is a tort?
10. Discuss why a hospital should have a risk management plan and a corporate compliance plan.

CHAPTER 21

The Importance of Diversity in a Healthcare Organization

Geronimo Rodriguez, Jr., and Melvin V. Greene

KEY TERMS

Diversity
Inclusion

Cultural competence

INTRODUCTION

This chapter defines **diversity**, **inclusion**, and **cultural competence**, and discusses how these concepts can help minimize healthcare disparities and improve services in hospitals. In addition, various leadership approaches highlight the challenges in this new and growing area of responsibility for healthcare administrators.

In the 21st century, the world is more interconnected and interdependent than in any other time in history. According to 2009 US Census projections (http://www.census.gov), by the year 2040 more than 50% of US residents will be people of color. In fact, in certain regions of the country, this prediction is already being realized in hospitals where the majority of patients are of various nationalities and cultures. The United States is more diverse than ever, highlighting the need for those in the healthcare field to learn to respect different values and to treat every individual with dignity and respect.

Before we can discuss these issues, we first need to define certain terms, as listed below:

- Diversity: the condition of being diverse: variety; the inclusion of diverse people (as people of different races or cultures) in a group or organization.
- Inclusion: the act of including; the state of being included.
- Cultural competence: often described as the combination of a body of knowledge, a body of belief and a body of behavior. It involves a number of elements, including personal identification, language, thoughts, communications, actions, customs, beliefs, values and institutions that are often specific to ethnic, racial, religious, geographic, or social groups. For the provider of health information or health care, these elements influence beliefs and belief systems surrounding health, healing, wellness, illness, disease, and delivery of health services. The concept of cultural competence has a positive effect on patient care delivery by enabling providers to deliver services that are respectful of and responsive to the health beliefs, practices, and cultural and linguistic needs of diverse patients (http://www.nih.gov/clearcommunication/culturalcompetency.htm).

Cultural competence can also be defined as the ability to interact effectively with people of different cultures. It comprises four components: (1) awareness of one's own cultural worldview, (2) attitude toward cultural differences, (3) knowledge of different cultural practices and worldviews, and (4) cross-cultural skills. Developing cultural competence results in an ability to understand, communicate with, and effectively interact with people across cultures (http://www.wikipedia.org).

International migration and immigration, and dramatic increases in the Hispanic and Asian American populations require hospitals to address language issues as they strive to be the best providers of health care. Historical discrimination against African Americans and other persons of color have tainted the trust relationship between hospitals and individuals who, in the past, were often poor and vulnerable.

For leaders in healthcare fields, January 1, 2011, is an important date. It is the earliest date The Joint Commission can release its new standards for hospitals. From August 2008 to January 2010, The Joint Commission gathered vital information on how hospitals address the cultural and language needs of their diverse patient populations. On the basis of this ongoing study, The Joint Commission drafted accreditation standards for hospitals that focus on effective communication, cultural competence, and patient-centered care (http://www.jointcommission.org).

A hospital's board of trustees, chief executive officer, and senior administrators play key leadership roles in deciding how to address the cultural competence needs of their communities. First and foremost, they must determine how diversity efforts should be integrated into the organization. Next, they should determine what languages are spoken in the community. By performing a comparative analysis of the general and leadership workforces by race, age, and gender, administrators can gauge whether the members of the hospital staff accurately reflect the community they serve.

Diversity is a complex issue that reaches beyond race and gender. Today, hospital leaders are challenged to blend the unique work styles of four generations of caregivers into a smoothly functioning team. Also, to serve their rapidly growing, multicultural communities, hospitals must create an environment that is compassionate, sensitive, and respectful of the spiritual needs of their patients.

Diversity is important because it offers a society, a community, and a culture the opportunity to gain new perspectives and experiences that can lead to cultural and societal changes. The creation of new ideas, processes, and best practices as a result of diversity can have long-term benefits. When combined with inclusionary practices and cultural competency in health care, diversity can enhance organizational effectiveness at all levels.

Here is an example of how one health care organization defines diversity, inclusion, and cultural competence as follows:

Diversity is:

1. Recognizing the differences, inclusive of diverse ideas and backgrounds, individuals bring to their work, and
2. Utilizing the varied dimensions, experiences, and ideas of our talented workforce to deliver culturally competent patient care.

Inclusion is:

1. Valuing our universal human "oneness" and interdependence,
2. Accepting the whole person and being free to bring our whole selves to work, and
3. Ensuring an understanding, appreciation, and respect of cultural differences and similarities within and among groups.

Cultural competence is:

1. Skills, behaviors, policies, and practices that enable healthcare staff to work and communicate effectively across cultures in situations that involve team members, patients, families, partners, visitors, and other stakeholders, and
2. The ability to acquire and use knowledge of health-related beliefs, attitudes, practices, and communication patterns with patients and their families, team members and other stakeholders.

Diversity is *not*:

- An affirmative action program. Diversity is not a government mandate or requirement. It is voluntary and tied to organizational strategy, plans, and results.
- A quota system. Diversity is voluntary.
- A narrow focus on just race and gender. Diversity is multidimensional and includes age, disability, education, geographical location, income, and religion.
- Diversity is not a human resources function. It is leader-led and owned by all associates with an organization.

Whereas these definitions may be applicable for some hospital organizations, one size does not fit all. A sustainable definition for diversity, inclusion, and cultural competence must be aligned with the mission, vision, and values of the organization and its focus on patient care.

THE ROLE OF LEADERSHIP

The success of diversity, inclusion, and cultural competence efforts begins and ends with leadership. Leaders set the tone required to move an organization from recognizing diversity to institutionalizing inclusion and cultural competence.

Here is what one health care leader, Charles Barnett, says about diversity and inclusion:

> As the communities we serve have become more diverse, the Seton Family of Hospitals has identified the diversity of and inclusion in our family as one of the core characteristics of our organization.
>
> Our workforce is evolving to reflect the diversity of our patients. By employing associates who understand the health beliefs and practices prevalent in the community, we can help patients feel more welcome and better understood.
>
> We also ask associates to better appreciate each other's differences and similarities. This is why we highlight different cultural aspects of diversity, providing associates with the opportunity to learn from—and grow with—one another.
>
> At our best, the Seton Family of Hospitals is in tune with even subtler dimensions of diversity—how individuals share information and listen, offer help and advice and perform in teams. When associates are fully committed to communicating effectively across cultures, we provide safer and more responsive patient care.
>
> *Charles J. Barnett, FACHE*
> *President and CEO*
> *Seton Family of Hospitals*

Healthcare leaders, including the hospital board of directors, must demonstrate a commitment to building a diverse workforce that is reflective of the community they serve, and developing an inclusive environment in which all associates are respected, valued, and engaged.

THE BUSINESS CASE FOR DIVERSITY

Healthcare organizations that connect diversity to social responsibility and business results will position themselves for success over time. Leaders who understand the importance of a diversity initiative to the organization's bottom line should embrace a comprehensive strategy to integrate such an initiative into their business plan. By doing so, healthcare organizations can benefit from increased productivity, higher retention, and decreased litigation and employee-relations complaints. The organization may also enjoy a competitive advantage when recruiting and hiring, resulting in lower recruitment and hiring costs, as well as a safer environment of care and increased creativity. This strategy may include sharing best practices, resulting in diverse teams that have lower attrition and can outperform homogeneous teams. It may also create opportunities for the organization to increase its market share in an increasingly multicultural community. All of these benefits add up to improved patient outcomes and lower operating expenses.

THE ORGANIZATIONAL APPROACH TO DIVERSITY AND INCLUSION

Hospital organizations have many options for implementing a diversity, inclusion, and cultural competence strategy. One approach is to create a stand-alone office and consolidate all related functions. Another method is to integrate an office of diversity into the business organization. Finally, a hybrid approach that ensures accountability at each leadership level may provide the best benefits. Table 21-1 highlights the pros and cons of each approach.

Organizational Framework for a Diversity Initiative

Consultants in healthcare organizational development and experts in diversity and inclusion have different opinions as to what constitutes the ideal framework for a diversity initiative. There are, however, several basic

Table 21-1. Organizational Approach to Diversity and Inclusion

Approach	Pros	Cons
Stand-alone	• Consolidates all functions under one leader • Single-leader accountability	Multiple resources may be required Minimal/no visible leadership
Integrated	• Leader-led; accountability to all leaders	No clear lines of authority Minimal leader visibility
Hybrid	• Clear accountability and responsibility at each leadership level • Focused on organization's mission, vision, and values • Leadership buy-in and investment	Resource/funding constraints

steps that should be part of the structure of a diversity initiative, as described below.

Step 1: Create an office of diversity that is comprised of one or more diversity and inclusion subject matter experts. These individuals are the strategic diversity leaders who will develop, implement, consult, monitor, and report the metrics of the diversity initiative.

Step 2: Identify executive sponsors from key members of senior leadership, including the chief executive officer, president, chief operating officer, and/or senior vice president. The office of diversity should report directly to one of these sponsors and have a dotted-line responsibility to the others. These reporting/communicating levels provide the best opportunities to eliminate the potential of burying the initiative in the organizational structure and also to eliminate the creation of a silo effect for diversity.

Step 3: Organize a diversity advisory committee or council (DAC). This diverse group of internal leaders and associates should provide advice, counsel, and support to the office of diversity. The members should rotate off the committee every 2 or 3 years.

Step 4: Integrate diversity into existing processes and systems (training, talent acquisition, performance measurements, promotions, and succession planning). Conduct a gap analysis to highlight areas where change is required in order to achieve desired results.

Step 5: Develop and implement programs that promote diversity, inclusion, and cultural competence. These include mentoring, intern management, diversity skills training for leaders and associates, associate affinity groups, cultural celebrations, community outreach, and supplier diversity.

Step 6: Establish metrics and reporting tools. Create and utilize diversity dashboards and/or balanced scorecards.

Healthcare organizations that are considering implementing a diversity initiative can utilize the business plan concepts and the framework described in this chapter to position themselves for a sustainable diversity journey.

Today, hospitals and other healthcare organizations are focused on patient care and patient outcomes more than ever. Healthcare reform will impact each region differently. The one thing that will remain constant is change itself.

Healthcare leaders who have implemented a diversity initiative will face certain challenges that evolve from creating inclusive organizations. These include responding to The Joint Commission's cultural competence model and cooperating with the Civil Rights Division of the Department of Health and Human Services in its efforts to ensure equal treatment of all patients regardless of race or national origin. Healthcare organizations will also be challenged to create a spiritually diverse environment, increase their capacity to respond to change, provide diversity management and a global workforce that reflects the communities they serve, and improve services for an increasingly multicultural population.

CHAPTER REVIEW

1. Identify and describe the impact of changes in demographics on the healthcare delivery system.
2. Define diversity, inclusion, and cultural competence, and explain the importance of each in terms of providing safe and quality patient care.
3. Describe the role of leadership in implementing and managing a diversity initiative.
4. Discuss the business case for diversity.
5. List the key elements of an organizational structure and framework for a diversity initiative.
6. Identify the overall purpose and advantage of implementing a diversity initiative.

CHAPTER 22

Hospital Accreditation and Licensing
Donald J. Griffin

KEY TERMS

Joint Commission
Medicare survey
Sentinel event

Joint Commission International
(JCI)

INTRODUCTION

How do patients and community residents know whether a hospital in their community is a good hospital? How does a patient know whether an outside organization has reviewed the systems, procedures, physicians, nurses, and other elements of the hospital to make sure the system is functioning properly? Fortunately, a group has been established whose sole purpose is to review hospitals. It then informs hospitals, patients, and the community whether a hospital is satisfactory. This process of review is called hospital accreditation, and the group that undertakes it is called The **Joint Commission** (formerly known as the Joint Commission on Accreditation of Healthcare Organizations [JCAHO], and before that the Joint Commission on Accreditation of Hospitals [JCAH]).

THE JOINT COMMISSION

The Joint Commission has identified seven national patient-safety goals for healthcare institutions, as listed below:

1. Improve the effectiveness of communication among caregivers.
2. Improve the safety of using high-alert medications.
3. Improve the safety of using infusion pumps.
4. Improve the effectiveness of clinical alarm systems.
5. Improve the accuracy of patient identification.
6. Eliminate wrong site, wrong patient, and wrong procedure surgery.
7. Reduce the risk of healthcare-acquired infections.

Any institution that wishes to participate in The Joint Commission accreditation program must demonstrate what steps it is taking to meet these goals.

This lists touches on only a very small number of patient safety areas and ways to reduce errors. Countless safety practices are followed in hospitals to ensure patient safety, and they often require a team effort involving every department in the hospital. These practices include medical staff credentialing to ensure that physicians are qualified for privileges, human resources to conduct random drug screens and criminal background checks of every employee, and education and training to ensure that caregivers are competent in the latest clinical techniques. In addition, hospitals should implement infant security measures to minimize the risk of abductions, infection control measures to minimize hospital-acquired infections, and surgery procedures such as obtaining informed-consent forms; confirming the right patient, right site, and right procedure; and ensuring that the surgeon is competent to perform the procedure.

Zero tolerance for errors and unsafe practices should be the goal of every healthcare institution.

The roots of The Joint Commission can be traced back to the Hospital Standardization Program established by the American College of Surgeons in 1918. The program was initiated to help surgeons understand and appreciate the uniform medical records format that would allow them to evaluate members who wished to apply for fellowship status in the American College of Surgeons. Subsequently, the Hospital Standardization Program joined with three other groups—the American College of

Physicians, the American Medical Association, and the American Hospital Association (AHA)—to form the JCAH. On January 1, 1952, the JCAH officially began its work of surveying hospitals and granting accreditation. After the first year, it was clear that the organization had to have a more dynamic nature, and its standards were amended slightly. Ever since then, the commission has done a credible job of keeping up with new standards in the United States and constantly revising its approach to those standards. In the early years (up until 1961), field studies were done by member organizations that were part of the JCAH. In 1961, the JCAH hired its own full-time field staff.

In 1964, the JCAH began to charge hospitals a survey fee to complete its field program. With the passage of Medicare legislation (Public Law 89–97) in 1965, the JCAH was given a necessary boost. The law mandated that hospitals participating in Medicare had to meet a certain level of quality of patient care as measured against a recognized norm. The JCAH was specifically referred to in the law and hospitals were told they could undergo either a **Medicare survey** or a JCAH survey. This was reaffirmed by the Social Security Administration in its standards of 1965.

While the JCAH introduced medical audit requirements in the early 1970s, it also adopted broad requirements concerning the review and evaluation of the quality and appropriateness of health care. In 1979, the JCAH established new standards that required hospitals to develop quality-improvement programs. The Joint Commission has since adopted these standards for all other types of healthcare organizations that it accredits, and its focus has essentially become quality improvement. The name change from the Joint Commission on Accreditation of Hospitals to the Joint Commission of Healthcare Organizations that occurred in September 1987, and subsequently to The Joint Commission in 2007, more accurately reflects its mission and the constituencies it serves. Today, The Joint Commission often surveys home health agencies, hospice care, and other types of healthcare providers.

During the 1980s, The Joint Commission became more involved in the use of information systems. It now uses a computerized system in its survey analysis process. The Joint Commission also has a database that can help explain variations in outcomes of hospital care and help improve quality of care.

ACCREDITATION OVERVIEW

How does a hospital become accredited? First, the hospital completes an application and asks The Joint Commission, located in Chicago, to survey the hospital. The Joint Commission then sends the applicant a comprehensive questionnaire that addresses its standards for a hospital. After the hospital returns the completed questionnaire, The Joint Commission assigns a survey team and sets a date for a site visit to the hospital.

The questionnaire is concerned with standards in three major areas:

1. The services and quality of services the hospital delivers to the patient. The Joint Commission reviews the medical staff organization and systems, including the nursing, dietary, pharmacy, respiratory care, imaging, physical therapy, and emergency department services. It determines whether the services provided are adequate for patients. It is important to note that laboratories are surveyed by their own association, the College of American Pathologists (CAP). Both The Joint Commission and Medicare recognize this in lieu of conducting their own surveys.
2. The principles of organization and administration. Does the hospital have an effective bylaws structure? Does it have written policies and procedures? Does it require its departments to meet on a regular basis and to present written reports? Is the board involved and does it provide adequate oversight?
3. The physical plant and the environment in the hospital. This includes such things as life-safety code problems, whether the hospital has adequate sprinkler systems, whether the corridors are large enough, and whether there are proper safety exits.

Recently, The Joint Commission has been spending a great deal of time and effort on quality-improvement reviews in patient-care areas. The surveyors review patient medical records and other reports to determine whether the care given is appropriate for a specific case.

The Joint Commission publishes a reference manual for hospitals called the Accreditation Manual for Hospitals (AMH). This manual contains the standards used by The Joint Commission to evaluate hospitals. The reader is cautioned that The Joint Commission periodically changes its standards to maintain best practices for hospitals. It is imperative that the hospital to be surveyed is current on the latest survey standards.

ACCREDITATION IN MORE DETAIL

After the hospital completes the survey and the questionnaire, a Joint Commission survey team is scheduled to visit the hospital. The survey team consists of a physician, a nurse, and sometimes a hospital administrator. If it is a large hospital, the survey team may consist of three members and will usually take 3 to 4 days to complete the survey. If it is a very small hospital, there may be two members (a physician and a nurse) and the survey may involve only a 2- to 3-day visit.

The survey is quite complete and well organized. Each member of the survey team has a specific area to observe and survey. During the survey, which is actually a walk-through of the hospital, the surveyors read procedure manuals and minutes of meetings, look at life-safety code issues such as smoke barriers and sprinkler systems, examine crash carts to ensure they are periodically inventoried and inspected at the change of each nursing shift, interview personnel, and note any deficiencies observed in the hospital. They then make recommendations. Before they leave the hospital, they give their list to the hospital administrator at a formal exit briefing. The survey team reviews with the administrator and key members of the administrator's staff exactly what they found in need of improvement and what they recommend. This is a very open, candid discussion on how the hospital can improve itself. The surveyors send their list and reports to Joint Commission headquarters, where they are reviewed in detail. Finally, The Joint Commission decides, based on the survey, whether the hospital should be accredited. There are three different levels of accreditation: accreditation with commendation, accredited, or conditionally accredited.

After a hospital has been accredited by The Joint Commission, it receives a certificate of accreditation indicating this achievement. If it receives a 3-year accreditation, it must, in the interim period before the next visit by Joint Commission, complete a detailed questionnaire identifying what was done to correct the deficiencies noted in the original survey. The interim questionnaire is sent to The Joint Commission in Chicago, where it is evaluated.

The Joint Commission is important in the evaluation of hospitals in the United States. It is unique because it is voluntary. The Joint Commission has been responsive to hospitals, as well as state and federal governments, and provides a silent service to patients and communities by maintaining high professional standards. It acts as an advisory group to hospitals and is influential in urging hospitals to improve their life-safety measures, their quality improvement programs, and their organizations.

WHAT DOES ACCREDITATION REALLY MEAN TO A HOSPITAL?

In becoming accredited, a hospital says to its community, patients, and staff that it wants to meet high standards and that it is willing to spend the time and effort to have The Joint Commission measure it against a set standard. Accreditation tells a hospital's employees and patients that they are in a high-quality environment and the personnel are qualified to provide care. Accreditation emphasizes that the hospital is a responsible institution that takes its obligations for patient care seriously and has asked an independent, objective group to review it.

SENTINEL EVENTS

The Joint Commission requires healthcare organizations to report **sentinel events**, which are defined as unexpected occurrences involving death, serious physical or psychological injury, or the risk thereof. This includes unanticipated death or major permanent loss of function not related to a patient's illness. It also includes events such as surgery on the wrong patient or body part, infant abductions, patients who commit suicide or are raped while in the hospital, or transfusion reactions caused by major blood group incompatibilities.

After reporting a sentinel event, the organization should conduct a root cause analysis to uncover the basic factor(s) that led to the problem. This should assist the organization in enhancing its performance outcomes and avoiding similar problems. In addition to a thorough investigation, the organization should determine best practices (as defined in the current literature and the seminars held by professional groups) and make changes to reduce the chance of future incidents. It should identify who will be responsible for making the necessary changes, set a time line for their implementation, educate the staff regarding the changes, and then monitor and evaluate the effectiveness of the changes.

JOINT COMMISSION INTERNATIONAL

Many hospitals in the United States voluntarily participate in an accreditation survey from The Joint Commission in order to (1) receive federal funding, (2) demonstrate to the public that they are a quality institution, and/or (3) improve their own internal processes.

Hospitals outside the United States have wanted a similar accreditation process so that they can demonstrate quality and thus attract patients and physicians. In 1999, The Joint Commission announced standards for international hospitals under the name **Joint Commission International (JCI)**. Hospitals outside the United States may apply for an accreditation survey, prepare for the survey, and then receive a site visit from a survey team. The accreditation visit is conducted in a manner similar to that employed in the United States.

LICENSURE

The Joint Commission's reviews and surveys are the primary forms of control over hospitals. In fact, the accreditation is somewhat like an informal license, particularly since the federal government, under Titles XVIII and XIX of the Medicare legislation (Public Law 89–97), has endorsed The Joint Commission's survey to certify payment for hospitals under Medicare. However, hospital systems also involve other forms of control.

Formal licensing is the most common form of regulation by the states. Generally, a license to operate a hospital is issued by a state agency, perhaps the health department. The licensing bureau or agency can retain records of a hospital's bed capacity and the capabilities of its other facilities. State health and welfare departments account for three quarters of the state agencies that have regulatory powers over hospitals. A state's licensure laws and regulations usually culminate in a licensure inspection that is similar to the inspection conducted by The Joint Commission. This can lead to an overlap in the regulatory systems. Frequently, state and Joint Commission inspectors inspect the same things, or the state will accept The Joint Commission's accreditation process and not conduct an inspection.

The Joint Commission reciprocally shares survey information with state and district licensure agencies regarding a hospital's accreditation surveys. In turn, these agencies report information about potential standard-related problems in accredited hospitals to The Joint Commission. Reciprocally sharing information enables both The Joint Commission and licensure agencies to identify hospitals that have performance problems and require further review.

MEDICARE CERTIFICATION

In addition to licensure, another form of control for hospitals is the process of Medicare certification. In 1965, the federal government enacted Social Security amendments (Titles XVIII and XIX) and stipulated that hospitals had to conform to certain general compliance guidelines before they could be certified to participate in federal insurance programs. For example, hospitals could follow these guidelines to establish an around-the-clock nursing staff, improve medical supervision, and ensure the proper use of clinical records. This step led to the formal Medicare program.

MEDICARE SURVEYS

Hospitals that do not wish to participate in a Joint Commission survey (usually because these surveys are expensive, involving fees to The Joint Commission, and require considerable preparation time) may opt to undertake a Medicare survey. If it does not successfully complete either a Joint Commission or Medicare survey, the hospital will not qualify for Medicare funding.

REGISTRATION

Registration is a weak form of control for healthcare systems. Some hospital authorities might not even regard it as a control. However, registration systems can be useful in that they allow third-party payers, consumers, and federal agencies to review the rosters of hospitals and other healthcare institutions. The most commonly used registry for hospital systems is the one maintained by the AHA. The AHA collects and maintains extensive data in the form of hospital profiles. It is also involved in registering hospitals in planning areas. For example, the AHA reviews new construction, proposed mergers, and proposals for sharing of services. The AHA publishes an annual hospital statistics report that includes data from many of its registration activities.

CHAPTER REVIEW

1. What is The Joint Commission and how does it differ from the JCI?
2. A Joint Commission survey team usually consists of _____.
3. What is a recognized alternative to The Joint Commission survey?
4. What is a sentinel event?
5. How does state licensing differ from accreditation?

CHAPTER 23

Hospital Marketing
Donald J. Griffin

KEY TERMS

Public relations

Target markets

Branding

Focus groups

Marketing audit

Positioning

Four Ps

INTRODUCTION

It can be argued that hospital care is something everybody needs and therefore should not have to be marketed at all. Traditionally, hospitals, like the rest of the healthcare field, have avoided marketing. Although they have been willing to attempt to improve their public and community image, they have resisted advertising and competitive pricing. Yet with a finite patient population and many communities being overbedded, some hospitals are finding themselves in a fierce fight for their very survival, pitted against other hospitals, and are pulling out all the stops to maintain market share.

Marketing today is very sophisticated and requires a combination of self-analysis, market research, competitor research, and demographic research. Trends must be carefully noted and a strategy plotted to maximize market share. It comes down to knowing who you are ("you" being the hospital), who they are ("they" being the rival hospitals), and the needs of the target population. The target population could be patients, physicians, or insurance companies . . . after all, patients don't admit themselves. Hospitals have no patients unless physicians admit the patients, and many patients must visit a certain hospital based on their insurance coverage.

Marketing studies suggest that hospitals should try to determine both the physicians' and the community's needs, and then attempt to meet those needs by developing appropriate services, testing, and treatment programs.

Other factors, such as soaring health costs, increased participation by patients in meeting their own healthcare needs and selecting their providers, and higher expectations from healthcare consumers, have driven hospitals to increase their marketing efforts.

WHAT IS MARKETING?

Marketing is a system of activities that combines product, place, price, and promotion to properly distribute goods and services to a target population. A market exchange can be viewed as an individual being persuaded to give another individual something in order to receive a service, good, or privilege in return. Four of the more active areas of marketing are (1) public relations, (2) advertising, (3) research, and (4) sales.

Public Relations—Only One Part of the Marketing Effort

Public relations (PR) is generally defined as creating or improving the public image of a person or organization, and establishing goodwill between that person or organization and the public.

For many years, hospitals have understood the need to develop and retain positive relationships with their patients, their potential donors, and their community at large. PR can improve a hospital's image, generate public interest in the institution, and aid in fundraising efforts. Most hospitals have some sort of PR program, whether formal or informal. Many have a full-time PR staff. The main objective of this staff is to position the hospital to receive favorable publicity in the community. To accomplish this, staff members might invite a local newspaper reporter to tour the hospital, or they could develop strong contacts at local television and radio stations, thereby improving relationships with the media.

The PR department is an advisory department. Generally, there is a PR director in charge of the department. The PR department works closely with all other hospital departments, but the PR function is clearly the responsibility of hospital management. The technical aspects of PR, such as creating brochures or writing press releases, are usually left to a technical expert. A PR program need not necessarily be costly or elaborate, but it must be well thought out and systematically developed with managerial input if it is to be effective and get the message across in a proper manner.

In terms of PR, a community hospital has two target populations. The first is the internal market—the hospital's board of trustees, its employees, medical staff members, volunteers, patients, and friends of the hospital. It is relatively easy to "sell" a positive image of the hospital to this population, and this is traditionally done by circulating certain types of publications within the hospital, such as newsletters.

The more difficult segment to reach is the hospital's external market. This includes potential patients of the hospital, members of the community, and potential contributors to the hospital. This public market is not as clearly defined as the internal market and presents a much more difficult challenge for PR directors and hospital management.

Most hospitals are involved in publishing some type of PR material and literature. Hospitals commonly publish booklets containing patient or employee information. Frequently they publish their own internal newspapers, institutional brochures, or even annual reports for the internal group. The hospital administrator and management team initiate most of these internal publications. The hospital's patients have the greatest need for this type of published material and information, but unfortunately for the hospital, it usually has only a short period of time to get the message across to most of its patients.

Some hospitals televise informative videos, and nearly every hospital has a website that can be very useful in building a good image (and can also be an important recruiting tool). Written publications are still important and may include the following:

- *A patient information booklet.* This booklet contains information to familiarize the patient with the hospital environment, gives the "dos and don'ts" of being a patient, and also offers visitor information. This booklet should strive to be a warm communiqué, and it provides an excellent opportunity to promote a positive image.
- *An employee information handbook.* This handbook lists the rules of employment, the employees' rights and obligations, and often the fringe benefits available to employees. This is a PR opportunity.

- *A hospital newsletter.* Typically, the hospital newsletter is prepared by a local printer and is generally not of the same quality as the traditional newspapers with which we are familiar. The newsletter may be published infrequently, perhaps once a month or once a quarter. The reporting staff is usually made up of amateur writers and reporters from within the hospital. However, it is a source of information, and if done properly, it can be enjoyed by all employees.
- *An institutional brochure.* This is available to internal groups, the board of trustees, and volunteers. It usually describes the history, mission, vision, and core values of the institution.
- *The annual report.* When a hospital publishes a formal annual report, it is usually done with quality printing and a high degree of expertise in its layout. The report is used for internal purposes of the medical staff, board of trustees, and employees, and it is frequently sent to other hospitals and to certain members of the public. Annual reports summarize the operational highlights of the year and usually list key management and medical staff.

Hospitals generally develop a relationship with the public through the use of mass media and press releases. The hospital has specific objectives it wants to accomplish—mainly to keep the public informed, to improve or build a positive image for the hospital in the community, and perhaps to have an influence on what the mass media are reporting in the healthcare arena. The PR department commonly uses press releases to keep in touch with the media and, accordingly, the public.

When a hospital embarks upon a capital fundraising campaign or an annual fundraising effort, it must solicit the public, usually in written form. Although some hospitals might not consider this a function of the PR department, it clearly is, since many letters of solicitation are sent out. Often, costly folders or brochures are also developed and sent, usually by direct mail, to raise funds.

Hospital Advertising

Advertising can be utilized to build the hospital's image or to sell a particular product. For example, a hospital may purchase billboards depicting a picture of the hospital with the tag line "Ready when you need us." This is clearly an *image* advertisement. As an alternative, the hospital may sell a particular *product*, such as its emergency department depicted on the same type of billboard, with the tag line "Seen in 30 minutes or your visit is free." This clearly touts the speed and efficiency of the emergency department crew. Both types of ads have their appropriate places.

Hospitals are becoming increasingly involved in advertising. Today, hospitals spend more than half of their marketing budgets on advertising. In fact, advertising has a major role to play in the entire marketing process, for both not-for-profit and for-profit activities. Hospital advertising is a great way to promote facts related to hospital services and facilities.

Hospitals are finding that they can tailor advertising to their professional needs and select very specific **target markets**. For example, they can target their advertising efforts toward physicians who may be interested in utilizing the hospital. Or they may use advertising as a way to increase activity in less frequently used areas of the hospital. For example, prospective obstetrical patients may be attracted by images of a family-centered maternity room displayed in the local newspaper, on television, or on the Web.

In general, hospital advertising (1) informs the public, (2) persuades the public, and (3) reminds the public. Mass production has created an economy of abundance. In this context, hospitals are competitive institutions. The federal government reports that there are too many hospital beds in this country. Therefore, it is logical to conclude that hospitals will turn to a lesson already learned by for-profit retail industries: people can be persuaded to use one service instead of another. Hospitals can make their products or services known, and sell their benefits and features. They can employ advertising to remind the public to continue to use their services, as well as to remind them why they were satisfied with the hospital and what brought them there in the first place.

There are many reasons for hospitals to spend money on advertising. For one, the hospital's patients may need information on how to prevent disease and illness. They may need guidance on how to practice good nutrition or how to self-administer a breast examination. Another reason is that hospital patients need to understand how the healthcare system works, and how preventive medicine programs function with interaction from healthcare professionals. For example, patients might want to know where cancer screening is available and where children can receive immunizations. Advertising helps to inform hospital patients how they can properly access the basic elements of the healthcare system. The hospital can also advertise to tell patients about new services or facilities, such as a newly remodeled emergency department, a new birthing center, or expanded clinic hours. Advertising can convey this type of information to improve not only the hospital's image but the entire hospital industry's image as well. Hospitals are likely to be interested in advertising along these lines because such efforts are closely related to their mission of health education.

SALES

As hospitals are becoming more businesslike and competitive, the sales function is growing in popularity. Some hospitals now have a dedicated sales force that reports directly to marketing executives or others in top management. These sales forces have proved to be effective, especially regarding certain restrictive services or products such as occupational health, smoking cessation, sports medicine, and weight loss. Hospitals also use telemarketing and, of course, the invaluable hospital website as sales tools.

This same sales force can be effective for recruiting physicians and educating doctors who are not on staff about the wonderful array of services the hospital offers.

BRANDING

Many hospitals are engaged in **branding**, which identifies everything they do as originating from the same entity. To understand what branding is, let us look at the example of an industrial giant: Honda. After successfully manufacturing and marketing motorcycles, Honda then introduced automobiles and later generators, chain saws, and countless other motorized products, all bearing the brand name Honda. In like manner, large hospitals with good reputations open clinics, long-term care facilities, home health agencies, durable medical equipment stores, etc., under the same hospital name to assure the public that they will receive the same high-quality services they have come to expect from the hospital.

MARKET RESEARCH

Although market research is one of the most critical duties of the marketing department, it is one that hospitals often overlook. Market research is valuable because it provides information about local demographics, physicians the hospital may want to recruit, the wants and needs of the hospital's patients, and what the competition is doing. It can also generate information concerning perceptions, preferences, and potential demand. Hospitals use various market research techniques, including demographic analysis, direct mail and telephone surveys, personal interviews, and focus groups. **Focus groups** are usually volunteers of interest to the client who are paid to be interviewed about a particular issue. For example, a group of mothers might be asked, "Why did you choose to use Hospital A when you delivered your first baby?"

MARKET STUDIES AND AUDITS

Hospitals must become familiar with certain key concepts in the marketing process if they are to be successful. Perhaps the best place to begin is with a marketing study. A market study is simply a systematic, objective, critical way of appraising a market in which the hospital is interested. The marketing program can then be fine-tuned to target the market in question. A marketing study involves the following steps:

1. Identify the kinds of information to be gathered in order to evaluate market or patient relations.
2. Set about collecting this information.
3. Evaluate the information that was collected.
4. Evaluate the amount of resources and effort needed to have a significant presence in that market.

In similarity to an accounting audit, a market audit is an examination of how a process is being undertaken and, particularly in the context of marketing, how resources are being used. Where are we spending our resources, and are they still being correctly allocated in the best manner? Do we have the necessary websites in place? Are we allocating too much to television? Are we overlooking drive-time radio? Are there key billboards that we should purchase? What have our surveys shown about our effectiveness? Has our share of the market increased as a result of our expenditures?

Physicians are often the principal targets of a hospital's marketing program (after all, the hospital sits empty until a physician admits a patient), and a common **marketing audit** in use by hospitals is the physician audit. This gives hospital management information about how many physicians are admitting patients, the type of patients by payer category per physician compared to the same physician a year ago, how many surgeons are operating, etc. This will set a baseline by which the hospital can measure progress. Another type of marketing audit examines the number of dollars spent in comparison with the number of procedures, admissions, and surgeries performed.

After a marketing audit has been completed, it may become clear to the hospital that it has more than one kind of audience or public. The various populations with which the hospital works are called segments or market segments. A market segment is a group of patients or potential patients who can be assigned to a distinct category. For example, it is common to divide patients by type of insurance (Medicare, Medicaid, Blue Cross, etc.), by age, or by the service required (e.g., obstetrics, pediatrics, cardiac) Frequently, patients are categorized by income level or geographic location.

After completing an audit and identifying its different market segments, it is important for the hospital to realize that its patients, the community, and competing hospitals all have an image of the hospital. Where the hospital fits into this image spectrum is called the hospital's **positioning** strategy.

It is important for hospital management to understand the concept of positioning when it is trying to determine what programs the hospital should invest in or sponsor. To use an illustration from commercial business, Avis Rent a Car's position was not clear until the company finally adopted the slogan "We Try Harder." This move was highly successful because Avis did not position itself directly opposite its number one competitor, but in fact differentiated itself from its competition. In the context of hospitals, if a neighboring hospital has a superior cardiology unit, perhaps the hospital with the lesser cardiology unit should promote its outpatient pediatrics services. It could then position itself as being different from its competition, and become successful and strong while carving out its own unique niche.

With the concept of a marketing niche, segment, or positioning in mind, the marketing staff can proceed with the classic **four Ps** of marketing: product, place, price, and promotion. The objective is to put the right product (or service) in the right place at the right price with the proper promotion.

With regard to the right product, it should be remembered that hospitals do not really sell products—they sell services. They sell the benefit or satisfaction a patient may get from receiving their services. This is the hospital's product. Ideally, a hospital should conduct inventories or marketing audits frequently to determine what its products and benefits should be. Hospitals should regularly analyze their service programs.

A good example of the importance of place, or location, can be seen in satellite outpatient clinics or in medical office buildings situated near a hospital. These hospitals have placed their services in the right location. They are convenient and responsive to the patient.

Now that the federal government and other large insurers reimburse hospitals for patient care, price (the third P) may become less important to the hospital industry than it is to retail businesses. However, price is still important to the small portion of the market that purchases services directly—for example, elective surgery not covered by insurance. The market is somewhat sensitive to the cost for an hour in the operating room, a 4-day stay in the nursery, or a urinalysis. Cost still must be considered in the total marketing program, and especially when negotiating with HMOs.

The last P, promotion, refers to the classic marketing activities that hospitals undertake, such as advertising, as well as more innovative ways of promoting products (for example, offering premiums and incentives to certain people). Hospitals must be sensitive to the ethical issues involved in promoting health services.

It is important for hospital managers to understand in detail the strategies and tactics of the marketing process. If hospitals want to attract new physicians, develop effective programs, retain qualified personnel, and remain current in their delivery services, they will find that marketing can be a great asset.

FUNDRAISING

Most not-for-profit hospitals rely on donations and fundraising efforts as a source of needed funds. Fundraising may be divided into two general categories: (1) annual giving programs and (2) capital or special purpose campaigns. Hospitals often have a section or part of their organization devoted to fundraising. This section or department is referred to as the development office, and the annual giving program is usually conducted by the development staff. Hospitals frequently use outside consultants to assist them on special or capital campaigns. Many of the tactics used to solicit funds draw on proven marketing methods, including direct mail, a special section of the hospital's website, direct contacts, solicitation of individuals, and special events. Major sources targeted for contributions include wealthy individuals, large business corporations, and foundations.

CHAPTER REVIEW

1. What is a target market?
2. What are the four Ps of marketing?
3. Discuss focus groups.
4. Explain branding.
5. List five examples of written publications used in marketing efforts, and discuss the importance of each.
6. What is a marketing audit?
7. What are two hospital fundraising methods?
8. Discuss how marketing differs from PR.
9. Discuss how image advertising is different from product line advertising.
10. What is positioning and why is it important?

CHAPTER 24

Strategic Planning
Donald J. Griffin

KEY TERMS

Long-range plan
SWOT analysis
Mission statement
Vision statement

Execution
Implementation
Certificate of need (CON)

INTRODUCTION

A plan is a roadmap. Hospital planning requires a careful analysis of where and what the organization is, how it relates to its environment and competition, where it wants to go or to become, how quickly the developments will happen, and who is responsible for each segment in the process. To quote the famous baseball player Yogi Berra, "If you don't know where you are going, you could end up somewhere else." Planning is not only common sense, it is a good management strategy, particularly now that third parties and regulatory agencies are all pushing hospitals into a more competitive environment. Administrators see the changing demands of the population. The needs of physicians are increasing. The need to remain solvent and achieve appropriate reimbursements requires budgetary planning. Today, a hospital's survival is truly contingent upon its ability to make the correct strategic decisions for its future course of action.

THE EVOLUTION OF PLANNING

In the early 1950s, about 10 hospital councils, located mostly in large urban cities, began to make some progress on capital planning in their respective regions. After 1955, more and more agencies were structured to aid in community planning, and specific planning programs were set up for metropolitan hospital areas.

Planning continued to evolve through the 1950s and 1960s, and at that time, it was generally focused on developing new facilities in a rapidly expanding healthcare market. There was a major concentration on designing and constructing the physical plants for hospital systems. In the 1970s, planning efforts began to focus more on the development or expansion of programs, services, and products. In the 1980s, planning moved beyond the institution to the external environment, with an emphasis on developing relationships with outside healthcare providers. Today, partly because of the oversupply of beds in many areas and the tightening of government regulations, planning usually involves a great deal more than expansion. It is often used to ensure that a hospital's services are necessary, appropriate, and profitable, and will remain so in the future. Recently it has become common for hospitals to develop associations, shared services, or linkages with other healthcare providers as part of their planning process.

Hospitals are looking seriously at vertical and horizontal growth in the industry. For example, they are exploring home care, primary care, and other forms of subacute care that relate directly to the hospital (horizontal integration), as well as the use of clinics and long-term care facilities that could be sources of patients or places to send patients (vertical integration). Many hospitals are joining in not-for-profit multisystems of one kind or another.

THE HOSPITAL'S LONG-RANGE PLAN

It is to a hospital's advantage to make sound, practical plans for the future, particularly now that there are so many competitive forces, such as free-standing surgery centers owned by physicians and new governmental regulations impacting the hospital environment. The changing patterns of medical practice include a shift from acute inpatients to ambulatory medicine; the mushrooming of biomedical technology, with its accompanying impact on operational costs; and shifts in demographics and community needs. These changing patterns are especially important in urban areas where age, insurance coverage, and mobility are constant factors in hospital planning. Finally, changing economic conditions, particularly regarding the availability of money to carry out the hospital's plans, and increased legislation and regulations will affect the hospital. The hospital must factor all of these elements into the planning process in order to derive a list of options that will serve it in the future.

WHO SHOULD DO THE PLANNING FOR THE HOSPITAL?

The hospital's planning effort is usually led or initiated by the CEO, but it usually involves the active participation of the senior management team, the board of directors, and the medical staff. The CEO may also receive assistance from the hospital's own planning department, if it has one, or from outside consultants.

As the person who is primarily responsible for carrying out the board's decisions, the administrator or CEO participates actively in planning deliberations. Usually the CEO determines the planning process and suggests various options regarding long-range decisions to the board.

The medical staff's role is also critical. The medical staff must identify changes in the healthcare needs of the community and suggest new ways to meet those needs. They are also the ones who will be using any new technology purchased by the hospital. Medical staff members can serve as spokespersons for advanced technology and advise the board's planning committee on how this technology will influence the hospital's plan. Another byproduct of encouraging the participation of the medical staff is that it allows them to become acquainted with the problems faced by hospital management in planning for the future, usually in an environment of limited resources.

The Strategic Planning Process

Hospitals generally engage in sequential planning to create a strategic plan (also sometimes known as a 5-year plan). As a first step, an environmental scan is done to analyze the political, competitive, regulatory, social, economic, and technological environments. Next, the hospital's internal and external environments are assessed. This evaluation step is commonly referred to as a **SWOT analysis** (with SWOT standing for strengths, weaknesses, opportunities, and threats). Strengths and weaknesses reflect the internal environment, whereas opportunities and threats refer more to the external environment. An essential element is to examine the demographic trends of the area to note potential pitfalls.

Once the hospital's internal and external environments have been analyzed, the hospital must decide what it wants to do and be in a broad sense. This decision involves reviewing the hospital's mission statement to ensure that it is current. The **mission statement** describes what the hospital is all about, or what it stands for. The mission statement expresses the hospital's philosophy and details what community services, research, educational commitments, and major offerings the hospital will provide. Mission statements can often be condensed to a slogan that is short enough to fit on an employee's name badge, such as "Delivering excellent care, benchmarked to international standards." Mission statements are usually written through a joint effort of the CEO and the board of directors.

A **vision statement** is a statement of hope. It expresses where the hospital wants to be in the future, or where it sees itself in 10–15 years. Usually the CEO writes the vision statement.

The hospital then sets specific goals for accomplishing its mission, and determines the strategies and tactics it will use to accomplish those goals. A careful market analysis is usually undertaken to examine competitive factors. Timetables are agreed upon and certain personnel are given the responsibility of ensuring that a particular goal is achieved. After the plan is approved and implemented, it must be evaluated and refined on a regular basis, usually yearly or biyearly. In summary, strategic planning involves (1) performing an environmental scan, (2) conducting a SWOT analysis; (3) writing mission and vision statements, and communicating them to all employees and the public; (4) setting goals; (5) establishing a timetable; and (6) determining who is responsible for each goal that was set. This periodic review is necessary to ascertain whether the hospital is on track or new goals should be set. The best planning documents or stategic plans are of no value if they are not implemented. It is a waste of many people's time for a plan to merely set on a shelf or be stored on a memory stick and not be implemented. Of even more importance is the **execution** of the plan; to ensure the plan is carried out, a timetable of dates are set out and then key people are given responsibilities and are periodically monitored to see that they are carrying out the **implementation** of the plan.

LEVELS OF LONG-RANGE PLANNING

A hospitals plan may well have different levels of involvement. For example, the CEO and the board of directors might create the strategic plan, senior-level division executives (DON, CFO, COO, etc.) might create the tactical plan, and the department directors might flesh out the operational details.

BENEFITS OF PLANNING

Proper long-range planning will improve the hospital's ability to deal with problems or changes that arise in the future. Specifically, it will provide the following benefits:

- It will establish a systematic basis for allocating resources.
- It will ensure that the hospital continues to abide by its mission statement.
- It will ensure the viability of the hospital by integrating budgets with long-range strategic plans.
- It will give managers and administrators more control because they will have a better idea of where the organization is going; this will also guide management's day-to-day operations.
- It will give the hospital a standard for management against which it can evaluate and measure performance.

PLANNING NEW FACILITIES

As part of the planning process, hospitals must determine what sort of facilities they will need in the future. The facilities themselves should not drive the plan; rather, form should follow function. A master site and facilities plan must be agreed upon and followed if the hospital plan is going to be successful.

Planners today have a big advantage in that they can easily access vital data on the Web using a host of search engines. For example, if the hospital wishes to expand the neonatal intensive care unit, it can find formulas that predict the number of beds needed for any given time period based on the number of births, the number of current neonatal intensive care unit patients, and the anticipated population growth.

One other issue a healthcare facility planner must be aware of is the **certificate of need (CON)**. Many states have taken steps to address the problem of overbedding by limiting the number of facilities that can be built in certain communities. In such cases, healthcare entities must apply for a CON and demonstrate that the proposed service is currently lacking or insufficient. Other states, such as Texas, have abolished the CON process, reasoning that economic forces should be allowed to work.

CHAPTER REVIEW

1. What is a plan? What is the difference between a strategic plan and a tactical plan?
2. What is a mission statement? What is a vision statement?
3. Why must upper management be involved in planning? Could it not just retain a planning consultant?
4. How often should a hospital engage in strategic planning?

Part IX

Hospital Financial Issues

CHAPTER 25

Finance

Tiankai Wang

KEY TERMS

Billing and collection
Preclaims submission activities
Claim processing activities
Accounts receivable (A/R)
Claims reconciliation
Electronic data interchange (EDI)
Health information management (HIM)
Explanation of benefits (EOB)
Medicare summary notice (MSN)
Remittance advice (RA)
Revenue cycle management (RCM)
Key Performance Indicators (KPIs)
Healthcare Financial Management Association (HFMA)
Point-of-service (POS)
Collections

Discharged not final billed (DNFB)
False Claims Act
Certified public accountant (CPA)
Generally accepted accounting principles (GAAP)
Double entry rule
Cost conservatism principle
Accrual concept
Matching concept
Balance sheet
Income statement
Statement of cash flows
Average payment period (APP)
Liquidity ratio
Budgets—operating, capital, cash
Net present value (NPV)
Budget process (steps in the. . .)
Forecasting

INTRODUCTION

Finance is the lifeblood of hospitals. It is a key element in the efficient functioning of all aspects of the hospital system, from strategic planning to daily operations. The financial functions of a hospital include billing and collection, financial management, and budgeting. **Billing and collection** generate revenues for the hospital, financial management addresses financial planning, and budgeting involves control of expenditures.

SECTION A: BILLING AND COLLECTION

The billing and collection department is responsible for billing patients for services rendered in the hospital. The billing and collection process is called the medical claim cycle and consists of four phases: **preclaims submission activities**, **claim processing activities**, **accounts receivable (A/R)**, and **claims reconciliation** and collection. The medical claim cycle is illustrated in Figure 25-1.

Preclaims Submission Activities

The medical claim cycle begins when a person first enrolls in a medical plan. Table 25-1 shows the various types of insurance plans available.

The person, now called a patient, calls to schedule a medical appointment. The collection of data for a medical claim begins at this time. The receptionist, or scheduler, collects and documents insurance information in order to arrange the appointment with an authorized provider under contract with the patient's medical plan, and to determine whether any other requirements must be met. On the day of the appointment, the scheduler collects or verifies the patient-supplied medical billing information and sometimes information for preauthorization. In most cases, it is standard policy to contact each payer and verify that the billing information is correct and the policy or the patient's eligibility has not expired.

When the patient presents to the hospital, the receptionist collects the patient registration form, obtains any required signatures, copies the insurance card, and attaches an encounter form to the patient record. The encounter form (also called a charge slip, communicator, fee ticket, multipurpose billing form, or patient service slip) contains areas to check off or write in diagnoses and procedures, along with basic information about the patient and the patient's account. The receptionist is responsible for

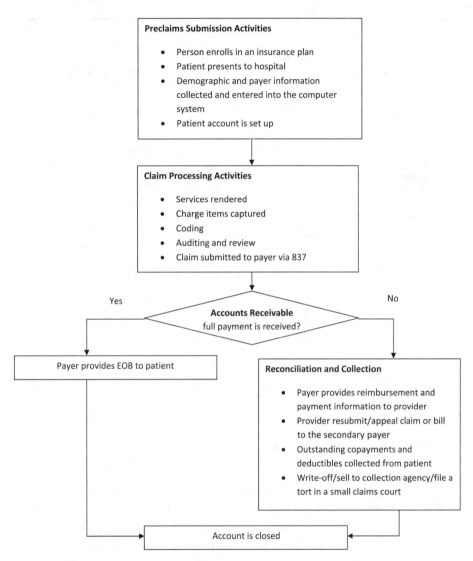

FIGURE 25-1. Medical claim cycle in hospital.

entering new information into the computer correctly and, if necessary, correcting inaccurate information.

Each patient is assigned a patient account. Hospitals are increasingly using electronic accounting software programs to handle patients' accounts. To create the account, the patient's data are entered into the software program. When all of the patient's data have been entered into the system, patient lists and many other documents can be generated in several ways.

Table 25-1. Classifications of Healthcare Plans

Voluntary healthcare insurance plans	Government-sponsored healthcare programs	Managed care
Private/commercial individual healthcare insurance plan	Medicare	Health maintenance organization (HMO)
Private/commercial employer-based healthcare insurance plan	Medicaid	Preferred provider organization (PPO)
Blue Cross and Blue Shield plans	Temporary Assistance for Needy Families (TANF) program Program of All-Inclusive Care for the Elderly (PACE) State Children's Health Insurance Program (SCHIP) TRICARE programs Civilian Health and Medical Program of the Veterans Administration (CHAMPVA) Indian Health Services (IHS) Workers' Compensation	Point-of-service (POS) plan Exclusive provider organization (EPO) Medicare Advantage

Claims Processing Activities

Claims processing activities include the capture of all billable services, claim generation, and claim correction. Charge capture is a vital component of the billing process. In addition to providing medical care, the authorized physician is responsible for (1) documenting the details of the encounter in the patient's medical record in a manner that meets legal requirements; and (2) approving the charges and instructions listed on the encounter form for the billing department.

The billing specialist records the transactions, including professional fees, payments (e.g., cash, check, or credit card), adjustments (e.g., write-off or courtesy), and balance due. The balance of the account is the amount owed on a transaction. The billing specialist may use a copy of the encounter form to record the transaction. However, if the hospital uses an electronic order entry system, the charge for the service or supply is automatically transferred to the patient accounting system and posted to the patient's claim.

Coding is a major part of the charge capture process. When filing a claim, the billing specialists are required to code with ICD-9-CM (or ICD-10-CM after October 1, 2013; please refer to the coding Chapter 17 for details on how coding is performed).

The Health Insurance Portability and Accountability Act (HIPAA) prohibits providers with more than 10 employees from sending paper claims. Hospitals have to submit claims electronically or contract with an outside billing agency to prepare and file the claims electronically. Both paper and electronic claims are constructed from data used in the reimbursement process. However, the electronic claim is sent by means of an **electronic data interchange (EDI)**, rather than by mail or fax. Electronic submission reduces claim filing errors, provides more security in submission, and allows the providers to be reimbursed more quickly. The electronic claim is submitted via an 837 form, which replaces the paper CMS-1500 form. Currently, the claim software includes a data field that allows the specialist to include a paper claim (CMS-1500) attachment. However, it is expected that in the near future, this will no longer be necessary.

Once all of the data have been posted to the patient's account, the claim can be reviewed for accuracy and completeness. Many hospitals have an internal auditing system that runs each claim through a set of edits designed for specific third-party payers. The auditing system identifies data that have failed an edit and flags the claim for correction. The auditing process prevents facilities from sending incomplete or inaccurate claims to the payer. **Health information management (HIM)** and billing specialists review the claims against the medical record to determine whether all services, diagnoses, and procedures were accurately reported. If errors are found, they can be corrected before the claim is submitted. Once it is reviewed and corrected, the claim can be submitted to the third-party payer for payment.

Sometimes an electronic medical claim is sent through a clearinghouse, where a series of edits are conducted before the claim is sent to the payer. If the claim has errors and is rejected by the clearinghouse, it is sent back to the hospital.

Accounts Receivable

The total amount of money owed for professional services rendered (i.e., the combined charges minus all payments) is called the A/R.

Once the claim is submitted to the third-party payer for reimbursement, the A/R shows up in the hospital account.

Once a claim is received by the third-party payer, the insurance processing of the claim begins. In addition to processing the claim for payment, the third-party payer prepares an **explanation of benefits (EOB)** that is delivered to the patient. The EOB is a statement that describes the services rendered, the payment covered, and the benefit limits and denials. For Medicare patients, a **Medicare summary notice (MSN)** is prepared. The MSN details the amounts billed by the provider, amounts approved by Medicare, how much Medicare reimbursed the provider, and what the patient must pay the provider in terms of the deductible and copayment. EOBs and MSNs are provided to both the facility and the patient.

Once the claim is processed by the third-party payer, a **remittance advice (RA)** is returned electronically to the provider. The RA reports claim rejections, denials, and payments to the hospital. Payments are typically transferred to the hospital bank.

If the patient has secondary insurance that is responsible for a portion of the bill, or has an outstanding balance for his or her portion, the hospital submits a claim to the secondary payer or the patient. A copy of the EOB or MSN received from the primary payer must accompany secondary claims. If applicable, the tertiary payer is billed after every effort has been made to collect payment from the secondary payer. When the full payment from the payer is received and verified, the account for the claim is closed; otherwise, it remains open and the hospital must reconcile the account.

Reconciliation and Collection

The hospital uses the EOB, MSN, and RA to reconcile accounts. EOBs and MSNs identify the amount owed by the patient to the hospital. RAs indicate rejected or denied line items or claims. The hospital can review the RAs and determine whether the claim error can be corrected. First, the reason/denial code on the EOB is checked to determine the cause. Next, the problem claim is examined and categorized into one of five compliance risk areas: (1) insurance policy requirements, (2) correct coding, (3) appropriate billing guidelines, (4) reasonable and necessary services, and (5) proper documentation. Once it has been categorized, the necessary steps are taken to correct the problem. Then hospital can resubmit the claim for additional payment.

Age analysis is a term used for the procedure of systematically arranging the A/R by age from the date of service. Accounts are usually categorized in time periods of 30, 60, 90, and 120 days and older. The older the account or the longer the account remains unpaid, the less of a chance the hospital will receive reimbursement for the claim.

When efforts to resolve denials or underpayment issues have not been satisfied, the next step is to appeal the claim. Hospitals can appeal a claim under billing guidelines and state and federal insurance laws and regulations within a certain time limit according to the EOB or contracts between the provider and payer.

After all insurance payments have been received, collection specialists check to see whether the patient is responsible for any of the remaining balance. Most managed care contracts do not allow a provider to bill patients for anything except a deductible or copayment amount. In addition, services that are deemed "noncovered" usually may be billed to the patient only if the patient signed a specific noncovered service payment agreement, or advance beneficiary notice (ABN), before the service was rendered.

When all expected payments from all sources, including the patient, have been received, any remaining balances are typically written off and the account for the claim is closed. Other collection options include selling the delinquent account to a collection agency or filing a tort in a small claims court.

Revenue Cycle Management

With the increasing importance of efficient revenue cycle and cash collection procedures to a hospital's bottom line, hospital managers are seeking ways to improve performance in those areas. **Revenue cycle management (RCM)** involves the supervision of all administrative and clinical functions that contribute to the capture, management, and collection of patient service revenue. The purpose of RCM is to improve the efficiency and effectiveness of the revenue cycle process, and to leverage the hidden potential in complex payment processes.

RCM staff members identify ways to improve A/R, discuss issues with appropriate personnel, develop educational materials (e.g., a revenue cycle manual), create a map or blueprint for new services, review denials, and discuss outcomes of the appeal process, **key performance indicators (KPIs),** and measures. The **Healthcare Financial Management Association (HFMA)** has worked with multiple stakeholders to develop a common set of revenue cycle financial KPIs, including net days in A/R, aged A/R as a percentage of billed A/R, **point-of-service (POS)** cash **collections**, cost to collect, cash collection as a percentage of adjusted net patient service revenue, bad debt, charity care, and days in total **discharged not final billed (DNFB)** (HFMA KPI Task Force, 2010).

Billing and Collection Compliance

A hospital's billing practices are subject to federal and state rules and regulations. Perhaps the single biggest risk area for hospitals is the preparation and submission of claims or other requests for payment from the federal health care programs. A hospital may be liable under the federal **False Claims Act** or other statutes for submitting false claims or statements, including liability for civil money penalties or exclusion (Federal Register, 2005). Since the enactment of False Claims Act in 1986, settlement against healthcare providers has reached over $700 million because of upcoding, unbundling, kickbacks, and billing for items and services that were not medically necessary (Potter, 2005). When HIPAA was enacted in 1996, the financial penalty was increased to $10,000 per item or service.

There are eight key components of a sound compliance program: (1) implementing compliance standards, (2) designating a compliance officer or committee, (3) conducting internal monitoring and (4) auditing, (5) conducting appropriate training and education for all staff members, (6) responding to detected offenses, (7) taking corrective action, and (8) maintaining open lines of communication (Derricks, 2004).

SECTION B: FINANCIAL MANAGEMENT

Functions and Organization

The hospital financial division is responsible for managing the overall accounting, treasury, financial reporting, and financial services operations of the hospital. This includes ensuring that the official accounting records of the hospital are up-to-date and accurate, creating and presenting financial reports to internal and external parties, providing financial supports to hospital management and development personnel, and safeguarding and preserving the assets of the hospital.

The process of financial management involves various players within the organization's financial arena. Figure 25-2 shows a typical organizational chart for a hospital financial division.

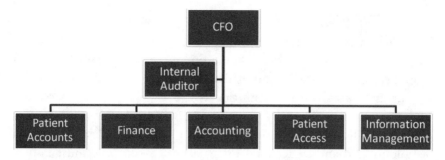

FIGURE 25-2. Organization chart of hospital financial division.

The details of this organizational system vary from hospital to hospital. In a small hospital, one individual may perform several separate functions, whereas in larger hospitals, one or two staff members, with the help of an accountant, may be responsible for all financial functions.

The individual who is responsible for supervising the financial management of the hospital is the chief financial officer (CFO). Typically, the CFO is at minimum a **certified public accountant (CPA)** or certified management accountant (CMA). The CFO may report directly to the chief executive officer (CEO) and has overall responsibility for related departments, including patient accounts, finance, accounting, patient access, and information management.

Most large organizations have an internal auditor. The internal auditor ensures that the accounting and reporting functions are performed in accordance with **generally accepted accounting principles (GAAP)**. GAAP are accounting principles that have substantial authoritative support. Substantial authoritative support is a question of fact and a matter of judgment. The power to establish GAAP actually rests with the Securities and Exchange Commission (SEC).

Financial Statements

Hospitals produce three different types of financial statements:

1. The balance sheet, which presents the dollar value of assets the hospital has acquired, and where it obtained the money to pay for them.
2. The income statement, which indicates what the hospital earned and how much was spent in giving care over a certain period of time (usually 1 year).
3. The statement of cash flows, which reveals how much cash the hospital has at the beginning and end of the reporting period, and how it achieved those balances.

Basic Accounting

Financial management is dependent on accounting. Every financial manager must know at least the rudiments of accounting. McLean (2003) summarized the importance of accounting for healthcare organizations as follows: First, accounting is the language of business, and business records are kept by accountants. Second, financial statements present the clearest picture of a hospital's previous financial health. To be able to read and understand financial statements, one must understand the accounting rules behind them. Finally, knowledge of financial accounting is important for the manager who is involved in cost analysis and budgeting.

Accounting is a very complex field. Here, we discuss only the basic accounting concepts needed to analyze financial statements, as described by Berman et al. (1994).

Fundamental Accounting Equation

The framework for financial accounting is based on the following equation:

$$\text{Assets} = \text{Liabilities} + \text{Owners' Equity}$$

Assets are all of the things of value owned by the organization, including cash (or cash equivalent), investments, inventory, land, buildings, equipment, and intangible assets. Liabilities are obligations, such as accounts payable, notes payable, accrued expenses, and long-term debt owed to outside entities. The owners' equity represents the share of the organization's assets owned by its owners. It is the difference between the value of the organization's assets and its liabilities. In not-for-profit hospitals, there is no shareholder or partner to claim the owners' equity account. As a result, that account is identified as the net assets. In this chapter, we will use examples from for-profit hospitals.

Double Entry

According to the **double entry rule**, which was first established in 1492, accounting records must reflect two aspects of each transaction: debit and credit. In accounting, debit and credit have no financial meaning; instead, they are the signal of the accounting entries. Thus, in order for accounting records to reflect the full effect of any transaction, two entries must be made.

Cost Conservatism

According to the **cost conservatism principle**, all financial transactions must be recorded as a monetary cost, and most assets should be valued conservatively, usually at their historical costs. For example, if the hospital purchases land and holds it for a long period of time, the value recorded in the asset account should not be increased to show changes in the land's market value. Rather, the land remains on the books at its historical cost as long as it is there. Some assets whose market values are easily observable are exempted from this standard. Marketable securities (stocks and bonds) are recorded at their current market value.

Accrual

The **accrual concept** acts as a guide in accounting for revenues and expenses. According to this concept, revenues are recorded in the accounts when they are realized, and expenses are recorded in the period during which they contribute to operations. In practice, for example, this means that supplies purchased and used at the end of a month should be recorded as expenses for that month. However, if the supply distributor has not sent out an invoice for the goods, the organization's accountants must estimate the value of the supplies and record it in that month's financial records. This concept permits income and expenses to be properly allocated to the appropriate fiscal period. In accrual accounting, revenues are recorded in the period in which the associated service is performed, and the expenses are recorded in the period in which they were incurred, regardless of whether any cash actually changed hands.

Matching

According to the **matching concept**, the accountant must match all associated revenues and expenses in the financial records in any given month to properly determine the net income. If hospitals did not have to match related items, revenues, and expenses, they would be able to manipulate income from various types of activity to produce whatever operating picture they desired.

Balance Sheet

The **balance sheet** is similar to a snapshot of the organization, in that it captures what the organization looks like at a particular point in time (usually the last day of the accounting period, i.e., the quarter, half year, or fiscal year). An organization with a strong balance sheet can withstand a short run of losses or reduced profits, whereas one with a weak balance sheet may find it difficult to do so. The investor's eye quite naturally looks first to the balance sheet and then to the income statement.

Table 25-2 presents an example of a balance sheet and serves as an overview of this section of the text. A significant amount of financial information can be extracted from the balance sheet alone. However, this information is also used in conjunction with other parts of the financial statements, as well as additional financial and volume-related data, to form a complete picture of the hospital's financial resources.

Income Statement

The **income statement** is known as the statement of operation. The income statement can provide information about the use of funds in the income process (i.e., expenses), the use of funds that will never be used to earn income (i.e., losses), the source of funds created by those expenses (i.e., revenues), and the source of funds not associated with the earnings process (i.e., gains).

The income statement is useful for determining profitability, value for investment purposes, and credit worthiness. The income statement is also useful for predicting information about future cash flows (e.g., the amounts, timing, and uncertainty of cash flows) based on past performance (Table 25-3).

Statement of Cash Flows

The **statement of cash flows** allows the reader to understand the financial statement elements that make up the change in cash in the organization's operating checkbook. The statement captures both the current operating results and the accompanying changes in the balance sheet (Helfert, 2001).

Transactions on the balance sheet also must be analyzed and converted from an accrual basis to a cash basis in preparation of the cash flow statement.

The statement of cash flows is divided into cash flow from operations, investing activity, and financing activity (see Table 25-4). These designations represent cash flows from the organization's principal activity (operations), investments and capital expenditures (investing), and proceeds of debt activity (financing).

Table 25-2. ABC Hospital Balance Sheet: December 31, 2009
(in Thousands of Dollars)

	2009	2008
Assets		
Current assets		
Cash	1,200	2,000
Marketable security	6,500	5,400
Net patient A/R	15,500	16,300
Inventory	2,000	1,900
Prepaid expenses	400	300
Other current assets	100	100
Total current assets	25,700	26,000
Long-term investments	95,500	87,000
Property and equipment		
Land	8,000	7,000
Buildings	70,000	60,000
Equipment	56,000	51,600
Less accumulated depreciation	32,000	21,000
Net property and equipment	102,000	97,600
Total assets	223,200	210,600
Liabilities and Shareholders' Equity		
Current liabilities		
Accounts payable	12,000	10,000
Notes payable	4,000	4,500
Interest payable	1,500	1,900
Accrued expenses	2,000	1,500
Total current liabilities	19,500	17,900
Long-term debt	120,000	123,400
Other long-term liabilities	4,000	4,100
Total long-term liabilities	124,000	127,500
Total liabilities	143,500	145,400
Shareholder's equity:		
Common stock $1 par value		
(1,500,000 shares authorized, 1,000,000 shares outstanding)	1,000	1,000
Capital in excess of par	9,000	9,000
Retained earnings	69,700	55,200
Total shareholders' equity	79,700	65,200
Total liabilities and shareholders' equity	223,200	210,600

Table 25-3. ABC Hospital: Income Statement for Year Ended December 31, 2009 (in Thousands of Dollars)

	2009	2008
Revenues		
Net patient service revenue	93,000	94,000
Facilities rental revenue	5,000	5,000
Other revenue	3,300	2,500
Total revenue	**101,300**	**101,500**
Expenses		
Salaries and benefits	44,000	42,300
Supplies	14,500	15,600
Insurance	4,500	3,900
Leases	3,100	4,600
Depreciation	11,000	12,500
Interest	3,800	1,700
Other expenses	5,900	7,200
Total expenses	**86,800**	**87,800**
Net Income	**14,500**	**13,700**

Financial Statement Analysis

Financial statements summarize comprehensive information and can reveal a great deal about a hospital's performance; therefore, a financial statement analysis is a critical factor in any decision made by the stakeholders. The financial statements of a hospital may be viewed by stockholders, donors, and sponsoring communities; creditors and bond rating agencies; government taxing authorities; third-party payers; accrediting organizations; network contractors, subcontractors, and suppliers; managers; and competitors. For example, the managers, lenders, and investors of a hospital need to know about the hospital's performance to make business decisions, and the creditors need to know whether the hospital will be able to pay back their loans. Government taxing authorities determine the tax on for-profit hospitals, evaluate not-for-profit hospitals' compliance, and oversee specific controls related to financial reporting.

A set of financial measures is developed to describe a hospital's major financial characteristics. These financial measures are expressed as ratios. Typical

Table 25-4. ABC Hospital: Statement of Cash Flows for Years Ended December 31, 2009, and 2008 (in thousands)

	2009	2008
Cash Flows from Operating Activities		
Net income	$14,500	$13,700
Adjustments		
Depreciation	11,000	12,500
Increase in net patient A/R	800	870
Increase in inventories	(100)	(350)
Decrease in accounts payable	2,000	1,200
Increase in prepaid expenses	(100)	0
Increase in accrued expenses	500	300
Net cash from operations	**$28,600**	**$28,220**
Cash Flows from Investing Activities		
Capital expenditures	**($15,400)**	**($6,200)**
Cash Flows from Financing Activities		
Increase in marketable securities	(1,100)	(700)
Increase in notes payable	(500)	100
Increase in long-term investment	(8,500)	(5,700)
Increase in long-term debt	(3,400)	(1,500)
Increase in interest payable	(400)	0
Increase in other long-term liabilities	(100)	0
Net cash from financing	**($14,000)**	**($7,800)**
Net increase (decrease) in cash	**($800)**	**($14,220)**

financial reports may contain as many as 30 financial ratios; however, empirical studies suggest that most individuals can only comprehend six to eight components of financial information when making a decision. Only one ratio is necessary to measure each respective financial character, because the other ratios are correlated. The major ratios are used to measure the hospital's profitability, asset efficiency, capital structure, fixed-asset age, working capital efficiency, and liquidity. Financial analysts can compare the hospital's financial ratios with those of a comparable hospital or with its previous financial status to evaluate its current financial situation (Zeller, Stanko, & Cleverley, 1997).

The bottom line for any organization is its ability to generate profits, and this is reflected in the profitability ratios. The most frequently used ratio is the total margin ratio (TMAR), which is the ratio of net income to the total revenue. For ABC Hospital, the TMAR ratio is 0.1431. Another popular profitability ratio is the return on assets (ROA), which is the ratio of net income to the total assets. For ABC Hospital, the ROA ratio is 0.0650. Other profitability ratios include the return on investment (ROI) and the operating margin (OMAR).

Asset efficiency can be measured by means of the inventory turnover (ITO) and total asset turnover (TATO). The ITO ratio is computed as the value of total revenues divided by ending inventory. For ABC Hospital, the ITO ratio is 50.56.

The TATO is more important because it indicates the extent to which the assets produce revenues. It is defined as the value of total revenues divided by the total assets. For ABC Hospital, the TATO ratio is 0.45. Other asset efficiency ratios include the fixed asset turnover (FATO) and the price-level adjusted fixed asset turnover (FATOPL).

The capital structure indicates the financial structure of a hospital. Low values for equity financing (EF) and high values for fixed asset financing (FAF) imply more debt. The most basic and useful capital structure ratio is the asset/equity (AE) ratio, which is defined as the value of total assets divided by the total equity. For ABC Hospital, the AE ratio is 2.8018. Other capital structure ratios include EF and FAF.

The fixed asset age represents the approximate age of a hospital's fixed assets. Hospitals with low average age-of-plant ratios will have either newer investment or a heavier mix of equipment with shorter depreciable lives and thus a higher depreciation rate. The **average payment period (APP)** is one of the ratios used to measure fixed-asset age. It is defined as Current Liabilities/[(Total Expenses − Depreciation)/365]. For ABC Hospital, the APP ratio is 129.88. Another asset age ratio is the depreciation rate (DEPR).

The working capital efficiency highlights the relative importance of a hospital's investment in current assets or working capital. The most commonly used liquidity ratio is the current ratio (CR), which is defined as the value of the current assets divided by the current liabilities. The higher the current ratio, the more capable is the company of paying its obligations. For ABC Hospital 2009, the CR ratio is 1.32. Other working capital efficiency ratios include the current asset turnover (CATO) and the short-term sources days cash on hand (DCHST).

The **liquidity ratio** measures a hospital's access to cash and investments that can be used for short- or long-term needs. Days cash on hand (DCH) is defined as (Cash + Marketable Securities)/[(Expenses − Depreciation)/ 365]. For ABC Hospital 2009, the DCH ratio is 51.29. Another liquidity ratio is the replacement viability (REPV).

SECTION C: BUDGETING

What Is a Budget?

A hospital's resources (e.g., capital, office space, material, and human resources) are limited, and hospitals must create a plan to maximize their utilization. This plan is called the **budget**. Moreover, a budget turns a plan into a program for the expenditure of funds (Seawell, 1992). Preparing the budget is an important step in planning. Spending the budget is how one turns a plan into reality.

In the budgetary process, the hospital's resources are allocated, staff members make an effort to keep the hospital running as close to the plan as possible, and then the results are evaluated. Budgets require the hospital managers to think ahead, examine alternatives, and choose those that will likely yield the best results.

The term "budget" is a broad concept that includes the operating budget, capital budget, and cash budget.

Operating Budget

The hospital establishes its operating budget by planning for the revenues it expects to receive for providing services to patients, as well as the expenses it will incur in doing so. For-profit hospitals generally receive resources, such as money, in exchange for services and goods. Such exchanges generate revenues for the hospitals. Not-for-profit hospitals may earn revenues in a similar fashion and may also receive revenues from contributions or grants.

When patients are treated at a hospital, they receive bills for the care provided. Suppose a patient pays $5000 for the care received. The hospital receives the $5000 in cash. The hospital is said to have earned revenue of $5000. The revenue reflects the amount of resources that have been received in exchange for the services the hospital provided.

To prepare an operating budget, the hospital must calculate its revenues and expenses. The CFO of the hospital must consider all possible resources of revenue or other supports, and calculates the revenues by predicting the volume of services to be provided and their unit price. By multiplying the price per unit by the volume of units, the CFO can provide the organization with an estimate of its revenues.

The CFO also needs to consider all of the costs incurred as well as additional expenditures required to incorporate elements of the hospital's plan. The budget for expenditures is calculated by aggregating all of the individual costs required to operate the facility.

The budgeted expenses of the organization are subtracted from the budgeted revenues to determine whether the hospital projects a surplus or deficit for the coming year. In some instances, a loss may be acceptable. A major investment may result in a loss in subsequent years. In the long term, a hospital needs to have a surplus operating budget to stay in business. Table 25-5 shows an example of a hospital's operating budget.

Capital Budget

A capital asset is anything the hospital acquires to provide services for more than one fiscal year. Capital assets typically include buildings, vehicles, information systems, major diagnostic and treatment equipment, and the development of new systems and products. The process of acquiring a capital asset is reflected in the capital budget.

According to the previous definition, a chair in the waiting area that cost $30 can be considered a capital asset because its life span is more than one fiscal year. However, hospitals only treat relatively costly acquisitions as capital assets. The chair would simply be included in the operating expenses for the year in which it was acquired, because it is relatively inexpensive.

At what dollar level should a purchase be capitalized, or, to put it another way, what is the capitalization threshold? Medicare has had a large impact in the area of capitalization policy. When Medicare was first established in 1966, it defined a capital asset as something having a useful life of at least 2 years and a cost of more than $500. Therefore, anything bought for less than $500 was by definition an operating expense. Since 1998, Medicare has allowed providers to consider a purchase with a useful life of at least 2 years and cost of $5000 and above to be considered capital (Human Health Service, 1998). The CFO of the hospital has the authority to set the capitalization threshold up to $5000.

Hospital CFOs and CEOs pay a great deal of attention to capital budgeting. Acquiring a capital asset represents a large expenditure for hospitals,

Table 25-5. ABC Hospital Operating Budget
(in Thousands of Dollars)

Account	Budget
Revenue	
Routine	29,682,230
Other	24,530
Total operating revenues	**29,706,760**
Salary expenses	
Salaries—regular	23,781,340
Salaries—overtime	170,276
Federal Insurance Contributions Act (FICA) tax	1,323,000
Health insurance	609,786
Pensions	1,112,000
Other	198,265
Total salary expense	**27,194,667**
Supply expenses	
Laboratory supplies	1,773,298
Equipment	94,323
Office supplies	10,003
Meetings	8221
Miscellaneous	6279
Total supply expense	**1,892,124**
Other expenses	**111,904**
Excess of revenues over expense	**508,065**

and has a significant impact on the financial performance and strategic development of the hospital. However, a capital asset will generate revenue for the hospital in future years. Thus, it is necessary to prepare a separate capital budget that allows the capital asset's costs and benefits to be assessed over its lifetime.

A wide array of criteria are used in capital budgeting decisions, including the **net present value (NPV)**, internal rate of return (IRR), payback period, and return on book value. The NPV leads to better capital budgeting decisions (Brealey & Myers, 2005; Hansen, Mowen, & Guan, 2007). Using the NPV as a measure, the CFO can select projects that will increase

Table 25-6. Proposed New Investment

	Angiography System with a 5-Year Life Span					
	Initial	Year 1	Year 2	Year 3	Year 4	Year 5
Cash in		$260,000	$270,000	$280,000	$290,000	$290,000
Cash out	$959,280	$0	$64,500	$64,500	$64,500	$64,500
Total	($959,280)	$260,000	$205,500	$215,500	$225,500	$225,500

the value of the hospital because they have a positive NPV. The following example illustrates how to use the NPV in capital budgets:

ABC Hospital is considering purchasing an angiography system. The expected cash flows for its 5-year life span are shown in Table 25-6.

The present value (PV) can be calculated by using a financial calculator, time value of money (TVM) tables, or software such as Microsoft Excel. In Year 1, the total cash flow is $260,000. The present value of the future value (FV) of $260,000 is $247,619 at a 5% discount rate (i) in one (n) year, that is:

$$PV = FV/(1+i)^n = 260,000/(1+5\%)^1 = 247,619$$

Similarly, the present values in subsequent years can be calculated. The NPV of a series of cash flows equals the sum of the discounted present values of each individual cash flow. As illustrated in Figure 25-3, the proposed project has a positive NPV of $23,095. Therefore, the hospital should make the investment.

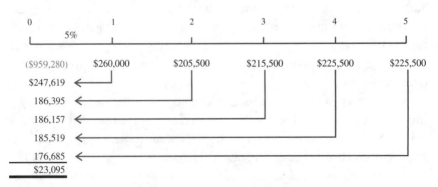

FIGURE 25-3. Calculate NPV.

Table 25-7. General Form for a Cash Budget

Beginning cash balance
Add:
Estimated cash receipts
Borrowing
Deduct:
Estimated cash payments
Repaying or investing
Estimated ending cash balance

Cash Budget

Hospitals keep cash on hand (in a bank account) for daily transactions such as meeting payroll, paying suppliers, and covering ongoing operating expenses. However, it is not wise to keep too much cash on hand, because that cash could be invested to generate a return. When establishing the cash budget, the CFO must estimate the minimum amount of cash that must be held to maintain operations efficiently (Hauser, Edwards, & Edwards, 1991). In order to do so, the CFO needs to calculate the monthly or daily amount of cash that remains after all anticipated expenses have been covered and all expected revenues have been collected. Projections of monthly and daily cash balances that result from expected cash inflows and outflows allow the organization to plan for temporary shortages and surpluses of cash that result from seasonal and cyclical factors.

Cash budgets follow the general form shown in Table 25-7, as suggested by Financial Accounting Standards Board Statement 95, and Table 25-8 shows an example of a cash budget.

Budget Process

Hospitals use different budget processes, ranging from comparatively simple to complex. In general, however, the **budget process** includes the activities described later in this chapter (see Fig. 25-4).

First, the budget is prepared. After it is reviewed by the body with the authority to adopt it, the budget is adopted with or without changes. It is common for the decision maker (e.g., the trustees or CEO of the hospital) to request or make changes prior to approval. Once it is approved, the budget is implemented. The managers of the hospital are responsible for ensuring that the adopted budget is carried out. Finally, the results are

Table 25-8. Example of a Cash Budget

ABC Hospital Cash Budget		
	January	**February**
Beginning balance	$12,000	$10,000
Estimated cash receipts		
Routine	$3,000	$3,000
Other	$2,000	$2,000
Total estimated cash	$17,000	$15,000
Less estimated cash payment		
Labor	$1,000	$1,000
Rent	$1,000	$1,000
Suppliers	$4,000	$500
Other	$1,000	$1,000
Total estimated cash payments	$7,000	$3,500
Estimated cash before borrowing repaying or investing	$10,000	$11,500
Borrowing/(repaying or investing)	$0	−$1,500
Estimated ending cash balance	$10,000	$10,000

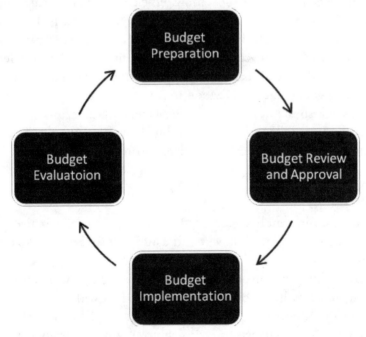

FIGURE 25-4. Budget cycle.
Source: International Budget Partnership.

evaluated. Often the actual results will vary from those predicted in the budget. All significant variations should be analyzed. This evaluation in turn will provide feedback to be used in preparing the next budget.

The budget process can be quite complicated and time-consuming (in some hospitals it can take months). To ensure that the budget is ready early enough to be implemented at the start of the coming year, many hospitals prepare a budget calendar or budget timeline. The timeline sets the deadline by which each major activity must be completed in order to ensure timely adoption of the budget (Table 25-9).

Budget Preparation

Several different types of budgets can be prepared. The most popular ones are the line-item budget, responsibility center budget (department budget), and program budget. After World War II, hospitals (especially non-profit hospitals) began to experiment with performance-based budgets (i.e., zero-based budgets), but these proved to be ineffective. Here, we only discuss only the first three approaches.

Line-Item and Responsibility Center Budgets

A line-item expense is a specific class or category of resource used by a hospital. For example, salaries and overhead are both line items. In con-

Table 25-9. Hospital Budget Timeline

Date	Action to be Completed
August 31	The budget committee is appointed.
September	The budget committee holds meetings; agrees on key definitions, assumptions, and document formats; determines and schedules any necessary training or key meetings; evaluates the previous year's budget; and forecasts revenues and expenses based on program goals and assumptions.
October 31	The budget proposal is completed.
November	The budget committee communicates with the department managers.
December 20	All negotiations and revisions are completed.
December 21	The budget is approved.
January	The budget is implemented.

Table 25-10. Example of a Line-Item Budget

ABC Hospital Budgets for 20XX (in Thousands of Dollars)	
Salaries	
Full-time	86,000
Part-time	28,000
Services	
Rental	20,000
Equipment	4,000
Utilities	6,000
Supplies	
Office	2,000
Meeting	200
Computer	800
Others	2,000
Total	**149,000**

trast, the responsibility center approach divides the budget into units for which individual managers are held accountable.

Line-item expenses represent specific individual types of expenses, such as wages or supplies (see Table 25-10). Responsibility centers are organizational subdivisions that are supervised by a specific person. Table 25-11 shows an example responsibility center budget.

Table 25-11. Example of a Responsibility Center Budget

ABC Hospital Budgets for 20XX (in Thousands of Dollars)	
Administration	12,000
Informational Services	5,000
Therapeutic Services	97,000
Diagnostic Services	29,000
Support Services	6,000
Total	**149,000**

Program Budget

Suppose a hospital specializes in three major programs: neurosurgery, plastic surgery, and ophthalmology. Budgets can be prepared that will show the expected revenues and costs of each program. This can be done for regular programs, special projects, and special services. If the hospital establishes budgets for different programs, it can prepare program budgets to evaluate each program's profitability and decide whether it can afford each program. For example, if the plastic surgery department performs mostly elective surgery, and the program loses money (as shown in the following budgets), the hospital might decide to eliminate the program (Table 25-12).

Budgeting Techniques

Forecasting (Fixed Budgets)

Hospitals establish budgets to plan for the future. Budgets are based on estimates of expected revenues and expenses. Consider a hospital budget. The budget revenue will depend on the number of patients who are admitted to the hospital. Part of the hospital budget revenue may depend on the average collection rate for bills. On the expenses side, the budget must include the cost to air-condition the hospital's facilities. That cost will depend on the average temperature throughout the summer. These are just a few of the many factors that must be considered in a hospital budget. The future depends on many unknown factors and events. When managers develop budgets, they must make forecasts, which are little more than guesses about what the future will be. However, there are statistical approaches to **forecasting** that can improve the accuracy of the predictions and indicate how variable the actual results might be.

Table 25-12. ABC Hospital Program Budgets for 20XX (in Thousands of Dollars)

	Neurosurgery	Plastic Surgery	Ophthalmology
Revenues	40,000	12,000	50,000
Expenses	37,000	15,000	45,000
Profit	3,000	(3,000)	5,000

In the example given earlier, the hospital CFO preparing the budget will forecast the number of patients, the collection rate for bills, and the average temperature. The more accurate the forecast, the more effective the budget will be.

Different approaches can be used to make a forecast. Forecasts often are the result of a combination of the output from an analytical model and the judgment of the forecaster. Most forecasts are accomplished by using historical information and projecting that information into the future. Forecasting techniques range from the very simple to the very complex; however, they all have the benefit of being based on a historical foundation.

Forecasts based on historical data fall into two categories: causal models and time-series models. The simplest approaches to forecasting are informal. For example, the summer next year will probably be just like the one this year. More effort and sophistication in the forecasting method can result in more accurate forecasts, but simple models often provide the most reliable results.

In causal models, changes in one variable are used to predict changes in another. For example, the CFO can examine the relationship between nurses' pay and the nurse turnover rate in past years. Based on this, he or she can predict what the turnover rate will be at the current salary level.

In time-series models, there is assumed to be a relationship between the item to be forecast and the passage of time. For example, the hospital might conclude that the trend of an increasing number of patients in the past few years will continue in future years.

In periods of relative stability, forecasting models usually provide an accurate forecast. However, when the external environment changes, these models will lose their magic power. For example, during an epidemic, the patient admission number cannot be predicted by the time-series model based on historical data.

Flexible Budgeting

The workload in a hospital is difficult to predict even with sophisticated models. A flexible budget is one that adjusts to changes in the volume of workload. It is more useful than a fixed budget.

The key to preparing a flexible budget is to determine which numbers in the budget are likely to change and which are likely to remain the same. Will the costs that vary change in direct proportion to volume changes, or

Table 25-13 ABC Hospital Flexible Budget November 20XX (in Thousands of Dollars)

	Original budget	Volume adjustment	Flexible budget
Revenue			
Inpatient revenue	82,000	7,112	89,112
Outpatient revenue	11,500	415	11,915
Other revenue	0	0	0
Total revenue	93,500	7,527	101,027
Expenses			
Labor	3,333	0	3,333
Administrative	5,333	517	5,850
Supervisory	2,500	243	2,743
Registered nurses	27,334	2,652	29,986
Technician	2,500	0	25,000
Secretarial	1,167	0	1,167
Other indirect	500	0	500
Contract	0	446	446
Other productive	42,667	3,858	46,525
Total labor	20,250	182	20,432
Nonlabor			
Total nonlabor	62,917	4,040	66,957
Total expenses	30,583	3,487	34,070
Net profit			

will their change be more or less than proportional? Management personnel must be able to understand revenue and cost structures enough to anticipate the changes caused by volume variations. Table 25-13 shows an example of a flexible budget.

CHAPTER REVIEW

1. Please list three types of budgets and explain what is contained in each.
2. What are the four parts of billing and collecting?
3. What are the steps in the budgeting process?
4. What are KPIs?
5. What do we mean by revenue cycle management?

6. Please list at least 3 important financial documents that the CEO should review each month.
7. Please explain the importance of the False Claims Act.
8. Please give an example of NPV to demonstrate your familiarity.

REFERENCES

Berman, H. J., Weeks L. E., Kukla S.F. (1994). *The Financial Management of Hospitals,* 8th ed. Chicago, IL: Health Administration Press.

Brealey, R. A., & Myers, S. C. (2005). *Principles of corporate finance.* Boston, MA: McGraw-Hill/Irwin.

Derricks, J. (2004) Audit the Auditors: Are Your Documentation, Coding and Billing Audit Findings Valid? *2004 IFHRO Congress & AHIMA Convention Proceedings.*

Federal Register. (2005) OIG Supplemental Compliance Program Guidance for Hospitals Vol. 70, No. 19/Monday, January 31, 2005/*Notices.* Retrieved October 11, 2010 from, http://oig.hhs.gov/fraud/docs/complianceguidance/012705HospSupplementalGuidance.pdf

Finkle, S. A. (2010). *Financial management for public, health, and not-for-profit organizations.* Upper Saddle River, NJ: Prentice Hall.

Hansen, D. R., Mowen, M. M., & Guan, L. (2007). *Cost management: Accounting and control.* Chula Vista, CA: Southwestern College Publications.

Hauser, R. C., Edwards, D. E., & Edwards, J. T. (1991). Cash budgeting: An underutilized resource management tool in not-for-profit health care entities. *Hospital and Health Services Administration, 36,* 439–446.

Helfert, E. A. (2001). *Financial analysis tools and techniques—a guide for managers.* New York: McGraw-Hill.

HFMA KPI Task Force. Leveraging KPI use for revenue cycle success. Retrieved February 19, 2010, from http://www.hfma.org/NR/rdonlyres/A5C9EA9E-0-D44-45A3-BE7F-C5812E34E2B8/0/1077_RevenueCycleKPI_w1.pdf

Human Health Service, Health Care Financing Administration. *OASIS User's Manual.* 1998. Retrieved October 11, 2010 http://www.cms.gov/OASIS/05_UserManual.asp#TopOfPage

McLean, R. A. (2003) *Financial Management in Health Care Organizations.* 2nd ed. Florence, KY: Thomson-Delmar Cengage Learning.

Potter, J. (2005) Where Bad Billing Can Lead You. *AHIMA's 77th National Convention and Exhibit Proceedings,* October 2005.

Seawell, LV. (1992). *Introduction to Hospital Accounting.* 3rd ed. Dubuque, IA: Healthcare Finance Management Association.

Zeller, T. L., Stanko, B. D., & Cleverley, W. O. (1997). A new perspective on hospital financial ratio analysis. *Healthcare Financial Management, 51,* 62–66.

CHAPTER 26

Generating Revenue— Third-Party Payers by Types and Percentages

Michael Nowicki

KEY TERMS

Third-party payers
Commercial indemnity plans
Health Maintenance
    Organization Act of 1973
Managed care
Point-of-service plans

Healthcare provider
Medicare and Medicaid
Per diem
Capitation
Charity care

INTRODUCTION

In 2008, payments to hospitals accounted for $718.4 billion (or 30.7%) of the $2,338.7 trillion the nation spent on health care that year. During that year, 83.3% of hospital charges were reimbursed by third-party payers (see Figure 26-1). **Third-party payers** are agents of patients who contract with a provider (the second party) to pay all or part of the bill for the patient (the first party).

---

* This chapter is based on Chapter 4, Third-Party Payment in Nowicki, Micheal *The Financial Management of Hospitals and Healthcare Organization 4th Edition*

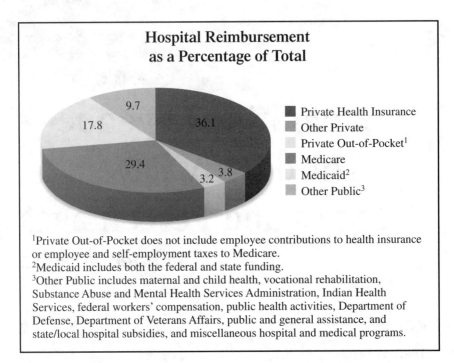

Hospital Reimbursement as a Percentage of Total

- Private Health Insurance
- Other Private
- Private Out-of-Pocket[1]
- Medicare
- Medicaid[2]
- Other Public[3]

[1]Private Out-of-Pocket does not include employee contributions to health insurance or employee and self-employment taxes to Medicare.
[2]Medicaid includes both the federal and state funding.
[3]Other Public includes maternal and child health, vocational rehabilitation, Substance Abuse and Mental Health Services Administration, Indian Health Services, federal workers' compensation, public health activities, Department of Defense, Department of Veterans Affairs, public and general assistance, and state/local hospital subsidies, and miscellaneous hospital and medical programs.

FIGURE 26-1. Hospital reimbursment as percentage of total.
Source: National Health Expenditures by type of service and source of funds, CY 1960–2008. Available at: http://www.cms.hhs.gov/NationalHealthExpendData/02_NationalHealthAccountHistorical.asp#TopOfPage.

HISTORY OF THIRD-PARTY PAYMENT

Prior to the 1920s, the second-party payment method was predominantly used for health care. This method is typically used in free markets where informed consumers are free to make choices in a manner similar to how consumers purchase automobiles. As this system applies to health care, the patient seeks care from the provider, and the provider provides care to the patient and then bills the patient. Second-party payment is economically efficient because under normal circumstances, patients will seek only the amount and quality of care they can afford.

Although the movement toward a third-party payment system started in the 1920s, it received considerable impetus from the Great Depression of the 1930s. The American Medical Association (AMA), fearing that third-party insurance would threaten doctors' relationships with their patients, declared that it would support third-party insurance only if hospitals and physicians were reimbursed separately. This resulted in direct service plans in which employers prepaid participating hospitals and physicians to provide care directly to their employees (both Baylor University Hospital and Henry J. Kaiser had plans of this type). The defeat of compulsory (national) health insurance under President Truman in 1935 and in 1948 meant that third-party health insurance in America would be exclusively voluntary and private until Medicare and Medicaid were enacted in 1965.

The mid-1940s saw the development of **commercial indemnity plans**, which allowed employers and/or employees to prepay to an insurance company that would then reimburse physicians and hospitals chosen by the patient for services provided. At first, premiums were established based on a community rating (everyone pays the same premium), but this was later changed to an experience rating (employees/employers pay a premium based on the insurer's previous experience with a class of employees). By the late 1950s, 66% of Americans had some form of health insurance, usually provided by employers (Starr, 1982). Today, with Medicare providing health insurance to the elderly and Medicaid providing health insurance to the poor, approximately 85% of Americans are now covered.

MANAGED CARE ENTERS THE SCENE

Although the beginnings of managed care date back to the direct service plans in the 1930s, growth in this area did not accelerate until much later. The **Health Maintenance Organization Act of 1973** required companies with 25 or more employees to offer managed care plans as an alternative to commercial indemnity insurance if a managed care plan was available. This was an attempt by the federal government to slow healthcare spending. **"Managed care"** is a broad term for plans that manage the cost of health care, the quality of health care, and the access to health care. Managed care organizations accomplish this in a variety of ways, including aggressive discounting agreements with physicians and hospitals, credentialing of physicians and hospitals, and controlling access to expensive services through the use of a primary care provider or gatekeeper physician. The most aggressively managed organizations are called health maintenance organizations (HMOs). These organizations can exert tight control over costs by employing their own physicians and owning their own hospitals.

Managed care plans grew dramatically in the late 1980s and early 1990s as employers sought ways to control their healthcare costs in order to compete in an increasingly competitive global economy. New tax laws also limited the amount employers could deduct for providing health insurance to their employees. By the late 1990s, public criticism of the aggressive cost-saving techniques used by managed care organizations resulted in less aggressive utilization reviews and different plans, such as point-of-service and consumer-driven plans. **Point-of-service plans** permit patients to seek care from providers who may offer fewer discounts to the insurer, and consumer-driven plans include high deductibles that allow patients to control their own healthcare account.

SETTING CHARGES

Providers establish charges, or prices, for their services in a variety of different ways. Although these charges should have a reasonable relationship to the cost of the services provided, they often do not. For instance, providers may set charges based on what other providers are charging. They may also set charges to offset losses resulting from bad debts, charity care, or public programs. Few third-party insurance companies and patients will pay these charges in full. Insurance companies demand large discounts from the provider in exchange for large volumes of patients. Medicare and Medicaid pay providers a fixed rate regardless of the charges. Various methods of payment are discussed here.

METHODS OF PAYMENT

Third parties and patients use a variety of different methods to pay providers for health services. These methods can be classified by the amount of cost risk and utilization risk borne by the provider.

Every **healthcare provider** has a list of charges (also called prices or rates) for care they provide to patients. Providers establish these charges in different ways (e.g., based on costs or what the market will bear), and if the third party or patient pays the charges, the provider assumes no financial risk.

The most frequently used method for paying healthcare providers is known as "charges minus a discount." Third-party payers negotiate to receive discounts from providers in return for large volumes of patients. The amount of the discount determines whether the provider will favor this method of reimbursement.

From 1965 until 1983, **Medicare and Medicaid** reimbursed providers based on the cost of care provided to their patients. Providers had to document their costs in reports submitted to Medicare and Medicaid. Allowable costs were reimbursed to providers, but Medicare and Medicaid rarely reimbursed providers their full costs of providing care. Therefore, providers were accepting a "cost risk," in that if their costs exceeded the cost that Medicare or Medicaid would reimburse, the provider would lose money. Many Blue Cross plans reimburse providers on a "cost plus" basis, meaning that Blue Cross reimburses provider costs in a manner similar to Medicare plus a small percentage that allows the provider to grow.

Another approach used for reimbursement is the per diem method. The third party reimburses the provider a set charge that is intended to cover the costs incurred for a day of care. Because the per diem charge is set in advance, or prospectively, the provider accepts not only the cost risk but also the utilization risk. This means that if a patient uses more services than are considered necessary in a day of care, the provider loses money. The **per diem** is commonly used in long-term care facilities.

The per diagnosis method is another prospective payment system. It is similar to per diem except that the basis of payment is a diagnosis rather than a day. Similarly to the per diem approach, the per diagnosis method involves both financial risks and rewards; however, providers cannot extend lengths of stays to recover excessive costs.

The **capitation** method is used not so much to pay for services already provided, but to ensure future care for members of a particular plan. The provider receives a payment per member per month whether that member receives care or not. This gives the provider an incentive to keep the member healthy, which is viewed as less expensive than caring for that person after he or she becomes ill. Capitation entails the most financial risk for the provider, but it also offers the most reward.

Bad debt is not really a method of payment; rather, it is a form of nonpayment. Providers that use accrual accounting assume a bad debt expense when they bill and expect payment from patients who have the ability to pay for services rendered but refuse to do so.

Charity care is another form of nonpayment. Providers assume charity care when they provide services to a patient who the provider knows at the time of service is unable to pay.

CHAPTER REVIEW

1. Discuss the impact of third-party payment on hospitals.
2. Discuss the history of third-party payment to hospitals.
3. Compare and contrast managed care and indemnity insurance.
4. Discuss the different ways in which providers set their charges.
5. Evaluate the various methods of payment to providers.
6. Describe the duties of director/manager of reimbursement.

REFERENCES

Starr, P. (1982). *The social transformation of American medicine*. New York: Basic Books.

Nowicki, M. (2007). *The financial management of hospitals & healthcare organizations*. Chicago: Health Administration Press.

Part X

Evaluating and Ensuring the Quality of Care

CHAPTER 27

Compliance and Performance Improvement in Hospitals
Lolly Lockhart

KEY TERMS

Patient safety	Culture of safety
Compliance improvement	Just culture
Performance improvement	National patient safety goals
Diagnosis related group (DRG)	Patient safety organizations
Adverse outcomes	(PSOs)
Medical errors	

INTRODUCTION

Efforts to improve **patient safety**, quality of service, and the performance of healthcare providers and facilities are a priority for all involved in healthcare delivery. Licensed hospitals are required to have a **compliance** and **performance improvement** program in place. This requirement is also a key aspect of the Medicare conditions of participation for hospitals that wish to be a Medicare provider. The emphasis on patient safety and quality of service has progressed over time. In Texas, hospital licensing laws require a patient safety committee to investigate adverse events and take measures to promote safety and performance improvement.

As early as 1910, Dr. Ernest Codman began a review of surgical cases to determine how to improve outcomes. Post–World War II, the Joint Commission for Healthcare Organizations, now known as The Joint Commission, developed quality standards for accredited facilities. During the 1950s, most accreditation surveys were limited to a review of the minutes of the medical staff and various hospital committees. With the advent of Medicare and Medicaid in 1965, the Health Care Financing Administration (now known as the Centers for Medicare and Medicaid Services [CMS]) began to conduct reviews that were mostly concerned with utilization, coding (using International Classification of Diseases, 9th Revision [ICD-9] codes), and investigations of complaints regarding quality of service. The utilization review simply asked physicians to document the need for continued admission, but there were no criteria for medically necessary admissions. Understandably, many Medicare recipients were admitted to acute-care hospitals for maintenance and to give their caretakers relief; however, the unnecessary admissions were costly to the program.

PEER REVIEW ORGANIZATIONS

In 1984, peer review organizations (PROs) were established to review Medicare admissions in terms of medical necessity with appropriate medical treatment, proper coding for billing, and quality of service. The PROs were given criteria with established review and data systems. The Texas Medical Foundation was the recipient of the Medicare scope of work grant as the PRO for Texas. The billing system was changed to **diagnosis related groups (DRGs)**, which grouped various admissions according to average costs. Payment was then made to hospitals based on the DRG rather than the actual costs of admission. The process was basically one of looking for outliers and "bad apples." Hospitals worked with their medical staffs to ensure that they were adhering to admission standards so that the hospital could receive reimbursements.

SYSTEM FAILURES

The PRO reviews gave rise to the concept that many **adverse outcomes** were due to system failures rather than individual failures. In the late 1980s and early 1990s, several adverse events received national attention.

In one case, a patient in Florida underwent amputation of the wrong leg. Actually, the patient was a diabetic who was scheduled to have both legs amputated. At the last minute, the patient asked the surgeon to remove the leg that hurt the most, rather than the one with the most gangrene. The surgeon agreed to do so, but failed to advise the staff. The signed consent form specified only the most painful leg, whereas the most gangrenous leg was amputated. Another case involved a woman being treated for cancer at a major cancer center. The physician ordered chemotherapy that was in excess of the standard amount. The pharmacist filled the prescription and the nurses administered it for several days before the patient died of an overdose.

These and other cases resulted in efforts to reduce errors, such as marking the surgical site at the time the consent is signed, and having the surgical team take a "time-out" before surgery to verify what procedure is being performed and to make sure that everyone is on the same page. The use of checklists was also promoted as a means of reducing errors, based on experience in the airline industry and among anesthesia providers.

HIPAA AND OIG

Federal compliance measures included the Health Insurance Portability and Accountability Act of 1996 (HIPAA) and the Office of the Inspector General (OIG) compliance program for hospitals (and a similar one for physician offices), established in 1998. HIPAA provides controls for release of confidential patient information, as well as four programs aimed at reducing fraud and abuse in health care. According to the OIG guidelines, which are not mandatory, facilities must document that they have established an effective program to prevent, detect, and respond appropriately to fraud and abuse. As an incentive to do so, they may receive a lighter sentence if they are subsequently held liable for fraud.

TO ERR IS HUMAN

In 1999 the Institute of Medicine (IOM) produced *To Err Is Human: Building a Safer Health System*. This publication raised awareness about adverse outcomes by reporting that almost 100,000 people were dying each year as a result of **medical errors** and misadventures in the healthcare system. Its recommendations focused on accountability and introduced the concept of a culture of safety and a just culture. To establish a **culture of safety**, a healthcare organization must make safety a top priority, involving teamwork on the part of both staff and patients, transparency, and account-ability. A **just culture** exists when the staff is free to report errors and near misses without fear of retaliation. This report generated much interest and activity on a number of fronts concerned with health and safety. A series of additional IOM reports have been issued that address specific areas of the healthcare system that require overhaul, including the safety net, emergency services, and mental health services. (Note: Executive summaries of the IOM reports may be downloaded for free at http://www.iom.edu).

ACCREDITATION

The Joint Commission changed its survey focus to patient care outcomes and added tracers whereby it can monitor the actual care of patients as they move through the system in hospitals and other healthcare settings. In 2002, The Joint Commission initiated annual **national patient safety goals** (NPSGs) to create a safer and more therapeutic environment for health care. Accredited entities report specific measures on these NPSGs. The Joint Commission updates the NPSG based on findings that the risks are reduced and new issues are identified for review. The current list of NPSGs can be found on The Joint Commission's website (http://www .jointcommission.org/). The CMS recognizes two national hospital ac-creditation programs—The Joint Commission and the DNV/National Integrated Accreditation for Healthcare Organizations (http://www .DNV.com)—to determine "deemed" Medicare provider status.

QUALITY IMPROVEMENT ORGANIZATIONS

In 2002, the PROs' scope of work was changed to focus on the healthcare environment, and the grant name was changed to quality improvement organizations (QIOs). These organizations emphasize prevention, early de-tection, and proper management of services that are high cost and/or have a high potential for errors and adverse outcomes. More recently, QIOs have been focusing on providing technical services to healthcare facilities other than hospitals, such as nursing homes, physician offices, home health agencies, and health plans. QIOs also assist in the implementation of safety measures and evidence-based clinical management guidelines.

KEEPING PATIENTS SAFE

In 2004, the IOM released *Keeping Patients Safe: Transforming the Work Environment of Nurses*, which addressed patient safety issues in the environment of care and expanded on the concepts of a culture of safety and a just culture. The report noted that nurses are the last line of defense in identifying and stopping procedures or treatments that are potentially harmful to patients. It also addressed key issues such as frequent failure to follow management practices necessary for safety, loss of trust in hospital administration by nurses, the need for self-governance in nursing, unsafe work and workspace design, and fear of retaliation for reporting errors. The report promoted nurses' involvement in addressing workplace issues concerned with patient safety and quality of care initiatives. The recommendations included transforming the work environment for nurses, thereby providing a safer environment for patient care.

PSOs

The Patient Safety and Quality Improvement Act of 2005 provides for **patient safety organizations (PSOs)** to collect, aggregate, and analyze reports of errors and near misses in a confidential database so that measures can be identified to promote safety. PSOs can perform external medical peer reviews to ensure objective reviews.

IHI AND ISMP

A number of other organizations also focus on safety in the healthcare environment. The Institute of Health Initiatives (IHI) and the Institute of Safe Medication Practices (ISMP) have provided leadership and programs for patient safety and improved patient outcomes.

WHERE ARE WE 10 YEARS AFTER *TO ERR IS HUMAN?*

It may seem that all of the bases have been covered and great progress has been made in the areas of patient safety, performance improvement, and fraud control. Unfortunately, that is not the case. Ten years after the publication of *To Err Is Human*, numerous reports suggest that progress has been "frustratingly slow." There are still reports of wrong-site surgeries, drug errors, and unexpected mortalities (https://ssl3.ama-assn.org; http://www.healthaffairs.org/).

WINKLER COUNTY NURSES

There is great need for increased reporting and for stronger legal protections for healthcare professionals and individuals who are willing to take advocacy action. A recent case underscores the need for additional protections. Three registered nurses in Winkler County, Texas, reported concerns about a physician's practice to the chief of staff and the administrator of their hospital. When they failed to take effective action to protect patients, the nurses reported the case (appropriately) to the Texas Medical Board (TMB). The physician shared his notice from the TMB with his friend, the sheriff, who was able, by questionable means, to identify the nurses. The administrator at the hospital fired two of the nurses (the third had already left because of the situation). The nurses were indicted by a grand jury that was not given the full story or told that the nurses were required by law and ethics guidelines to report their concerns. In spite of a strong letter from the TMB supporting the nurses and opposing action against them, the county attorney filed criminal charges against the two nurses (the charges against one were later dropped). The jury trial ended on February 11, 2010, with a finding of not guilty. Although the nurses have filed a civil lawsuit against the hospital, no amount of money can make up for the loss of their jobs (each having worked for the hospital for 20 years) and the loss of recognition for their actions to protect their patients' well-being and safety. As the TMB letter stated, the criminal lawsuit against the nurses will put a chill on others coming forward to report patient safety concerns. Stronger federal and state laws are now needed to protect whistle-blowers from retaliation, to encourage reporting, and to appropriately punish those who may attempt to restrict such reporting.

CONTINUING NEED TO PROMOTE PATIENT SAFETY

The healthcare industry must expand measures to reduce, if not eliminate, human errors. For example, manufacturers of medical tubing could prevent human error by making tubes designed for a particular function (e.g., a feeding tube cannot be connected to an IV set).

Cultural changes within organizations are necessary to ensure that errors and near misses can be reported without retaliation. Current laws require a healthcare professional who believes or has reason to believe that illegal, unethical, impaired, or unsafe practice has occurred or may occur to report to the proper authorities, which may be the employer or a state licensing agency. The code of ethics for health professionals makes it clear that they are responsible for advocating for patient safety and well-being. Federal and state provisions to protect whistleblowers from retaliation for reporting in good faith must be strengthened.

Effective external medical peer reviews are needed throughout the healthcare industry to confirm standards of care. Several programs are authorized to conduct external medical peer reviews for hospitals and clinics. Even large facilities find it difficult to secure objective peer reviews because the physicians tend to refer to one another and are less inclined to review one another. One such program is administered by the Rural and Community Health Institute (RCHI) of A&M Medical Center, Bryan-College Station, Texas. The RCHI, which was established in 2003, conducts blinded medical peer reviews for participating hospitals. The program is geared toward improving performance. If any deficiencies are noted during the review, the RCHI medical director will provide current evidence-based information to the hospital to share with the reviewed physician. The hospital's chief medical officer or chief executive officer receives the report and is responsible for using the information to promote quality and performance improvement.

The use of electronic medical records (EMRs), which includes red flags and reminders to prevent errors, may promote safety but it is limited in preventing many misadventures. There is no doubt that EMRs show great potential for improving communications and coordinating and monitoring patient care.

The use of barcodes to confirm that the right medication is being given to the right patient can reduce medication errors, provided that the nurses do not take shortcuts and work around the system.

Many errors are the result of miscommunication or lack of communication among healthcare providers and staff. Health team members must develop critical thinking skills and communicate their concerns to the appropriate people when patient safety is at stake. The message must be clear so that appropriate action can be taken for the patient. Miscommunications must be investigated and systemic changes must be implemented to promote effective communication.

Last but not least, patient safety can be enhanced by involving patients in self-management and encouraging them to assume responsibility for maintaining a healthy lifestyle, practicing prevention measures, and managing their medical conditions.

SUMMARY

All healthcare providers and facilities must increase their cultural awareness of issues and systems that are not consistent with patient safety and quality of care, and to make sure that effective programs and processes are in place. Seeking health care should not be a dangerous process.

CHAPTER REVIEW

1. What was the impact on health care when Medicare was established without criteria for the medical necessity of admissions?
2. What might hospitals expect when their payments are changed from cost-based to average costs (DRGs)?
3. Explore the implications of system errors versus individual errors.
4. Discuss how a hospital administrator and leadership team can create a culture of safety and just culture in the organization.
5. Discuss the impact of *To Err Is Human* on healthcare providers. What are the barriers to addressing adverse patient outcomes?
6. Secure a list of national patient safety goals from the Joint Commission website and discuss the reasons for those goals, as well as possible barriers to achieving them.
7. Discuss the impact of an effective nursing service on the quality of patient services and how that impact might be measured and validated.
8. Explore systemic and personal factors that can support health professionals in reporting substandard care, errors, and near misses, or impede them from doing so.
9. Identify ongoing activities that need to be implemented and monitored by all healthcare facilities to promote patient safety and performance improvement.

CHAPTER 28

The Importance of Bioethics

Eileen E. Morrison

KEY TERMS

Ethics

Bioethics

Autonomy

Beneficence

Nonmaleficence

Justice

Compassion fatigue

Do Not Resuscitate (DNR)

Professional integrity

Mission versus margin

Clinical ethics committee (CEC)

Institutional Review
    Board (IRB)

Patient-centered care

INTRODUCTION

Hospitals are different from all other work environments. Their mission is to provide care from a person's first breath of life to the last. To fulfill this mission, a hospital must function 24 hours a day, 7 days a week, 365 days a year. Those who work in this setting must be able to provide compassionate care for patients who suffer from a myriad of health issues and who represent every age, economic status, and ethnicity. They must also be able to communicate both good and bad news to patients and family members in a way that is respectful and empathetic.

Healthcare professionals who serve hospital patients also have their own concerns. They work in an environment where compassion is expected

335

regardless of the patients' circumstances or their own situations. They also face the increasing challenges of a higher patient census without higher patient revenue, the growing demand for sophisticated technologies, and the expectation that the hospital will provide efficient, effective, and high-quality care.

Given this complex environment, it is easy to see that hospitals are confronted with ethics issues from countless sources. For example, the community expects these organizations to maintain the highest moral and ethical standards while caring patients' needs and remaining fiscally sound. Because of the ethical responsibilities inherent in the nature of the business of hospitals, a discussion of bioethics is essential for fully understanding the issues involved.

This chapter presents a brief review of the definitions of **ethics** and **bioethics**, and a discussion of the essential principles of healthcare ethics. Examples of common bioethics issues are provided, and the concept of hospital ethics committees, including their design and functions, is reviewed. Finally, patient-centered care is examined as an ethics issue.

DEFINITION AND PRINCIPLES OF BIOETHICS

Debates about the definition and nature of ethics are not new. The ancient Greeks struggled to define how to live justly in society. They also formed theories to explain ethics and the practice thereof. Their thinking provided the foundation for numerous ethics theories, ranging from Aristotle's virtue ethics to Aquinas's natural law theory and Kant's ideas about duty-based ethics. Theorists such as John Stuart Mill (utilitarianism) and John Rawls (social justice) spent their lives studying how ethics applies to individual and societal decisions. What captured the attention of these great men? It was the fascination with ethics and its application in the real world.

Because there are so many definitions of ethics, it is necessary to create a few operational definitions for this chapter. In a philosophical context, ethics is determining what is right or wrong in any given situation and explaining why it is right or wrong (Summers, 2009). However, this definition applies to different areas, such as leadership ethics (how leaders determine right and wrong), organizational ethics (how organizations determine right and wrong), and professional ethics (how professionals determine right and wrong). This chapter examines the discipline of bioethics. This modern area of ethics focuses on the application of ethical theories and principles to problems involving people and their health. Bioethicists also work with physicians and hospitals to help determine the right decisions for complex patient-care issues.

Multiple ethics theories create the basis for four cardinal principles that can be used as tools to resolve the complex ethical dilemmas inherent to patient care. These principles are **autonomy, beneficence, nonmaleficence,** and **justice.** The core of the autonomy principle is respect for human beings. This respect is translated into allowing a person to make his or her own decisions. While this may seem to be a simple principle, it can be quite difficult to implement in healthcare settings.

Hospitals apply the principle of autonomy through informed consent, confidentiality, fidelity, and veracity (Morrison, 2011). Each of these applications may lead to ethical dilemmas for members of the hospital staff. For example, the term "informed consent" implies that a patient is competent, understands the procedures, and makes his or her decisions voluntarily. An ethics issue arises when the patient does not meet these criteria. For example, suppose a patient does not understand English. What is the ethical obligation of the hospital to that patient? Suppose a patient is coerced by family members into undergoing an unwanted procedure. What is the physician's ethical duty?

Similar ethics dilemmas occur in autonomy as applied through confidentiality. There is a need for professionals to have access to highly personal patient information. However, the hospital also has an ethical duty to protect patient confidentiality. With the advent of the electronic medical record, this duty is becoming increasingly more complex. Likewise, ethical issues occur when autonomy is expressed as fidelity and veracity. For example, how much information should a health professional provide to a patient? Is it ever ethical to shade the truth when the diagnosis is a terminal illness?

These few examples show that the cardinal principle of patient autonomy may be restricted in hospital situations. However, when decisions are made that restrict autonomy, they should be based on preventing or decreasing harm and/or providing benefit to the patient. Using this guide allows the hospital to honor the principle of autonomy while providing quality care.

The principles of beneficence and nonmaleficence (Munson, 2008) are often paired in ethics discussions. Nonmaleficence forms a core belief in medicine that has its origins in the age of Hippocrates. Professionals are cautioned to practice in ways that do not harm patients. If harm is necessary, such as in surgery, they are to cause the least amount of harm possible in their treatment. Application of this principle includes practice guidelines, due care standards, and risk assessment for patients.

From the patients' view, beneficence is expected. When patients seek help in a hospital setting, they believe that professionals are there for their benefit. They expect to receive compassion, appropriate treatment and pain relief, education about their conditions, and respect. However, healthcare professionals can sometimes experience what is known as **compassion fatigue**. This occurs when they are physically or emotionally exhausted and no longer see patients as people. Patients become a set of vitals to be taken or one more call button to be answered. When this occurs, beneficence is strained and this ethical principle can be violated.

To lessen the likelihood of staff members developing compassion fatigue, hospital administrators must ensure that their shifts are not too long and their morale is not too low. They also have to be aware of the patients' experience by conducting administrative rounds that include patient and staff visits. Practicing beneficence is essential for a positive hospital image. Therefore, it is a good business decision as well as a fundamental ethics practice.

It is sometimes difficult to practice the principle of justice in hospitals. The desire to provide needed care, decrease patients' pain and suffering, and promote healing is at the core of healthcare practice. Practitioners are trained to give this needed care without regard to financial or social status, ethnicity, or education level. Therefore, for the professional, justice is providing needed care to those in need of it (Morrison, 2011).

However, there is another facet to justice. Distributive justice involves balancing the benefits and burdens. When this is achieved, there is justice. This concept becomes even more important when one considers that hospitals are businesses. This means that they must make a profit in order to continue to provide services and pay salaries. Profits are not made by treating people who have little or no ability to pay. Therefore, there is a constant ethics dilemma between the need to provide care and the need to make profit. This dilemma will only increase in complexity as hospitals begin to implement the new healthcare reform measures.

Autonomy, nonmaleficence, beneficence, and justice are the four guiding principles for hospitals. Although these principles are essential to the practice of ethics, they are not always easy to implement. Practicing ethically requires both the knowledge of these principles and the courage to make them a part of clinical and administrative decisions. The following sections examine some of the bioethics issues that hospitals face and how they try to address them.

BIOETHICS ISSUES FOR HOSPITALS

Hospitals face bioethics issues that are numerous and heartbreakingly difficult. Since they are involved in patient care from the beginning of life to its end, patient-based ethics issues occur on an almost daily basis. For example, Munson (2008) discusses the ethical dilemma of treating or withholding treatment for certain infants with serious medical conditions, such as severe prematurity, spina bifida (opening of the spine), and anencephaly (the absence of hemispheres of the brain). Arguments for withholding treatment include the notion that these infants are not persons, and the costs of treatment are not reflected in the benefits for the child and the family. Others argue that these infants should be treated as people because they have potential. Therefore, their best interests should be considered. Although theoretical arguments are necessary, the reality is that bioethical decisions in cases involving infants are difficult and affect both the family and the professionals involved in them. Therefore, determination of best interests, communication, and ethics-based policies are essential when these situations occur.

Numerous bioethics issues also occur at the end of life. For example, patient autonomy becomes an issue when there is a disagreement about a patient's wishes for treatment at the end of life. This is especially true when patients can no longer articulate their preferences and there is no documentation (e.g., a **Do-Not-Resuscitate [DNR]** order) specifying them. There are also complex issues involving patients' right to die and to be able to commit physician-assisted suicide. In addition, there are issues relating to advance directives and their implementation. In practice, the difficulty of dealing with all of these issues can create an emotional experience for families and staff members.

Another example of bioethics is the concept of **professional integrity** and conscience (Ashcroft, Dawson, Draper, & McMillan, 2007). Healthcare professionals possess more than just essential clinical skills. They are also people of integrity who want to provide the best care to all of their patients. However, in certain circumstances, patient care may conflict with the professional's conscience. Examples of these conflicts include participating in abortions, prescribing postcoital contraception, and refusing to discontinue treatment that prolongs life. Some hospitals have established conscience clauses that exempt professionals from being involved in situations that violate their conscience. This would seem to be an equitable solution to this issue; however, such policies must balance the patients' needs with those of the professional. For example, when AIDS first became a part of health care, some professionals refused to have any contact with patients with this disease. Although this decision may have stemmed from a matter of conscience, it may also have been based on fear or a lack of information. What effect did their refusal have on the care and treatment of AIDS patients?

These are just a few of the many patient-centered ethics issues faced by hospitals. Hospitals also face bioethical issues that are connected to the nature of their business. For example, there is the ongoing problem of balancing the mission of the hospital with the need to make a profit. To better address this issue, it is important to remember that hospital services are considered scarce resources. This is because although there is a need for such services, not all Americans can pay for them. Furthermore, sometimes even when funds are available, certain much-needed services, such as organ transplants and kidney dialysis, cannot be provided.

One must consider the potential demand in addition to the scarce resources involved in hospital practice. Hospitals are one of the few businesses that must operate around the clock, all year long. There are no holidays in hospitals. This business model is necessary because anyone could need hospital services at any time. A hospital must always be ready.

However, a hospital is more than a business—it is also a social institution. Hospitals are an integral part of their communities and may be subsided through their tax-exempt status. Further, community members often feel that they have a moral right to be treated in the hospital. This means that communities have certain expectations. From a moral rights and ethics standpoint, the community expects to receive quality care that includes respect for persons, prevention of undo harm, beneficent care, and just treatment. They also expect that each patient's overall experience will be positive even if it involves the death of a family member.

How do these issues affect the hospital's bottom line? They create unique fiscal and managerial issues. For example, other businesses can reduce staff and close down parts of their operations to reduce expenses in difficult times. A hospital cannot take this kind of action. For example, it cannot lay off its entire nursing staff to save money. To do so would compromise patient care and perhaps cause unnecessary deaths. It also cannot refuse to care for patients who seek care in the emergency room even when they have no ability to pay. These patients add to expenses but do not produce necessary revenue for the business side of the hospital.

Costs are also continuing to rise with the advent of sophisticated technologies, improvements in medical treatments, increased use of sophisticated drugs and equipment, and limits on payments from government and managed-care payers. In addition, there is the constant issue of the medically uninsured, who, despite their lack of insurance coverage, have medical needs. There is also a gap in understanding about the actual cost of health care among individual patients and the community in general. This leads to the misperception that hospitals make tremendous amounts of money and can easily treat all those who need their services.

From a bioethics standpoint, the **mission versus margin** (or service versus profit) dilemma discussed here presents a struggle between distributive justice and autonomy. From a distributive justice standpoint, hospitals must concentrate on making fiscally sound decisions that will allow them to cover their expenses and make enough profit to stay in business. These decisions not only benefit patient care, they also allow hospitals to provide employment for the community they serve. In terms of autonomy, hospitals have a mission to serve. They must respect the needs of patients and provide quality care regardless of a person's ability to pay.

This difficult bioethics dilemma is a constant one for today's hospitals. It also promises to become an even greater one as healthcare reform becomes a reality. Greater expectations will be placed on hospitals to be more efficient, effective, and quality-driven in their services. They will also be required to serve a larger number of patients with justice, respect, compassion, and nonmaleficence. The future holds many bioethics challenges and opportunities.

HOSPITAL ETHICS COMMITTEES AND BIOETHICS

How do hospitals respond to the multiple bioethics issues they face? First, the hospital must establish a culture in which ethics is the norm, not the exception. It must be driven by a mission, vision, and values that reflect more than the achievement of a solid bottom line. Patients should be central to operations, and every employee should feel a sense of commitment to their care. To achieve these goals and maintain ethics-based practices, hospitals often rely on the assistance of ethics committees (Ashcroft et al., 2007; Monagle & West, 2009; Morrison, 2011).

Ethics committees are appointed bodies that assist hospitals in dealing with both patient and organizational ethics issues. In a large hospital, the ethics committee may have several subcommittees that deal with specific areas of bioethics. For example, a **clinical ethics committee (CEC)** provides patient case consultation. The hospital may also have an **institutional review board (IRB)** that addresses ethics issues related to hospital-based research. In smaller hospitals, one ethics committee serves all of these functions.

The membership of general ethics committees is designed to represent both medical and administrative views. Representation from the medical staff may include a neurologist, oncologist, psychiatrist, or other physician. Nursing staff members are also represented by supervising nurses or the director of nursing. In addition, members of the hospital administration and social services staff are included. Commonly, a member of the clergy or a bioethicist will serve on the committee. Finally, a community representative (often a hospital board member) is selected to represent the views of the larger community.

The membership of a CEC may be slightly different because this committee provides direct consultation on specific cases and is often on call; therefore, it is more limited in size. Typically, this committee includes the attending physician, the patient and/or family members, the main nurse in the case, and a bioethicist or member of the clergy (Monagle & West, 2009).

What are the functions of an ethics committee? The primary duty of an ethics committee is to assist in making appropriate bioethical decisions within a hospital. These decisions often involve patient care, but can also include education and policy. In the area of education, the committee works to ensure that hospital staff members are instructed in bioethical principles and practices. Committee members also foster communication between clinicians and administration personnel concerning the hospital's values and their implementation. In some cases, hospital ethics committees also provide ethics education to patients, family members, and the larger community.

Ethics committees may also have a role in decisions regarding the use of scarce resources and providing quality care. In this role, they address issues related to limiting or eliminating services to save money. As reimbursements from Medicaid and Medicare become smaller and technological costs increase, ethics committees will be called upon to address more than patients' quality of life in their recommendations. This change in emphasis may require a different commitment on the part of ethics committees in the future.

According to Monagle and West (2009), ethics committees help to develop the ethics culture of a hospital. They represent the conscience of the hospital because they translate its mission, vision, and values into recommendations for ethics-based practice. Institutions can sometimes be tempted to compromise quality for the sake of efficiency, and the ethics committee serves to remind hospitals that patients are human beings and not product lines. It recommends policies and actions that reinforce the hospital's true nature and the healthcare staff's true calling.

Another function of the ethics committee is to help establish hospital policies. This function can include formulating policies directly related to organizational ethics and its practice. In addition, the committee may review existing or new policies that involve a bioethics component. For example, a subcommittee might analyze the current DNR policy and make recommendations for clarification. The entire ethics committee would then review the analysis and recommendations. If approved, these recommendations would then be sent to the administration for adoption.

Consultation is perhaps the most dramatic and visible function of the ethics committee. In some hospitals, an advisory group or a CEC is formed as needed to assist physicians with difficult bioethics cases. Occasionally, family members will also ask for assistance in these cases. The group members gather necessary information about the case and apply bioethical theories and principles to it. Based on the results of their deliberation, they make a recommendation for action and provide the rationale for it. With the advent of complicated technologies and an increase in end-of-life concerns, the consulting role of ethics committees has increased in importance. The most common issues, not surprisingly, revolve around autonomy and end-of-life concerns.

Although ethics committees have an important role in hospitals, they can sometimes present problems. Finances are an issue. As the budget is squeezed and the demand for quality care increases, some hospitals may find it difficult to justify the time and expense required to maintain an ethics committee. Hospitals must assess the value of having a committee and decide whether they can continue to justify the costs. In addition to fiscal concerns, the nature of bioethical issues is becoming increasingly more complex. This means that there are no universal or simple answers, and the work of the committee is accordingly more difficult. In addition, many committee members may not understand the business side of health care, which makes it difficult for them to assist in making decisions that apply in the real world of hospital practice.

Despite these problems, hospital ethics committees serve a valuable function in the culture of the hospital. They serve as its conscience by keeping it on track with its true purpose. Ethics committees can also assist in policy review and development to ensure that the hospital's policies reflect the ethics position articulated in its mission statement. Of course, they are invaluable in assisting physicians, patients, and families who are struggling with difficult issues, especially at the end of life.

Ethics committees use discussion, review of ethics theory and principles, and decision-making models to achieve consensus and provide direction for resolving bioethical dilemmas. A variety of decision-making models are available; however, it is important for each committee to choose one and use it consistently. An example of a decision-making model can be found on the American College of Healthcare Executives' website (http://www.ache .org). This model involves clarifying the nature of the conflict, identifying stakeholders, and finding out the facts of the situation (Nelson, 2005). Once this is done, the applicable ethical theories and principles are discussed, leading to a series of ethics-based options. These options are evaluated and the best possible one is selected for implementation and evaluation. This is just one of many models, but it demonstrates the need for ethics committees to attend to detail and use ethics reasoning in their decision making.

HOSPITALS, PATIENT-CENTERED CARE, AND BIOETHICS

Traditionally, hospital care in America was guided by decisions made predominantly by the professional staff, including physicians, nurses, and administrators. Because of their (perceived) superior wisdom, these professionals were allowed to make decisions on behalf of their patients. Patients were expected to be compliant and express gratitude for their care. Today, patients also expect the professionals responsible for their care to have their best interests at heart, to act with beneficence, and to respect their personhood. However, given the nature of the modern hospital, with its sophisticated technology, specialized units, and harried staff, the paternalistic delivery of care does not always meet expectations. Patients often feel ignored, devalued, and demeaned.

Thanks to increasing information from various sources, such as the mass media and the Internet, and greater awareness of the hospital system, patients are becoming more than patients; they are becoming healthcare consumers. This change is altering the way they respond to care and increasing their expectations. Of course, they want the best possible care and the newest technologies. However, they are no longer content to be a "head in the bed" or the "colon in room 321." They want to be heard, respected, informed, and treated with dignity and kindness. This desire is expressed in the movement toward **patient-centered care.**

The model for patient-centered care originated in the work of Angelica Thieriot and her Planetree Foundation (Frampton, Gilpin, & Charmel, 2003). Hospitals that choose to implement patient-centered care have adopted all or parts of her model, which is known as the Planetree model. The elements of this model include an emphasis on the human interaction aspect of health care and its effect on healing. Healthcare professionals recognize that beneficent patient–professional interactions not only increase patient satisfaction, they also promote healing. In addition, staff members find that having an emphasis on human interaction increases their ability to make a difference. As a result, staff satisfaction is increased, resulting in greater morale and productivity.

In addition to human interaction, the Planetree model empowers patients by increasing their access to information. This means that hospitals provide libraries and resource centers, as well as improved patient communication, to enhance healing. In addition, the model recognizes the importance of family and friends as a part of patient healing. This means that family members or designated others can assist hospital staff by participating in care partner programs and advisory councils.

The Planetree model also recognizes the importance of food as a part of healing. The value of good nutrition is recognized by means of education programs, personalized services such as room service menus, and attention to food presentation. This concept extends to the hospital cafeteria, which is no longer located in an inhospitable site and does not simply ladle out "hospital food." Instead, it becomes a refuge for both staff and family members, and a source of nutritional information.

The inner resources of healing are not ignored in the Planetree model. This means that the role of spirituality is acknowledged and spiritual interventions such as counseling, meditation, prayer, and ritual are honored. In addition, the healing arts, as demonstrated through the visual arts and music, are part of the Planetree model. Creating an environment that includes these elements helps to fight the pain, fear, loneliness, and noise of the modern hospital. Examples of the application of the healing arts include colors in patient rooms, art in patient areas, and musician visits to patient rooms (Frampton et al., 2003).

The Planetree model also recognizes the power of touch in the healing process. Caring is communicated by offering therapeutic massage to those patients who choose to have it. This service is also offered to employees as a stress reduction tool. In addition to massage, the Planetree model also recognizes the value of integrative medicine practices. Although traditional-medicine proponents are not always supportive, some Planetree hospitals include medication, visualization, acupuncture, and humor as part of their services.

Finally, the Planetree model is concerned with the overall design of the hospital. Is the hospital environment a place where healing is enhanced? Does it help patients and staff members feel nurtured and sustained?

Hospitals attend to these environment issues by addressing navigation through the hospital, contact with nature, and sensory engagement. Hospitals that use the Planetree model try to create an environment that is welcoming to patients, family members, and staff.

What is the response to patient-centered care? Although not all hospitals have adopted the entire Planetree model, many have implemented at least some elements of it. One of the most obvious results of this implementation is greater patient satisfaction scores and reports. Some hospitals also report shorter lengths of stay for patients. In addition, staff satisfaction levels have increased because caregivers feel they are engaged in their chosen vocation (Frampton et al., 2003).

However, not all hospitals have implemented patient-centered care. Some professionals question the merits of giving patients a significant degree of control over what happens to them in a hospital. They dislike the changes brought about by this system and fear a loss of control and respect. Administrators worry about the potential costs of implementing any aspect of the Planetree model and question its ability to produce a return on the investment. This delivery system sounds good, but is it truly a good business practice?

Whether one agrees or disagrees with patient-centered care, its ethical implications merit discussion. A bioethics analysis involves four basic principles: autonomy, beneficence, nonmaleficence, and justice. In terms of patient autonomy, this care delivery method makes good sense. It is designed to show respect for persons, because patients are treated with dignity, compassion, and sensitivity. Instead of treating patients like children, this model respects them and supports their ability to make informed decisions. This autonomy also extends to staff members because the Planetree model respects their expertise and allows them to make a difference in patient care.

Beneficence is also a highly visible element of patient-centered care. It reflects the expectation that the hospital will do all it can to enhance the patient's healing experience. The patient becomes the heart of the hospital's daily activities. Even when the patient outcome is death, the people involved are treated with respect, compassion, and kindness. Families remember this and add to community trust and loyalty.

Nonmaleficence is also present in patient-centered care delivery. When the patient is the focus of the hospital, greater care is taken to avoid causing harm or to reduce any necessary harm. Often, harm can be reduced by giving patients information about the procedures they are about to undergo, encouraging the use of care partners, and giving family members better access to patients. In addition, staff members may suffer less harm from burnout and compassion fatigue because they know they are providing better care and are valued by the patients and their families, and the hospital itself.

Finally, justice needs to be considered with respect to patient-centered care. If the hospital chooses to make patients the center of its operations, will it increase the likelihood that they will get the care they deserve? Does this mean that the ability to be just, as the patient views justice, is increased? Patient-centered care should increase patient justice in hospital settings because there is a perception that what is deserved is received.

How does patient-centered care fit with the concept of distributive justice (balancing benefits and burdens)? To answer this question, hospitals have to determine the cost burden of providing patient-centered care, including fiscal and organizational changes. Although this cost may be minimal, each hospital will have to decide the worth of patient-centered care based on a cost–benefit analysis. If the benefits outweigh the costs, then hospitals can use distributive justice to make the decision to implement all or parts of the model.

The trend toward patient-centered care has great appeal for the health-care consumer. It demonstrates that hospitals are more than professional-centered workplaces or profit centers. They are places where patients matter and healing happens. However, healthcare reform and the de-mands to do more with less will challenge hospitals' ability to move from business as usual to patient-centered care. Current and future patients hope that hospitals will take the bioethical high road and continue to adopt this care delivery system.

SUMMARY

In this chapter, we have discussed bioethics as it applies to hospital settings and introduced the terms and principles that form the basis of ethical deci-sion making in both policy and patient situations. Examples of various is-sues were provided to demonstrate the complexity of applying ethics to patient care. The hospital's response to bioethical issues, the ethics com-mittee, was discussed with a focus on the membership, roles, responsibili-ties, and decision-making processes of this body. Finally, the patient-centered care model was presented and analyzed in terms of its bioethical implica-tions. It is hoped that this discussion will lead to further explorations of the intriguing field of bioethics as it applies to hospitals.

CHAPTER REVIEW

1. What is the difference between ethics and bioethics?
2. How does a hospital protect its patients' autonomy?
3. How is nonmaleficence practiced in hospitals?
4. What does the hospital patient expect with respect to beneficence?
5. What are some examples of bioethical issues faced by hospitals?
6. What are the roles of the ethics committee in a hospital?
7. How does patient-centered care relate to bioethics?

REFERENCES

Ashcroft, R. E., Dawson, A., Draper, H., & McMillan, J. R. (2007). *Principles of health care ethics* (2nd ed.). West Sussex, England: John Wiley & Sons Ltd.
Frampton, S. B., Gilpin, L., & Charmel, P. A. (2003). *Putting patients first: Designing and practicing patient-centered care.* San Francisco, CA: John Wiley & Sons.

Monagle, J. F., & West, M. P. (2009). Hospital ethics committees: Roles, memberships, structure, and difficulties. In E. E. Morrison (Ed.), *Health care ethics: Critical issues for the 21st century* (2nd ed., pp. 251–266). Sudbury, MA: Jones and Bartlett.

Morrison, E. E. (2011). *Ethics in health administration: A practical approach for decision makers* (2nd ed.). Sudbury, MA: Jones and Bartlett.

Munson, R. (2008). *Intervention and reflection: Basic issues in medical ethics* (8th ed.). Belmont, CA: Thompson Higher Education.

Nelson, W. A. (2005). An organizational ethics decision-making process. *Healthcare Executive, 20*, 8–14.

Summers, J. (2009). The theory of healthcare ethics. In E. E. Morrison (Ed.), *Health care ethics: Critical issues for the 21st century* (2nd ed., pp. 3–40). Sudbury, MA: Jones and Bartlett.

REFERENCES (CHAPTER 1)

Chilliers, L. & Retief, G. (2005). The evolution of hospitals from antiquity to the Renaissance. *Acta Theologica Supplementum*, Vol. 7 (2005).

Chilliers, L. & Retief, G. (2002). The evolution of the hospital from antiquity to the end of the middle ages. *Curationis*. 2002 Nov;25(4):60-6.

Risse, G. (1999). *Mending Bodies, Saving Souls: A History of Hospitals*. New York. Oxford Press.

Rosen, G. (1993). *A History of Public Health*. Baltimore, Maryland. The Johns Hopkins University Press.

Starr, P. (1982). *The Social Transformation of American Medicine*. Printed in the United States.

Case Studies

This appendix contains 20 case studies that should challenge you in your quest to understand the modern medical center and its environment. All of the cases are presented from the perspective of the reader as the CEO of a hospital. Some of the cases present bioethical dilemmas, whereas others address challenges related to marketing, planning, management, legal issues, the medical staff, and other issues.

The cases are designed to illustrate both common and unusual problems that can arise in the management of a hospital, and to stimulate discussion among the members of the team assigned to the case. This is done to simulate how the CEO and management team would address the issue within their hospital. Not all of these cases can be resolved from the text material alone. This also reflects the real world: executives often face problems for which they have no experience, training, or precedence to go by. The reader is certainly invited to use other resources.

The 20 case studies are as follows:

1. Towel? What Towel?
2. Water, Water Everywhere (three parts)
3. Problems for the New Administrator (three parts)
4. I'm Calling the EEOC and Filing a Complaint
5. Controls and Indicators for the Ship
6. The Case of Jill
7. You're on the Hospital Board!
8. You're the New CEO!
9. The Need to Communicate
10. Ooops!

11. Adding a New Service to the Hospital
12. The Case of Baby B
13. New Board Member Suggestion
14. I Hurt
15. Changes
16. The Crash
17. HIPAA Violations
18. An Application for Privileges
19. The Case of the Relocated Management Team
20. Do We Have Permission?

CASE 1: TOWEL? WHAT TOWEL?

You arrive at your office and find Dr. Ratliff waiting to see you. Dr. Ratliff is an experienced pathologist and one of the best physicians in the hospital. When he looks worried, you understand it is time to worry.

He begins by saying, "Chief, I was in my office this morning when surgery sent what appeared to be a large hairy softball. I bisected it and found a large green towel with the hospital's name on it." How could this have happened? Stunned, you ask the physician to continue.

Dr. Ratliff explains, "Well, you know the tax assessor's wife, Mrs. Bradley? She had a hysterectomy about 3 months ago; Dr. Estelle did the surgery. Apparently, he uses a rather unusual technique. After the patient is opened, one of the surgery technicians uses a folded, rolled-up towel to retract the patient's tissue while the operation is conducted. Since Mrs. Bradley is overweight, some of her tissue covered the towel, so no one noticed it, and Dr. Estelle closed her up."

You think for a moment and then ask, "Why didn't the nurses do a towel count at the completion of the surgery?"

Dr. Ratliff replies, "I thought the same thing and asked that of the surgery director. He told me, 'Hey, we count sponges, clamps, and other instruments, but we don't count towels. How can anyone leave an 18 × 240 green surgery towel in a patient? From now on, however, you had better believe that we'll count every towel.'"

You ask, "How did the patient discover that the towel was inside her?" Dr. Ratliff continues, "It seems that the patient began to notice a protruding lump, and the lump kept getting bigger. She went to a different doctor because she and Dr. Estelle had a falling-out regarding her bill. This time she went to Dr. Gibson. Dr. Gibson palpated the area, x-rayed it, then opened her up and found the towel. He says that he has not yet spoken with her; she is still in recovery."

Discussion

What action is appropriate in this case? Whom should you contact? Does the patient have an action that meets the four criteria for negligence? If she files suit, whom might her attorney name as defendants? How can you act quickly to mitigate the possible damages?

CASE 2: WATER, WATER EVERYWHERE

This case study is presented in three parts. You will derive the most value from the case if you stop reading when directed and discuss the points that have just been made.

Part 1

As you left your office Friday afternoon, you were delighted that it had been raining for nearly a week. Your 177-bed hospital is located in an arid part of the state that gets very little rain each year. The city's water supply comes from San Gabriel Creek, a spring-fed creek emanating from underground. In fact, this creek is the reason why the Spaniards founded the city of San Gabriel nearly 400 years ago. The spring pumps 90 million gallons of water a day as the creek winds its way majestically through the center of the city of San Gabriel.

Sunday night at about 11:30, your phone rings and awakens you from a deep sleep. The vice president of nursing, Mr. Arthur, is on the line. In your absence, Mr. Arthur serves as the acting CEO. Although his voice is under control, you have never heard him sound so serious.

"Chief, do not try to come to the hospital; you won't make it. The entire town is flooded and the hospital is receiving casualties. San Gabriel Creek overflowed its banks and many houses have been torn from their foundations. The authorities are predicting that when the sun comes up, there will be hundreds of bodies floating all over town."

You agree that you probably cannot make it to the hospital, and you also think that Mr. Arthur will need to be relieved from his capacity as acting CEO when morning comes. You go back to bed and ponder what you have just heard.

Discussion

Stop. Please do not read further until you have answered the following question: What priorities will you set in the morning? After you have discussed this question, continue to Part 2.

Part 2

When morning comes, the floodwaters have receded and you are able to drive to the hospital. Upon arrival, you find approximately 80 very wet people sleeping in the hallways. You gather a team together consisting of the chief engineer, vice president of nursing, assistant administrator, ancillary and support services director, and public relations director, and receive damage reports from each.

The chief engineer reports that the hospital has not been directly affected by the flood because of its location near the top of a hill. He does reveal bad news, however: the city has lost its entire water supply because the city water pumps are flooded. They may be out of service for as long as 30 days. The pumps are old and parts are no longer available; they will have to be replaced.

Mr. Arthur discloses that 12 people were killed in the flood. More than 700 homes were swept away, but most people were able to evacuate swiftly. The hospital emergency department received 50 casualties during the night, nearly all of which involved lacerations.

When you ask Mr. Arthur about such surprisingly low casualties compared to the initial prediction, he reports, "The Red Cross arrived around 4 a.m. and set up emergency facilities at the civic center. There are about 500 people sleeping there. Our own staff, with the exception of about 10 to 12 people, was able to report to work this morning."

Ms. Nelson, the ancillary and support services director, has some grim information: "There is no water supply to the hospital. We have lost our ability to do surgery because the air chillers, which are water-cooled, are not working. The surgery suite is no longer cool and the sterile packs are no longer sterile due to the high humidity. Lacking the proper working facilities, patients cannot use their restrooms and dietary services cannot prepare meals."

Discussion

Stop. Please do not read further until you have discussed the following questions: What priorities should you set? What action should you take?

Part 3

That morning, you join a team of about 30 community leaders who have agreed to meet at the San Gabriel airport each morning. This team is comprised of key government officials and members of the sheriff's department, the state department of public safety, the police department, the border patrol, the Red Cross, the hospital, etc. The leadership of this group has been ceded to the state department of public safety due to the resources it can provide and its experience in matters of this nature. The department has brought in search dogs and its helicopter pilots have been looking for additional victims. To date, 3 more bodies have been found, resulting in a total of 15 dead.

It has been confirmed that the water supply will be nonexistent for at least 30 days. Bottled water is being brought to the city and given to anyone who needs it. Many are driving outside of town to use showers provided by citizens with water wells.

The hospital has taken its surgical instruments to the local Air Force base, which has the ability to sterilize instruments in its dispensary. To obtain its own water supply, the hospital has borrowed a water-pumping fire truck from the city and connected it by a large hose to a water tanker truck from the Air Force base. The water truck pumps water through a city water pipe leading into the hospital. Every 2 hours, the water truck leaves and is replaced quickly by another water truck sitting directly behind it. In effect, your hospital has the only water supply in the entire city.

Discussion

How do you think outside agencies evaluating the hospital would rate the hospital's response at each stage of the disaster? Why? What do you think the hospital should do to minimize such disasters in the future? What lessons have been learned from this?

CASE 3: PROBLEMS FOR THE NEW ADMINISTRATOR

Background

El Verde Memorial is a 98-bed acute-care hospital in a rural town of 35,000 citizens. It is located in Rojo County, a western U.S. area of approximately 55,000 residents. The facility is the sole provider of medical care, as well as ambulance services, for the county. It includes an emergency department, an OB department, pediatric services, three surgery suites, and other standard departments.

The hospital is owned by the hospital district, an entity that was created by the state and is partially supported by taxes. It is governed by a board of directors whose seven members are elected by the citizens of Rojo County for 2-year terms. The board hires the administrator, who serves at its will.

The citizens are proud of their hospital, which dates to 1954, having been constructed with Hill-Burton funds. The town is in the southern part of the state and is in a very rural area, 150 miles away from any larger city, near the border of Mexico.

This rural municipality has 14 general practitioners (MDs and DOs), three general surgeons (two of whom are in practice together), two cardiologists, three internal medicine specialists, one urologist, three OB/GYNs, and two pediatricians. All own their own buildings and practices. There are also three certified registered nurse anesthetists (CRNAs) who provide operating-room coverage for the surgeons.

The primary economic base for the county is sheep ranching. The sheep are shorn for wool and are shipped annually to market by rail. There are no feedlots; rather, the county prides itself on organic farming and ranching, with many families contributing to the county's total output. There is a small military base, a US Border Patrol headquarters, a mall, and a recreation lake that attracts many tourists. The town's population grows dramatically in winter with many Canadians and retirees from the northern states fleeing south to escape their colder climates. As the new hospital CEO, you are facing a major challenge during your first few months in office.

Part 1

The problem is that the hospital has no medical office building (MOB). This presents an obstacle to your attempts to recruit new physicians to move to El Verde. Where will you tell new physicians to locate their practices?

You submit a memorandum to the hospital's board of directors proposing that an MOB be constructed immediately next to the hospital, on property already owned, and that it be connected to the hospital by an overhead walkway.

You find that the medical staff initially is very surprised about this proposed construction, and then is openly hostile to it. They argue that this facility will diminish the value of their personal investments in their own offices, and they will be at a distinct disadvantage in trying to compete with new physicians in a building next to the hospital.

Finally, the chief of the medical staff says, "Are you aware of the economic might we physicians have? We are some of the biggest depositors in the El Verde Bank, and we can switch our money to Big Lake Bank. How do you think the two board members who work at El Verde Bank will feel about you when they learn our reason for switching banks? The board can unappoint you just like it appointed you!"

Discussion

Administrators are often confronted with issues when the medical staff acts against the financial interests of the hospital, such as by constructing a freestanding outpatient surgical center or an imaging center in the immediate vicinity of the hospital. In this case study, the hospital is acting contrary to the best interests of some of the physicians by erecting an MOB to attract new physicians. Should a compromise be sought, and if so, what terms would you suggest? Should an independent third party be invited to build and then lease the MOB to keep the hospital uninvolved? Could this third party be the physicians?

Part 2

A second problem you face is that of out-migration of potential patients. Many citizens have told you that the hospital is fine for people of lesser economic means, but those who can afford it will seek health care at larger facilities in larger cities. To help fight this problem, the board of directors has given you a mandate to enhance the quality of care. In the board's opinion, you should immediately recruit an anesthesiologist instead of continuing to depend on the three CRNAs. When you tell this to the surgeons, they say, "We have used the CRNAs for 15 years; we will not use an anesthesiologist." In their best Western vernacular, they tell you, "We are gonna ride the horse that brung us!"

Discussion

Is it likely that the new anesthesiologist will be successful if the surgeons remain loyal to the CRNAs? What about other physicians who could use the services of the anesthesiologist? Could the anesthesiologist provide anesthesia services for functions other than surgery, such as caring for patients who require pain management? Could he or she teach the CRNAs new techniques? Could the hospital provide new patient services in which the CRNAs have no experience, such as open-heart surgery?

Part 3

Finally, the physicians ask you to side with them in requesting a change in the legislation that created the hospital.[1] In this hospital district, physicians are expressly prohibited by law from running for a seat on the board. The hospital's medical staff formally requests that the administrator and hospital support their move to have the legislation changed.

Discussion

Would you want physicians serving on the board of directors? What would be the pros and cons of having physicians on the board? Do you think anyone in the community or on the current board of directors would oppose the idea?

---

[1] Hospital districts in this state are created by legislative acts. The act creating the district sets forth what the hospital and its board can and cannot do, how often elections are held, how the administrator is hired, etc. In this case, a seven-person board was created to oversee the hospital, but physicians were specifically prohibited in the original enabling legislative act from serving on the hospital board. To change the enabling legislation, a bill would have to be introduced by a congressional representative, passed by the legislature, and then signed by the governor.

CASE 4: I'M CALLING THE EEOC AND FILING A COMPLAINT

You are the new, female CEO of an 80-bed rural hospital. One of the employees asks if she can speak to you for a moment. Having an open-door policy and wishing to know all of the employees, you smile and say, "Of course," and usher her into your office.

She seems a little sheepish and then states, "Speaking woman to woman, I'm sure you'll understand my plight. My department director seems to be attracted to me, and I have continually repelled his advances. He is much older than I am, is not attractive, is married, and frankly, the thought of him irritates me. Moreover, he is not a good boss. I am not trying to get anyone in trouble, but the other night I saw on late-night television a discussion of something called sexual harassment. That is what I think is going on. I am in a hostile work environment, and if he doesn't quit, I'm calling the EEOC and filing a complaint."

Discussion

What steps will you take? What policies should be in place? Will you interview anyone, and if so, whom? If the person who has complained to you chooses to call the EEOC before you investigate, what should you expect and what will you do? Should you call the hospital's attorney? What protection should be afforded the department director?

CASE 5: CONTROLS AND INDICATORS FOR THE SHIP

You are the CEO of a 342-bed acute-care hospital with several clinics. While reflecting on your experiences during the past year, you decide to create plus and minus columns listing the things you are pleased with and things you have vowed to change.

In the plus column, you realize that you have several solid senior management team members and many competent department directors. Because of the location of the hospital, you enjoy zero competition. You have good capital equipment and a solid infrastructure. The hospital's reputation in the community is good; in fact, your hospital is viewed as the region's principal medical center.

In the minus column, however, you realize that most of your senior management team, including yourself and the chief medical director, have been reduced to "firefighters." You find yourself constantly jumping from one problem area to another, never having enough time to enjoy your job, to explore new possibilities, or to visit physicians, government officials, members of the public, or employees. You are literally pinned down in your office, worrying about vendors will be able to deliver out-of-stock items, dealing with broken equipment, and responding to unhappy patients and family members. Many employees are also unhappy, as demonstrated in the recent employee satisfaction survey.

As you begin to consider your options for change, you happen to read an article stating that hospitals are like ocean liners, in that there are many departments and operations, and all are meant to serve the public. In short, you and your management team are the equivalent of the senior leadership of a large cruise ship, and you are at the helm. This helps you realize that just like the ship's captain, you cannot be everywhere at the same time, and yet it is critical that you understand what is going on everywhere. What is ahead? Are you approaching an iceberg? Are heavy winds rising? Are the passengers happy? Is the crew about to stage a mutiny?

These thoughts help you and your senior team realize that you need gauges, instruments, and warning indicators that you can monitor periodically. You need information that is simple and concise, and can be trended to reveal what is really happening on the ship.

One of your team members suggests that in addition to macro indicators such as the average daily census, you need micro indicators from each department. These indicators can alert you to when the ship is going off course. You want a fixed set of controls and indicators that will enable you to be *proactive* and stop problems before they arise, rather than to *react* to problems and continue your firefighting.

Discussion

What do you and your team suggest? What set of macro indicators are you going to monitor? What specific micro indicators do you want your department directors to watch? Why did you select these indicators? How often should they be monitored?

CASE 6: THE CASE OF JILL

Jill is a patient who was admitted 2 weeks ago with pneumonia. She has lived in a local long-term care facility for the past 12 years.

Jill is 15 years old and entered the long-term care facility after suffering a major head injury when she was 3 years old. She has an extremely low IQ, cannot speak, is blind, and sits either in bed or in a wheelchair, quietly rocking back and forth. Jill's cognitive prognosis is for no change, due to the extensive brain damage. She is in the long-term care facility because her father travels extensively and her mother, who is also physically challenged, is unable to care for Jill.

Your hospital has given Jill good care and her pneumonia has subsided. However, the long-term care facility has notified you that they no longer have a bed for Jill; the facility is at capacity and for the near future will not be admitting patients. Jill does not belong in your hospital; she no longer needs acute care, but discharging her to a long-term care facility does not seem to be an option. Home health care is also not an option because Jill needs care for most of the day.

As the social worker and discharge planner think about what to do, they notice that Jill's color has changed and her skin tone appears to be jaundiced. They refer this new problem to Jill's physician, who orders a battery of tests. Jill is diagnosed with renal disease and an order for dialysis is written.

When the dialysis needle is placed in Jill's arm, she cries out in pain, lashes out, and is very combative. Because she is blind and does not understand the world around her, Jill cannot comprehend what is happening to her, but it is easy to see that her pain is acute.

After three dialysis sessions, Jill's parents come to the hospital at the request of her physician. They are told the following options are open to Jill: (1) she can receive dialysis three times a week for the next 20 to 30 years because she is otherwise healthy, or (2) the dialysis can be discontinued and Jill would be expected to die within the next 12 months.

After conferring with their minister, Jill's parents decided to discontinue the dialysis treatments. They reason that Jill has a low quality of life, which is not expected to change. The benefits of the treatment are not worth the pain that Jill would have to bear.

Upon learning of the parents' decision, you decide to convene the bioethics committee, which will act as an impartial advisory body. The committee is comprised of you (the CEO), a physician, a nurse, a social worker, the hospital attorney, and one of the committee's volunteer ministers.

Jill's physician objectively presents her case to the committee and describes the two options. The committee members ask questions and then confer with Jill's parents, who present their views. The committee then decides to confer privately.

As the committee members confer, the hospital's attorney suggests a third option. The state could be contacted and Jill could be removed from the care of her parents. The attorney anticipates that the state would then place Jill in a state institution and would continue to provide dialysis treatment.

Discussion

Discuss Jill's case in detail, as the bioethics committee would, and weigh all options. What recommendations would you make?

CASE 7: YOU'RE ON THE HOSPITAL BOARD!

You are proud to be a citizen of Marcos San Loco, a very progressive, beautiful, and growing city of about 35,000 people. The principal industry is making seatbelts for automobile manufacturers. As a concerned and responsible resident, you feel it is your civic duty to run for membership on either the local school board or the local hospital board. Because your children are now in college and there are so many issues that rivet your attention in the healthcare reform debate, you decide the hospital board is for you.

In speaking with your friends, neighbors, and fellow employees, you gain their support and some campaign contributions, and are on your way. Because you are a lifelong resident and own your own business, which bears your name, you are a shoo-in to be elected. You win coveted seat #2 on the board of directors of Loco Medical Center.

As you discuss issues with your fellow board members, you find that:

1. Although the administrator has built a new wing, added three profitable services, and recruited two primary care practitioners to the area, she is not liked by the employees. Many feel she is too "big city" for them, constantly saying things like, "Well, we didn't do it this way in Antonio San Lupe" (a large hospital in a nearby city). Many of these employees are your friends.

2. The hospital will not accept payments from citizens who belong to the Good Wellness healthcare plan. The Good Wellness HMO plan originated in Antonio San Lupe and is widely recognized and honored by most of the local medical offices. However, when you question the administrator of the hospital, she informs you that Good Wellness pays very poorly—in terms of both promptness and the amount it will pay per case, which is nearly at Medicaid rates. She does not want to do business with Good Wellness, which means that members of the plan must drive to Antonio San Lupe, about 45 minutes away, if they need hospital services.

Discussion

Discuss what the newly elected board member should do, if anything, about the hospital administrator. Does she represent progress that the Marcos San Loco healthcare system needs, or is she someone who does not fit in with the culture and should be terminated?

Please discuss the pros and cons of the Good Wellness plan. Should the hospital break even with these patients, or should the patients drive to another hospital? Are there alternatives?

CASE 8: YOU'RE THE NEW CEO!

After 4 years of undergraduate work and 2 years of working toward a master's degree in healthcare administration, you graduated and got a job as the COO of a hospital in Antonio San Lupe. You worked hard for several years and then applied to the board of directors of a hospital in a small neighboring town, Marcos San Loco, to be the CEO. You were hired and have operated the hospital in the black for 3 years.

The county holds a new election and you find that only two of the original seven board members who hired you have been reelected. Four decided to retire from the board and one was defeated in the election.

As you meet with the five new board members for their orientation, you are taken aback by their lack of knowledge about health care; you have the impression that most couldn't even recognize a hospital if they saw one. The new members are a popular high school football coach, a car salesman, a vice president of a bank, a retired aircraft mechanic, and a fourth-grade teacher. They may not be the most knowledgeable people in terms of health care, but they were certainly the best vote getters.

As you are considering your new situation, you find out that two of the board members are feeling self-important and are actually telling some of the nurses to give special treatment to friends of theirs who are currently patients in the hospital. Furthermore, the new members are listening to the complaints of employees whom you consider your "problem children"—long-term employees who are reluctant to embrace change.

You also know that keeping the hospital in the black is your number one priority. If you accept the current terms of the Good Wellness plan, the cost of caring for members of the plan could have a very negative impact on your bottom line.

Discussion

Because you answer to the board members, how do you plan to tell them that although they set policy, *you* manage the day-to-day operations? How do you plan to address those employees who are discussing their likes and dislikes openly and frequently with your board members? Finally, what do you plan to do about Good Wellness and the fact that many of the town's citizens are driving to Antonio San Lupe for care?

CASE 9: THE NEED TO COMMUNICATE

You are the administrator of a 201-bed acute-care facility located in a medium-sized city somewhere in middle America. Your hospital provides the normal array of services and you think your management team does a good job. Acting on a suggestion from a staff member, you decide to ask your marketing department to undertake some research. You ask the staff to form two focus groups: one comprised of a dozen physicians randomly chosen from the active medical staff, who have handled at least 10 admissions apiece during the past year, and one comprised of a dozen citizens. The citizens will be recruited by posting a sign in a large neighborhood supermarket seeking paid volunteers. Questions for both groups will be open-ended and elicit responses as to how the hospital is perceived by each group.

After a couple of months, the marketing department prepares the following report:

Summary: Physician Group

The physician focus group met during lunch with an experienced moderator. They were asked to provide information about the hospital, specifically their chief likes and dislikes. While nearly all voiced the opinion that the facility was up-to-date, had modern technology, and employed well-trained staff, their chief complaint was that they were never informed of what the hospital was about to undertake, they were always in the dark, and they always felt left out of decision making. To be specific, one physician commented, "I have been on staff for 3 years and wondered what the construction at the rear of the hospital was all about. I just found out it is a new outpatient dialysis unit."

Another physician spoke up and complained, "The new CT scanner that was ordered is a Hemotso. If I had known that, I might have persuaded the hospital to switch to Hitachi; it does better spin-echo imaging. It seems that no one ever tells us anything, and we are the ones charged with taking care of the patients."

The responses from the remaining physicians were similar.

Summary: Consumer Group

This group of 12 was comprised of five men and seven women of varying ages. All lived less than 5 miles from the hospital, and eight had used the hospital within the last 12 months. The focus group session was conducted during lunch, the volunteers were paid $50 for their participation, and the group was asked open-ended questions regarding their perceptions of the hospital.

While everyone thought the hospital had the best reputation of any hospital in the city, they all voiced the opinion that they knew little about the hospital. When asked, "What new service provided by the hospital do you feel is the most important?" only one commented on the cardiac catheter unit. Most could not name *any* new service, and the only other service that was named at all was the emergency department.

You feel disappointed by the perceptions of the two groups, but you also believe this is an opportunity to launch new and better communication efforts, both internally and externally.

Discussion

What do you plan to do to improve communication with the physicians and other employees? What do you plan to do to communicate with the public? Please be specific and set out a strategy, budget, and timetable for each group.

CASE 10: OOOPS!

You are the CEO of the Loco Medical Center in Marcos San Loco. You enjoy a good relationship with most of the businesses and agencies in the city. You are a fundraiser for the Girl Scouts, sit on the board of directors for the battered women's shelter, and regularly contribute to local charities.

Because of these relationships, the chief officer of the Border Patrol confides in you that he strongly suspects one of his employees is using drugs, both on and off the job. He tells you that he has a random drug screening policy and that he plans to demand a sample when he suspects that the employee is using drugs, and that he will send the sample to your laboratory.

This in fact transpires and the employee produces a sample in compliance with the policy. This sample is collected correctly, logged in and placed in the proper chain of custody, and then delivered to the hospital laboratory for testing.

When the chief officer phones the laboratory for the results, he is told that the specimen has been misplaced and cannot be accounted for. He angrily asks how this could have happened and wonders if you are aware of how many relatives of agents work in the hospital.

Discussion

Was it ethical of the chief officer to tell you he suspected that one of his agents was using drugs?

What can you do to ensure that samples like this do not vanish? Who might you hold responsible if they do?

Should you institute a nepotism policy? What if you discover that many relatives work within the hospital?

CASE 11: ADDING A NEW SERVICE TO THE HOSPITAL

It is February 2006 and you are the CEO of a medium-sized acute-care medical center. You have been at the hospital for 6 years and are pleased that Gamma Knife (GK) procedures will be added to the list of services offered by the hospital. In fact, you are expecting the first patient to be scheduled for this procedure about August 2007.

The Gamma Knife is a new technology for this area of the country. One of your challenges is to inform the public about the nature and purpose of the procedure, how it can benefit a patient, the risks involved, and the positive and negative aspects of the surgery.

The hospital's marketing director has just joined the organization from a sales position at Ferrari's of Miami. He is a genius at public relations and marketing, but, in his own words, he "knows zero about health care."

In addition to recruiting the correct personnel to do the procedure, you must lead a team of hospital employees in taking an integrated approach to delivering this new service. This team must ensure that the laboratory, radiology, anesthesia, surgery, ICU, safety, pharmacy, materials management, physical therapy, and patient education departments all work together for the patients' benefit.

Discussion

Please present steps that you deem appropriate to lead your team of employees toward successful implementation of the GK procedure. You must also build awareness in the public regarding the new procedure and who might be candidates for the GK. How will you do this?

CASE 12: THE CASE OF BABY B

As you arrive at work on a Monday morning, you find the vice president of nursing, Ms. Pipkin, RN, waiting outside your office with a very worried look—a sign that all did not go well during the weekend. As the CEO of the hospital, you have relied on her judgment for several years and you think well of her. You have learned that when she gets upset, it is usually for a good reason.

Ms. Pipkin opens the dialogue by saying, "We had a baby taken from the pediatrics ward during the weekend. I didn't beep you or call because the baby was taken by the nurse manager of pediatrics." You quietly compose yourself and ask the nursing vice president to continue.

"Patti is the nurse manager in question," she said. "Recently, she and her husband, Tim, were told by their physician that Patti is unable to get pregnant. On Friday night, a 14-year-old girl gave birth here. She then stated to everyone concerned, 'When I leave this hospital I am not taking that baby home with me. Call the state, call anyone you want, but I am leaving the baby here and you can do with it what you want.'"

"Patti is a veteran nurse and is well versed in the law," Ms. Pipkin continued. "Patti understands that the girl, even though she's only 14, becomes emancipated after giving birth, and legally can sign her baby over to anyone she chooses. Patti found the necessary forms and explained to the girl that she, Patti, would be a very fit parent; she is the nurse manager of pediatrics and understands children very well; and she and her husband, Tim, wanted children but just learned that could not have any. With a stroke of a pen, the new mother signed over her baby to Patti, and Patti took the baby home on Saturday morning."

You confer with Ms. Pipkin further and then call the hospital's attorney, the local district attorney, the state nursing board, the state hospital association, and the state attorney general's office. After lengthy discussions, each group replies that it can find no rule or statute that has been violated. One person wisecracks that a nurse should not accept gifts from patients, but all decline to become involved because they can see no breach of duty or care, or a broken law.

The state attorney general's office tells you that the state always conducts an investigation when a couple is given a baby. The state will send a social worker to visit and assess the potential parents and the environment they can provide. If the parents are declared unfit, the baby will be placed in a foster home pending adoption; if they are deemed to be fit, they will be allowed to adopt the baby.

Discussion

Did Patti have an ethical duty to not solicit the baby? How will the community feel about her action? Should the hospital adopt a new policy regarding such matters? Should the hospital take any action regarding Patti's employment?

CASE 13: NEW BOARD MEMBER SUGGESTION

As the CEO, you have gotten used to the new board members of the Marcos San Loco hospital, and they appear to be getting used to you.

One of the board members has been doing some reading regarding patient admissions to hospitals and comes to you with what he believes to be a money-making idea. Physicians are not required to treat people who cannot afford to pay for their services. However, indigent persons can be admitted into a hospital if they are first seen in the emergency department. The Emergency Medical Treatment and Active Labor Act (EMTALA) prohibits hospitals from turning away indigent people in need of care.

The board member suggests to you that the emergency department should be closed at once. Without an emergency department, the hospital's financial picture would greatly improve because it would be providing almost no indigent care.

Discussion

Discuss what action you plan to take.

CASE 14: I HURT

As part of your expansion efforts, you have added a cardiac catheterization laboratory to the hospital. For the catheterization procedure, the patient is placed on a table. After an injection of Demerol to make the patient woozy and to ease any discomfort, a catheter line is inserted into the femoral artery and snaked upward until it reaches the patient's heart. At this point, dye is injected, and through the use of something akin to a fluoroscopy machine the cardiologist can observe and film in real time the interior of the patient's beating heart to determine which vessels might be occluded. This will enable the cardiologist to diagnose the problem and perhaps recommend surgery or a stint to improve the patient's health and/or comfort.

A physician who has just performed the above procedure drops by your office to discuss some concerns. He says that after the shot of Demerol, the patient did not get woozy as expected, and in fact, as the line was inserted, cried out, "I hurt!" "This sometimes happens," the physician said. "I thought that perhaps I had started the line insertion too soon. However, very interestingly, the same thing happened to the next patient in exactly the same manner. I honestly believe you have someone in your cath lab crew who is diverting Demerol for his or her own use and replacing the drug with saline solution that is then injected into the patient."

Discussion

Discuss the pros and cons of the physician's ideas.

CASE 15: CHANGES

As the CEO of Marcos San Loco, you arrive at work to find the health information management director waiting to see you. You usher him into your office and he shuts the door, which is never a good sign from a department director.

He begins the conversation by saying, "I am extremely upset with Dr. Corta. You'll remember I complained about him last month. He used Wite-Out on the patient's medical record to cover up a prescription error—he had ordered 25 cc of a medication when he should have ordered 5 cc. Luckily, the pharmacist caught the mistake before the patient was given an overdose, and phoned Dr. Corta. Dr. Corta then used Wite-Out to cover the 2 in the medical record. I cautioned him that he should never, ever to do that, and that he should only draw a single ink line across the 2 and then write the correction in the medical record. Well, this time, he was treating a patient and then he left the hospital with the medical record. The nurses saw him put it under his lab coat, walk off the ward, and then use the exit to go to his car.

Discussion

What should you do? Is this a matter for the medical director to handle? What if Dr. Corta denies having the medical record? If the medical record includes material related to litigation, where should it be kept?

CASE 16: THE CRASH

As the CEO of Marcos San Loco, you are experiencing a pleasant week. Admissions have increased, the average length of stay is within bounds, and the medical staff is smiling about their recent softball victory over the city attorneys. All in all, things seem good.

As you walk around the hospital on your daily rounds, you notice that one particular hallway wall has really been bleached by the sun. This wall is on the wing near the physical therapy department. Light has been streaming in through large picture windows, and over the years the wall has faded much more than the other walls along the hall.

Arriving back at your office, you phone the hospital's maintenance director and mention the particular area in question. You then meet her in that area and jointly discuss painting the wall during the weekend when only a few physical therapy sessions are conducted with inpatients (and none with outpatients).

The maintenance director agrees that this is a good idea, and suggests sending one of the employees to buy paint.

A couple of hours later, one of your board members calls. It seems that the employee who was sent to buy paint has been involved in an automobile accident with the board member's wife. As the employee was backing out of his parking spot at the paint store, driving the hospital's truck, he backed into her car. To complicate the matter even further, the employee's girlfriend and her child were also in the truck at the time of the accident.

Discussion

Discuss the hospital's possible liability for damaging the board member's car. What do you plan to do to avoid similar problems in the future?

CASE 17: HIPAA VIOLATIONS

Things have been going pretty well in Marcos San Loco. It's fall, school has begun, and your hospital is a proud booster of the local high school football team.

As you are settling into your morning routine, your phone rings and it is the local PTA president. He says, "Hi, Polly, it seems that we have a problem. Several of our, shall we say, 'more adventuresome teens' have contracted some sexually transmitted diseases. I came across this news because one of your laboratory workers who ran the analyses told her husband and he mentioned it to me when we were playing golf yesterday. I wouldn't have phoned you except I saw a news story last week on TV about patient confidentiality issues and some law called HIPAA. I thought you would want to know before some government inspector called you or, worse yet, one of your board members."

Discussion

Do you see this as a problem? What should be done? Who should be held responsible? How can you ensure that things like this do not happen in the future?

CASE 18: AN APPLICATION FOR PRIVILEGES

As the CEO of Marcos San Loco Medical Center, you are anxious to recruit a new urologist. The current urologist, Dr. Sandler, is not well liked by the medical staff and is thought to deliver questionable care. You are not afraid to find another provider because if Dr. Sandler gets upsets and leaves the community, it may be even easier to find someone because there would then be no competing interests.

You contact a urologist named Dr. Smaney, who is practicing in a small community about 50 miles away. It seems that, yes, Dr. Smaney would like to see more patients and can drive to Marcos San Loco 2 days a week. You have a spare suite in the new MOB and arrange for Dr. Smaney to occupy the office.

After you carefully check Dr. Smaney's credentials and ensure that he is set up to practice, the chief of the medical staff drops by your office for a short discussion. He begins, "You know Polly, there is a problem with the coverage for Dr. Smaney. Yes, he seems to be a good doctor and his patients think he's a great guy. Our physicians also want to refer patients to him, but there is a little problem. When he does surgery and keeps the patient overnight in the hospital, who is going to cover his patient if the patient has a problem in the middle of the night? Dr. Smaney lives 50 miles away and it would take at least an hour for him to get here. Meanwhile, no one has his expertise or desire to provide coverage . . . why, the patient could bleed out and expire before Smaney could make the drive! I've talked with the surgeons and all of us are uncomfortable with this arrangement."

Discussion

Should Dr. Smaney's surgical privileges be revoked? Is there another solution? Certainly you don't want patients to be hospitalized 50 miles away. What do you suggest?

CASE 19: THE CASE OF THE RELOCATED MANAGEMENT TEAM

You and your senior management team have done an extraordinary job in managing the company's medical center in Wisconsin. In fact, on several occasions the company president has singled you out for special commendations.

One of the company's key regional vice presidents flew into town yesterday and requested an emergency meeting with you and your senior management team. It seems there is a crisis at the company's medical center in Missouri.

In meeting with the vice president, you learn that the hospital CEO in Missouri has a terminal disease, two of his senior management team members have recently retired, and two others resigned yesterday for other opportunities. There is a critical management vacuum at the top. This has caught the company by surprise and the company has no game plan. However, the company president was consulted and suggested to the regional vice president that you and your team be shifted to take over the Missouri facility.

In your meeting with the vice president, she states, "I have confidence in your management abilities and therefore I am reassigning you immediately to the Missouri hospital. You and your team are to report there tomorrow to assume key command and control positions. You will be there for a minimum of 9 months or until other staff can be recruited to take your place, and you have full authority and responsibility to make any changes you wish. I can tell you that the hospital has a 27% nursing staff shortage, and the contracted pharmacy company that has been managing the pharmacy has given notice that it will be leaving in 60 days. On top of that, eight physicians are not renewing their contracts at the end of the year (it is now August 4), engineering has informed us that the emergency power system is nonoperational and cannot be repaired because it is too old, and the finance director is in jail, charged by the government with embezzling hospital funds for his personal use."

You also learn in a follow-up meeting that if you do a good job in Missouri, there will be key positions waiting for you and your team in the home office. However, if you fail, you likely will be relocated to Sand Dune Hospital, a 37-bed facility in Death Valley.

Discussion

What do you think are the central issues of concern? What do you plan to undertake each month? What information will you immediately request upon arrival? How do you plan to address employees who were very loyal to the previous administration team and convince them to stay with the company?

CASE 20: DO WE HAVE PERMISSION?

You are the CEO of Marcos San Loco Medical Center and are attending a medical staff dinner. Because many of the medical staff know you have a law degree (you are a hospital administrator who also went to law school so you could better understand contracts, employment law, malpractice, etc.), the staff wants to explore the issue of patient consent. Please address these questions from the medical staff:

1. If a patient comes into the emergency department unconscious, can we legally treat him or do we need to wait until the patient becomes conscious?

2. If a minor comes into the emergency department and his parents are Jehovah's Witnesses who are ordering the physicians not to give their child blood, even though a blood transfusion is essential to save the child's life, must we obey the parent's wishes? What else could we do to obtain consent?

3. If a patient is treated before she gives written consent, will oral consent suffice?

4. What could happen to us, the medical staff, if we treat a patient without getting her consent?

5. If a patient is conscious but is intoxicated, can we treat him?

6. If a patient is married but is a minor according to the state's statutory age of consent, can he give valid consent for treatment?

7. If a patient is a minor and thus is below the state's statutory age of consent, but has just delivered a baby, can she give valid consent for the treatment of herself and the baby?

Glossary

Accreditation. A process used by The Joint Commission to evaluate the quality of patient care at hospitals and health facilities.

Accredited hospital. A hospital that meets specific operating standards set by The Joint Commission or the American Osteopathic Association. Typically, the seal of accreditation is displayed in the lobby of a hospital.

Act of God. An unpredictable act of nature uninfluenced by human intervention; an unplanned, undesired event, usually associated with catastrophic outcomes.

Acute care hospitals. Hospitals that specialize in the care of severely ill or injured patients.

Admission. The formal acceptance of inpatients into a hospital or other inpatient health facility. Such inpatients are typically provided with room and board, as well as continuous nursing services, and stay at least overnight.

Admitting department. The hospital department that obtains inpatients' demographic and financial information for registration purposes; schedules preadmission testing; coordinates patient room assignments; records all patient movements, including transfers and discharges, for the purpose of maintaining accurate census data; and disseminates patient information to other hospital departments.

Advance directives. Instructions given by individuals specifying what actions should be taken for their health in the event that they are no longer able to make decisions due to illness or incapacity, and appointing a person to make such decisions on their behalf.

Adverse drug reaction. Any adverse event for which there is a reasonable possibility that a drug caused the event. This unplanned and unwanted result may have occurred because the drug was not given in the recommended manner to a patient, thus resulting in harm or having the potential to cause harm. Effects range from "nuisance effects," such as dry mouth, to severe reactions. For safety reporting to the FDA during the investigational stage, the term "reasonable possibility" means that there is evidence to suggest a causal relationship between the drug and the adverse event.

Advertising. The act or practice of attracting public attention with the specific intent to generate interest or induce a purchase. Advertising is generally accomplished by means of the mass media.

Against medical advice (AMA). When patients are noncompliant or do something against the orders or advice of their physician, such as leaving the hospital before the treating physician writes a discharge order, he or she is considered to be acting against medical advice.

Agency contract nurse. A nurse who works for an outside agency that contracts with hospitals to provide registered nurses, licensed practical nurses, and nursing assistants.

Alliance. A formal agreement between two or more hospitals and/or hospital systems for specific purposes. These arrangements usually operate under a set of bylaws or other written regulations.

Allied health. A discipline that includes the study of health and health outcomes, and implementation of policies and procedures in ways that support the direct study of health care.

Allied health professional. A health worker other than a physician, dentist, podiatrist, or nurse, who is specially trained and, in some cases, licensed (e.g., a physician's assistant). Depending on the hospital or health facility, this individual may perform tasks that could be performed by a physician. An allied health professional always works under the supervision of a health professional.

Ambulatory. Pertaining to or capable of walking and moving; able and strong enough to walk and use limbs to move.

Ambulatory care. Medical or health services provided on an outpatient basis. It usually implies that the patients are ambulatory and came to the facility for a specific outpatient treatment or service. (Synonym: outpatient care.)

Ambulatory care center, freestanding. A facility that is not located on a hospital campus and offers medical, surgical, diagnostic, and rehabilitative care on an outpatient basis.

Ambulatory hospital. A program based in the hospital or other institution offering intensive medical, psychiatric, nursing, or rehabilitative services to patients during daytime hours.

Ambulatory surgery, hospital. Minor elective surgical procedures provided by a hospital on an outpatient basis. Because patients are admitted and discharged on the day of surgery, such programs reduce hospital costs. (Synonyms: short procedures unit (SPU), same-day surgery, come-and-go surgery, and outpatient surgery.)

Ambulatory surgical facility, freestanding. A facility that is separate from the hospital and provides surgical treatment to outpatients who do not require overnight hospitalization. Note: The offices of private physicians or dentists are not included in this category unless such offices have a distinct area that is used solely for outpatient surgical treatment on a routine, organized basis. (Synonym: freestanding surgicenter.)

American College of Healthcare Executives (ACHE). Professional society for hospital and healthcare managers and executives, founded in 1933. Up until 1985 it was known as the American College of Hospital Administrators (ACHA). Headquarters: One North Franklin Street, Chicago, IL 60606.

American Hospital Association (AHA). A nationwide association founded in 1898 to promote public welfare by ensuring better hospital care for all people. The AHA conducts research and educational programs in areas of healthcare administration, hospital economics, hospital facilities and design, and community relations. In addition, the AHA represents hospitals as a national spokesperson for legislation. The AHA has several separate professional divisions, including the American Academy of Hospital Attorneys and American Society for Hospital Central Service Personnel. The AHA also offers policy guidance to governmental agencies. Headquarters: One Franklin Street, Chicago, IL 60606.

American Medical Association (AMA). A nationwide professional association of licensed physicians, founded in 1847. The AMA monitors the quality of medical practice; provides information on drugs, medical therapy, research, food and nutrition, cosmetics, and medical quackery; determines the conditions of medical practice and payment; and acts as a watchdog over the growing governmental interest in the nation's health. The AMA also offers policy guidance to governmental agencies. Headquarters: 535 Dearborn Street, Chicago, IL 60610.

Americans with Disabilities Act (ADA). A 1990 federal act prohibiting discrimination against people with physical disabilities.

Ancillary services. Therapeutic or diagnostic services provided by specific hospital departments (other than nursing service), including but not limited to imaging, laboratories, and anesthesiology. Other ancillary services include but are not limited to respiratory therapy, electroencephalography, heart station, rehabilitative medicine, and pharmacy.

Anesthesiology. The branch of medicine that deals with the administration and study of anesthetics. It involves the administration of local, general, or regional anesthesia before and during surgery.

Anesthesiology department. Hospital department staffed by anesthesiologists and nurse anesthetists who administer anesthesia and anesthetics to patients so that surgical or other authorized procedures may be performed.

Annual report. A yearly publication prepared and issued by a hospital, detailing the state of the institution's operations and financial position. Typically, the hospital's accomplishments, as well as its future plans and programs, are highlighted.

Assisted living. A housing arrangement for individuals who are not capable of completely caring for themselves but do not need constant care from others.

Audit medical and patient care. A periodic and systematic review of quality care within a hospital, usually performed by a committee or a designated person according to an established procedure.

Autonomy. Quality or state of being self-governing, self-directed freedom or moral independence.

Average census. The average number of patients who receive medical or nursing care during a specific reporting period (typically 1 year or 1 month).

Average daily census. The average number of inpatients receiving care each day during a reporting period, excluding newborns. Bed counts of patients are most often done at midnight.

Average length of stay (ALOS). The average number of days of service rendered to each patient who is discharged during a given time period. This figure is computed by dividing the total number of days spent in the hospital by patients discharged in a given time period by the total number of inpatients discharged during that time period. Example: 120 total patient days for 20 patients discharged. The average length of stay is 120 ÷ 20 = 6 days.

Baccalaureate degree program, nursing. A formal program of study in a 4-year college or university that educates students in the nursing field. Typically, the college's nursing school provides both classroom and laboratory teaching. The college's own hospital or its affiliated hospital provides the clinical teaching. Upon graduation from the program, individuals are awarded a bachelor of arts or bachelor of science degree in nursing. Graduates are then eligible to take the state nursing examinations for licensure as registered nurses. (Synonym: bachelor of science in nursing [BSN].)

Bad debt. An account that cannot be collected from a patient even though the patient has or may have the ability to pay. This results in a credit loss for the hospital, clinic, or other healthcare facility. These losses may be reflected as an allowance from revenue or as an expense of doing business.

Balance sheet. A summary listing of an institution's assets, liabilities, and net worth showing the financial condition of the hospital or business at a specific point in time. For hospitals, the net worth is commonly referred to as the fund balance.

Battery. The tort of harmful, forceful touching in a socially unacceptable manner without permission; also a set or series of clinical tests.

Bed. A bed located in a hospital or nursing home used for inpatients. Beds are used as one important measure of an institution's capacity and size.

Bed allocation policy. A hospital's method of assigning inpatient beds. A hospital may establish its own policy. Policies may be established to maximize occupancy or hospital resources, segregate clinical areas (e.g., medicine, surgery, obstetrics, and gynecology), minimize bad debts or maximize revenue, and/or support the hospital's teaching programs (interns and residents) by assigning beds according to teaching needs.

Bed size. The number of hospital beds, vacant or occupied, maintained regularly for use by inpatients during a reporting period (the typical reporting period is 12 months). To determine this amount, first add the total number of beds, which is available every day during the hospital's reporting period. Then divide that amount by the total number of days in the reporting period. (Synonym: statistical beds.)

Bedside telemonitoring equipment. Sophisticated medical equipment used at a patient's bedside for a variety of functions, including recording electrocardiograms, measuring heart and respiratory rates, and recording blood pressure. Although such monitors are equipped with easy-to-use indicators and controls, they should be operated only by medical/nursing personnel who have been trained to use them.

Beeper system. A communications system used by medical and health-care professionals to stay in touch with the hospital or office staff. The system uses radiowave pagers (digital and voice recorders, or a combination of both). Within the hospital, the paging system or beeper system is usually coordinated through the telephone office.

Beneficence. Actions that promote the well-being of others. In the medical context, this means taking actions that serve the best interests of patients.

Best practice. A technique, method, process, activity, incentive, or reward that is considered to be more effective at producing a particular outcome than any other technique, method, process, etc.

Blood bank. A medical laboratory that collects blood from donors and then refrigerates the blood until it is needed for transfusion. The unit also analyzes blood from donors to determine compatibility; this process is referred to as typing and cross-matching.

Blood bank technologist. A trained individual who works under the direction of a laboratory director, physician, or pathologist. Responsibilities include collecting, classifying, storing, and processing of blood; preparing components from whole blood; detecting and identifying antibodies in blood from patients and donors; and selecting and delivering blood suitable for transfusion.

Blue Cross (BC). A private insurance plan that provides coverage for hospital costs. Most Blue Cross members sign up for coverage at their workplace under a group plan.

Board certified. A professional title of considerable merit awarded to a physician who passes an examination administered by the professional organization that regulates his or her specialty. Physicians cannot take the examinations until they meet requirements established by the specialty board, making them board eligible.

Board of trustees. See *Governing body*.

Bond ratings. General measures of a bond's quality, provided to guide investors in making investments. Bonds that are rated Aaa/AAA are judged to be of the best quality because they carry the smallest degree of investment risk. Bonds are generally rated by one of two companies: Standard & Poor's or Moody's.

Brand name drug. A drug that has been assigned a registered trademark, trade name, or patent name by the manufacturer. Note: A drug's brand name differs from its generic name, which is the official scientific name by which the drug is known. Drugs are advertised to physicians chiefly by brand name. (Occasionally, states may have an antisubstitution law that forbids pharmacists from substituting a physician's prescribed brand name drug with either an equivalent brand name drug or a generic drug made by a different manufacturer, even though either one may be less expensive than the prescribed drug.)

Budget. The dollar amounts required to meet a hospital's immediate administrative objectives, as well as its operation and financing plans for a given time period, (usually 1 year). It is the hospital's plan for that period expressed in dollars and cents.

Budget, cash. Details the hospital's anticipated receipts and cash disbursements for the forthcoming budget period. It is usually used to forecast the amount of cash required to meet operating expenses and to determine the amount of cash that will be available for capital purchases, acquisitions, and investing.

Business office manager. The individual who supervises and coordinates the operations of a hospital's business office, including office functions such as bookkeeping, typing, clerical services, word processing, record keeping, files, and reports in accordance with hospital standards.

Bylaws. The rules, regulations, and ordinances enacted by an organization to provide the basis for its own self-government. In a hospital, two major sets of bylaws are the governing body bylaws (or hospital bylaws) and the medical staff bylaws.

Capital budget. A financial plan detailing anticipated capital expenditures principally for equipment (medical and nonmedical) and building renovation and construction. The sources of these funds are identified as part of the capital budget. Potential sources are operating funds, restricted funds, and outside financing such as leases or debt financing and fund-raising.

Cardiac Care Unit (CCU). A specialized cardiac unit reserved for observation and recovery of patients who have undergone an intensive cardiac procedure or who have critical cardiac problems (e.g., heart attack). Units are equipped with electrocardiographic and hemodynamic monitoring equipment.

Certification. The process by which a government or private agency or a health-related association evaluates individual, institutional, or educational programs and verifies that they meet predetermined standards.

Certified laboratory assistant (CLA). Individuals who perform routine clinical laboratory procedures and work under the supervision of a medical technologist or pathologist.

Chart. The medical dossier of a patient, or file of information on transactions in personal health care. See *Medical record.*

Chief executive officer (CEO). The individual responsible for the overall management of the hospital. The CEO is appointed by the governing body to ensure that the mission and goals of the institution are carried out according to the bylaws of the hospital. The job includes planning, organizing, and directing all hospital activities in accordance with objectives and policies established by the board, developing ongoing and future hospital programs, presenting annual budgets, and creating and implementing sound organizational plans. (Synonyms: administrator, president, hospital administrator, hospital director, superintendent.)

Chief financial officer (CFO). The individual responsible for an organization's overall financial plans and policies, and administration of accounting practices. The CFO oversees the hospital's treasury; budgeting; audit, tax, and accounting functions; and real estate purchases. Specific responsibilities include developing and coordinating all necessary and appropriate accounting and statistical data for all departments.

Chief operating officer (COO). The second-highest management position in the hospital. The COO is responsible for managing day-to-day internal hospital operations, and in the absence of the CEO assumes that person's duties. (Synonyms: assistant administrator, executive vice-president, senior vice president.)

Children's hospital. A hospital that specializes in inpatient and outpatient care limited to the treatment of diseases and injuries of children.

Chronic illness. Any illness that has continued for a long period and may recur in the future. Alterations in such illnesses occur slowly.

Civil Rights Act of 1964. A federal act that prohibits discrimination against any person on the basis of color, race, religion, or gender by any public facility or government agency that receives federal funding.

Clinic. An independent organization of physicians and allied health personnel, or a hospital-operated facility designed to provide preventive, diagnostic, therapeutic, rehabilitative, or palliative services on an outpatient basis.

Clinical engineer. A professional with an associate or bachelor of science degree in biomedical engineering. This individual utilizes engineering techniques to repair or develop equipment, instruments, processes, and systems for the medical care of patients and the overall maintenance and improvement of healthcare systems. Some biomedical engineers develop lasers, pacemakers, and artificial organs such as hearts and kidneys; others adapt computer systems to hospital systems to increase operating efficiency. Typically, they work in hospitals, private medically related industries, or medical settings. (Synonym: biomedical engineer.)

Clinical nurse specialist. A registered nurse with both a master's degree and clinical expertise in a clinical area (e.g., surgical, critical care, medicine, or cardiology).

Clinical outcomes. A form of medical and/or nursing evaluation that measures the patient care process against criteria such as the status of the patient at discharge.

Clinical privileges. Permission granted to physicians and selected other practitioners that authorizes them to provide specific diagnostic, therapeutic, medical, dental, podiatric, or surgical services within the hospital.

Community hospital. A hospital that is established to meet the medical and health needs of a specific geographic area. Usually these hospitals are nonprofit, but they may also be proprietary (for profit). Community hospitals are generally nonfederal, short-term, general-care hospitals.

Comprehensive outpatient rehabilitation facility (CORF). A facility that provides comprehensive outpatient rehabilitation services, including physician's services, physical therapy, occupational therapy, speech-language pathology, respiratory therapy, prosthetic supplies, and home environment evaluation. These services are reimbursable under Medicare Part B.

Computerized axial tomography (CAT) scan. A radiographic technique that is more sensitive than conventional x-ray systems for detecting variations among soft tissues with similar densities. It provides highly detailed, cross-sectional, three-dimensional images that can be used to establish the area and depth of an abnormality.

Confidential information. Information whose unauthorized disclosure could be prejudicial to a person or organization, or national interest; usually subject to penalty when there is a breach, depending on the importance and sensitivity of the information.

Consent forms. Documents that patients are asked to sign giving permission to the hospital or its physicians to perform procedures during the patient's hospital stay, whether as an outpatient or inpatient. There are two general types of consent forms: one for general treatment and diagnosis, and one for special medical or surgical procedures. The most important element in the consent process is that the physician must clearly explain the procedures to be performed to the patient and obtain the patient's consent to the procedures. This is known as an informal consent form.

Continuing medical education (CME). Postgraduate education aimed at maintaining, updating, and extending healthcare professionals' knowledge and skills. Many professional organizations and state licensing boards require physicians and nurses to participate in CME activities.

Contract management. A system whereby hospital management contracts with an outside company to perform certain management services, such as dietary, housekeeping, and data processing services. It is also possible to employ contract management for the total management of a hospital. (Synonym: contract service.)

Controller. The person who oversees the traditional financial activities of the hospital, including general accounting, reimbursement, and budgeting. In smaller institutions, this position may be combined with that of the chief financial officer (CFO). In larger institutions, the controller reports to a CFO.

Copayment. An additional payment made by an individual who has health insurance.

Corporate compliance committee. A hospital-wide committee that conducts audits regularly to ensure that the hospital is in compliance with all federal, state, and local laws.

Corporate restructuring. The regrouping of a hospital's corporate hierarchy by creating holding companies or foundations in order to guard assets, provide flexibility for diversification, accomplish a broader mission, increase effectiveness, and permit capital accumulation. (Synonym: corporate reorganization.)

Cost reimbursement. Payment to hospitals and other providers by a third-party carrier for costs incurred by the providers; cost rates are calculated after the service is rendered.

Cost reports. Cost-analysis documents prepared by a healthcare facility to be submitted to third-party payers as part of contract agreements. These reports are used as the basis for cost reimbursement.

Credentials committee. The committee that interviews applicants for medical staff positions, reviews their credentials, and delineates their privileges.

Damages. Loss or harm resulting from injury to a person, property, or other valued item.

Darling case. A landmark legal case, *Darling v. Charleston Community Hospital*, in which the court found that the hospital was responsible for overseeing and monitoring the quality and process of medical care in the institution, and that these functions were not exclusively the responsibility of the medical staff.

Delinquent medical records. Inpatient medical records that have not been completed within a given time period (usually 15 to 30 days) after the patient's discharge.

Department of Medical Records. The hospital department that is responsible for cataloging, maintaining, processing, and controlling patient hospital medical records. This unit may be responsible for the statistical and qualitative preparation and analysis of the information in the medical record to aid in the evaluation of patient care. The department also prepares records subpoenaed by the courts and interprets medical–legal aspects of records to protect the interests of the hospital.

Development office. The office that is responsible for directing, planning, and coordinating direct fund-raising activities and programs for the hospital. This section may also be responsible for the hospital's public relations activities. (Synonym: fund-raising office.)

Diagnostic related group (DRG) rate. A dollar amount used by Medicare to pay hospitals for services rendered. It is based on the average of all patients belonging to a specific DRG adjusted for economic factors, inflation, and bad debts.

Diagnostic related groups (DRGs). Recognized categories of illnesses that are used for classification of clinical procedures and billing purposes.

Dietary department. The hospital department that is equipped, designed, and staffed to prepare food to meet the normal and therapeutic nutritional needs of the patients and hospital staff. (Synonym: food service department.)

Dietician. A professional who is educated and trained to deal with the scientific aspects of human nutrition and diets. The dietician develops specific food and nutritional plans for patients.

Diploma school of nursing. A 2- to 3-year professional nursing program, generally affiliated with a hospital, that leads to a diploma.

Director of nurses. Old term for the person who oversees the nursing service; now known as the vice president of nursing services.

Director of volunteers. An individual (frequently a department head) who organizes and directs the training and utilization of volunteers within a hospital. This includes recruiting, assigning, and coordinating volunteers in their work assignments, and maintaining records of volunteer hours worked and the types of services performed.

Discharge. Release from an inpatient healthcare facility that requires a physician's order and consultation with the patient about follow-up care.

Discharge planning. The planning and organization process undertaken by a committee of a hospital medical staff that addresses a patient's discharge into the community, home, or appropriate healthcare facility. This process begins at the time of admission or, in elective cases, prior to admission.

Elective admission. The admission of a patient to a hospital prior to the actual scheduled date of admission. This admission can be delayed without potential risk to the health of the individual.

Electrocardiography (EKG). A cardiac procedure used at the heart station to diagnose irregularities in heart action. It records changes in electrical current during a heartbeat and provides important diagnostic information.

Electroencephalography (EEG). A procedure used to measure the brain's electrical signals. This is useful for diagnosing epilepsy, brain tumors, strokes, and other metabolic abnormalities.

Electronic health record (EHR). A vital document or file generated and maintained within an institution, such as a hospital, integrated delivery network, clinic, or physician's office, for the purpose of accessing and sharing patient data among authorized healthcare providers.

Emergency admission. The admission of a patient to a hospital immediately or within a very short period of time in order to save the patient's life or to protect the patient's health and well-being. Other general categories of admission are urgent (usually requiring admission within 12–24 hours) or elective (when a patient can wait for admission without any adverse effects).

Emergency center, freestanding (FEC). A facility structured, equipped, and staffed to offer primary, urgent, and emergency services. These facilities often offer laboratory and radiographic services as well, and may have transfer agreements with area hospitals that allow the FEC to send severely ill patients to the hospital once they are stable.

Emergency department (ED). The department or unit of a hospital that provides immediate medical services necessary to sustain life or prevent critical consequences. This area sometimes also provides nonurgent, walk-in care. The department is usually staffed 24 hours a day by physicians and nurses. (Synonym: emergency service.)

Emergency Medical Treatment and Active Labor Act (EMTALA). A federal law mandating that all patients who present to an emergency department must be at least stabilized and/or transferred to the appropriate facility, regardless of their ability to pay.

Emergency patient. An outpatient who presents to a hospital or free-standing emergency department for immediate treatment.

Employment Retirement Income Security Act (ERISA). A 1974 federal act that protects employee benefits.

Epidemiology. Study of the distribution and detection of health-related states or events in specific populations.

Equal Employment Opportunity Commission (EEOC). An independent US federal agency that enforces laws against workplace discrimination. Its mandate was specified under Title VII of the Civil Rights Act of 1984.

Equal Pay Act. Federal act prohibiting pay differences between men and women doing the same work.

Ethics. The branch of philosophy that deals with with distinctions between right and wrong.

Evidence-based medicine (EBM). The process of obtaining relevant information from the medical literature and other reliable sources to determine the "best available" or "gold standard" method to address a specific clinical problem.

Executive committee. The senior committee of a governing body (hospital board or medical staff). It may also be the ruling body.

Expenses. The sum of all incurred costs for services used or consumed in performing some activity during a given time period and from which no benefit will accrue beyond the stated period.

Expert witness. A person who testifies in court about matters related to their special skills or knowledge derived from training and/or experience.

Fair Labor Standards Act. A law that sets nationwide minimum wages and maximum hours for workers.

False-negative. A test result that appears negative but fails to reveal the correct situation.

False-positive. A test result that appears positive but fails to reveal the correct situation.

Family history. In the context of health care, the history of significant diseases that run in a patient's family, such as a hereditary disease or predisposition to certain diseases.

Fiduciary. A person who undertakes a solemn duty to act for the benefit of another under a given set of circumstances (e.g., the members of the governing body of a hospital have a fiduciary responsibility to the community).

Financial statement. A summary of the financial activities of a hospital. The balance sheet includes itemized listings of the hospital's assets and liabilities, and the net worth of the hospital. The income statement, or profit and loss statement, lists the hospital's income or revenue and its expenses or costs.

Fluoroscopy. A technique that uses x-rays to view real-time moving images of the internal structures of a patient's body on a fluorescent screen.

Formulary. A list of drugs (usually indicated by their generic names) that are considered to be medically appropriate treatment for specific purposes. A formulary may also be a list of drugs for which a third party will or will not pay.

Full-time equivalent (FTE). A term that indicates the number of hours a full-time employee would be expected to work in a given year (i.e., 40 hours a week or 2080 annual hours). This term is used in assessments involving hospital budgeting, position control, and productivity.

Gatekeeper. A person or system who regulates or controls access to a healthcare service or healthcare data or information.

General fund/fund accounting. A technique that accounts for separate entities in a hospital fund, used to record transactions arising out of general operations in the day-to-day financial and operational activities of the hospital. (Synonym: hospital accounting.)

Generic drug. The official scientific name for a drug.

Governing body. The body that is responsible for an institution's overall operations. Its essential functions include defining objectives, mandating policies, maintaining the programs and resources necessary to implement policies, monitoring progress to guarantee the policy objectives are met, and hiring the CEO. Note: The board of trustees should not be mistaken for the lay advisory board. (Synonyms: the board, board of directors, board of trustees, board of governors.)

Graduate nurse (GN). A nurse who has graduated from an approved program of professional nursing but has not yet received registered nurse (RN) licensure.

Group practice. A formal association of physicians who provide either specialty or comprehensive medical care on an outpatient basis. (Synonyms: single specialty group, general practice group, multispecialty group.)

Group purchasing. An arrangement whereby a two or more hospitals band together, often through a third party (e.g., the group purchaser) to purchase goods and services at the lowest price, because the arrangement makes it feasible for them to engage in quantity purchasing. (Synonym: shared purchasing.)

Health. "A state of complete physical, mental and social well-being and not merely the absence of disease or infirmity" (1948 preamble of the World Health Organization [WHO]).

Health administration. The management of resources, procedures, and systems to meet the needs and wants of a healthcare system. (Synonyms: healthcare administration, hospital administration.)

Healthcare facility. Any licensed facility that is organized, maintained, and operated for the diagnosis, prevention, treatment, rehabilitation, convalescence, or other care of human illness or injury (physical or mental), including care during and after pregnancy.

Health information technology. The comprehensive management of health information and its secure exchange among consumers, providers, government and quality entities, and insurers; allows information to be interpreted and disseminated effectively. See *Informatics*.

Health Insurance Portability and Accountability Act (HIPAA). This 1996 act contains new federal regulations intended to increase the privacy and security of patient information during electronic transmission or communication of protected health information (PHI) among providers or between providers and payers or other entities.

Health maintenance organization (HMO). Third-party payer plans. There are two fundamental types of HMO plans: (1) the group model, in which HMOs contract with several group practices and share the risk of the venture with the physicians; and (2) independent practice associations (IPAs), which are loose-knit organizations that contract with individual physicians to treat patients in their offices, often on a fee-for-service basis.

Health system. An organization of human resources, facilities, and medical technology. (Synonym: medical system.)

Heart diagnostics (or heart station). The unit or section of a hospital that coordinates cardiac tests and procedures, some of which may be done on an outpatient basis (e.g., EKGs).

Hill-Burton Act. The legislative act that led to federal legislation and programs offering federal support for construction and modernization of hospitals and other health facilities. This program was initiated by Public Law 79-725, the Hospital Survey and Construction Act of 1946, and has been amended often.

Home care nurse. A registered nurse (preferably with a BSN and 2 years of hospital experience) who intermittently visits patients at their homes to carry out a nursing care plan approved by a physician. Typical duties include injections, incision care, rehabilitation activities, patient education, and other skilled care. (Synonym: visiting nurse.)

Home health care. A formal program offering medical and nursing care, therapeutic services, and social services to patients in their homes. (Synonym: home care services.)

Hospice care. A program providing palliative and supportive care for terminally ill patients and their families either directly or on a consulting basis with the patient's physician or another community agency. Emphasis is placed on system control, preparation for death, and support of the survivors. Care may be provided by a freestanding hospice, or the hospice program may be based in a facility such as a hospital.

Hospital. An institution that provides medical and health care every day around the clock. Its primary function is to provide inpatient and outpatient services, including diagnostic and therapeutic services, for a variety of medical and surgical conditions. Some also provide emergency care. Hospitals can be teaching or nonteaching, specialty (e.g., psychiatric) or nonspecialty (e.g., general), proprietary (for-profit), or not-for-profit (government, local, or private) entities. The majority of hospitals in the United States are short-term, acute-care, general, and nonprofit hospitals.

Hospital bylaws. The written guidelines, rules, and regulations that govern the activities and policies of the hospital.

Hospital chaplains. Members of the clergy who provide religious services to patients and their families, and members of the hospital staff.

Hospitalist. A physician who practices medicine within the hospital setting.

Hospital ledger. A record that details the various accounts of a hospital, categorized as assets, liabilities, revenues, and expenses. Entries are made periodically (generally monthly) from various journals. The general ledger allows for financial analysis over a long period.

Human resources. The hospital department that is responsible, in conjunction with other hospital departments, for recruitment, selection, orientation, and employee training programs. The department is also responsible for maintaining personnel records and statistics, initiating and maintaining salary and wage administration, and recommending personnel policies and procedures to the hospital administrator. (Synonym: personnel department.)

Implied consent. Consent given by implication or inference rather than in a direct statement; behavior that gives rise, by silence or inaction, to a presumption that consent has been given. Unconscious patients in the emergency room are considered to have given implied consent to be treated.

Incident report. A written report detailing an accident or error that occurs during the care of a patient. To ensure accuracy, the nurse and/or physician in charge must complete the form as soon as possible after the accident. (Synonym: accident report.)

Income statement of revenue and expenses. A summary of the operations of a hospital in terms of revenue generated from patient services and other sources and the expenses incurred to render those services. (Synonyms: profit and loss statement, income statement.)

Independent laboratory. A freestanding laboratory that is not affiliated with any physician's office or hospital.

Infection control. The process of identifying, controlling, and preventing hospital-acquired (nosocomial) infections. This is usually the responsibility of a hospital medical staff committee, with the support of an infection control practitioner.

Infection control committee. The hospital or medical staff committee that is responsible for overseeing infection control activities in the institution. The committee usually consists of representatives from the medical staff, clinical laboratory, administration, nursing staff, and, at times, the housekeeping department.

Informatics. The study of the use and processing of data, information, and knowledge.

Informed consent. Consent given by a patient to receive treatment after his or her physician has fully explained the nature of the patient's condition and the proposed procedure, the purpose of the procedure, the probability of risks and benefits, alternatives to the treatment, and the associated risks and benefits of not receiving the treatment.

Inpatient. A patient who has been admitted for at least one night to a hospital or other health facility for the purpose of receiving diagnostic treatment or other medical service.

Inpatient component. An element of the hospital–medical care system (e.g., a hospital bed). (Synonym: hospital component.)

Intensive care unit (ICU). A special medical and nursing section of a hospital with extensive monitoring and treatment equipment that enables minute-to-minute observation and treatment of critically ill or injured patients.

Intermediate care facility (ICF). An institution or section of an institution that provides nursing care or rehabilitative services to patients who do not require inpatient hospital care.

Intern. A graduate of a medical or dental school enrolled in the first year of postgraduate education in an accredited training program, usually in a hospital. (Synonym: postgraduate year, first-year resident.)

International Classification of Diseases (ICD). The standard classification system established by the World Health Organization to provide universal clinical or case definitions for diseases, illnesses, and injuries. Medical diagnoses are based on this system. ICD-10 will go into effect in October 2010.

Internship (medical). A period of on-the-job training for physicians and other health professionals. The internship is usually begun soon after the individual graduates from medical school and lasts 1 year.

Investor-owned hospital. A privately owned medical facility that operates for profit. (Synonyms: for-profit hospital, proprietary hospital.)

Job description. A summary of the key features, elements, or requirements of a specific job category. This summary is generally written after a review of the job (or job analysis) is completed.

Joint Commission, The. The preferred title of The Joint Commission on the Accreditation of Hospital Organizations. See *Joint Commission on the Accreditation of Health Care Organizations (JCAHO)*.

Joint Commission International (JCI), The. The body of The Joint Commission that extends accreditation services and products to other countries.

Joint Commission on the Accreditation of Health Care Organizations (JCAHO), The. Now known as The Joint Commission, this is an independent, not-for-profit organization that has accredited and certified more than 17,000 healthcare organizations and programs in the United States.

Joint venture. A business enterprise conducted by an organization or association of two or more parties. Such an organization may make its membership liable for the organization's debts.

Laboratory department. The unit or department in a hospital or healthcare facility that is staffed, equipped, and designed to perform clinical tests and procedures through detailed analysis and examination of specimens. The laboratory is usually divided into sections such as anatomical pathology, clinical chemistry, cytopathology, hematology, and microbiology. (Synonyms: clinical laboratory, laboratory service, medical laboratory, laboratory, lab.)

Laboratory report. A document identifying the results of diagnostic tests performed in a clinical laboratory. Such reports, requested by a physician, are generally used to determine baseline clinical data on a patient or to determine a patient's diagnosis.

Length of stay (LOS). The time an inpatient remains in a hospital or other health facility from the date of admission to the date of discharge.

Licensure. Permission granted to an individual or organization by a competent authority (usually public) to engage in a practice, occupation, or activity that would otherwise be unlawful.

Limited liability. A statutory damage limit for acts of negligence.

Long-range plan. A corporate or managerial plan for the operation of a hospital or institution for the long term (usually 3 to 10 years), including any planned changes in services to be provided, service areas, and proposed buildings or remodeling plans. (Synonym: corporate strategy.)

Long-term acute care. Hospitalization for an extended period of time (usually 25 days).

Long-term care. Health care that is provided to qualified patients who require extended medical assistance and services, as in the case of a significant chronic or debilitating disease or injury.

Long-term care facility. A site that provides housing for individuals who require rehabilitation or continual care; includes nursing homes, rehabilitation centers, inpatient behavioral health facilities, and long-term chronic care hospitals.

Magnetic resonance imaging (MRI). A diagnostic procedure in which large magnets and radio signals are used to produce tomography [NC1] images of a patient's anatomical structures. This diagnostic tool also allows a patient's chemical disturbances to be evaluated at the cellular level. The original term for this procedure was nuclear magnetic resonance (NMR).

Maintenance department. The unit, division, or department of a hospital that is responsible for repair and servicing of a hospital's physical plant, including the hospital grounds, buildings, and equipment. It may also include the provision, distribution, and monitoring of water, light, heat, power, and other building service systems throughout the physical plant.

Malfeasance. The commission of a wrongful act.

Malpractice. Medical care provided by a healthcare professional that deviates from accepted norms or national standards.

Malpractice suit. Legal proceeding by a plaintiff alleging malpractice.

Management information system (MIS). System in which data are collected from many areas of the hospital to provide all levels of hospital management with timely, meaningful information on hospital operations.

Market research. The gathering and analysis of data related to the marketing of a product/service to fulfill a company's mission and objectives.

Marketing. A system of planning, promoting, and distributing needed and wanted services to both present and potential customers, including physicians, patients, insurance companies, and employers.

Marketing audit. A marketing tool that provides an extensive view of a hospital's services, image, and market segments.

Marketing plan/program. The process of presenting products/services to the marketplace, including product definition, location, price, and promotion, including public relations and advertising.

Material safety data sheets (MSDS). Documents detailing all hazardous and potentially dangerous chemicals that are kept on site, as required by the Occupational Safety and Health Administration.

Medicaid (MA). Title XIX of the Social Security Act, which contains the principle legislative authority for the Medicaid program to provide health care for the indigent.

Medical College Admission Test (MCAT). A standardized test required or strongly recommended by nearly all U.S. medical schools as part of the admissions process. The results of this test are evaluated by admission committees to determine a student's ability to handle medical school course work.

Medical director. The physician on the hospital medical staff who is either appointed by the board, elected by the medical staff, or employed by the institution to serve as the medical administrative head of medical staff affairs. If the physician is elected by the medical staff, he or she may be called the president of the medical staff. (Synonym: chief of staff.)

Medical error. A failure of the healthcare system or practitioner to complete a planned action as intended, thus causing harm or potential harm; acting outside a recognized standard of care.

Medical necessity. Procedures, treatments, or practices deemed to be necessary to meet a reasonable standard of care.

Medical office building (MOB). A building that is either freestanding or attached to a hospital where a physician or other health practitioner can establish an office. An MOB is sometimes used as a marketing tool for hospitals to attract and retain physicians.

Medical record. A complete medical record usually contains patient information such as (1) clinical (diagnosis, treatment, progress, etc.); (2) demographics (age, sex, birthplace, residence, etc.); (3) sociocultural (language, ethnic origin, religion, etc.); (4) sociological (family, occupation, etc.); (5) economic (method of payments, fee-for-service, etc.); (6) administrative (site of care, provider, etc.); and (7) behavioral (satisfaction with services provided, being on time, etc.).

Medical school. An institution of higher learning accredited by the Association of American Medical Colleges. Medical colleges are accredited to provide courses in the arts and science of medicine and related subjects, and are empowered to grant an academic degree in medicine.

Medical staff appointment. The appointment by the hospital board of trustees of a physician or dentist to a hospital's medical staff based on the approval of the credentials committee of the medical staff. Appointment includes delineation of clinical privileges. There are different categories of medical staff membership: active, courtesy, consulting, and honorary.

Medical staff, attending. A category of a hospital's medical staff that includes physicians and dentists who contribute actively to the hospital by admitting and caring for patients on a regular basis. The medical staff may also include other practitioners, such as podiatrists. These individuals are eligible to vote and hold office in the medical staff organization.

Medical staff bylaws. A document required by The Joint Commission outlining the activities, functions, roles, purpose, rules, and regulations of a hospital's medical staff. The bylaws identify and define the key operating committees of the medical staff and their functions.

Medical students. Individuals who are enrolled in an accredited medical school and studying to become physicians.

Medical technologist. An individual who is trained in the use of clinical laboratory equipment to test human body tissues and fluids, culture bacteria to identify disease-causing organisms, analyze blood factors, and trace cancer with radionuclides. Medical technologists specialize in blood banking microbiology, chemistry, and nuclear medical technology.

Medicare. Title XVIII of the Social Security Act, Public Law 89-97. A federal program that pays providers for medical care and other health services for individuals who are 65 years of age or older, or disabled, regardless of income. The program has two parts: hospital insurance (Part A) and medical insurance (Part B). Part B is also known as supplementary medical insurance (SMI).

Medicare Part A. Refers to the Title XVIII of Health Insurance for the Aged of the Society Security Act, Public Law 89-97, which became effective July 1, 1966, and applies to services rendered by a provider (e.g., hospital) to an eligible beneficiary. This part is commonly referred to as hospital insurance.

Medicare Part B. Refers to Title XVIII of Health Insurance for the Aged of the Social Security Act, Public Law 89-97, which became effective July 1, 1966, and applies to services rendered by a physician to an eligible beneficiary. This part is commonly referred to as supplementary medical insurance.

Merger. A business, corporation, or hospital secures the capital stock of another business; the merged corporation's stock is usually then dissolved.

Misdiagnosis. An error on the part of the doctor or any health professional authorized to make a diagnosis in determining the cause of a disease, illness, or injury.

Mission. The stated purpose for which an organization exists.

Morbidity. Objective or subjective departure from a physiological or psychological state of well-being, usually associated with the occurrence of a disease or illness.

Morbidity and mortality committee. Hospital committee that reviews unusual deaths and patterns in deaths.

Morgue. The area of a hospital that houses patients who have died. It is usually connected to an autopsy room.

Mortality. Death as a result of a disease of injury.

Multihospital system. A central association that owns and/or leases or controls, by contract, two or more hospitals. Such systems allow for easier access to capital markets, mutual purchasing for greater economies of scale, and mutual use of technical and management personnel. There are two types of multihospital systems: not-for-profit (which includes church-affiliated) or investor-owned, for profit.

Narcotics and barbiturates. Medications that are under the control of the Drug Enforcement Administration (DEA). (Synonym: controlled substances.)

National Institutes of Health (NIH). An agency of the United States Department of Health and Human Services that focuses on medical research to improve health and save lives.

National Resident Matching Program. Official process for placing medical school graduates in their first year of graduate medical education. The program matches the preferences of medical students for certain internships and residencies with available hospital positions. The matching process is carried out under complete confidentiality. It is frequently called "the match."

Negligence. Failure to take care according to certain standards.

Next of kin. One or more persons in the nearest degree of relationship to another person.

Noncompliance. Failure to comply with procedures recommended by healthcare professionals; such lack of compliance may result in harm to the patient or impair or prolong the recovery period.

Noninvasive procedure. A medical treatment or practice that does not break the skin or enter an internal body cavity.

Nonmalfeasance. The duty to do no harm.

Nosocomial infection. An infection that a person develops as a result of being in the hospital. It is unrelated to the patient's admitting condition.

Not-for-profit hospital. A hospital that is organized as a nonprofit corporation. Not-for-profit hospitals include state and local government-owned facilities, as well as religious institutions. (Synonyms: nonproprietary hospital, voluntary hospital.)

Nuclear medicine. The field of medicine concerned with the diagnostic, therapeutic, and investigative use of radioactive compounds. It is sometimes considered a subspecialty of radiology.

Nurse. A registered nurse (RN) or licensed practical nurse (LPN). The term usually refers to an RN, who has more education and responsibility than an LPN.

Nurse manager. A registered nurse who is responsible for overseeing the operations of a single nursing unit 24 hours a day, 7 days a week. The nurse manager supervises the personnel in this patient care unit, is accountable for the quality of the nursing care on the unit, controls the supplies for the unit, and usually schedules the nursing staff in the unit. Generally, nurse managers have a staff of nurses working for them. (Synonym: nurse manager, patient care manager.)

Nurse scheduling. The process in nursing management of determining which nursing personnel will be on duty each shift, and the time period they will work. The schedule usually applies for a specified period (4 to 6 weeks) and is tailored to each nursing unit's needs. The needs are often determined by a patient classification or acuity system.

Nurse staffing. The process in nursing management that is primarily concerned with scheduling the correct amount of nursing hours needed to adequately staff a particular nursing unit.

Nurses' station. The part of the nursing unit that serves as the center for administration, record keeping, and communication. Often this is where patient records for the entire nursing unit are kept.

Nursing. The act of providing nursing care to patients, their families, and, in the broader sense, communities. Some nursing care activities may be performed by licensed practical nurses and nurses' aides. The hospital nursing function is organized under a nursing service department, headed by a director of nursing or vice president of nursing.

Nursing, primary care. A system in which a professional nurse, in collaboration with other members of a nursing team, assumes responsibility for overseeing the total care of a group of patients.

Nursing service department. The department that is responsible for providing nursing care to meet patients' physical and psychological needs and to collaborate with patients' physicians in developing and implementing patient treatment plans.

Nursing staffing standard. A frame of reference for ensuring proper nurse staffing on a patient unit. These staffing standards are usually expressed in terms of nursing hours per patient day. (Synonym: nursing norm.)

Nursing supervisor. A registered nurse who supervises or directs the activities of two or more nursing units. A nursing supervisor usually manages and directs the nursing services' activities during the evenings, nights, and weekends. (Synonym: patient care coordinator.)

Nursing team. A team composed of registered or graduate nurses, practical nurses, aides, and orderlies who provide bedside care to a group of patients under the supervision of a team leader who is a registered nurse.

Nursing unit. The area of the hospital in which the nursing service functions. In hospitals, these divisions are often located on nursing or patient floors and may be arranged along medical/surgical specialty lines. The nursing personnel in charge of these units are called nurse managers. They report to a nursing supervisor, assistant director of nursing, or, in some cases, directly to the director of nursing. Nursing units come in a variety of sizes and shapes, but most have somewhere between 20 and 40 inpatient beds.

Occupancy rate. A measure of inpatient hospital use; the ratio of inpatient beds occupied to inpatient beds available for occupancy.

Occupational Safety and Health Administration (OSHA). Federal agency established by a 1970 act to ensure that all employees in the United States have a safe and healthful workplace.

Occupational therapist (OT). A registered professional who is trained to work with individuals with physical injuries or illnesses, psychological or developmental problems, or problems associated with the aging process. An OT requires a bachelor's degree in occupational therapy.

Occurrence. General term describing how often a disease, event, or situation occurs.

Operating budget. A financial plan detailing estimated income and expenses for a given time period (usually one fiscal year). Proposed income is classified by revenue sources; proposed expenses are accounted for by natural classification, such as salaries, benefits, and supplies.

Osteopath (DO). A physician has received education similar to that of an MD but has graduated from a school of osteopathic medicine.

Outpatient. A patient who receives ambulatory care at a hospital or other health facility without being admitted as an inpatient.

Outpatient department. An organized unit of a hospital, or a general or specialty hospital clinic, that delivers outpatient services.

Outreach. The process by which a hospital interacts with its surrounding communities. This may involve meeting community or patient needs, locating new services within the community, or offering educational health and wellness programs in addition to medical care programs. Hospitals may assign personnel to work in outreach activities.

Pandemic. An epidemic that occurs over a wide area, crossing international boundaries, and often affects a large number of people.

Parent company. A separate corporate and legal entity/organization used by healthcare organizations for a variety of reasons, such as to be able to react to opportunities in the marketplace. Hospitals form holding companies by a process of corporate reorganization. (Synonyms: holding company, foundation.)

Participatory medicine. A cooperative model of health care that encourages and expects the active participation of all parties (patients, caregivers, healthcare professionals, etc.) to ensure a full continuum of care.

Pathogen. Usually refers to a germ or microbe that can cause illness.

Pathology services. Microbiological, serological, chemical, hematological, biophysical, cytological, immunohematological, and pathological examinations performed on materials from human bodies. These clinical and anatomical examinations provide information for the diagnosis, prevention, or treatment of a disease or assessment of a medical condition. (Synonyms: pathology department, clinical laboratories.)

Patient. Any individual who has been determined by a physician or an authority with similar medical credentials to be ill or injured.

Patient accounts and billing department. The department that is responsible for managing patient accounts, hospital receivables, and patient bills. (Synonym: business office.)

Patient day. A unit of measure that denotes the room and board and services provided to an inpatient during one 24-hour period. The numbers of such days in a month are called patient days per month.

Patient representative. An individual who works with patients, their families, hospital departments and staff, medical staff, and administration in investigating patient complaints and problems with a patient's hospital care. (Synonym: ombudsman.)

Patient safety. A healthcare discipline that focuses on the reporting, analysis, and prevention of medical errors that can lead to adverse healthcare events; prevention of harm caused by errors of commission and omission.

Patient Safety and Quality Improvement Act (PSQIA) of 2005. This act was enacted to address growing concerns about patient safety by encouraging voluntary and confidential reporting of adverse medical events and unsafe conditions.

Patient's Bill of Rights. An outline of the treatment and care a patient has the right to expect during hospitalization. The American Hospital Association provides hospitals with a 12-point bill of rights, which they can modify to accommodate local laws or customs.

Pediatric unit. A hospital clinical care unit with facilities, equipment, and personnel for the care of infants, children, and adolescents, excluding obstetrical and newborn care.

Peer review organization (PRO). A federally funded organization established by the Social Security Act of 1983 that performs utilization and quality reviews to monitor hospitals and physicians. The organization also monitors all healthcare services provided to Medicare beneficiaries. Peer review organizations replaced the professional standards review organizations (PSROs) established in 1972. Now known as quality improvement organizations (QIOs).

Pharmacy. The art, science, and practice of preparing, preserving, compounding, and dispensing drugs, as well as giving appropriate instructions for and monitoring their use. Also a location (place) where pharmaceuticals are prepared and dispensed. (Synonym: apothecary.)

Pharmacy and therapeutic committee. A committee of hospital medical staff personnel concerned with the development and monitoring of pharmaceutical and therapeutic policies and practices, particularly as regards drug utilization within a hospital. The committee generally includes the hospital pharmacists.

Physiatrist. A specialty physician who is trained in physical medicine and rehabilitation and is responsible for the physical medicine and/or physical therapy departments.

Physical therapist (PT). A registered professional who plans and administers physical therapy treatment programs for medically referred patients to restore function, release pain, and prevent disability following disease, injury, or loss of body parts. PTs use the treatment modalities of electricity, heat, cold, ultrasound, massage, and exercise. The educational preparation is a bachelor's or master's degree.

Physician. Any individual with a medical doctorate degree (MD or DO).

Physician's assistant (PA). An individual who extends the services of a supervising physician by taking medical histories, performing physical examinations, and, in circumscribed areas, diagnosing and treating patients.

Placebo. Inert medication or procedure designed to resemble, as much as possible, its active counterpart in clinical research.

Placebo effect. The effects of using a placebo may be partly attributed to the power of suggestion and the expectations of the research participants that health benefits will occur.

Polygraph Protection Act. Federal law prohibiting most employers from subjecting employees to lie detector examinations.

Potency. Strength of a specific drug, toxin, or hazard.

Power of attorney. A legal instrument authorizing a person to act as the attorney or agent of the grantor.

Preadmission certification. Review and approval of the necessity and appropriateness for proposed inpatient service. The term also refers to actual admission to an institution prior to the proposed admission time.

Preadmission testing (PAT). Diagnostic tests performed in hospital outpatient areas prior to a patient's admission to the hospital. This system is used to verify the need for a hospital admission and/or reduce the inpatient's length of stay.

Preferred provider arrangement (PPA). A direct contractual arrangement among hospitals, physicians, insurers, employers, or third-party administrators in which providers join together to offer health care for a certain group of people. These contracts normally have three distinguishing features in common: discounts from standard charges, monetary goals for single subscribers (insurers) to utilize contracting providers, and broad utilization review programs. (Synonym: preferred provider organization.)

Pregnancy Discrimination Act. A federal act that protects pregnant women from discrimination based on their pregnancy.

Prescription medicine. Medicine that is prescribed by a physician and is dispensed by a pharmacist.

Private practice. A medical practice wherein both the practitioner and the practice are independent of any external policy control.

Privileged communication. Statements made to a physician, attorney, spouse, or anyone else in a position of trust. Such communication is protected by law and cannot be revealed without the permission of the parties involved.

Professional standards review organization (PSRO). An organization that was created by the Social Security Amendments of 1972 and charged with the responsibility of operating professional review systems to determine whether hospital services were medically necessary, provided properly, carried out on a timely basis, and met with professional standards. It was conceived as a nationwide network of locally based physicians' groups. It was disbanded in 1983 due to excessive operating costs and little documented impact on patient care.

Prophylactic. Measures or products designed to preserve health and prevent the spread of disease.

Prospective payment system (PPS). A method of payment to hospitals in which rates for services are established in advance based on a DRG system or some other methodology.

Protected health information (PHI). According to the Health Insurance Portability and Accountability Act (HIPAA), any information about the health status, provision of health care, or payment for health care that can be linked to a specific individual.

Protocol. Plan or set of steps to be adhered to in investigations or in an intervention program.

Provider. A qualified person who delivers proper health care in a systematic way professionally to any individual in need of healthcare services.

Psychiatric hospital. A specialty institution primarily concerned with providing inpatient and outpatient care and treatment for the mentally ill.

Public health. A social institution, a discipline, and a practice designed to protect, promote, and restore the people's health.

Public relations (PR). The process of developing goodwill with members of the public; in the hospital, the public can include patients, physicians, employees, business and industry, and the community.

Purchasing department. The department of a hospital that is responsible for evaluating and procuring supplies and equipment. (Synonym: procurement department.)

Quality assurance. Procedures, audits, checks, and corrective actions undertaken to ensure that methods used for testing, measuring, recording, sampling, and analyzing meet established standards of performance for work processes and outcomes.

Quality care. The degree to which patient care services increase the probability of desired patient outcomes.

Quality improvement. A general term used to describe, measure, document, and continuously improve works processes, products, or any services used by customers and stakeholders.

Quality improvement program (QIP). An institutional program that generally involves a continuous process and regular review of the quality of patient care provided by the institution.

Quarantine. Limitation or restriction of the activities of persons or animals that have been exposed to any communicable disease within the period of communicability.

Radiation therapy. A medical treatment that uses ionizing radiation to destroy cancer and other tumors or neoplasm with minimal damage to surrounding healthy tissue. (Synonym: radiotherapy.)

Radiology. The branch of medicine that deals with the use of x-rays and other forms of radiant energy for the diagnosis and treatment of disease. (Synonyms: x-ray, medical imaging.)

Radiology department. The unit in a hospital that is specifically designed, equipped, and staffed to use x-rays and other radioactive elements for the diagnosis and treatment of patients. This department is under the direct supervision of a radiologist (physician). This department could also include radiation therapy and/or nuclear medicine sections. (Synonyms: x-ray department, medical imaging department.)

Reasonable costs. Costs approved by third-party payers for reimbursement to a hospital, which are then included as a hospital's allowable costs determined by the cost report. (Synonyms: cost reimbursement, total cost.)

Reckless endangerment. Engaging in conduct that creates a substantial risk of serious physical injury to another person, such as firing a gun into a crowd or driving an automobile on a sidewalk.

Rehabilitative medicine. Medical specialty concerned with the diagnosis and treatment of certain musculoskeletal defects and neuromuscular diseases; includes physical therapy, occupational therapy, speech therapy, and closely related specialties.

Reliability. Consistency or the extent to which results obtained from measurement can be replicated or repeated using exactly the same protocol or methods.

Reportable diseases. A group of illnesses that are required by statute to be reported to federal, state, and local public health agencies.

Residency. Training after graduation from an approved medical college that leads to certification in a specialty field of medicine. This training must be approved by the American Medical Association or the American Osteopathic Association.

Resident. A physician who has completed an internship or last year of medical school and is receiving further supervised full-time hospital training in a specialty area of medicine. (Synonyms: house staff, postgraduate year [PGY].)

Respiratory care department. An organizational unit of a hospital designed to provide ventilator support and associated services to patients. (Synonyms: respiratory therapy department, inhalation therapy department.)

Risk-benefit analysis. Using a single scale to analyze and compare the expected positive benefits and negative risks of an action or lack of an action.

Risk management. Identifying, studying, and controlling risks to patients, employees, and the hospital; serves as an early warning system for identifying potential causes of liability.

Risk management committee. One of a hospital's quality improvement committees. The committee develops policies and procedures to ensure a safe environment, conducts surveillance programs to monitor all adverse occurrences, and reviews incidence reports.

Room and board. A hospital revenue category that includes revenue from room, board, and general nursing services. (Synonym: routine services or daily patient services; daily room and board.)

Root cause analysis (RCA). A structured process to identify the causal or contributing factors underlying adverse events or other critical incidents.

Safe. A state of existence free from harm.

Safety. A condition or goal by which intended and unintended errors are minimized and mitigated or prevented so that risk of harm to patients and healthcare workers is absent or is calculated to be low.

School of nursing. A broad term used today as a catchall phrase for various forms of education offered to individuals pursuing a nursing career.

Security department. The unit or department of a hospital that is responsible for protecting patients, their families, and hospital staff, as well as safeguarding the facility, equipment, and supplies.

Self-pay. Individuals, institutions, or corporations assume the entire responsibility for payment of hospital and medical bills that otherwise might be covered by an insurance policy. (Synonym: self-insured.)

Semiprivate accommodations. A hospital room with two or more beds (usually three or four); these rooms generally cost less than private or single-bed accommodations.

Sentinel events. Unexpected hospital mishaps resulting in death or serious physical injury that must be reported to the JCAHO and investigated, seeking the root cause and instituting preventive changes.

Sexual harassment. Intimidation or coercion of a sexual nature, or creating a quid pro quo ("something for something") situation, resulting in a hostile work environment. The EEOC is charged with investigating allegations and, if necessary, enforcing penalties.

Shared purchasing. A co-op arrangement between hospitals to reduce the cost of purchases. (Synonym: group purchasing.)

Skilled nursing facilities (SNF). Facilities that provide long-term care to individuals who require nursing care but not hospitalization. They include extended care facilities reimbursable by Medicare, as well as nursing homes reimbursable by Medicaid.

Social Security Administration (SSA). Established in 1946. The bureau of the federal government that is responsible for overseeing Medicare, the financing of which is under the direction of the Health Care Financing Administration (HCFA). The SSA is also responsible for administering a number of other programs, including the Old Age Survivors and Disability Insurance Program.

Social services department. The hospital unit that works with patients, their families, and the institution's professional staff to assist patients with personal, socioeconomic, and environmental problems related to their medical conditions.

Special diets. Foods or menus specially planned and prepared for individuals who need nutritional therapy to improve their overall health or to control disease. Such diets are usually prescribed for a patient by a physician. Special diets can include modifications in consistency (liquid, soft), or content (sodium- or fat-restricted, high/low calorie/protein, and diabetic).

Speech therapist. A professional, registered therapist who evaluates, diagnoses, and counsels individuals with communication disorders.

Stakeholders. Patients and their families, healthcare professionals, and support personnel, including attorneys, insurers, suppliers, vendors, financial institutions, etc.

Stark 1. Statute prohibiting referral of patients to an entity in which the physician or physician's family member has a monetary interest.

Stark 2. Technical amendment modifying Stark 1 and creating certain safe harbors.

Statute of limitations. The maximum time after an event that legal proceedings based on that event can be initiated.

Student nurses. Individuals who are preparing for careers as licensed practical nurses (LPNs) or registered nurses (RNs). In addition to classroom studies, nursing students must complete many hours of hands-on clinical training in a variety of settings. They are closely supervised by both experienced nurses and instructors as they perform routine patient care activities. Nursing schools usually contract with hospitals, nursing homes, and other healthcare institutions to provide clinical training sites for their students.

Survey. A process of examining information in a systematic way, but not under experimental control.

Symptom. Subjective evidence of a disease that a person experiences, such as anxiety, fatigue, or pain.

Syndrome. A group of signs and symptoms that occur together and characterize a condition or disease.

Synergy. A situation in which the combined effect of two or more factors is greater than the sum of their solitary effects.

Target. An explicitly stated or aspired outcome that will be achieved by a specific date.

Tax Equity and Fiscal Responsibility Act (TEFRA) of 1982. Public law 97-248, which covers many far-reaching Medicare amendments as applied to hospital reimbursement policies. This law was a first step in placing hospitals on a prospective pricing system (PPS) rather than the previous cost reimbursed, retrospective cost system.

Tax exempt revenue bonds. A source of debt financing for hospitals with two major features: the interest received by bondholders is not subject to federal income tax, and the organization receiving the financing secures the bonds with its gross revenues.

Teaching hospital. A hospital that provides undergraduate or graduate medical education, usually with one or more medical or dental internships and/or residency programs in affiliation with a medical school.

Telemedicine. The use of telecommunications such as wire, radio, optical, or electromagnetic channels to transmit voice, data, and video to facilitate medical diagnoses, patient care, and/or medical learning.

Tertiary care. Services provided by highly specialized providers such as neurosurgeons, thoracic surgeons, and intensive care units. These services frequently require highly sophisticated technology and facilities.

Third-party administrator. An independent organization that provides administrative services, including claims processing and underwriting, for other entities, such as insurance companies or employers.

Third-party payer. Public or private organization that pays or insures health or medical expenses on behalf of beneficiaries or recipients.

Tort. Legal term for the harmful consequences of a noncriminal act.

Unambiguous event. Event that is clearly defined and easily identified.

Unit clerk. The individual who performs routine clerical or reception work on a nursing unit, including receiving patients and visitors, scheduling appointments, working with records, and assisting in communications.

Universal precautions. The clinical practice and care level that assumes all patients are highly infectious, for the purpose of preventing spread of an infection, promoting workplace safety for healthcare workers, and improving general patient safety.

Urgent admission. Admission of a patient to the hospital for a clinical condition that requires admission for diagnosis and treatment within 48 hours, because otherwise the patient's life or well-being could be threatened. The other two categories for admission are emergency and elective.

Urgent care center. A freestanding facility that provides care for minor emergency (not life-threatening) situations or basic health services on a nonscheduled basis. (Synonyms: urgicenter; "doc in the box," freestanding emergency department, walk-in clinic.)

Utilization. A quantitative measure of the actual use of equipment, facilities, programs, services, and personnel. This measure can be a simple rate, such as the number of admissions per day for a particular unit, or a complex evaluation of an institution's efficiency in allocating its resources, known as a utilization review (UR).

Utilization review (UR). The process of examining the appropriateness of a patient's hospital admission, services provided during the patient's length of stay (LOS), and the hospital's discharge practices. This type of review is required by The Joint Commission, Medicare, Medicaid, and many other third-party payers and regulatory agencies.

Utilization review committee. A committee of the medical staff or the hospital composed of physicians, nurses, administrative representatives, and allied health personnel. The committee's function is to review the medical records of inpatients and discharged patients to determine the medical necessity for their treatment and hospital stay. This committee may also be involved in reviewing the discharge plans for hospitalized patients. This committee is one element in a hospital's quality improvement program.

Vaccination. Immunization against an infectious disease.

Vice president/assistant administrator. An individual who holds an upper-level management position in a hospital and is responsible for certain units or functions within the hospital. This person reports directly to the hospital administrator, president/CEO, or the associate administrator.

Volunteer. An individual who works without financial compensation and performs a variety of tasks within various hospital departments. Members of the hospital auxiliary are volunteers.

Whistle-blowing. The disclosure by employees of illegal, immoral, or illegitimate practices by employers to people or organizations able to take action.

Workers' Compensation. A form of insurance that provides compensation medical care for employees who are injured in the course of employment, in exchange for mandatory relinquishment of the employee's right to sue his or her employer for the tort of negligence.

World Health Organization (WHO). Created in 1946 and headquartered in Geneva, Switzerland, this specialized agency of the United Nations acts as a coordinating authority on matters of public health.

Useful Websites

ETHICS-RELATED WEBSITES

Bioethics	http://www.bioethics.net

LEGAL-RELATED WEBSITES

American Society of Law, Medicine & Ethics	http://www.aslme.org
Health Law Resource	http://www.netreach.net/~wmanning/
NoLo	http://www.nolo.com

GOVERNMENT-RELATED WEBSITES

Agency for Healthcare Research and Quality	http://www.ahrq.gov/news/
Centers for Disease Control and Prevention	http://www.cdc.gov
Centers for Medicare & Medicaid Services	http://www.cms.hhs.gov/default.asp
U.S. Department of Health and Human Services	http://www.hhs.gov/

MEDICAL-RELATED WEBSITES

Health Insurance Portability and Accountability Act   http://www.cms.gov/hipaaGenInfo/

The Joint Commission   http://www.jointcommission.org/

Associations

American Hospital Association   http://www.aha.org
American Medical Association   http://www.ama-assn.org
American Nurses Association   http://www.ana.org
World Health Organization   http://www.who.int

Journals

Journal of the American Medical Association   http://www.jama.com

New England Journal of Medicine   http://content.nejm.org/

News

BBC   http://www.bbc.co.uk
USA Today Health   http://www.usatoday.com/news/health/healthdigest.htm

Index

Note: Page numbers followed by *f* indicate figures and those followed by *t* indicate tables.

A

accounting ratios, 305–307
accounts receivable (A/R), 295–298
accreditation of hospitals. *See* hospital accreditation, licensing
Accreditation Manual for Hospitals (AMH), 227, 266
accrual concept, 301
acute care, defined, 142–143
acute-care community hospitals
    building of specialty hospitals, 17–22
    downsizing, mergers, closures, 14–17
    nursing personnel shortage, 22, 32*f*
    profit margins, 17
acute-care statistics, 207
administrative services. *See also* facilities support; hospitals, essential services
    accreditation, licensing, 263–270
    corporate compliance, 254
    diversity, cultural competence, 255–262
    hospital attorney, 253
    hospital liability, 250–251
    hospital marketing, 273–281
    human resources department, 242–248
    legal services, 249–251
    risk management, 249–250
    strategic planning, 283–288
admitting privilege, 54, 56
advance beneficiary notice (ABN), 297
advance directives, 55
advanced cardiac life support (ACLS), 107, 147, 156
advanced practice nurse (APN), 87

advanced practice registered nurse (APRN), 87–88
adverse outcomes, 328–329
advocacy, advocate, 193
African Americans, 256
aging, geriatric care, 113–116
Aiken, L., 87
ALARA (as low as reasonably achievable), 128
alliances, 35
allied health staff, 67, 75–76
almshouses, 6–7
ambulation, 136, 136*t*, 142
American Academy of Nursing, 97
American Academy of Professional Coders, 209
American Academy of Wound Management, 142
American Association of Blood Banks (AABB), 122
American Association of Hospital Social Workers, 192
American Association of Medical Colleges (AAMC), 68
American Association for Respiratory Care (AARC), 147, 152–153
American Board of Bioanalysis, 122
American Board of Clinical Chemistry, 122
American Board of Microbiology, 122
American Board of Physical Therapy Specialties, 142
American Board of Surgery, 69
American College of Healthcare Executives (ACHE), 42–43, 344

American College of Physicians, 264–265
American College of Surgeons, 264
American Federation of Labor and
    Congress of Industrial Organizations
    (AFL-CIO), 248
American Health Information Management
    Association, 209
American Hospital Association (AHA)
    allied health personnel, 76
    JCAH, 265
    nursing standards, 95
    registered hospitals, 15t, 270
American Medical Association (AMA)
    allied health personnel, 76
    founding of, 10, 70
    JCAH, 265
    National Joint Peace Practice
        Committee, 95
    residency programs, 68–69
    third-party payment, 320
American Medical Technologists
    (AMT), 123
American Nurses Association (ANA)
    functions of, 89
    National Joint Peace Practice
        Committee, 95
    nurse retention, 97
    nursing education, 86
    nursing standards, 95
American Nurses Credentialing Center
    (ANCC), 97–98
American Physical Therapy Association,
    135, 142
American Recovery and Reinvestment Act
    (ARRA), 202, 205
American Registry of Radiologic
    Technologists, 129
American Society for Clinical Pathology
    (ASCP), 123
American Speech-Language-Hearing
    Association (ASHA), 160
Americans with Disabilities Act (ADA), 246
anatomical pathology, 120, 124
ancillary services
    clinical laboratory, pathologist, 119–126
    diagnostic imaging, therapeutic
        radiology, 127–134
    pharmacy, 167–175
    physical therapy, 135–143

respiratory therapy, 145–157
    speech-language pathology, 159–165
annual report, 276
aphasia, 160–161
appointment process, physicians, 71–72
approved residency programs, 68–69
Aquinas, Thomas, 336
Aristides, Aelius, 4
Aristotle, 336
arthritis treatment center, 115
as low as reasonably achievable
    (ALARA), 128
Asian Americans, 256
associate degree nurses (ADNs), 86
Association for the Advancement of Medical
    Instrumentation (AAMI), 226
asthma educator-certified (AE-C), 153
attorney for hospital, 253
auscultation, 4
autonomy, 337–339, 347
average length of stay (ALOS), 13, 15–17,
    16f, 24, 207
average payment period (APP), 306

B
baccalaureate degree nurses (BSNs), 86–87
bad debt, 323
balance sheet, 299, 301–302, 303t
barbiturate control, 173
Barnett, Charles J., 257, 259
Baylor Hospital, 101
Baylor University Hospital, 321
bed mobility, 136, 136t, 141–142
bedside terminals, 109–110
Bellevue Hospital School of Nursing, 86
beneficence, 337–339, 347
Berra, Yogi, 283
billing, collection
    accounts receivable, 295–296
    claims processing activities, 294–295
    compliance, 298
    healthcare plan classifications, 294t
    medical claim cycle, 293f
    preclaims submission activities, 292–294
    RCM, 297–298
    reconciliation, 296–297
bioethics
    definition, principles, 336–339
    hospital ethics committees, 341–344

introduction to, 335–336
issues for hospitals, 339–341
patient-centered care, 344–348
biomedical engineering department,
  225–226
biomedical equipment specialists, 226
blood banks, 121–122
Blue Cross, 11, 323
Blue Shield, 11
board of directors, 33–35, 37
  cultural competence, 257
  fiduciary duty, 30, 36
  functions of, 38–42, 39*f*
  medical staff, relationship, 38, 40–41
  operation, 41–42
  strategic planning, 285–287
Boyd, Thomas, 6
branding, 278
brand-name drugs, 173–174
BRCA1, BRCA2, 125
breaches, confidentiality, 205
budget, budgeting
  capital budget, 308–310
  cash budget, 311, 311*t*, 312*t*
  defined, 307
  flexible, 316–317, 317*t*
  forecasting, 315–316
  line item, responsibility center budgets,
    313–314, 314*t*
  operating budget, 307–308, 309*t*
  preparation, 313–315
  process, 311–313, 312*f*
  program budget, 315, 315*t*
  proposed new investment, 310*t*
  techniques, 315–317
  timeline, 313*t*
Bureau of Labor Statistics, 184

C
Cabot, Richard, 191–192
Cannon, Ida, 191–192
capital budget, 308–310
capitation, 323
cardiac critical care unit (CCU), 106–107
care, ensuring quality. *See* quality of care,
    evaluating/ensuring
case management in nursing, 94–95
case management in social services, 193
case nursing, 92–93

cash budget, 311, 311*t*, 312*t*
Centers for Disease Control and Prevention
    (CDC), 90
Centers for Medicare and Medicaid
    Services (CMS)
  accreditation, 328, 330
  codes, 210
  hospital security, 228
  patient records, 203
centralized purchasing, 217
centralized requisitions, 218
certificate of clinical competence (CCC), 160
certificate of need (CON), 287–288
certified hand therapist (CHT), 142
certified management accountant (CMA), 299
certified midwife (CM), 82
certified nurse midwife (CNM), 82
certified public accountant (CPA), 299
certified pulmonary function technologist
    (CPFT), 153
certified registered nurse anesthetists
    (CRNA), 88
certified respiratory therapist (CRT),
    152–153
Certified Social Worker in Health Care
    (C-SWHC), 195
certified wound specialist (CWS), 142
chain of command, 27–30
charity care, 324
chief executive officer (CEO), 29–31, 33–37
  cultural competence, 257
  ex officio board member, 45
  finances, 299, 308
  future of, 47
  historical functions, 43–44
  inside activities, 44–46
  introduction to, 42–43
  medical staff relationship, 45
  outside activities, 46–47
  selecting assistants, 47
  selection, evaluation, 38–40
  strategic planning, 285–287
chief financial officer (CFO), 31, 287,
    307–309, 311, 316
chief nursing executive, 102
chief nursing officer (CNO), 31, 102
chief operating officer (COO), 31, 33,
    47, 287
chief resident, 69

Children's Health Insurance Program
(CHIP), 56
Civil Rights Act, 245
Civil Rights Division, Department of
Health and Human Services, 262
claim processing activities, 294–295
claims reconciliation, 296–297
cleft palates, 160
clinical department, 72–74
clinical engineering. *See* biomedical
engineering department
clinical ethics committee (CEC), 342–343
clinical laboratory
accreditation, 121–122
certification, 120–121
future of, 125–126
introduction to, 119–120
personnel, 122–124
professional laboratorian, 126
proficiency testing, 122
quality improvement, 124–125
structure, function, 120
Clinical Laboratory Improvements Act
(CLIA), 120–123
clinical laboratory scientist (CLS),
122–123, 126
Clinical Modification (CM), 202, 209
clinical nurse leader (CNL), 88
clinical nurse specialist (CNS), 29, 87–88
clinical pathology, 120–122
clinical privileges, 71–72, 75–76
clinician, 193–194
closed medical staff, 73
closed-circuit television (CCTV), 231–232
Code of Ethics for Nurses (ANA), 89
codes, CPT, 209
codes, telecommunications, 181
Codman, Ernest, 328
cognitive-communication disorder, 163
collaborative practice nursing, 95
collections. *See* billing, collection
College of American Pathologists (CAP),
121, 266
commercial indemnity plans, 321
Commission on Accreditation in Physical
Therapy Education, 138
communication disorders, 159–161, 163, 165
community hospitals, 13–23. *See also*
acute-care community hospitals

comorbidity, 136, 136*t*, 139, 142
compassion fatigue, 338
compliance. *See* hospitals, compliance/
performance improvement
compounding drugs, 167, 175
Comprehensive Accreditation Manual for
Hospitals (CAMH), 227, 266
comprehensive emergency management
(CEM), 234–235
computed tomography (CT), 130
computer-aided traditional scheduling, 100
confidentiality, patient records, 204–206
consultant, 194
continuing education credits (CEUs),
153–154
continuing medical education (CME), 70
contract services, 226
coronary care units, 106–107
corporate compliance, 254
Cortes, Hernando, 6
cost conservatism principle, 301
Council on Academic Accreditation in
Audiology and Speech-Language
Pathology (CAA), 160
Council on Social Work Education
(CSWE), 196
covered entities (CEs), 204–205
credentials committee, 71, 74
criminal background checks, 247
critical care specialty (CCS), 153
critical-care services, respiratory
therapy, 147
cultural competence
addressing, 257
defined, 256, 258
introduction to, 255–258
leadership role, 257–259
strategy for, 260–262
culture of safety, 330
current procedural terminology (CPT)
codes, 209
custodian of records, 203–204, 210
cyclical scheduling, 99–100
cytologic technician, 124

D
Dabelko, H. I., 196
Darling v. Charleston Community
Memorial Hospital, 40

defensive medicine, 250
delayed-egress doors, 230
Department of Health, Education, and Welfare, 250
Department of Health and Human Services, 120, 262
designated record set (DSO), 204
diagnosis related groups (DRGs), 328
diagnostic imaging department
  CT scans, 130
  diagnostic x-rays, 128–129, 133
  importance of, 133–134
  introduction to, 127–128
  mission, 128
  MRI, 130–131
  nuclear medicine, 131
  radiation oncologists, 132
  radiation therapists, 132–133
  radiologic technologists, 129–130
  radiologists, 129
  specialties, 130–131
  therapeutic radiology, 131–132
diagnostic x-rays, 128–129, 133
dietary services, 182–183
differentiated practice nursing, 95
direct-entry midwife (DEM), 82
director and officer (D&O) insurance, 36
director of nurses (DON), 31, 102, 287
discharge plan, 59
discharge summary, 203, 208
discharged not final billed (DNFB), 298
district nursing, 94
diversion, 62
diversity
  business case for, 259–260
  defined, 255, 257
  introduction to, 255–258
  leadership role in, 257–259
  organizational approach, 260–262, 260t
diversity advisory committee (DAC), 261
Do Not Resuscitate (DNR), 55, 339, 343
doctor of physical therapy (DPT), 138
Doctor of Science in Physical Therapy (DScPT), 142
double entry rule, 300
Drug Price Competition and Patent Term Restoration Act, 174
Drug-Free Workplace Act, 175

drugs
  compounding, 167, 175
  dispensing errors, 172, 251–252
  distribution system, 170–171
  generic vs. brand-name, 173–174
  narcotic, barbiturate control, 173
  random screens, 247
  security of, 174–175
  selling to hospitals, 174
Duke University, 80
Durable Power of Attorney for Healthcare Decisions, 55

E
educator, 194
elderly, geriatric care, 113–116
elective admittance, 54–56
electronic data interchange (EDI), 295
electronic health record (EHR), 202, 205, 211
electronic medical records (EMRs), 333
emergency department
  cost of running, 62
  golden hour, 61–62
  introduction to, 57–59, 63
  protection of, 230–231
  vs. trauma center, 60–61, 61t
emergency management
  command, 235–236
  communications, 237
  multiagency coordination system, 236
  organizational adoption, 235
  overview, 234–235
  preparedness exercises, 237
  preparedness planning, 236
  preparedness training, 236–237
  public information systems, 236
  resource management, 237
Emergency Medical Treatment and Active Labor Act (EMTALA), 57
emergency operations plans (EOPs), 235, 237
employee assistance program (EAP), 244
employee information booklet, 275
Employment Retirement Income Security Act (ERISA), 246
endoscopic assessments, 163–164
environment of care, 227
Environmental Protection Agency (EPA), 220
environmental services department, 219–220

Equal Employment Opportunity Commission (EEOC), 245–247
Equal Pay Act, 246
ethics, 336, 341–344. *See also* bioethics
Europe, ORs, 253
evidence-based patient care, 146
ex officio members, 45
executive committee, 71, 74
executive housekeeper, 219
explanation of benefits (EOB), 296–297

F
facilities support. *See also* administrative services; hospitals, essential services
    biomedical engineering department, 225–226
    contract services, 226
    environmental services department, 219–220
    laundry department, 221–222
    maintenance department, 222–223
    materials management department, 216–219
    parking facilities, 224–225
    plant engineering, 224
    security, safety, 227–238
Fair Labor Standards Act (FLSA), 246
False Claims Act, 298
Federal Emergency Management Agency (FEMA), 231, 234–236
Federal Trade Commission (FTC), 73
Federally Qualified Health Centers (FQHCs), 56
financial management
    accrual concept, 301
    balance sheet, 301–302, 303t
    basic accounting, 300–301
    cost conservatism principle, 301
    double entry rule, 300
    financial division, organizational chart, 299f
    financial statement analysis, 304–307
    financial statements, 299
    functions, organization, 298–299
    fundamental accounting equation, 300
    income statement, 302, 304t
    matching concept, 301
    statement of cash flows, 302, 305t
financial statement analysis, 304–307

financial statements, 299
fire safety, 233–234
first responder, 57
first-party payment, 319
fixed budgets, 315–316
flat organizational structure, 92, 102
flexible budgeting, 316–317, 317t
Flexner, Abraham, 10–11
Flexner Report, 10
Florence Nightingale Nursing School, 86
fluoroscopy, 129
focus groups, 279
Food and Drug Administration (FDA), 172–174
forecasting, budgeting, 315–316
for-profit hospitals. *See* proprietary hospitals
four Ps, 280–281
Franklin, Benjamin, 6
full-time equivalent employees (FTEs), 96, 242–244
functional independence, 136t, 139
functional nursing, 93
fundamental accounting equation, 300

G
generally accepted accounting principles (GAAP), 299
generating revenue
    hospital reimbursement, 320f
    introduction to, 319–320
    managed care, 321–322
    payment methods, 322–324
    setting charges, 322
    third-party payers, 319–321
generic drugs, 173–174
geriatric care, 113–116
geriatric care management program, 116
geriatric psychiatry department, 115
golden hour, 61–63
Gonzales v. John J. Nork, MD, and Mercy General Hospital of Sacramento, CA, 40
governing body, hospitals. *See* hospital leadership, organization
government hospitals, 14
Great Depression, healthcare payments, 320
group purchasing, 217
Guide to Physical Therapy Practice (American Physical Therapy Association), 135

H

Hand Therapy Certification Commission, 142
Hatch-Waxman Act, 174
Health Care and Education Reconciliation Act, 22
Health Care Financing Administration, 328. *See also* Centers for Medicare and Medicaid Services (CMS)
Health Care Quality Improvement Act, 76
health information management (HIM), 295
  EHR, 202, 205, 211
  introduction to, 201–202
  patient record purpose, 202–204
  patient record storage/archiving, 210–211
  privacy, confidentiality, security, 204–206
health information management (HIM) department
  abstracting, coding, 209–210
  hospital statistics reporting, 207
  introduction to, 201–202, 206
  MPI, 206
  patient record completion, 208–209
  patient record storage/archiving, 210–211
  release of information, 210
Health Information Security and Privacy Collaboration (HISPC), 205
Health Insurance Portability and Accountability Act (HIPAA), 186, 204–205, 209–210, 232, 246, 295, 329
Health Maintenance Organization Act, 321
health maintenance organizations (HMOs), 80, 321
healthcare, diversity. *See* diversity
Healthcare Financial Management Association (HFMA), 297–298
healthcare plan classifications, 294t
healthcare provider, charges, 322
healthcare reform. *See* Patient Protection and Affordable Care Act
healthcare system, history. *See* hospitals, history
Henry VIII, 6
Hill-Burton Act, 11

Hippocrates, 4, 338
Hispanic Americans, 256
histologic technician, 124
holistic outlook, 81
hospice unit, 115
hospital accreditation, licensing
  accreditation, 266–268, 330
  introduction to, 263
  Joint Commission, 264–265
  Joint Commission International, 269
  licensing laws, 327–328
  licensure, 269–270
  Medicare certification, surveys, 270
  registration, 270
  sentinel events, 268
hospital acquired infection (HAI), 207
hospital finances
  billing, collection, 292–298
  budgeting, 307–317
  financial management, 298–307
  generating revenue, 319–324
  introduction to, 292
hospital leadership, organization. *See also* hospital team
  alliances, 35
  board of directors, 30, 33–42
  CEO, 29–31, 33–48
  chart, 30–31, 32f
  COO, 31, 33, 47
  corporate restructuring, 34
  governing body, 35–48
  management principles, 28–30
  management pyramid, 28f
  medical staff, 33, 40–41, 45
  multihospital systems, 34–35
  product-line management, 30f
  team of three, 33–34
hospital marketing
  advertising, 276–278
  branding, 278
  explained, 274–278
  four Ps, 280–281
  fundraising, 281
  introduction to, 273–274
  market research, 278–279
  market studies, audits, 279–281
  sales, 278
Hospital Standardization Program, 264

hospital team. *See also* hospital leadership, organization
  geriatric care, 113–116
  medical staff, 67–76
  nursing services, 85–110
  physician extenders, 79–83
hospital-based primary care center, 55
hospitalist, 75
hospitals
  acute-care community, 14–23
  AHA registered, 15*t*
  attorneys, 253
  bed numbers, 14*t*
  classification, 13–14
  costs, payer type, 18*f*
  death/mortality rate, 207
  geriatric care, 113–116
  government, 14
  importance of, 13
  liability for physicians' acts, 250–251
  negative total/operating margins, 20*f*
  newsletters, 276
  particularistic, 7, 10, 42
  payment shortfall, 19*f*
  proprietary, 7, 10, 17–22, 35–36
  public, 7, 10
  revenue/expense, annual change, 21*f*
  specialty, 13, 17–22
  statistics reporting, 207
  unions, 248
  voluntary, 7
  vs. acute care, 142–143
hospitals, accessing
  admitting privilege, 54, 56
  emergency department, 57–59
  emergency department *vs.* trauma center, 60–61, 61*t*
  entrance methods, 53–54
  FQHCs, 56
  golden hour, 61–62
  incarceration facilities, 56
  physician referrals, 54–56, 63
  planned admittance, 54–56, 63
  trauma department, 59–61
  unplanned admittance, 56–57
hospitals, compliance/performance improvement
  accreditation, 330
  current situation, 331–334

IHI, ISMP, 331
  introduction to, 327–328
  medical errors, 329–330
  patient safety, 331–334
  PROs, 328, 330
  PSOs, 331
  QIOs, 330
  system failures, 328–329
  Winkler County nurses, 332
hospitals, essential services. *See also* administrative services; facilities support
  dietary services, 182–183
  interpreters, 186–187
  introduction to, 179
  pastoral services, 183–185
  patient representatives, 186
  patient transportation services, 185–186
  reception, 179–181
  telecommunications, 181–182
  volunteer services, 187–188
hospitals, history
  current, 11–12
  early American, 6–11
  early medicine, 3–6
  first hospitals, 4
  post-WWII, 11–12
hospitals, safeguarding
  emergency management, 234–237
  fire safety, 233–234
  general safety, 232–233
  introduction to, 227–228
  security, 228–232
  summary, 237–238
housekeeping services. *See* environmental services department
human resources department
  employee performance appraisal, 245
  functions of, 242–244
  introduction to, 242
  laws, acts, issues, 245–248
  occupational licensure, 248
  salaries, wages, benefits, 244–245
  unions, 248

I

incarceration facilities, 56
incident command post (ICP), 236
incident command system (ICS), 235–237

inclusion
  defined, 256, 258
  introduction to, 255–258
  leadership role in, 258–259
  organizational approach, 260–262, 260*t*
income statement, 299, 302, 304*t*
Indian Health Service, 14
infection-control nurses, 90
infectious/hazardous waste removal, 220
information technology (IT) security, 232
inside activities, CEO, 44–46
Institute of Health Initiatives (IHI), 331
Institute of Medicine (IOM), 329–331
Institute of Safe Medication Practices
  (ISMP), 331
institutional brochure, 276
institutional review board (IRB), 342
integrated emergency management system
  (IEMS), 235
intensive care unit (ICU), 105–106, 109
International Classification of Diseases,
  202, 209, 328
International Commission on Radiological
  Protection (ICRP), 133
interpreters, 186–187
interventional radiology, 131
inventories, inventory management, 218, 218*t*
ionizing radiation, 127–128, 133–134

J
jail facilities, 56
Joint Commission
  accreditation, 139, 147, 154, 266–268, 328
  allied health personnel, 76
  board of directors, 41
  clinical laboratories, 122
  cultural competence, 257, 262
  hospital security, safety, 227–228, 233–234
  licensure, 269–270
  medical staff, 70–71, 73
  Medicare surveys, 270
  NPSGs, 330
  overview of, 264–265
  patient records, 203
  sentinel events, 268
  survey, 29
Joint Commission International (JCI), 269
Joint Commission on Accreditation of
  Hospitals (JCAH), 263, 265

Joint Commission of Healthcare
  Organizations (JCAHO), 263,
  265, 328
Jones, John, 6
just culture, 330
justice, 337–339, 347

K
Kaiser, Henry J., 321
Kant, Immanuel, 336
*Keeping Patients Safe: Transforming the Work
  Environment of Nurses* (IOM), 331
key performance indicators (KPIs), 297–298
Koch, Robert, 10, 119

L
laboratories, clinical. *See* clinical laboratory
Labor-Management Relations Act, 248
laminar flow hood, 171
laundry department, 221–222
laundry manager, 221
level I-IV trauma centers, 60
licensed baccalaureate social worker
  (LBSW), 195
licensed clinical social worker (LCSW), 195
licensed master social worker (LMSW), 195
licensed practical nurse (LPN), 29, 86
licensed vocational nurse (LVN), 29,
  86, 88
licensing of hospitals. *See* hospital
  accreditation, licensing
line item budgets, 313–314, 314*t*
line managers, 30
linen control, distribution, 221–222
liquidity ratio, 306
Lister, Joseph, 9–10
Living Will, 55
long-range planning, 284–285, 287

M
Magnet Hospitals, 97
Magnet Recognition Program, 98
magnetic resonance imaging (MRI), 130
maintenance department, 222–223
mammography, 131
managed care plans, 321–322
management of hospitals. *See* hospital
  leadership, organization
management pyramid, 28*f*

Mance, Jeanne, 6
marketing audit, 279–281
marketing hospitals. *See* hospital marketing
marketing publications, 275–276
Massachusetts General Hospital, 7, 191
Massachusetts General Hospital School of
    Nursing, 86
master patient index (MPI), 206
Masys, Daniel, 201
matching concept, 301
materials management department
    centralized purchasing, 217
    inventories, inventory management,
        218, 218*t*
    leasing, 217
    purchasing section, 216–217
    receiving station, 217–218
    shared purchasing, 217
    storage, warehousing, 218–219
mechanical ventilation, 149*t*
Medicaid
    founding of, 11, 321
    FQHCs, 56
    reimbursements, 17, 24, 322–323
    specialty hospitals, 22
    standards, 328
medical claim cycle, 293*f*
Medical College Admission Test
    (MCAT), 68
Medical Directive forms, 55
medical director, 75
medical errors, 251–252, 329–330
medical home, 55–58, 63
medical laboratory scientist (MLS), 123
medical laboratory technician (MLT), 123
medical malpractice, 249–250, 253
medical social workers
    education, 195–196
    licensure, 194–195
    patient care, 196–197
    training, development, 196
    types, 192–194
medical staff. *See also* hospital leadership,
        organization; hospital team
    allied health personnel, 75–76
    bylaws, 71–73
    closed *vs.* open, 73
    CME, 70

committees, 73–74
    executive committee, 71, 74
    geriatric care, 113–116
    hospital organization, 33, 40–41, 45
    hospitalist, 75
    introduction to, 67–68
    medical director, 75
    membership status, 72*f*
    organization, 70–73
    organized medicine, 70
    physicians, becoming, 68–69
    physicians, legal restrictions, 76
    strategic planning, 285–286
medical technologist (MT), 123
Medicare
    certification, 270
    founding of, 11, 46, 321
    FQHCs, 56
    hospital finances, 308
    JCAH, 265
    legislation, Joint Commission, 269
    PROs, 328
    reimbursement, 17, 24, 322–323
    skin care issues, 89
    specialty hospitals, 22
    standards, 327–328
    survey, 270
Medicare summary notice (MSN), 296
medication dispensing errors, 172, 251–252
memory care center, 115
methicillin-resistant *Staphylococcus aureus*
    (MRSA), 90
midwives, 79, 82–83
Mill, John Stuart, 336
mission statement, 286–287
mission *versus* margin, 341
modified barium swallow study (MBSS),
    163–164
modular nursing, 94
molecular diagnostics, 125
Monagle, J. F., 343
multihospital system, 34–35
Munson, R., 339

N
narcotic control, 173
National Association of Social Workers
    (NASW), 195

National Board for Respiratory Care (NBRC), 152–153
National Certification Agency, 123
National Coordinating Council for Medication Error Reporting and Prevention, 172
National Council on Radiation Protection and Measurement (NCRPM), 133
National Fire Protection Association (NFPA), 230, 233–234
National Foundation for Trauma Care, 59
National Incident Management System (NIMS), 231, 235–237
National Joint Peace Practice Committee, 95
National Labor Relations Board (NLRB), 248
National League for Nursing (NLN), 89
national patient safety goals (NPSGs), 330
National Physical Therapy Examination for Physical Therapist Assistants, 138
National Practitioner Data Bank, 71, 76
National Resident Matching Program, 68–69
National Trauma Foundation, 61
neonatal intensive care unit (NICU), 106
neonatal-pediatric specialist (NPS), 153
net present value (NPV), 309–310, 310f
networking, 47
neurological intensive care unit (NICU), 106, 108
New England Hospital for Women and Children, 86
Nightingale, Florence, 8, 85–86
nonacute special care units, 108–109
nonionizing radiation, 127, 133–134
nonmaleficence, 337–339, 347
North American Nursing Diagnosis Association (NANDA), 95
North American Registry of Midwives, 82
nuclear medicine (NM), 131
Nuclear Regulatory Committee (NRC), 133
nurse managers, 30
nurse practitioners (NPs), 29, 79, 81, 87
nurse staffing, 96–98
Nurse Staffing Advisory Committee, 98
Nurse-Friendly program, 98

nurses' aides, 29, 91
nurses' station, 104
nursing
    case, 92–93
    case management, 94–95
    collaborative practice, 95
    department organization, 101–102
    differentiated practice, 95
    early traditions, 85–86
    functional, 93
    ICUs, 105–106, 109
    informatics specialist, 90
    introduction to, 85
    licenses, 246
    modes of delivery, 92–95
    modular/district, 94
    patient-care unit, 102–105
    personnel shortage, 22, 32f, 92–93, 97–98
    primary care, 94
    product-line management, 30f
    roles, 89–90
    scheduling, 98–101
    special-care units, 105–109
    staffing, 96–97
    staffing issues, 97–98
    standards, 89, 95–96
    team, 93–94
    telemonitoring, bedside terminals, 109–110
    work shifts, 100–101
nursing education
    ancillary help, 90–92
    degrees, 86–89
    nursing roles, 89–90

O

obstetrics, gynecology, midwives, 79, 82–83
Occupational Health and Safety Administration (OSHA), 233, 245
occupational licensure, 248
Office of the Inspector General (OIG), 329
open medical staff, 73
operating budget, 307–308, 309t
operating rooms (ORs), 253
organizational structure, hospitals. See hospital leadership, organization
orientation, 243–244

otolaryngology, 161, 164–165
outpatient care, 15
outside activities, CEO, 46–47
oximetry, 147

P
pain management program, 115
Papanicolaou (Pap) smears, 120
par level system, 218–219, 222
parking facilities, 224–225
particularistic hospitals, 7, 10, 42
Pasteur, Louis, 9–10
pastoral services, 183–185
pathologists
    certification, 120–121
    functions, 120
    introduction to, 119–120
    laboratory personnel, 122–124
    professional laboratorian, 126
pathology assistant, 124
Patient Protection and Affordable Care Act,
    22, 24
patient records
    completion, 208–209
    contents, 202–203
    as legal documents, 203–204
    ownership, 203
    privacy, confidentiality, security, 204–206
    purpose, 202–204
    storage/archiving, 210–211
Patient Safety and Quality Improvement
    Act, 331
patient safety organizations (PSOs), 331
patient support services
    health information management,
        201–211
    hospital essentials, 179–188
    social services department, 191–198
patients
    bioethics, 344–348
    care, evidence-based, 146
    information booklet, 275
    outpatient care, 15
    patient-care unit, 102–105
    patient-centered care, 344–348
    physical therapy, 139–141
    rapport, SLPs, 162
    representatives, 186

safety, 232, 331–334
SLP assessments, 162–165
social services, 196–197
transportation, 185–186
Patient's Bill of Rights, 55
Patient's List of Responsibilities, 55
peer review organizations (PROs),
    328, 330
Penn, William, 6
Pennsylvania Hospital, 6
per diagnosis charges, 323
per diem charges, 323
performance improvement. *See* hospitals,
    compliance/performance improvement
person-in-environment perspective, 194, 196
pharmacies
    drug distribution system, 170–171
    drug security, 174–175
    function of, 168
    generic *vs.* brand-name drugs, 173–174
    introduction to, 167
    medication dispensing errors, 172
    narcotic, barbiturate control, 173
    P&T committee, 170
    pharmacist education, 169
    quality improvement, 175
    selling hospitals drugs, 174
    staff, 168–169
    telepharmacy, 168
pharmacists
    education, 169
    introduction to, 168–169
    robotic, 171
pharmacy assistants, 168–169
pharmacy technicians, 168–169
pharmacy and therapeutics (P&T)
    committee, 170
PharmD degree, 169
phlebotomy, 120, 123
physical therapist aides, 138
physical therapist assistants (PTAs), 138–139
physical therapists (PTs)
    compliance, accreditation, 139
    defined, 135–137
    education, licensure, 138–139
    guiding documents, 142t
    patients, 139–141
    special considerations, 141–143

physical therapy
  delivery locations, 140*t*
  department services, 137
  glossary of terms, 136*t*
  historical perspective, 137
  information resources, 143*t*
  introduction to, 135–137
  patients, 139–141
  personnel, 138–139
  special considerations, 141–143
physician assistants (PAs), 79–81, 83
physician extenders
  introduction to, 79
  midwives, 79, 82–83
  NPs, 79, 81, 83
  PAs, 79–81, 83
physicians
  appointment to medical staff, 71–72
  becoming, 68–69
  CME, 70
  defensive medicine, 250
  hospital liability for, 250–251
  legal restrictions, 76
  referrals, 54–56, 63
  residency programs, 68–69
physiologic reserves, 136*t*, 139
physiotherapy. *See* physical therapy
Planetree Foundation, 345
Planetree model, 345–346
planned admittance, 54–56, 63
plant engineering, 224
point-of-service plans, 322
point-of-service (POS) cash collections, 298
Polygraph Protection Act, 247
polymerase chain reaction (PCR) test, 125
position control plan, 242–243
positioning strategy, 280
postgraduate year 1 resident (PGY1), 69
postoperative infection, 207
power plant, 224
preadmission workup, 54, 63
preclaims submission activities, 292–294
Pregnancy Discrimination Act (PDA), 247
preparedness training, 236–237
preventive maintenance, 223, 225
primary care nursing, 94
principle of ALARA (as low as reasonably
  achievable), 128

private pay, 17
product-line management, 30*f*
professional integrity, 339
proficiency testing, 122
program budget, 315, 315*t*
proprietary clinics, 55
proprietary hospitals, 7, 10, 17–22,
  35–36
protected health information (PHI),
  204–205, 211
public hospitals, 7, 10. *See also* acute-care
  community hospitals
public relations (PR), 274–276
publications, marketing, 275–276
purchasing section, 216–217
Pursuit of Excellence, 98
pyramid organization, 28*f*
pyxis, 104–105

Q
quality assurance (QA) nurse, 89–90
quality improvement, clinical laboratory,
  124–125
quality improvement organizations
  (QIOs), 330
quality of care, evaluating/ensuring. *See*
  bioethics; hospitals, compliance/
  performance improvement

R
radiation oncology, 132–133
radiation therapists, 132–133
radiography, 128–129
radiologic technologists, 129–130
radiologists, 129
random drug screens, 247
ratios, accounting, 305–307
Rawls, John, 336
reappointments, 74
receiving station, 217–218
reception, receptionist, 179–181
reconciliation, collection, 296–297
registered nurse (RN), 29, 86–89
registered nurse practitioner (RNP), 87
registered polysomnographic technologist
  (RPSGT), 153
registered pulmonary function technologist
  (RPFT), 153

registered respiratory therapist (RRT), 152–153, 156–157

religious hospitals. *See* particularistic hospitals

remittance advice (RA), 296

residency programs, 68–69

respiratory care practitioner (RCP), 150–152

respiratory therapists
credentials, 152–154
education, 152–153
functions of, 146–147, 155–157
licensing, accreditation, 153–154
scope of practice, 148–150*t*

respiratory therapy
bed to RCP ratio, 151
diagnostics, 154–155
introduction, history, 145–147
mission, 146–147
product line, 147, 148–150*t*, 155
staffing, 147–151

respondeat superior, 44, 251

responsibility center budgets, 313–314, 314*t*

revenue cycle management (RCM), 297–298

risk management
medical malpractice, 249–250
quality improvement, 249
team approach, 249

robotic pharmacists, 171

Roentgen, William, 127

Rural and Community Health Institute (RCHI), 333

S

sanitation specialists, 219–220

scheduling, 98–101

School of Philanthropy, 192

second-party payment, 319–320

Securities and Exchange Commission (SEC), 299

security. *See also* hospitals, safeguarding
access control, 229–230
assessment, 228–229
emergency department protection, 230–231
identification, 231–232
infant, patient protection, 232

introduction to, 227–228
IT security, 232
management plan, 229
surveillance, 231

self-scheduling, 100

Semmelweis, Ignaz, 9

senior citizens, geriatric care, 113–116

senior programs, 115

sentinel events, 268

sexual harassment, 247–248

shared purchasing, 217

Sisters of St. Joseph, 6

skilled nursing facility, 116

sleep disorders specialist (SDS), 153

sliding fee scale, 56

Smith, Nathan, 10

Social Security Administration, 265

social services
compliance, regulation, 194–196
introduction to, 191–192
licensure, 194–195
medical social workers, 192–194
patient care, 196–197
summary of, 199
worker education, 195–196
worker training, development, 196

Society for Social Work Leadership in Healthcare, 195

span of control, 29

special-care units, 105–109

specialization, 29

specialty board, 69

specialty hospitals, 13, 17–22

speech-language pathologist (SLP)
certification, 160
education, 160
patient assessments, 162–165
roles of, 159–161
staffing, 161–162
swallowing assessments, 163–165

St. Thomas Hospital, 86

Stark Law, 22

state hospital licensing, 269–270

statement of cash flows, 299, 302, 305*t*

Stead, Eugene A., 80

strategic planning
benefits of, 287
evolution of, 284

implementation, execution, 286
introduction to, 283
long-range levels, 287
long-range plans, 284–285
new facilities, 287–288
process of, 285–286
staff roles, 285–286
SWOT analysis, 285–286
strengths, weaknesses, opportunities, and
    threats (SWOT) analysis, 285–286
stroke, SLPs, 160
surgical intensive care unit (SICU),
    106, 108
surveillance systems, 231
swallowing disorders, 159–163, 165

T
Taft-Hartley Act, 248
tall organizational structure, 92, 102
target markets, 277, 279
team nursing, 93–94
team of three, 33–34
telecommunications department, 181–182
telemonitoring, 109–110
telepharmacy, 168
Texas Medical Board (TMB), 332
Texas Medical Foundation, 328
Texas Nurses Association (TNA), 98
therapeutic radiology, 127–128, 131–134
Thieriot, Angelica, 345
third-party payers
    defined, 319
    history of, 320–321
    payment methods, 322–323
thoracic intensive care unit (TICU),
    106–108
*To Err Is Human: Building a Safer Health
    System* (IOM), 329, 331
tort law, 250
traditional scheduling, 99
transfer, 136*t*, 137, 141–142
trauma, 59
trauma department
    cost of running, 62
    golden hour, 61–62
    introduction to, 59–61, 63

level I-IV trauma centers, 60
trauma center model, 60*f*
vs. emergency department, 60–61, 61*t*
Truman, Harry S., 321

U
ultrasound, 131
unions, hospitals, 248
unit dose system, 171
United States, diversity, 255–256
United States, ORs, 253
unplanned admittance, 56–57
urgent clinic, 55
US National Library of Medicine, 80

V
Vendidad, 5
Veterans Administration (VA), 14, 28
vice president (VP), 29, 47–48, 47*f*
vice president (VP) of Corporate
    Compliance, 48
vice president (VP) of nursing, 31, 102
vice president (VP) of Regulatory
    Affairs, 48
videofluoroscopy, 164
vision statement, 286
voice recognition (VR) software, 208
voluntary admittance, 54–56
voluntary hospitals, 7
volunteer services, 187–188

W
W. K. Kellogg Foundation, 95
weekend-alternative shifts, 101
West, M. P., 343
Winkler County nurses, 332
work order, 223
work shifts, nurses, 100–101
workers' compensation, 248
wound-care nurses, 89

X
x-rays, 128–130, 133

Z
Zimmerman, J., 196